RHETORIC AND ETHIC

Also by Elisabeth Schüssler Fiorenza

Sharing Her Word: Feminist Biblical Interpretation in Context (1998)

Jesus, Miriam's Child, Sophia's Prophet: Critical Issues in Feminist Christology (1994)

Searching the Scriptures, vol. 1: A Feminist Introduction (editor, 1993)

Searching the Scriptures, vol. 2: A Feminist Commentary (editor, 1994)

Discipleship of Equals: A Critical Feminist Ekklesia-logy of Liberation (1993)

But She Said: Feminist Practices of Biblical Interpretation (1992)

Revelation: Vision of a Just World (1991)

Bread Not Stone: The Challenge of Feminist Biblical Interpretation (1985)

Justice and Judgment: The Book of Revelation (1985, 1998)

In Memory of Her: A Feminist Theological Reconstruction of Christian Origins (1983, 1994)

Lent: Proclamation (1981)

Invitation to the Book of Revelation (1981)

The Apocalypse (1976)

Priester für Gott: Studien zum Herrschafts- und Priestermotiv in der Apokalpyse (1972)

Der vergessene Partner: Grundlagen, Tatsachen und Möglichkeiten der beruflichen Mitarbeit der Frau in der Heilssorge (1964)

Rhetoric and Ethic

The Politics of Biblical Studies

Elisabeth Schüssler Fiorenza

FORTRESS PRESS
Minneapolis

To
Harvey Guthrie
Ronald F. Thiemann
Krister Stendahl
Who in various ways have made this work possible

RHETORIC AND ETHIC
The Politics of Biblical Studies

Scripture translations from the Revised Standard Version of the Bible, copyright © 1946, 1952, and 1971 by the Division of Christian Education of the National Council of Churches of Christ in the United States of America are used by permission.

Cover design by David Meyer
Author photo by Jennifer McClory
Typesetting by Peregrine Graphics Services

Library of Congress Cataloging-in-Publication Data

Schüssler Fiorenza, Elisabeth
    Rhetoric and ethic : the politics of biblical studies / Elisabeth Schüssler Fiorenza.
      p. cm.
    Includes bibliographical references (p.).
    ISBN 0-8006-2795-4 (alk. paper)
      1. Bible N.T.—Feminist criticism. 2. Bible—Socio-rhetorical criticism. 3. Bible—Hermeneutics. I. Title.

    BS2379 .S38 1999
    220.6'082—dc21   99-052709

The paper used in this publication meets the minimum requirements for American National Standard for Information Sciences—Permanence of Paper for Printed Library Materials, ANSI Z329.48–1984.

Manufactured in the U.S.A.   AF 1-2795
    04   03   02   01   00   99   1   2   3   4   5   6   7   8   9   10

Contents

Figures

Preface

In this volume I propose a fundamental change in how we understand and employ the biblical text, based on a critical understanding of language as a form of power. I ask readers to re-envision biblical studies as a theory and practice of justice. I ask biblical scholars to contribute, as critical transformative intellectuals, to claiming the power of the word for those engaged in global struggles for justice and well-being. As readers take up the argument, they may find helpful at the outset a quick sketch of how I am using some key terms, more fully explained in the text:

ekklesia: originally a Greek political term denoting the democratic assembly or congress of full citizens. In the Christian Testament, *ekklesia* is the name for church. With *ekklesia* I intend to signify the radical equality that characterizes the "already and not yet" of religious community and democratic society.

Christian Testament (CT): I use *Christian* rather than *New Testament* and *Hebrew Bible* rather than *Old Testament* in order to avoid triumphalist Christian supersessionism. Both Christian Testament and Hebrew Bible constitute the Christian Bible or Scripture.

G*d: Similarly to Jewish custom, I write G*d in this broken way to emphasize the inadequacy of our language to speak about the divine.

kyriarchal/kyriocentric: derived from the Greek term for lord, this coinage underscores that domination is not simply a matter of patriarchal, gender-based dualism but of more comprehensive, interlocking, hierarchically ordered structures of domination, evident in a variety of oppressions, such as racism, poverty, heterosexism, and colonialism.

scientistic: I use this term adjectivally to signal the positivistic ideological framework of much that passes for "science." Inasmuch as scholarly and scientific inquiry and discourse function to legitimate overarching kyriarchal oppressions, invoking a false value-neutrality and objectivity, they are effectively positivist or scientistic, not genuinely scientific.

Wo/man and *wo/men:* I use this broken form to avoid an essentialist depiction of "woman" and to stress the instability of the term. Wo/man is not only defined by gender but also by race, class, and colonial structures of domination. Moreover, I use the term in an inclusive way. 'Wo/man' denotes not one simple reality, and 'wo/men' is often equivalent to 'people'.

Acknowledgments

Almost a decade ago Dr. Marshall Johnson of Fortress Press suggested to me that I develop my presidential address to the Society of Biblical Literature into a book. After Marshall retired from the press, Michael West of Fortress took over gently prodding me to get on with the project. I am grateful to both of them for keeping this project alive, and I want to thank especially him and Ann Delgehausen for shepherding the manuscript through its various stages of production.

That all rhetoric is a material practice becomes obvious especially in the process of producing and polishing a manuscript. I am grateful to my secretarial assistant Paula Shreve for her expert handling of numerous e-mail attachments and for her cheerful support throughout the process. I also want to thank my research assistants Emily Neill and Emily Holmes for library assistance as well as for feedback and proofreading of the various drafts. However, I am especially indebted to Lyn Miller, who in the final stages worked long hours to edit the chapters, get the manuscript in shape, and produce the bibliography. A million thanks to all of them.

I would like also gratefully to acknowledge the *Journal of Biblical Literature,* Sheffield University Press, *New Testament Studies,* and E. J. Brill, with whom I published earlier versions of chapters 1, 4, 5, and 6, respectively, and to *Critical Inquiry* for permission to reprint Paul Hernadi's literary compass in chapter 5.

This book is dedicated to three scholars who have at crucial times supported my work: Dr. H. Guthrie, former Dean of the Episcopal Divinity School, persuaded me to join the faculty, arguing that wo/men's full citizenship in the church is not just a question of ordination but of theological transformation; Dr. Ronald F. Thiemann, former Dean of the Harvard Divinity School, whose vision of a pluralistic university divinity school and the public vocation of the scholar/teacher has inspired this work and supported me over the years; and Dr. Krister Stendahl, in whose honor the chair was created that would allow me to pursue my interests in historical and contemporary biblical interpretation.

Last but not least, I want to thank Francis for his unwavering support and especially for making Salisbury possible, as well as Chris for more than a month of hardworking companionship at the North Shore.

Introduction

For a Biblical (Wo/man) Scholar to Speak in the *Ekklesia* . . .

As in all the *ekklesiai* of the saints,
the women should keep silence in the *ekklesiai*.
For they are not permitted to speak,
but should be subordinate, as even the law says.
If there is anything they desire to know,
let them ask their husbands at home.
For it is shameful for a woman to speak in the *ekklesia*.
What! Did the word of God originate with you,
or are you the only ones it has reached?
                                                 1 Cor. 14:33-36 RSV

Let a woman learn in silence with all submissiveness.
I permit no woman to teach or to have authority over men;
she is to keep silent.
For Adam was formed first, then Eve; and Adam was not deceived,
but the woman was deceived and became a transgressor.
Yet woman will be saved through bearing children,
if she continues in faith and love and holiness, with modesty.
                                                 1 Tim. 2:11-15 RSV

Conceptualized as a further explication of my presidential address before the Society of Biblical Literature (SBL),[1] this book has been more than ten years in the making. It is not so much concerned with biblical exegesis and a close reading of texts as with change of hegemonic discourses and disciplines; it is about scholarly values, emancipatory visions, and critical accountability. In it I argue for a reconceptualization of the scientistic antiquarian ethos of biblical studies as an academic discipline by re-articulating biblical interpretation in rhetorical-ethical terms. The individual chapters circle around three key concepts of the postmodern—representation, ethics, and politics. Although the book is conversant with postmodernism,[2] it does not derive its inspiration from postmodern debates.[3] Rather, the arguments of its pages

---

1. See chapter 1.
2. For a critical feminist evaluation of postmodernism, see Somer Brodribb, *Nothing Mat(t)ers: A Feminist Critique of Postmodernism* (Melbourne: Spinifex Press, 1992).
3. The Bible and Culture Collective, *The Postmodern Bible* (New Haven: Yale University Press, 1995).

are energized and compelled by marginalized discourses and "minority" theories, especially by those engendered by feminist re-visions, to borrow a term from Adrienne Rich.[4] Such re-visions of the discipline, I submit, must be feminist, political, and contextual.

Feminist Struggles against Silencing

The epigraphs at the beginning of this chapter are biblical texts that traditionally are attributed to Paul but are considered in modern exegetical literature to be not of Pauline provenance.[5] They bespeak the centuries of wo/men's silencing that have shaped all western academic and religious discourses. The works of Paul, like those of Aristotle and other intellectual fathers of the western tradition, have been celebrated as "classics" of western culture, although they have provided the arguments for wo/men's second-class citizenship or no citizenship at all. This tradition of silencing has legitimated wo/men's subordinate position in western societies and in the Christian churches. Moreover, these Pauline texts share in the hegemonic ethos of antiquity that characterizes the ideal wo/man through cultural codes that require wo/men's submission.

Like ancient and modern rhetorical traditions, the biblical tradition has become almost exclusively a western tradition of vocal, virile, public—and privileged—men, a tradition from which wo/men have been excluded for the most part. This biblical tradition shares in "the dominant ideology of most of the ancient world [which] offered women no place in public discourse. The exclusion of women from politics and power was one side, the other was their lack of right to be heard."[6] Thus these Pauline texts share in the hegemonic ethos of antiquity and have mediated theologically the image of the ideal wo/man through cultural codes that required "a closed mouth (silence), a closed body (chastity) and an enclosed life (domestic confinement)."[7]

For much of subsequent western history wo/men were prohibited from speaking in public. At the same time it must not be overlooked that there have always been some wo/men who have challenged this tradition of silencing throughout the centuries. Yet, once they began to speak, their words were not preserved, and many insights and works by wo/men are lost forever.[8] Nevertheless, that does not mean that wo/men have not spoken in public in past times nor that they have collaborated in their own silencing.

---

4. See Krista Ratcliffe, *Anglo-American Feminist Challenges to the Rhetorical Tradition: Virginia Woolf, Mary Daly, Adrienne Rich* (Carbondale: Southern Illinois University Press, 1996).

5. See the discussion in Helmut Koester, *Introduction to the New Testament*, 2 vols. (Philadelphia: Fortress Press, 1982).

6. Ratcliffe, *Anglo-American Feminist Challenges*, 16.

7. Cheryl Glenn, *Rhetoric Retold: Regendering the Tradition from Antiquity through the Renaissance* (Carbondale: Southern Illinois University Press, 1997), 1.

8. See Dale Spender, *Women of Ideas and What Men Have Done to Them* (London and Boston: Ark Paperbacks, 1983).

Insofar as the public realm of rhetoric was competitive, driven by rationality and the desire to persuade others, those wo/men who spoke in public had to adopt a "masculine" persona in modernity, since the "feminine persona" was restricted to the private sphere of the house. For instance, in the nineteenth century the "the cult of true womanhood," or as I would call it, the ideology of the "white lady," defined wo/men as the "other," as the repository of spiritual values such as obedience, humility, and self-sacrifice.[9] Two distinct subcultures emerged that defined the public realm: the world outside the home was men's place, whereas the place of the "white lady" was home and church, areas that were supposed to be free from "dirty" politics and economic exploitation. The space of the "white lady" is the place where the spiritual and emotional needs of husbands and children are to be met.

Freeborn wo/men who were forced to work outside the home, therefore, were no longer considered to be "ladies," but were tainted as "women." They lost their moral superiority. Slave wo/men were not considered to be "ladies" at all, but were simply regarded as chattel. Hence they had to overcome a double resistance when speaking to audiences who did not consider them as full citizens who could speak in public, nor as fully human rational beings who could be entrusted with decision-making powers.

Audiences that were mixed, or "promiscuous," as they were called in the nineteenth century, had an especially difficult time accepting African American wo/men speakers both because they were female and because they belonged to the race of slaves. As wo/men they were not supposed to speak in public, and as slaves they were not supposed to speak at all because they were considered to be property and deficient in "human" nature. Euro-American wo/men who sought moral reform and founded abolitionist and suffragist societies, who made public speeches, held conventions, and published newspapers entered the public sphere and in so doing lost their claims to purity and piety.

Today such "silencing" is accomplished differently. Even a cursory glance at the literature can show that the contributions of critical feminist biblical studies are rarely recognized and even less acknowledged by the white-malestream academy and religious institutions, although feminist scholarship has much to contribute to the epistemological transformation of academic scholarship in religion. To place "women" or "feminist" in the title of an article or book[10] ensures that the work will be relegated to the "women's section" of reviewers and libraries as of interest only to wo/men. Once they are relegated to the wo/men's section (the wo/men's quarters) of libraries and bookstores, feminist works cannot be seen as having theoretical significance for the scholarly field of religious studies on the whole or for a wider audience.

---

9. See Aileen S. Kraditor, *Up from the Pedestal: Selected Writings in the History of American Feminism* (Chicago: Quadrangle Books, 1968).

10. For instance, neither the review article of Duane F. Watson, "Rhetorical Criticism of the Pauline Epistles since 1975," *Currents in Research: Biblical Studies* 3 (1995): 219–48, nor that of Dennis Stamp, "Rhetorical Criticism of the New Testament: Ancient and Modern Evaluation of Argumentation," in *Approaches to New Testament Study,* ed. Stanley E. Porter and David Tombs (Sheffield: Sheffield Academic Press, 1995), 129–69, mentions my feminist works on rhetoric.

The history of feminism in western societies and religions therefore could be written as a history of struggle to claim the power of the word for wo/men. Feminist scholarship and theories are best conceptualized, I argue, in terms of such rhetorical struggles[11] for wo/men's public speaking in the *ekklesia*, the democratic assembly or congress of full citizens. Consequently, feminist studies explicitly adopt a critical theoretical framework that stresses the agency and authority of wo/men as intellectual religious subjects. If the field of biblical studies were reconceptualized in light of feminism as a theory and practice of justice, it could attend to the rhetorical functions of biblical texts and their interpretations in their particular historical-social situation. Their rhetorical aims, theoretical arguments, and theological goals could be understood as both empowered and limited in significant ways by the sociopolitical and academic-religious contexts in which the Bible is read and used.

By placing wo/men at the center of its attention, biblical studies would be able to explore the political-public context of biblical texts and the values they advocate. What Eloise A. Buker has said about philosophy also applies to biblical studies:

> By beginning with the simple assumption that women are as central to cultural life as men are, and by seeking to articulate just gender relationships, one modifies philosophical foundations such as liberalism, Marxism, psychoanalysis, existentialism and socialism. . . . In this sense, feminist theories perform a radical hermeneutics that appropriates other philosophies in order to reflect on issues arising from women's confrontation with injustices.[12]

However, as many feminist theorists have pointed out, "woman" is not a unitary category but is ambiguous and ideologically typed. The category "woman-wo/men," like those of gender, race, or class, is rhetorically-politically produced in the interest of relations of domination and subordination. That the category and understanding of wo/men is not just ambiguous and divided in itself but also inflected by race, class, and colonial relations is underscored by bell hooks:

> Historically white patriarchy rarely referred to the racial identity of white women because they believed that the subject of race was political and therefore would contaminate the sanctified domain of "white" woman's reality. By verbally denying white women racial identity, that is, by simply referring to them as women when what they meant was white women, their status was further reduced to that of non-person. . . . White feminists did not challenge the racist-sexist tendency to use the word "women" to refer solely to white women; they supported it. For them it served two purposes. First, it allowed them to proclaim white men world oppressors while making it appear linguistically that no alliance existed between white women and white men based on shared racial imperialism. Second, it made it possible for white women to act as if alliances did exist between themselves and non-white women.[13]

---

11. For the analysis of the wo/men's movement as rhetorical, see Karlyn Kohrs Campbell, "The Rhetoric of Women's Liberation: An Oxymoron," in John Louis Lucaites, Celeste Michelle Condit, Sally Caudill, eds., *Contemporary Rhetorical Theory: A Reader* (New York: Guilford Press, 1999), 397–410.

12. Eloise A. Buker, "Feminist Social Theory and Hermeneutics: An Empowering Dialectic," *Social Epistemology* 4 (1990): 23–39.

13. bell hooks, *Ain't I a Woman: Black Women and Feminism* (Boston: South End Press, 1984), 140.

Hence feminism, as I understand it, cannot just be concerned with gender inequities and gender marginalization but must also address other forms of domination, such as racism, poverty, religious exclusion, heterosexism, and colonialism, all of which are inflected by gender and inflect gender.[14] Although there are so many divergent forms and even contradictory articulations of feminism today that it is appropriate to speak of feminisms in the plural,[15] most feminists agree nevertheless that contemporary feminism is not only a political movement that is akin to other emancipatory movements but also an intellectual process for theorizing the situation of wo/men in kyriarchal[16] societies and religions.[17]

The neologism *kyriarchy-kyriocentrism* (from Greek *kyrios* meaning lord, master, father, husband) seeks to express this interstructuring of domination and to replace the commonly used term *patriarchy,* which is often understood in terms of binary gender dualism. I have introduced this neologism as an analytic category in order to be able to articulate a more comprehensive systemic analysis, to underscore the complex interstructuring of domination, and to locate sexism and misogyny in the political matrix or, better, patrix of a broader range of oppressions.

Such an analytic allows one to deconstruct the kyriocentric dualisms of western cultures, which are often unwittingly re-inscribed through a cultural gender analysis. It allows one to understand these dualisms as discourses of legitimization that become necessary in the face of a radical democratic alternative that envisions humanity and the political in terms of radical equality. Such an analysis of the structures of domination in terms of kyriarchy frees wo/men from the compulsion to negotiate identity in essentialist gender terms. It allows one to understand gender not just as an ideological concept but as an ever-shifting position and social formation constituted by structures of domination and networks of power.

Conversely, this analytic category does not restrict itself to gender analysis but seeks to comprehend the complex multiplicative interstructuring of gender, race, class, and colonial dominations and their imbrication with each other. It seeks to expose the embeddedness of wo/men's oppression in the entire domain of western society, culture, and religion and thereby to reveal that the subordination and

---

14. See also the excellent contribution of Ken Stone, "Biblical Interpretation as a Technology of the Self: Gay Men and the Ethics of Reading," in *Bible and Ethics of Reading*, ed. Danna Nolan Fewell and Gary A. Phillips, Semeia 77 (Atlanta: Scholars Press, 1997), 139–55.

15. For an exploration of the diverse voices in feminist theology, see the contributions in *Feminist Theology in Different Contexts*, ed. Elisabeth Schüssler Fiorenza and Shawn Copeland, Concilium (Maryknoll, N.Y.: Orbis Books, 1996).

16. I have coined this neologism in order to complexify the dualistic definition of patriarchy in terms of gender alone. See my books *But She Said: Feminist Practices of Biblical Interpretation* (Boston: Beacon Press, 1992) and *Sharing Her Word: Feminist Biblical Interpretation in Context* (Boston: Beacon Press, 1998) as well as the introduction to *Searching the Scriptures: A Feminist Commentary* (New York: Crossroad, 1993–1994).

17. In order to mark the inadequacy of our language to speak about the divine, I write G*d in such a broken form. For a discussion of the term G*d, see Francis Schüssler Fiorenza and Gordon Kaufman, "God," in *Critical Terms for Religious Studies*, ed. Mark C. Taylor (Chicago: University of Chicago Press, 1998), 136–59.

exploitation of wo/men is crucial to the maintenance of kyriarchal cultures and religions. Hence any adequate theory or praxis of emancipation and liberation must explicitly take into account the multiplicative interlocking structures—heterosexism, racism, colonialism, class exploitation, and ageism—of domination and marginalization.

In order to avoid an essentialist reading of *wo/man*, I have begun to write *wo/men* in a broken form. I have done so in order to point to the ambiguity and heterogeneity of meaning implied by this designation. Such a form of writing also seeks to contravene the effects of dominant androcentric "generic" language[18] by using the expressions *wo/men* as inclusive of men, *s/he* as inclusive of he, and *fe/male* as inclusive of male. Such a language use seeks to signify that the term *wo/men* has a meaning equivalent to that of people. Moreover, it signals that *wo/man* does not mean feminist, for not all wo/men are feminists, and men in turn can engage feminist theories and support feminist struggles. Similarly, the word *feminist* is a controverted term.

In academic circles it is still assumed that feminist studies deal only with women and not with real scholarly topics. Moreover, feminist theory and theology are often labeled as ideological because of their advocacy stance. Feminist studies, it is alleged, misuse scientific methods in corroborating their preconceived and predetermined results and hence are ideological, with ideology understood as "false consciousness." Feminist scholarship in turn often retorts that such an allegation only hides and mystifies the biased kyriocentrism of malestream scholarship.

Since those who practice feminist studies understand themselves as "interested" and openly take sides for wo/men, they are often classed as unscientific. This prejudice comes to the fore, for instance, in an e-mail letter I received a couple of days ago inquiring as to whether I had published "real" biblical scholarship that is not explicitly feminist. Yet, not only general readers but also biblical scholars will operate with such an often unspoken assumption. Even some feminist scholars still feel compelled to "prove" the legitimacy and validity of their arguments by showing how these "fit" into the hermeneutical frameworks and epistemological theories of the "great men" in the field.[19] They often do so by suppressing or downplaying the pioneering work of other feminist scholars.

However, as long as feminist biblical scholarship marginalizes and silences itself in such a way, it cannot develop its full force for change.[20] The voices from

18. See Deborah Cameron, ed., *The Feminist Critique of Language: A Reader* (New York: Routledge, 1998).

19. See, e.g., the widely anthologized and frequently quoted article by Sheila Greeve Davaney, "Problems with Feminist Theory: Historicity and the Search for Sure Foundations," in *Embodied Love: Sensuality and Relationship as Feminist Values*, ed. Paula M. Cooey, Sharon A. Farmer, and Mary Ellen Ross (San Francisco: Harper & Row, 1987), 79–95. Even Rebecca S. Chopp, "Feminist Queries and Metaphysical Musings," in *Modern Theology* 11 (1995): 47, feels compelled to legitimate feminist theology as critical theory by placing it into the framework of American pragmatism. Both overlook that at least my own work has been eclectic, utilizing elements of diverse theories but integrating them in terms of my own critical feminist liberationist perspective and theoretical framework.

20. Erin White, "Figuring and Refiguring the Female Self: Towards a Feminist Hermeneutics," in *Claiming Our Rites: Studies in Religion by Australian Women Scholars*, ed. Morny Joy and Penelope Magee

the margins of biblical scholarship are not able to destabilize the center as long as they themselves seek to fit into the hegemonic ideological frameworks of the discipline. Rather than subscribe to the hegemonic politics of biblical studies, the voices from the margins must seek to destabilize the center. To do so they must braid together a rhetoric and ethics of inquiry with a critical reflection on issues arising from wo/men's confrontation with injustice and silencing.

The feminist philosopher Elisabeth List has delineated feminism as follows: "The place of feminist thought is always the place of woman who thinks herself and the world."[21] This means in theological terms that feminist studies are the intellectual space where wo/men are "thinking" about G*d, the world, and themselves. My preferred understanding of feminism, however, is expressed in the pithy statement of a popular feminist bumper sticker that defines feminism as the "radical notion that wo/men are people." This adage alludes to the radical democratic dictum "we the people." Wo/men are not beasts of burden, sex objects, temptresses, or "babies," but fully entitled and responsible citizens. Such a critical feminist perspective insists that wo/men and other nonpersons—to use an expression of Gustavo Gutiérrez[22]—who throughout the centuries were, and still are, marginalized and silenced in academy and church, are theological subjects and agents. With this definition of feminism as the claim to full citizenship for all, I have already indicated that my own theoretical framework is a radical democratic political and religious one.

In my view feminism is a theory and practice of justice that seeks not just to understand but to change relations of marginalization and domination. The prohibition of all wo/men from public speaking and the restriction of politics and rhetorics to elite freeborn males has constructed academic scholarship and biblical studies as a masculine gendered discipline and rhetorical culture. It also has defined

(Adelaide: Australian Association for the Study of Religions, 1994), 35–155, chides feminist biblical studies for not being sufficiently hermeneutical. After claiming that "feminist scholarship lacks extended discussion of hermeneutical questions," she goes on to assert that Phyllis Trible's and my own work "focus on the text" and in my case "on the communities of women and men who produced the text," but that we do not focus "on the relation between text and (female) self-identity" (136). In her elaboration of my alleged position, she does not refer to either my books *Bread Not Stone: The Challenge of Feminist Biblical Interpretation* (1984; 10th anniv. ed., Boston: Beacon Press, 1995), *But She Said* (published 1992), or *Revelation: Vision of a Just World* (Minneapolis: Fortress Press, 1991), nor to any of my other hermeneutical-epistemological essays. Instead, she (mis)reads *In Memory of Her: A Feminist Theological Reconstruction of Christian Origins* (10th anniv. ed., New York: Crossroad, 1993) in a positivist historical vein and claims that I do not "sufficiently recognize the place of both text and present context in the construction of any community of the past" (138). She concedes that her critique might seem "niggardly" [*sic*] but then goes on to show how much better off we would be if we had read Ricoeur, although a reading of *Bread Not Stone* and my discussion of, e.g., Sandra Schneider's proposal could have shown that I have considered this approach but found it wanting. However, at no point does she mention that the basic difference between our feminist hermeneutical proposals is neither my lack of hermeneutical sophistication nor my abandoning of experience but the theoretical difference between a feminist analysis in terms of gender and one in terms of the multiplicative structures of kyriarchal oppression and kyriocentric symbol systems.

21. Elisabeth List, *Die Präsenz des Anderen*, Gender Studies (Frankfurt: Edition Suhrkamp, 1992), 42.

22. See James B. Nikoloff, ed., *Gustavo Gutiérrez: Essential Writings* (Minneapolis: Fortress Press, 1996).

the parameters of western thought and Christian theology in elite white malestream terms. Since throughout the centuries all wo/men were excluded both from speaking in public and from authoritatively shaping cultural, academic, and religious discourses, theology and religious studies have become defined by elite males only.

The academic discipline of biblical studies, its self-understanding and methodological practices, have been constructed in depoliticized, privatized, and spiritualized terms, since it was shaped by and through the exclusion of wo/men. If biblical studies were to change into a public discourse, it would seek not just to describe and understand but to change and transform the unjust situation of wo/men's religious and academic silencing, marginalization, and exploitation. Biblical studies would then be able to acknowledge openly its political function rather than to continue to hide behind a value-neutral and disinterested scientistic ethos of scholarship.

As long as either the dogmatist or the scientistic ethos with their exclusivist structures of silencing determine biblical scholarship, one must be wary of the "cheap grace" of reconciliation. The politics of exclusion and silencing that has shaped the very ethos of the discipline is overlooked in Daniel Patte's response to the challenge of my SBL presidential address to the academy. Although the book[23] is well intentioned and comes highly recommended, it does not grapple with the fact that kyriocentric Euro-American malestream scholarship is part of the problem rather than part of the solution. If one has once understood a kyriocentric analysis of structures of domination, one can no longer formulate an advocacy position for white Euro-American male scholars in analogy to the advocacy stance for those who throughout history and still for the most part today have been silenced and marginalized in the academy and biblical religions.

The Politics of Biblical Studies

Reviewing in 1992 scholarship on the ethics and theology of the Christian Testament and partially responding to my SBL address, Jan Botha explored the practices of biblical scholarship in political terms. As a South African he did so in relation to the historic developments and changes that were under way at that time in South African society. Because text-immanent approaches were predominant in the 1970s and 1980s, he argued, "New Testament scholarship has become irrelevant within the political, ecclesiastical, and even theological context of South Africa."[24]

---

23. Daniel Patte, *Ethics of Biblical Interpretation: A Reevaluation* (Louisville: Westminster/John Knox Press, 1995). Rather than critically analyzing the marginalizing discourses of malestream biblical studies and their silencing powers, Patte reaffirms the solidarity of white male exegetes and claims scientific as well as theological authority for them. Their work has the task to bring to critical, i.e., scientific consciousness the interpretations of "ordinary" readers. Thereby he re-inscribes not only the status divisions between professional and "ordinary" readers that are at the heart of the silencing and exclusionary tendencies of the discipline but also those between scientific, i.e., (white male) scholars and hermeneutical, i.e., advocacy readings.

24. Jan Botha, "Aspects of the Rhetoric of South African New Testament Scholarship Anno 1992," *Scriptura* 46 (1993): 80.

Botha adopted rhetorical analysis for investigating how the in-house discussions of the academic "guild" in the 1990s responded to the needs of South African society and church in transition. He observed that a consensus was emerging among scholars that "each New Testament writing must be read individually in its own specific context if one wants to analyze its theology or ethics."[25] Whereas New Testament scholars expertly reconstruct the sociopolitical, historical-religious contexts of individual biblical writings, they are less skilled, he pointed out, in reading their own sociopolitical, cultural, historical, and religious contexts.

As in the South African academy, so also the North American academy, biblical scholarship has become a hullabaloo of often contradictory methodological voices. Yet,

> the demand to be "scientific" seems to lure [South African] New Testament scholarship to focus again—and almost exclusively—on the first-century contexts of the New Testament writings. And precisely this fact causes the guild's readings of the New Testament not to be of immediate interest for people outside the guild, which, in its turn, confirms the critique . . . that [South African] New Testament scholarship is not socially relevant.[26]

Since I believe that the situation of South African biblical scholarship is not the exception but the rule, I want to explore in this book the methodological conditions and epistemological changes necessary to sustain a paradigm shift in biblical studies. Such a paradigm shift would enable the discipline not only to contribute to the readings and use of the Bible in the public square but also to articulate biblical values and visions that can contribute to a cosmopolitan spiritual center of global dimensions.

To that end, I argue, the field of biblical studies needs to return to its scholarly roots and to remember that it began as biblical criticism, as critical biblical studies. What do I mean by *critical?* Since the words *critique* and *critical* are often understood in a negative, deconstructive, and cynical sense, I use these terms in their original sense of crisis. This expression is derived from the Greek word *krinein/krisis,* which means judging and judgment, evaluation and assessment. A critical approach is interested in weighing, evaluating, and judging texts and their contexts, in exploring crisis situations and seeking their adjudications. Its goals and functions are opposite to those of a positivist approach of "pure" science.

Moreover, in contrast to "scientistic" biblical studies, critical biblical scholarship is not compelled by merely antiquarian interests. Rather, for the sake of "theology" (ideology) critique it focuses both on the rhetoricality of all scholarly inquiry and on the rhetoricity of texts and the power relations in which they are embedded.[27] Biblical scholarship that seeks to reclaim its critical edge, I argue, is best understood as a critical rhetorics of inquiry that approaches all intellectual perspectives and methodological turns in the academy with an ethical reflexivity that has been pioneered by feminist and other "minority" studies.

25. Ibid., 91.
26. Ibid., 93.
27. See chapters 5 and 6.

This point has been brilliantly made by Tania Oldenhage. Instead of asking how to read the Bible after the Holocaust, her article investigates "the ways in which the events of the Holocaust have affected readings of the parables of Jesus"[28] during the last fifty years. Her careful analysis shows how biblical scholars of quite different theoretical persuasions writing at quite different times (such as Joachim Jeremias, Dominic Crossan, and the Collective that produced *The Postmodern Bible*) have not recognized the legacy of anti-Judaism cropping up in their work because they did not critically reflect on their scholarly practices in a post-Holocaust context.

In short, I want to explore in the following chapters the methodological conditions and epistemological changes that would foster such a critical reflexivity and enable the discipline of biblical studies to intervene in and to contribute to the readings and use of the Bible in the public discourses of society and churches, synagogues, or mosques.[29] As a public discourse, biblical studies could

- explicitly reflect on its sociopolitical religious location and ideological functions

- understand biblical discourses as inscriptions of struggle and reconstruct them as public debates of the *ekklesia*

- identify the languages of hate and the death-dealing ideologies inscribed in Scriptures

- identify biblical visions and values that would contribute to a radical democratic understanding of society and religion

- explore cultural practices such as film, music, or art and their use of the Bible[30]

- foster an understanding of biblical authority that allows for the questioning of the text in a critical practice of the discernment of the Spirit

- create public discourses and debates that could intervene in the discourses of the religious right and other antidemocratic groups

- refashion biblical education in such a way that it engenders scholars and religious leaders who are critical public intellectuals

Such a change in the ethos and praxis of the discipline also would engender a change in the self-understanding of the biblical scholar. In order to become a critical transformative intellectual[31] rather than just a professionalized one,[32] s/he must

28. Tania Oldenhage, "Parables for Our Time? Post-Holocaust Interpretations of the Parables of Jesus," in *The Bible and the Ethics of Reading*, ed. Fewell and Phillips, 227–41; quote is on p. 227.

29. Ronald F. Thiemann, *Religion in Public Life: A Dilemma for Democracy* (Washington, D.C.: Georgetown University Press, 1996).

30. For the use of the Bible in film see the fascinating work of Adele Reinhartz.

31. Stanley Aronowitz and Henry Giroux in *Education under Siege* (South Hadley, Mass.: Bergin, 1985), 45, argue that critical pedagogies require and construct "transformative intellectuals" who "can emerge from and work with any number of groups, other than and including the working class, that advance emancipatory traditions and cultures within and without alternative public spheres."

reclaim the public space of the *ekklesia* as the arena of biblical and religious studies, I contend. Since *ekklesia* is not primarily a religious but a political term,[33] such a change would position biblical scholarship in the public sphere of the polis and transform it into a critical discourse that seeks to further the well-being of all the inhabitants of the *cosmo-polis* today.

Such a redefinition has as its goal a critical culture of equality. It can build rhetorically on the ancient Greek democratic notions of *polis* and *ekklesia,* but would need to change them from signifying exclusion and privilege[34] to signifying radical democratic equality. If biblical studies were positioned in the space of the *ekklesia* redefined in egalitarian inclusive terms, they could speak both to the public of the church, synagogue, or mosque as well as to the civic public of society at large. Feminist theory and theology are an indispensable resource, I submit, for achieving such a transformation of biblical studies.

Hence in the following chapters I seek to explore the feminist contributions to fashioning a critical-political ethos of biblical scholarship and for re-articulating biblical studies as a public discourse. Only such a reconceptualization of biblical scholarship, I contend, would make it possible for marginalized scholars to speak and to be heard in the *ekklesia,* the public assembly of decision-making citizens. By *politics* and *political* I do not mean politics in the usual sense of "party politics," construed as manipulative machinations and behavior in which people engage without scruples in order to enhance their own powers and interests. Rather, I argue, political/politics must be redefined in feminist terms by those who have been marginalized and excluded. It will come as no surprise to anyone familiar with my work that I believe feminist theory and theology to be an indispensable resource for achieving the transformation of biblical studies into truly critical studies.

Understood as a public-political discourse, biblical studies would be able, I argue, not just to investigate the literary and historical elements and contexts of a biblical text but also to critically reflect on what kind of role the Bible plays today in the social construction of reality and in the discursive formations that determine individuals, religious communities, and society on the whole. In order to do so, it needs to abandon its own practices of silencing and excluding as well as to critically reflect and recognize its sociopolitical locations and functions.

Thus the arguments of this book seek to participate in the destabilizing efforts of the margins by critically exploring the scientistic hegemonic ethos of the center and by braiding together a critical rhetorical, political, and ethical analysis for biblical interpretation. If one wants to move from a scientistic-academic to a critical public discourse fueled by reflection on issues arising from wo/men's confrontation with injustice, it becomes necessary to braid diverse methods and theories of ethical

32. William Dean, in *The Religious Critic in American Culture* (Albany: State University of New York Press, 1994), xiv, argues that scholars in religion must become public intellectuals. He understands the religious critic in analogy to the social critic and the culture critic.

33. K. L. Schmidt, "*ekklesia,*" in *Theological Dictionary of the New Testament,* ed. Gerhard Kittel (Grand Rapids, Mich.: Eerdmans, 1964) 3:514–16.

34. See Page duBois, *Torture and Truth: The New Ancient World* (New York: Routledge, 1990).

and rhetorical inquiry that would make it possible to effect a critical feminist transformation in the self-understanding and institutional practices of the discipline.

For this reason I have decided to broach the topic here once more by elaborating the contributions of a critical feminist rhetorical analysis to the refurbishing of
the ethos of biblical studies. I hope that by recontextualizing some of my published
articles on ethics and rhetoric, I will be able to break through the attempt to silence
and mute feminist theoretical work in the discourses of the discipline.

As I have done before, I argue here that only if biblical studies relinquishes its
posture of value neutrality and claims of scientific status, will it be able to turn into
full-fledged critical rhetorical studies.[35] Only if it moves out of its academic "ivory
tower" and becomes a publicly responsible discourse, will biblical scholarship be able
to recognize the voices from the margins and those submerged by the kyriocentric
records of biblical and contemporary hegemonic "texts."

With this book I seek to contribute further to the development of a critical (feminist) ethic and rhetoric of inquiry that is scientific and objective.[36] Only an inquiry
that is able to explore all aspects of wo/men's reality and to take into account the intellectual distortions that are wrought by practices of exclusion and marginalization can
make this claim. A feminist ethics of justice therefore is not less but more objective.
For those theologically engaged, it should not be very difficult to find biblical warrants
for such an ethics of justice. This ethics of justice must be extended both to contemporary situations and to the biblical past. It seeks to engender solidarity not just with
contemporary wo/men struggling for justice and well-being but also with those whom
biblical texts address, argue with, or silence and marginalize.

The arguments of this work do not progress in a straight line but move in circles
and spirals. As the waves of the sea again and again return to the shore but with a difference, so also the theoretical explorations of this book circle around the project of
a rhetoric of inquiry in order to erode the positivist shore of biblical studies. They
seek to move the argument by returning again and again to some of the same critical touchstones: rhetoric, ethics, and politics.

This book's chapters move in two big waves. The first part circles around the theoretical and methodological paradigm shift that has been under way in biblical studies for quite some time, a shift from a scientist positivist to a rhetorical-political paradigm of interpretation. The second part seeks to explore the theoretical and
methodological issues raised by such a paradigm shift in and through a critical reading of Paul and his politics of meaning. Both parts have as touchstone and lighthouse
the proposals of the first chapter, to which they repeatedly return.

The first chapter, "The Ethics of Interpretation: Decentering Biblical Scholarship,"
sets the rhetorical parameters and articulates the hermeneutical questions that are

35. Such critical-rhetorical studies must be distinguished from the proposal for a textualized socio-
rhetorical interpretation advocated by Vernon K. Robbins. See, e.g., his *Exploring the Texture of Texts: A
Guide to Socio-Rhetorical Interpretation* (Valley Forge, Pa.: Trinity Press International, 1996).

36. See Bonnie G. Smith, "Gender, Objectivity and the Rise of Scientific History," in *Objectivity and
Its Other,* ed. Wolfgang Natter, Theodore R. Schatzki, John Paul Jones III (New York: Guilford Press,
1995), 51–66.

picked up and variegated in the other chapters. Except for some additional notes, it is only a slightly changed reprint of my SBL presidential address and as such must be read as a rhetorical-historical event rather than just as a theoretical exploration. Since I was the first wo/man scholar to be elected president of the Society of Biblical Literature in its hundred-year history, I was determined to mark this historic event by focusing my presidential address on critical feminist liberationist concerns.

Using as my rhetorical point of departure Virginia Woolf's query as to whether and under what conditions wo/men should join the processions of educated men, and Rudolf Bultmann's statement that World War I did not influence his theology, I sought to explore the possibilities of bringing to bear the perspectives and insights of the margins on the hegemonic center of biblical scholarship in order to change it. Such a change, I argue, would involve a re-vision of the self-understanding and ethos of the discipline and the creation of biblical studies as a public-political discourse.[37] The following chapters develop and circle around this demand for a paradigm shift in the ethos and rhetorical practices of the discipline.

In the second chapter I look more closely at the paradigm shift from a scientistic to an emancipatory ethos of biblical scholarship that is under way in biblical studies. I outline four paradigms—the dogmatic-authoritative, the historical-positivist, the cultural-hermeneutical, and the rhetorical-emancipatory—which are presently competing for determining biblical interpretation, and I develop further the rhetorical-emancipatory or rhetorical-ethical paradigm of interpretation.

The third chapter explores the conditions and possibilities of a critical rhetoric of inquiry. It highlights the areas in which feminists have challenged the scientistic value-free understanding of religious studies as of special significance for an ethical-political paradigm shift in religious studies: the challenge to a positivist ethos, the feminist challenge to kyriarchal relations of domination, the hermeneutical definition of religion, and the modern definition of religion in gender and colonialist terms. These challenges have been made possible by four intellectual turns in the academic ethos of science: the hermeneutical, the political, the ideological-critical, and the rhetorical.

Chapter 4 explores the question as to why the rhetorical turn in biblical studies has not been able yet to link hands with feminist, liberationist, and postcolonial studies in order to bring about a paradigm shift in biblical studies. The "feminine"coding of both rhetoric and religious studies, I argue, compels scholars to assert the "masculine"ethos of biblical studies as a "hard" science. If rhetorical criticism would engage with feminist theory a "full-turn" of biblical studies would be possible.

After the more theoretical explorations of the first part, I have brought together in the second part of the book analyses of Pauline texts understood as rhetorical practices. I explore first a methodological model of rhetorical analysis with regard to 1 Corinthians (chapter 5), inquire then as to the possibility of historical knowledge of Paul and his audiences in a rhetorical paradigm (chapter 6), engage the

---

37. See also Robert M. Fowler, "Postmodern Biblical Criticism," *Foundations & Facets Forum* 5, 3 (1989): 3–31.

rhetoric of inquiry for a feminist ideology critique of the interpretations of Gal. 3:28 (chapter 7), and conclude with an exploration of how to re-vision biblical theology by discussing Paul and the politics of interpretation in chapter 8.

Several of the chapters owe their existence to an international community of biblical scholars and religious audiences engaged in justice work. While all of the chapters are positioned in the forum of the university and struggle with academic frameworks and theories, they nevertheless are of significance not only for professional exegetes but also for all those concerned with a cosmopolitan biblical ethics of justice and well-being. While commonsense wisdom asserts "sticks and stones may break my bones but words can never hurt me," we all know that this is not true. Words, especially sacred words full of authority like those of the Bible, have great power to harm or to encourage. As anyone working with wo/men suffering from domestic and sexual violence can tell, the words of Holy Scripture keep many religious wo/men in such places of violence. In the interest of wo/men suffering from abusive relationships and practices of domination, all biblical texts must carry the label: "Caution, could be dangerous to your health and survival!"

Consequently, a rhetoric and ethics of justice has the task to clear the intellectual terrain in such a way that wo/men are enabled to read the Bible as well as other cultural and religious texts "as if their lives depended on it." The following story, reported by Rabbi Jonathan Magonet, underscores this point:

> In 1968 our progressive Jewish youth movement hosted a group of young Czech Jews for a conference near Edinburgh. . . . We studied some Bible texts and they were incredibly good at understanding them, picking up all the nuances very quickly. I was surprised as they had never studied the Bible before. "It's easy," they explained. "You see, in Czechoslovakia, when you read a newspaper, first you read what is written there. Then you say to yourself, 'If that is what they have written, what *really* happened? And if that is what really happened, what are they trying to make us think? And if that is what they are trying to make us think, what should we be thinking instead?' You learn to read between the lines and behind the lines. You learn to read a newspaper as if your life depended upon understanding it—because it does!" Sometimes the same applies to the Bible, you just have to learn how to read.[38]

In short, the theoretical explorations of this book seek to articulate the intellectual frameworks or lenses that make possible such a reading not only of the Bible but of other authoritative cultural and religious texts. It is possible, I contend, for the previously silenced and marginalized to change the center, because a shift from a scientistic-positivist to a rhetorical-ethical paradigm is under way in the methodological and theoretical self-understanding of the discipline. This book thus continues my efforts to advocate for a theoretical and institutional change that would foster a biblical rhetoric and ethics of justice and well-being. Biblical scholars are called to contribute as critical transformative intellectuals to a radical democratic biblical vision for the overcoming of domination in the global *cosmopolis* that is our spiritual home.

---

38. Jonathan Magonet, *A Rabbi's Bible* (London: SCM Press, 1991), 25.

Part One

Theoretical Explorations

Chapter 1

The Ethics of Biblical Interpretation: Decentering Biblical Scholarship

It is a commonplace that presidential addresses have primarily rhetorical functions.[1] They are a ceremonial form of speech that does not invite responsive questions or questioning responses. Such presidential rhetoric is generally of two sorts: either it addresses a particular exegetical, archaeological, or historical problem, or it seeks to reflect on the status of the field by raising organizational, hermeneutical, or methodological questions. The latter type sometimes attempts to chart the paradigm shifts or decentering processes in biblical scholarship that displace the dominant ethos of research but do not completely replace it or make it obsolete.

Almost eighty years ago, in his presidential address entitled "The Bearing of Historical Studies on the Religious Use of the Bible," Frank Porter of Yale University charted three such shifts: (1) The first stage, out of which biblical scholarship had just emerged, was the stage in which the book's records are imposed upon the present as an external authority. (2) The second stage, through which biblical scholarship was passing in 1908, was that of historical science, which brings deliverance from dogmatic bondage and teaches us to view the past as past, biblical history like other histories, and the Bible like other books. (3) Porter envisioned a third stage "at which, while the rights and achievements of historical criticism are freely accepted, the power that lives in the book is once more felt."[2] He likens this third stage to the reading of great books, whose greatness does not consist in their accuracy as records of facts, but depends chiefly on their symbolic power to transfigure the facts of human experience and reality. In the past fifteen years or so, biblical studies has followed Parker's lead and adopted insights and methods derived from literary studies[3] and philosophical hermeneutics, but it has, to a great extent, refused to relinquish its rhetorical stance of value-free objectivism and scientific methodism.

This third literary-hermeneutical paradigm seems presently in the process of decentering into a fourth paradigm that inaugurates a rhetorical-ethical turn. This fourth paradigm relies on the analytical and practical tradition of rhetoric in order

---

1. This chapter was first published in *JBL* 107 1 (1988): 3–17.

2. Frank C. Porter, "The Bearing of Historical Studies on the Religious Use of the Bible," *HTR* 2 (1909): 276.

3. Amos N. Wilder articulated this literary-aesthetic paradigm as rhetorical. See his SBL presidential address, "Scholars, Theologians, and Ancient Rhetoric," *JBL* 75 (1956): 1–11; and his book, *Early Christian Rhetoric: The Language of the Gospel* (Cambridge, Mass.: Harvard University Press, 1971).

to insist on the public-political responsibility of biblical scholarship. It seeks to utilize both theories of rhetoric and the rhetoric of theories in order to display how biblical texts and their contemporary interpretations involve authorial aims and strategies, as well as audience perceptions and constructions, as political and religious discursive practices. This fourth paradigm seeks to engender a self-understanding of biblical scholarship as communicative praxis. It rejects the misunderstanding of rhetoric as stylistic ornament, technical skills, or linguistic manipulation, and maintains not only "that rhetoric is epistemic but also that epistemology and ontology are themselves rhetorical."[4] Biblical interpretation, like all scholarly inquiry, is a communicative practice that involves interests, values, and visions.

Since the sociohistorical location of rhetoric is the public of the polis, the rhetorical paradigm shift situates biblical scholarship in such a way that its public character and political responsibility become an integral part of our literary readings and historical reconstructions of the biblical world. "The turn to rhetoric" that has engendered critical theory in literary, historical, political, and social studies fashions a theoretical context for such a paradigm shift in biblical studies.[5] Critical theory, reader-response criticism, and poststructuralist analysis,[6] as well as the insight into the rhetorical character and linguisticality of all historiography, represent the contemporary revival of ancient rhetoric.

The ethics of reading, which respects the rights of the text and assumes that the text being interpreted "may say something different from what one wants or expects it to say,"[7] is highly developed in biblical studies. Therefore, I will focus here on the

4. Richard Harvey Brown, *Society as Text: Essays on Rhetoric, Reason, and Reality* (Chicago: University of Chicago Press, 1987), 85. See also, for example, *The Rhetoric of the Human Sciences: Language and Argument in Scholarship and Public Affairs,* ed. John S. Nelson, Allan Megill, Donald McCloskey (Madison: University of Wisconsin Press, 1987); Hayden White, *Tropics of Discourse: Essays in Cultural Criticism* (Baltimore: Johns Hopkins University Press, 1978); Ricca Edmondson, *Rhetoric in Sociology* (New York: Cambridge University Press, 1985); John S. Nelson, "Political Theory as Political Rhetoric," in *What Should Political Theory Be Now? Essays from the Shambaugh Conference on Political Theory,* ed. John S. Nelson (Albany: State University of New York Press, 1983), 169–240.

5. See my article "Rhetorical Situation and Historical Reconstruction in I Corinthians," *NTS* 33 (1987): 386–403 (see chapter 5); and Wilhelm Wuellner, "Where Is Rhetorical Criticism Taking Us?" *CBQ* 49 (1987): 448–63, for further literature.

6. For bringing together the insights of this paper, I have found especially helpful the works of feminist literary and cultural criticism. See, for example, Seyla Benhabib and Drucilla Cornell, eds., *Feminism as Critique: On the Politics of Gender* (Minneapolis: University of Minnesota Press, 1987); Gayatri Chakravorty Spivak, *In Other Worlds: Essays in Cultural Politics* (New York: Methuen, 1987); Teresa de Lauretis, ed, *Feminist Studies/Critical Studies* (Bloomington: University of Indiana Press, 1986); Elizabeth A. Flynn and Patrocinio P. Schweickart, eds., *Gender and Reading: Essays on Readers, Texts, and Contexts* (Baltimore: Johns Hopkins University Press, 1986); Gayle Greene and Coppélia Kahn, eds., *Making a Difference: Feminist Literary Criticism* (New York: Methuen, 1985); Elizabeth A. Meese, *Crossing the Double Cross: The Practice of Feminist Criticism* (Chapel Hill: University of North Carolina Press, 1986); Judith Newton and Deborah Rosenfelt, eds., *Feminist Criticism and Social Change: Sex, Class, and Race in Literature and Culture* (New York: Methuen, 1985); Marjorie Pryse and Hortense J. Spillers, eds., *Conjuring: Black Women, Fiction, and Literary Tradition* (Bloomington: University of Indiana Press, 1985); Chris Weedon, *Feminist Practice and Poststructuralist Theory* (London: Blackwell, 1987).

7. J. Hillis Miller, "Presidential Address 1986: The Triumph of Theory, the Resistance to Reading, and the Question of the Material Base," *Modern Language Association Proceedings* 102 (1987): 284.

ethics of biblical scholarship as an institutionalized academic practice. I will approach the topic by marking my present rhetorical situation as a "connected critic"[8] who speaks from a marginal location and that of an engaged position. Then I will explore the rhetoric of SBL presidential addresses with respect to the shift from a scientific antiquarian to a critical-political ethos of biblical scholarship. Finally, I will indicate what kind of communicative practice such a shift implies.

Social Location and Biblical Criticism

In distinction to formalist literary criticism, a critical theory of rhetoric insists that context is as important as text. What we see depends on where we stand. One's social location or rhetorical context is decisive for how one sees the world, constructs reality, or interprets biblical texts. My own rhetorical situation is marked by what Virginia Woolf, in her book *Three Guineas*, has characterized as the "outsider's view":

> It is a solemn sight always—a procession like a caravanserai crossing a desert. Great-grandfather, grandfathers, fathers, uncles—they all went that way wearing their gowns, wearing their wigs, some with ribbons across their breasts, others without. One was a bishop. Another a judge. One was an admiral. Another a general. One was a professor. Another a doctor. . . . But now for the past twenty years or so, it is no longer a sight merely, a photograph . . . at which we can look with merely an esthetic appreciation. For there, trapesing along at the tail end of the procession, we go ourselves. And that makes a difference.[9]

Almost from its beginning women scholars have joined the procession of American biblical scholars.[10] In 1889, not quite one hundred years ago, Anna Rhoads Ladd became the first female member of this Society. Ten years later, in 1899, Mary Emma Woolley—since 1895 chair of the Department of Biblical History, Literature, and Exegesis at Wellesley College, and from 1900 to 1937 President of Mount Holyoke College—is listed in attendance at the annual meeting. In 1913 Professor Eleanor D. Wood presented a paper on biblical archaeology, and in 1917 Professor Louise Pettibone Smith, who also served later in 1950–51 as secretary of the Society, was the first woman to publish an article in the *Journal of Biblical Literature* (*JBL*). Mary J. Hussy of Mount Holyoke College had held the post of treasurer already in 1924–26. At the crest of the first wave of American feminism, women's membership

8. Michael Walzer characterizes the "connected critic" as follows: "Amos' prophecy is social criticism because it challenges the leaders, the conventions, the ritual practices of a particular society and because it does so in the name of values shared and recognized in that same society" (*Interpretation and Social Criticism* [Cambridge, Mass.: Harvard University Press, 1987], 89).

9. Virginia Woolf, *Three Guineas* (New York: Harcourt, Brace, Jovanovich, 1966), 61.

10. For the following information, see Dorothy C. Bass, "Women's Studies and Biblical Studies: An Historical Perspective," *JSOT* 22 (1982): 6–12; Ernest W. Saunders, *Searching the Scriptures: A History of the Society of Biblical Literature, 1880–1980* (Chico, Calif.: Scholars Press, 1982), 70, 83f.; and Carolyn De Swarte Gifford, "American Women and the Bible: The Nature of Woman as a Hermeneutical Issue," in *Feminist Perspectives on Biblical Scholarship*, ed. Adela Yarbro Collins (Chico, Calif.: Scholars Press, 1985), 11–33.

in 1920 was around 10 percent. Afterward it steadily declined until it achieved a low of 3.5 percent in 1970. Presently the Society does not have a database sufficient to compute the percentage of its white women and minority members.

The second wave of the women's movement made itself felt at the annual meeting in 1971, when the Women's Caucus in Religious Studies was organized; the first co-chairs were Professor Carol Christ of the American Academy of Religion (AAR) and myself. A year later, at the International Congress of Learned Societies in Los Angeles, the Caucus called for representation of women on the various boards and committees of the Society, the anonymous submission and evaluation of manuscripts for *JBL*, and the establishment of a job registry through the Council on the Study of Religion (CSR). At the business meeting two women were elected to the council and one to the executive board. Fifteen years later, I am privileged to inaugurate what will, it is hoped, be a long line of women presidents, consisting not only of white women but also of women of color,[11] who are woefully underrepresented in the discipline. The historic character of this moment is cast into relief when one considers that in Germany not a single woman has achieved the rank of ordinary professor in one of the established Roman Catholic theological faculties.[12]

However, the mere admission of women into the ranks of scholarship and the various endeavors of the Society does not necessarily assure that biblical scholarship is done in the interest and from the perspective of women or others marginal to the academic enterprise. Historian Dorothy Bass, to whom we owe most of our information about women's historical participation in the SBL, has pointed to a critical difference between the women of the last century who joined the Society as scholars and those women who sought for a scientific investigation of the Bible in the interest of women.[13] Feminist biblical scholarship has its roots not in the academy but in the social movements for the emancipation of slaves and of freeborn women. Against the assertion that God has sanctioned the system of slavery and intended the subordination of women,[14] the Grimké sisters, Sojourner Truth, Jarena Lee, and others dis-

11. To my knowledge in 1987 only one African American and one Asian American woman had yet received a doctorate in biblical studies. Even now, to my knowledge, no African American, Asian American or Latina/o American, male or female, has served as president or officer of the Society. At a recent conference on "African Americans and the Bible" at Union Theological Seminary in New York, April 8–11, 1999, Professor Randall Bailey presented in a lecture on "The Current Status of Scholarly Black Biblical Interpretation in the U.S." the following statistics: currently seventeen African Americans hold doctorates in Hebrew Bible and sixteen in New Testament Studies; of the six who are wo/men, one is in New Testament (and one more to graduate this spring) and five in Hebrew Bible. These statistics, which have not changed much in the twelve years since I presented this address, prove that the ethos of the discipline is kyriocentric.

12. In the meantime several wo/men have been appointed to Roman Catholic faculties. However, they have achieved their appointments under the condition that they publicly declared their assent to the papal prohibition of the ordination of wo/men. Since there is no academic freedom on German Catholic faculties, one cannot hope for a critical change of the discipline.

13. Bass, "Women's Studies," 10–11.

14. Barbara Brown Zikmund, "Biblical Arguments and Women's Place in the Church," in *The Bible and Social Reform,* ed. Ernest R. Sandeen (Philadelphia: Fortress Press, 1982), 85–104. For Jarena Lee, see William L. Andrews, ed., *Sisters of the Spirit: Three Black Women's Autobiographies of the Nineteenth Century* (Bloomington: Indiana University Press, 1986).

tinguished between the oppressive anti-Christian traditions of men and the life-giving intentions of God. Many reformers of the nineteenth century shared the conviction that women must learn the original languages of Greek and Hebrew in order to produce unbiased translations and interpretations faithful to the original divine intentions of the Bible. Nineteenth-century feminists were well aware that higher biblical criticism provided a scholarly grounding of their arguments. Women's rights leaders such as Frances Willard and Elizabeth Cady Stanton were the most explicit in calling on women to learn the methods of higher biblical criticism in order to critique patriarchal religion.

Although Elizabeth Cady Stanton and the editorial committee of *The Woman's Bible* sought to utilize the insights and methods of "higher criticism" for interpreting the biblical texts on women, no alliance between feminist biblical interpretation and historical-critical scholarship was forged in the nineteenth century. Cady Stanton had invited distinguished women scholars "versed in biblical criticism" to contribute to *The Woman's Bible* project. But her invitation was declined because, as she states, "they were afraid that their high reputation and scholarly attainments might be compromised."[15] This situation continued well into the first half of the twentieth century. In the 1920s, Rev. Lee Anna Starr and Dr. Katherine Bushnell, both outside the profession, used their knowledge of biblical languages and higher criticism to analyze the status of women in the Bible and the theological bases for women's role in Scripture.[16]

The androcentric character of biblical texts and interpretations was not addressed by a woman scholar until 1964 when Margaret Brackenbury Crook, a longstanding member of the SBL and professor of Biblical Literature at Smith College, published *Women and Religion*.[17] Although Brackenbury Crook repeatedly claimed that she did not advocate feminism or animosity toward men but that as a scholar she was simply stating the facts on the basis of evidence, she did so in order to insist that the masculine monopoly in biblical religions must be broken and that women must participate in shaping religious thought, symbols, and traditions.

In the context of the women's movements in the seventies and eighties, women scholars have not only joined the procession of educated men but have also sought to do so in the interest of women. We no longer deny our feminist engagement for the sake of scholarly acceptance. Rather, we celebrate tonight the numerous feminist publications, papers, and monographs of SBL members that have not only enhanced our knowledge about women in the biblical worlds but have also sought to change

15. Elizabeth Cady Stanton, ed., *The Original Feminist Attack on the Bible: The Woman's Bible* (1895, 1898; facsimile ed., New York: Arno, 1974), 1. 9; see also Elaine C. Huber, "They Weren't Prepared to Hear: A Closer Look at *The Woman's Bible*," *Andover Newton Quarterly* 16 (1976): 271–76; and Anne McGrew Bennett et al., "The Woman's Bible: Review and Perspectives," in *Women and Religion, 1973: Pre-printed Papers for the Working Group on Women and Religion,* comp. Joan Arnold Romero (Tallahassee: AAR, 1973), 39–78.

16. Lee Anna Starr, *The Bible Status of Women* (New York: Fleming Revell, 1926); Katherine C. Bushnell, *God's Word to Women: One Hundred Bible Studies on Woman's Place in the Divine Economy* (North Collins, N.Y.: Ray Munson, 1923).

17. Margaret Brackenbury Crook, *Women and Religion* (Boston: Beacon, 1964); see also Elsie Thomas Culver, *Women in the World of Religion* (Garden City, N.Y.: Doubleday, 1967).

our methods of reading and reconstruction, as well as our hermeneutical perspectives and scholarly assumptions. The Women in the Biblical World Section has since 1981 consistently raised issues of method and hermeneutics that are of utmost importance for the wider Society.[18]

And yet, whether and how much our work has made serious inroads in biblical scholarship remain to be seen. The following anecdote can highlight what I mean. I am told that, after I had been elected president of the Society, a journalist asked one of the leading officers of the organization whether I had been nominated because the Society wanted to acknowledge not only my active participation in its ongoing work but also my theoretical contributions, both to the reconstruction of Christian origins and to the exploration of a critical biblical hermeneutic and rhetoric.[19] He reacted with surprise at such a suggestion and assured her that I was elected because my work on the Book of Revelation proved me to be a solid and serious scholar.

Interpretive communities such as the SBL are not just scholarly investigative communities but also authoritative communities. They possess the power to ostracize or to embrace, to foster or to restrict membership, to recognize and to define what "true scholarship" entails. The question today is no longer whether women should join the procession of educated men, but under what conditions we can do so. What kind of ethos, ethics, and politics of the community of biblical scholars would allow us to move our work done in the interest of women from the margins to the center of biblical studies?

I hasten to say that I do not want to be misunderstood as advocating a return to a precritical reading and facile application of biblical texts on and about *Woman*. Rather, I am interested in decentering the dominant scientistic ethos of biblical scholarship by recentering it in a critical interpretive praxis for liberation. Ethos is the shared intellectual space of freely accepted obligations and traditions as well as the praxial space of discourse and action.[20] Since ethos shapes our scholarly behavior and attitudes, it needs to be explored more explicitly in terms of its rhetorical aims, which seek to affect a common orientation among its practitioners. The rhetoric of previous addresses of SBL presidents can serve as a text for engaging us in a critical reflection on the ethos as well as the rhetorical aims of biblical studies.

The Rhetoric of Biblical Scholarship

Only a few presidential addresses have reflected on their own political contexts and rhetorical strategies. If my research assistant is correct,[21] in the past forty years, no

18. The two volumes of *Searching the Scriptures* that I have edited owe their conceptualization to a series of panel discussions in preparation for the centennial of *The Woman's Bible*.

19. See my books, *In Memory of Her; Bread Not Stone; But She Said; Discipleship of Equals: A Feminist Ekklesialogy of Liberation* (New York: Crossroad, 1993); and *Sharing Her Word*.

20. See Calvin O. Schrag, *Communicative Praxis and the Space of Subjectivity* (Bloomington: Indiana University Press, 1986), 179–214.

21. I want to thank Ann Millin, Episcopal Divinity School, for checking SBL presidential addresses for references to and reflections of their political contexts; thanks also to Margaret Hutaff, Harvard Divin-

president of SBL has used the opportunity of the presidential address for asking the membership to consider the political context of their scholarship and to reflect on its public accountability. Since 1947, no presidential address has explicitly reflected on world politics, global crises, human sufferings, or movements for change. Neither the civil rights movement nor the various liberation struggles of the so-called Third World, neither the assassination of Martin Luther King, Jr., nor the Holocaust has been the rhetorical context for biblical studies. Biblical studies appears to have progressed in a political vacuum, and scholars seem to have understood themselves as accountable solely—as Robert Funk puts it—to the vested interests of the "fraternity of scientifically trained scholars with the soul of a church."[22] This ethos of American biblical scholarship after 1947 is anticipated in the following letter of Rudolf Bultmann written in 1926:

> Of course the impact of the war has led many people to revise their concepts of human existence; but I must confess that that has not been so in my case.... So I do not believe that the war has influenced my theology. My view is that if anyone is looking for the genesis of our theology he [sic] will find that internal discussion with the theology of our teachers plays an incomparably greater role than the impact of the war or reading Dostoievsky [sic].[23]

My point here is not an indictment of Bultmann, who more than many others was aware that presupposition-less exegesis is neither possible nor desirable. Rather, it allows me to raise the question: Does the immanent discourse between teachers and students, between academic fathers and sons—or daughters for that matter— between different schools of interpretation jeopardize the intellectual rigor of the discipline? Do we ask and teach our students to ask in a disciplined way how our scholarship is conditioned by its social location and how it serves political functions?

In his 1945 address, President Enslin of Crozer Theological Seminary ironizes the British snobbishness of Sir Oliver Lodge, who thought that the only American worth speaking to was Henry Cabot Lodge.[24] He nevertheless unwittingly supports such a scholarly in-house discourse by advocating an immersion in the works of the great scholars of the past while at the same time excoriating the "demand for the practical in biblical research." He rejects the requirement that biblical research "strengthen

ity School, for proofreading the manuscript. I am also indebted to Francis Schüssler Fiorenza for his critical reading of several drafts of this paper.

22. Robert W. Funk, "The Watershed of the American Biblical Tradition: The Chicago School, First Phase, 1892–1920," *JBL* 95 (1976): 4–22.7.

23. Letter to Erich Forster, pastor and professor in Frankfurt, as quoted by Walter Schmithals, *An Introduction to the Theology of Rudolf Bultmann* (Minneapolis: Augsburg, 1968), 9–10. See also Dorothe Soelle, "Rudolf Bultmann und die politische Theologie," in *Rudolf Bultmann. 100 Jahre,* ed. Hartwig Thyen et al. (Oldenburger Vorträge; Oldenburg: H. Holzberg, 1985), 69ff.; and Dieter Georgi, "Rudolf Bultmann's Theology of the New Testament Revisited," in *Bultmann: Retrospect and Prospect. The Centenary Symposium at Wellesley,* ed. E. C. Hobbs, HTS 35 (Philadelphia: Fortress Press, 1985), 82ff.

24. Morton S. Enslin, "The Future of Biblical Studies," *JBL* 65 (1946): 1–12. Already Julian Morgenstern had argued "that in Germany biblical science is doomed." Since in Europe biblical studies are in decline, North America, that is, the U.S. and Canada, "must become the major center of biblical research" ("The Society of Biblical Literature and Exegesis," *JBL* 61 [1942]: 4–5).

faith and provide blueprints for modern conduct" as one and the same virus which has poisoned German scholarship and made it liable to Nazi ideology. He therefore argues that biblical critics must be emotionally detached, intellectually dispassionate, and rationally value-neutral. Critical detachment is an achievement that turns the critic into a lonely hero who has to pay a price in comfort and solidarity. However, Enslin does not consider that this scholarly ethos of dispassionate industry, eternal questioning, utter loneliness, detached inquiry, patient toil without practical results, and the unhampered pursuit of truth "under the direction of men [sic] whom students can trust and revere" could be the more dangerous part of the same political forgetfulness that in his view has poisoned German biblical scholarship.

This scientistic ethos of value-free detached inquiry insists that the biblical critic needs to stand outside the common circumstances of collective life and stresses the alien character of biblical materials. What makes biblical interpretation possible is radical detachment and emotional, intellectual, and political distancing. Disinterested and dispassionate scholarship enables biblical critics to enter the minds and world of historical people, to step out of their own time, and to study history on its own terms, unencumbered by contemporary questions, values, and interests. Apolitical detachment, objective literalism, and scientific value-neutrality are the rhetorical postures that seem to be dominant in the positivistic paradigm of biblical scholarship. The decentering of this rhetoric of disinterestedness and presupposition-free exegesis seeks to recover the political context of biblical scholarship and its public responsibility.

The scientistic ethos of biblical studies was shaped by the struggle of biblical scholarship to free itself from dogmatic and ecclesiastical controls. It corresponded to the professionalization of academic life and the rise of the university. Just as history as an academic discipline sought in the last quarter of the nineteenth century to prove itself as an objective science in analogy to the natural sciences, so also did biblical studies. Scientific history sought to establish facts objectively, free from philosophical considerations. It was determined to hold strictly to facts and evidence, not to sermonize or moralize, but to tell the simple historic truth—in short, to narrate things as they actually happened.[25] Historical science was a technique that applied critical methods to the evaluation of sources, which in turn were understood as data and evidence. The mandate to avoid theoretical considerations and normative concepts in the immediate encounter with the text was meant to assure that the resulting historical accounts would be free of ideology.

In this country, Ranke was identified as the father of "the true historical method," which eschewed all theoretical reflection. Ranke became for many American scholars the prototype of the nontheoretical and the politically neutral historian, although he himself sought to combine theoretically his historical method with his conservative political views.[26] This positivist nineteenth-century understanding of histori-

25. George G. Iggers, *The German Conception of History: The National Tradition of Historical Thought from Herder to the Present* (rev. ed., Middletown, Conn.: Wesleyan University Press, 1983).

26. Robert A. Oden, Jr., "Hermeneutics and Historiography: Germany and America," in *SBL 1980 Seminar Papers*, ed. Paul J. Achtemeier (Chico, Calif.: Scholars Press, 1980), 135–57.

ography as a science was the theoretical context for the development of biblical scholarship in the academy. Since the ethos of objective scientism and theoretical value-neutrality was articulated in the political context of several heresy trials at the turn of the twentieth century, its rhetoric continues to reject all overt theological and religious institutional engagement as unscientific, while at the same time claiming a name and space marked by the traditional biblical canon. Such a scientistic posture of historical research is, however, not displaced when it is decentered by an objectivist stance that arrogates the methodological formalism of literary or sociological science. The pretension of biblical studies to "scientific" modes of inquiry that deny their hermeneutical and theoretical character and mask their historical-social location prohibits a critical reflection on these rhetorical theological practices in their sociopolitical context.

Although the dominant ethos of biblical studies in this century seems to have been that which is paradigmatically expressed in Bultmann's letter and Enslin's address, there have nevertheless also been presidential voices that have challenged this self-understanding of biblical scholarship. Already in 1919, James Montgomery of the University of Pennsylvania had launched a scathing attack on the professed detachment of biblical scholars when addressing the Society:

> We academics flatter ourselves on what we call our pure science and think we are the heirs of an eternal possession abstracted from the vicissitudes of time. We recall Archimedes working out his mathematical problems under the dagger of the assassin, or Goethe studying Chinese during the Battle of Jena. But we dare not in this day take comfort in those academic anecdotes nor desire to liken ourselves to the monastic scholars who pursued their studies and meditations in their cells undisturbed by the wars raging without. . . . [27]

Almost twenty years later, at the eve of World War II, Henry Cadbury of Harvard University discussed in his presidential address the motives for the changes in biblical scholarship. He observed that most members of the Society were horrified by the perversions of learning and prostitutions of scholarship to partisan propagandistic ends in Nazi Germany. He noted, however, that at the same time most members were not equally aware of the public responsibility of their own scholarship and of the social consequences of their research. Cadbury therefore challenged the membership to become aware of the moral and spiritual needs in contemporary life and to take responsibility for the social and spiritual functions of biblical scholarship.[28]

At the end of World War II, Leroy Waterman of the University of Michigan also called in his address for the sociopublic responsibility of scholarship. Biblical scholarship must be understood as situated in a morally unstable world tottering on the brink of atomic annihilation. Students of the Bible should therefore take note of the deep moral confusion in their world situation and at the same time make available "any pertinent resources within their own keeping." While biblical scholars cannot

---

27. James A. Montgomery, "Present Tasks of American Biblical Scholarship," *JBL* 38 (1919): 2.
28. Henry J. Cadbury, "Motives of Biblical Scholarship," *JBL* 56 (1937): 1–16.

forsake their research in "order to peddle their wares," they also cannot remain in the ivory tower "of privileged aloofness."

Waterman argued that biblical studies and natural science have in common the "claim to seek truth in complete objectivity without regard to consequences."[29] But biblical scholarship and natural science sharply diverge with respect to their public influence. Whereas science has cultivated a public that is aware of the improvements science can effect for the increase of human welfare or its destruction, biblical scholarship has taken for granted the public influence of the Bible in western culture. Therefore, it has cultivated as its public not society as a whole but organized religion, "whose dominant leadership has been more concerned with the defense of the status quo than with any human betterment accruing from new religious insights."[30] The task of biblical studies in this situation is therefore to make available to humanity on the brink of atomic annihilation the moral resources and ethical directives of biblical religions. At the eve of the Reagan-Gorbachev summit on nuclear arms reduction, Waterman's summons of the Society to public responsibility is still timely.

The Ethos of Biblical Scholarship:
Critical Rhetoric and Ethics

Although I agree with his summons to public responsibility, I do not share Waterman's optimistic view of positivist science. The reluctance of the discipline to reflect on its sociopolitical location cannot simply be attributed, as Waterman does, to the repression of biblical scholarship by organized religion. It is as much due to its ethos of scientistic positivism and professed value-neutrality. Scientistic epistemologies covertly advocate an apolitical reality without assuming responsibility for their political assumptions and interests. "Scientism has pretensions to a mode of inquiry that tries to deny its own hermeneutic character and mask its own historicity so that it might claim a historical certainty."[31]

Critical theory of rhetoric or discursive practices, as developed in literary, political, and historical studies, seeks to decenter the objectivist and depoliticized ethos of biblical studies with an ethos of rhetorical inquiry that could engage in the formation of a critical historical and religious consciousness. The reconceptualization of biblical studies in rhetorical rather than scientistic terms would provide a research framework not only for integrating historical, archaeological, sociological, literary, and theological approaches as perspectival readings of texts but also for raising ethical-political and religious-theological questions as constitutive of the interpretive process. A rhetorical hermeneutic does not assume that the text is a window to historical reality, nor does it operate with a correspondence theory of truth. It does

---

29. Leroy Waterman, "Biblical Studies in a New Setting," *JBL* 66 (1947): 5.
30. Ibid.
31. David Tracy, *Plurality and Ambiguity: Hermeneutics, Religion, and Hope* (New York: Harper & Row, 1987), 31.

not understand historical sources as data and evidence but sees them as perspectival discourses constructing their worlds and symbolic universes.[32]

Since alternative symbolic universes engender competing definitions of the world, they cannot be reduced to one meaning. Therefore, competing definitions are not simply either right or wrong,[33] but they constitute different ways of reading and constructing historical meaning. Not detached value-neutrality but an explicit articulation of one's rhetorical strategies, interested perspectives, ethical criteria, theoretical frameworks, religious presuppositions, and sociopolitical locations for critical public discussion are appropriate in such a rhetorical paradigm of biblical scholarship.

The rhetorical understanding of discourse as creating a world of pluriform meanings and a pluralism of symbolic universes raises the question of power. How is meaning constructed? Whose interests are served? What kind of worlds are envisioned? What roles, duties, and values are advocated? Which social-political practices are legitimated? Or which communities of discourse are accountable? Such and similar questions become central to the interpretive task. Once biblical scholarship begins to talk explicitly of social interests, whether of race, gender, culture, or class, and once it begins to recognize the need for a sophisticated and pluralistic reading of texts that questions the fixity of meaning, then a double ethics is called for.

An ethics of critical reading changes the task of interpretation from finding out "what the text meant" to the question of what kind of readings can do justice to the text in its historical context. Although such an ethics is aware of the plurality of historical- and literary-critical methods as well as the plurality of interpretations appropriate to the text, it nevertheless insists that the number of interpretations that can legitimately be given to a text are limited. Such a historical reading seeks to give the text its due by asserting its possible historical meanings over and against later dogmatic usurpations. It makes the assimilation of the text to our own experience and interests more difficult and thereby keeps alive the "irritation" of the "original" text by challenging our own assumptions, worldviews, and practices.

In short, the methods of historical- and literary-critical scholarship and its diachronic reconstructions distance us in such a way from the original texts and their historical symbolic worlds that they relativize not only them but also us. By illuminating the ethical-political dimensions of the biblical text in its historical contexts, such an ethics of critical reading allows one not only to relativize through contextualization the values and authority claims of the biblical text but also to assess and critically evaluate their rhetoric. It would be misunderstood if it were to search for "origins" or try to "fix" the text's meaning once and for all. Rather, it always must heed the warning of Alicia Ostriker:

32. See the discussion of scientific theory choice by Linda Alcoff, "Justifying Feminist Social Science," *Hypatia* 2 (1987): 107–27.

33. Maurice Mandelbaum, *The Anatomy of Historical Knowledge* (Baltimore: Johns Hopkins University Press, 1977), 150.

The hermeneutics of indeterminacy is what seems to be potentially most significant for the future. Suppose we take seriously the rabbinic saying that "There is always another interpretation." If this is the case, then my interpretation, yours, his, hers, must always be contingent, never final. There is not and cannot ever be a "correct" interpretation, there can only be another, and another. . . . . Human civilization has a stake in plural readings. We've seen this at least since the eighteenth century when the notion of religious tolerance was invented to keep the Christian sects from killing each other. The notion of racial tolerance came later. Most people haven't caught on, though. Most people need "right" answers, just as they need "superior" races. And groups tend to lose their enthusiasm for pluralism when they are no longer persecuted minorities but become dominant majorities. At this particular moment, it happens to be feminists and other socially marginal types who are battling for cultural pluralism. Still, this is an activity we're undertaking on behalf of humanity, all of whom would be the happier, I believe, were they to throw away their addiction to final solutions.[34]

Hence the rhetorical character of biblical interpretations and historical reconstructions requires an ethics of accountability that stands responsible not only for the choice of theoretical interpretive models but also for the ethical consequences of the biblical text and its subsequent interpretations. If scriptural texts have served—and still do—not only to support noble causes but also to legitimate war, to nurture anti-Judaism and misogyny, to justify the exploitation of slavery, and to promote colonial dehumanization, then biblical scholarship must take the responsibility not only to interpret biblical texts in their historical contexts but also to evaluate the construction of their historical worlds and symbolic universes in terms of a religious scale of values. If the Bible has become a classic of western culture because of its normativity, then the responsibility of the biblical scholar cannot be restricted to giving "the readers of our time clear access to the original intentions" of the biblical writers.[35] It must also include the elucidation of the ethical consequences and political functions of biblical texts and their interpretations in their historical as well as in their contemporary sociopolitical contexts.

Just as literary critics have called for an interpretive evaluation of classic works of art in terms of justice, so students of the Bible must learn how to examine both the rhetorical aims of biblical texts and the rhetorical interests emerging in the history of interpretation or in contemporary scholarship in terms of the vision of justice and well-being for all. This requires that we revive a responsible ethical and political criticism that recognizes the ideological distortions of great works of religion. Such a discursive ethics does not just evaluate the ideas or propositions of a work but also seeks to determine whether its very language and composition promote stereotypical images and linguistic violence. What does the language of a biblical text "do" to a reader who submits to its world of vision?[36]

---

34. Alicia Suskin Ostriker, *Feminist Revision and the Bible* (Cambridge: Blackwell, 1993), 123.

35. Krister Stendahl, "The Bible as a Classic and the Bible as Holy Scripture," *JBL* 103 (1984): 10.

36. See Wayne C. Booth, "Freedom of Interpretation: Bakhtin and the Challenge of the Feminist Criticism," in *The Politics of Interpretation*, ed. W. J. T. Mitchell (Chicago: University of Chicago Press, 1983), 51–82.

In order to answer this question, the careful reading of biblical texts and the appropriate reconstruction of their historical worlds and of their symbolic universes need to be complemented by a theo-ethical[37] discussion of the contemporary religious functions of biblical texts that claim scriptural authority today in biblical communities of faith. An ethics of accountability calls for an open forum in which biblical texts and interpretations can be problematized, interrogated, and re-visioned. To open up biblical texts and the historical reconstructions of their worlds for public discussion requires that students of the Bible learn to traverse not only the boundaries of theological disciplines but also those of other intellectual disciplines.[38]

To enable scholars to do so, biblical studies will have to overcome the institutionalized dichotomy between graduate training in the university and ministerial education in schools of theology. M.A. and Ph.D. students interested in teaching in seminaries and church-related schools need to become skilled in critical-theological reflection just as M.Div. and D.Min. students should be versed in the analysis of religion and culture. Moreover, in view of the insistence that all professions and research institutions should become conscious of the values they embody and the interests they serve, students in religious studies as well as in theology must learn to engage in a disciplined reflection on the societal and public values[39] promoted by their intellectual disciplines.

Finally, the growth of right-wing political fundamentalism and of biblicist literalism in society, religious institutions, and the broader culture feeds antidemocratic authoritarianism and fosters personal prejudice. In the light of this political situation, biblical scholarship has the responsibility to make its research available to a wider public. Since literalist biblical fundamentalism asserts the public claims and values of biblical texts, biblical scholarship can no longer restrict its public to institutionalized religions and to the in-house discourse of the academy. Rather, biblical scholarship must acknowledge the continuing political influence of the Bible in western culture and society.

If biblical studies continues to limit its educational communicative practices to students preparing for the professional pastoral ministry and for academic posts in theological schools, it forgoes the opportunity to foster a critical biblical culture and a pluralistic historical consciousness. Therefore, the Society should provide leadership as to how to make our research available to those who are engaged in the communication of biblical knowledge, who have to confront biblical fundamentalism in their professions, and especially to those who have internalized their oppression through a literalist reading of the Bible. Such a different public location of biblical

---

37. For this expression, see K. G. Cannon, *Black Womanist Ethics* (Atlanta: Scholars Press, 1988).

38. See Francis Schüssler Fiorenza, "Theory and Practice: Theological Education as a Reconstructive, Hermeneutical, and Practical Task," *Theological Education* 23 (1987): 113–41.

39. See also Ronald F. Thiemann, "Toward an American Public Theology: Religion in a Pluralistic Theology," *Harvard Divinity Bulletin* 18, 1 (1987): 3–6, 10.

discourse requires that the Society actively scrutinize its communicative practices and initiate research programs and discussion forums that could address issues of biblical education and communication.

In conclusion, I have argued for a paradigm shift in the ethos and rhetorical practices of biblical scholarship. If religious studies becomes public deliberative discourse and rhetorical construction oriented toward the present and the future, then biblical studies becomes a critical reflection on the rhetorical practices encoded in the literatures of the biblical world and their social or ecclesial functions today. Such a critical-rhetorical paradigm requires that biblical studies continues its descriptive-analytic work utilizing all the critical methods available for illuminating our understanding of ancient texts and their historical location. At the same time, it engages biblical scholarship in a hermeneutic-evaluative discursive practice by exploring the power-knowledge relations inscribed in contemporary biblical discourses and in biblical texts themselves.

Such an approach opens up the rhetorical practices of biblical scholarship to the critical inquiry of all the disciplines of religious studies and theology. Questions raised by feminist scholars in religion, liberation theologians, theologians of the so-called Third World, and by others traditionally absent from the exegetical enterprise would not remain peripheral or nonexistent for biblical scholarship. Rather, their insights and challenges could become central to the scholarly discourse of the discipline.

In short, if the Society were to engage in a disciplined reflection on the public dimensions and ethical implications of our scholarly work, it would constitute a responsible scholarly citizenship that could be a significant participant in the global discourse seeking justice and well-being for all. The implications of such a re-positioning of the task and aim of biblical scholarship would be far-reaching and invigorating.

Chapter 2

Changing the Paradigms:
The Ethos of Biblical Studies

It has now been more than twenty years since I diagnosed a paradigm shift under way in biblical studies,[1] a shift from a scientist-positivist to a hermeneutic-pastoral paradigm.[2] In the meantime this hermeneutic-pastoral paradigm has evolved into a hermeneutic-cultural one, which is rivaled by a rhetorical-political ethos of interpretation. The prevalent hermeneutical division of labor between the exegete who describes what the text meant and the pastor/theologian who articulates what the text means has been seriously challenged in the past two decades and proven to be epistemologically inadequate. Although it was Krister Stendahl who advocated this division of labor between biblical scholar and theologian/pastor in his famous article on biblical theology,[3] he did so not in order to immunize historical-critical scholarship from critical theological reflection but in order—as he puts it—to liberate the theological enterprise from what he perceived as "the imperialism of biblical scholars" in the field of theology.[4]

However, twenty years later Stendahl saw the problem somewhat differently when he called for scholarly attention to the "public health" aspect of biblical interpretation. Reflecting on the fact that his own exegetical-theological thinking has circled around two New Testament issues—Jews and women—he points to the clearly detrimental and dangerous effects that the Bible and Christian tradition have had as

1. Parts of this chapter were presented in 1996 at the Twenty-Fifth Annual Meeting of the Korean Association of Christian Studies, Yunsug, Korea, and in a lecture to the Philippine Theological Association in Manila. I am grateful to Professor Chung Hyun Kyung for making my visit to Korea possible and for sharing with me the rich cultural historical heritage of her native country.

2. See my articles: "Women in Early Christianity: Methodological Considerations," in *Critical History and Biblical Faith in New Testament Perspectives*, ed. T. J. Ryan (Villanova, Pa., CTS Annual Publication, 1979), 30–58; and "For the Sake of Our Salvation: Biblical Interpretation as Theological Task," *in Sin, Salvation, and the Spirit: Commemorating the Fiftieth Year of the Liturgical Press*, ed. Daniel Durken (Collegeville, Minn., Liturgical Press, 1979), 21–39, although I have changed the nomenclature over the years. Such a change in naming always also entails a shift in content and accentuation.

3. Krister Stendahl, "Biblical Theology, Contemporary," in *The Interpreter's Dictionary of the Bible*, vol. 1, ed. Keith Crim (Nashville: Abingdon, 1962), 418–32.

4. Krister Stendahl, *Meanings: The Bible as Document and as Guide* (Philadelphia: Fortress Press, 1984), 1.

5. Krister Stendahl, "Ancient Scripture in the Modern World," in Frederick Greenspahn, ed., *Scripture in the Jewish and Christian Traditions: Antiquity, Interpretation, Relevance* (Nashville: Abingdon Press, 1982), 201–14, especially 204.

a major problem for scriptural interpretation.[5] This call for a public-ethical-political self-understanding of biblical studies has become even more pressing today after the Moral Majority in the 1970s and the Christian New Right in the 1980s and 1990s have made biblical injunctions an object of public debate.[6]

Coming from a quite different experience and standpoint in the academy than Stendahl, I have sought in my own work to contribute to the articulation of such a critical ethical-political paradigm for biblical interpretation. Exploring wo/men's positioning in the margins[7] of biblical scholarship and Christian theology, my work has pioneered a critical feminist biblical interpretation for liberation. Such a feminist critical and evaluative interpretation for liberation seeks to recover both biblical texts and the biblical past as shaped not just by the exclusion but also by the agency of wo/men,[8] and it seeks to do so for the sake of the present and the future.

A critical feminist hermeneutics does not simply "apply" or translate the solutions of the past to the problems of the present; its historical imagination seeks to reconstruct the sociopolitical worlds of biblical writings and contemporary biblical interpretations in order to open them up for critical inquiry and theological reflection. Studying the biblical past in order to name the destructive aspects of its language and symbolic universe as well as to recover its unfulfilled historical possibilities becomes a primary task for biblical scholarship today. A new paradigm seems to be evolving, which I would call either ethical-political, public-rhetorical, or feminist-postcolonial emancipatory, and which Fernando Segovia has named as the paradigm of cultural studies.[9] In order to elaborate this emerging critical evaluative paradigm theoretically, I want to explore the questions, methods, and strategies involved in biblical interpretation in terms of what Stendahl has called the "public health department" of biblical studies.

However, I will argue that in order to have a "public health department," biblical studies must be refashioned in such a way that it constitutes a public and not just an

6. The literature is extensive. See, for instance, Walter H. Capps, *The New Religious Right: Piety, Patriotism, and Politics* (Columbia: University of South Carolina Press, 1990); Lawrence Grossberg, *We Gotta Get Out of This Place: Popular Conservatism and Postmodern Culture* (New York: Routledge, 1992); Sara Diamond, *Spiritual Warfare: The Politics of the Christian Right* (Boston: South End Press, 1989); James Davison Hunter, *Culture Wars: The Struggle to Define America* (New York: Basic Books, 1991); Michael Barkun, *Religion and the Racist Right: The Origins of the Christian Identity Movement* (Chapel Hill: University of North Carolina Press, 1994); Douglas D. Rose, ed., *The Emergence of David Duke and the Politics of Race* (Chapel Hill: University of North Carolina Press, 1992).

7. R. S. Sugirtharajah, "Introduction: The Margin as a Site of Creative Revisioning," in *Voices from the Margin: Interpreting the Bible in the Third World*, ed. R. S. Sugirtharajah (rev. ed., Maryknoll, N.Y.: Orbis Books, 1995), 1–8.

8. I have resorted to writing wo/men in such a fragmented way in order to indicate the ambiguity and the inclusivity of the term. What wo/men means depends on its racial, class, and ethnic-cultural inflection. In addition, wo/man includes man and s/he includes he. Hence, I use wo/men in the same sense as the term "human," which is typed as elite male. See my book *Sharing Her Word*.

9. Fernando F. Segovia, "Cultural Studies and Contemporary Biblical Criticism: Ideological Criticism as a Mode of Discourse," in *Reading from This Place*, vol. 2, *Social Location and Biblical Interpretation in Global Perspective*, ed. Fernando F. Segovia and Mary Ann Tolbert (Minneapolis: Fortress Press, 1995), 1–17.

CHANGING THE PARADIGMS / 33

academic or theological-religious discourse. Refashioning its exegetical, historical, and hermeneutical inquiry, I argue, biblical studies must engage in critical readings and evaluations of biblical discourses in terms of a public, radical democratic ethos. It must ask: How has this text been used and how is it used today to defy or corroborate hegemonic political systems, laws, science, medicine, or public policy? How has biblical interpretation been used and how is the Bible still used either to challenge or to protect powerful interests and to engender sociocultural, political, and religious change? How is the Bible used to define public discourse and groups of people? What is the vision of society that is articulated in and through biblical texts? Is, and how is, Scripture used to marginalize certain people, to legitimate racism and other languages of hate, or is it used to intervene in discourses of injustice? Such questions must become as central as exegetical-historical and literary-anthropological questions still are and have been.

To commit biblical research to asking such questions, I suggest, would engender a transformation in the self-understanding of biblical studies. It would effectively change biblical studies into a rhetorical-ethical public discourse. To do so one needs, however, to carefully analyze what stands in the way of such a paradigm shift. I have pointed out repeatedly in my work that the scientistic-positivist ethos that is still virulent in religious and biblical studies is the main obstacle to a paradigm shift from a scientistic-hermeneutical to a rhetorical-political, from a kyriarchal Eurocentric to a radical egalitarian cosmopolitan model of interpretation.

Although this paradigm shift has been under way for quite some time and has brought ferment or upheaval—depending on one's political perspective—to the once stable field of biblical and religious studies, it has not been able to unseat the positivist scientific, supposedly disinterested, ethos of the discipline. Hence it also is not yet able to champion a view of biblical studies that would no longer restrict its audience either to the academy or to organized religion. Instead, it would attempt to make available to a wider public research that is ethically accountable.

Feminist scholarship has blazed the trail for such a rhetorical, ethico-political paradigm of biblical and religious studies. However, the pioneering contributions of feminist theory are seldom recognized in the malestream discourses deliberating the status of the discipline. Critical feminist scholarship not only encounters resistance in the academic centers of biblical and religious studies but also often receives only a token acknowledgment in the malestream discourses of the margins.[10]

"Decentering biblical scholarship"[11] has proven to be a difficult task not least because the hegemonic institutions of biblical studies have subtly contravened it. For instance, although there were positive responses to my SBL presidential address, they have come mostly from the margins. I have never been invited again to hold an official function in the SBL, nor have I been asked for suggestions as to how the

---

10. I think here, for instance, of the rewriting of the discipline by Blount, Segovia, or Sugirtharajah, whose work I greatly admire although it gives only token recognition to the breakthrough brought about by critical feminist biblical studies.

11. See chapter 1 for such a programmatic statement.

proposals of my address could be implemented. However, not just traditional historical scholarship, but also "newer" fields, such as the social scientific study of early Christianity, continue to advocate a positivist ethos[12] as the only true scholarship. Without institutional change a paradigm shift cannot be accomplished. Scholarly discourses thus go on to re-inscribe the dominant divisions between academic biblical studies as "objective and impartial" and theological biblical studies as partial and unscientific because they speak from within a particular tradition or community. "Scientific" biblical studies position themselves in a modern academic context whereas theological studies seem to belong to a premodern situation. However, this dichotomy between "scientific" and theological biblical studies becomes relativized if seen in a postmodern and postcolonial context.

The Intellectual-Cultural Contexts of Biblical Studies

The categories postmodern[13] and postcolonial[14] are often seen as equally characterizing the intellectual context and cultural[15] climate of progressive biblical studies and theology. In both instances, however, the qualifier *feminist* still needs to be added because both intellectual formations, the postmodern and the postcolonial, are prone to operate out of a kyriarchal traditional or modern framework. To portray the present social location of biblical and religious studies, be they academic or theological, as postmodern or postcolonial invites close scrutiny of modernity. Yet, the prefix *post* in both terms seems to connote something quite different if one understands the meaning of the word *post* in its original sense. The general English meaning communicates that one has moved beyond the situation characterized by the word prefixed with "post." For instance, postdoctoral studies means further studies beyond the doctoral degree.

Just as postdoctoral studies affirm and continue doctoral studies, so the postmodern ethos and process of scholarship is determined by and based on its modern predecessors. As in postdoctoral studies one moves beyond the doctoral stage, so in postmodern studies one moves beyond the ethos and mindset of modernity not in order to abolish the achievements of modernity but in order to deepen and enhance them. Modernity as a deeply European event

---

12. The work of Bruce Malina is representative for such an approach. See, e.g., his article "Rhetorical Criticism and Social-Scientific Criticism: Why Won't Romanticism Leave Us Alone?" in *Rhetoric, Scripture and Theology: Essays from the 1994 Pretoria Conference*, ed. Stanley E. Porter and Thomas H. Olbricht (Sheffield: Sheffield University Press, 1996), 72–101.

13. It is impossible to even attempt to cite the literature. I have found very helpful here the essays collected by James Good and Irving Velody, eds., *The Politics of Postmodernity* (Cambridge: Cambridge University Press, 1998).

14. In place of many other works, I refer here to the discussions in Arif Dirlik, ed., *The Postcolonial Aura: Third World Criticism in the Age of Global Capitalism* (New York: Westview Press, 1997).

15. See Arif Dirlik, "Culturalism as Hegemonic Ideology and Liberating Practice," in *The Nature and Context of Minority Discourse*, ed. Abdul R. Jan Mohamed and David Lloyd (New York: Oxford University Press, 1993), 394–431.

is all about the massive changes that took place at many levels from the mid-sixteenth century onwards. . . . Modernity questions all conventional ways of doing things substituting authorities of its own based in science, economic growth, democracy, or law. And it unsettles the self; if identity is given in traditional society, in modernity it is constructed. Modernity started out to conquer the world in the name of Reason; certainty and social order would be founded on new bases. . . . The achievement of modernity is astonishing. In the space of a few decades a transformation began in Europe that would alter the world in unprecedented and irreversible ways.[16]

Modern "scientific" studies, however, have promoted in the name of "pure reason" a mode of inquiry that denies its own rhetorical character and masks its own historicity in order to claim scientific historical certainty and value-detached objectivity.[17] This modern posture of value-neutral inquiry in the interest of pure reason and its claims to universality has been thoroughly challenged by diverse postmodern discourses, such as philosophical hermeneutics, the sociology of knowledge, ideology critique, and critical theory.[18]

Allow me to clarify this point further with reference to the conceptualization of critical inquiry in the western Enlightenment tradition. The ideal of the European-American Enlightenment was critically accomplished knowledge in the interest of human freedom, equality, and justice under the guidance of pure and abstract reason. Its principle of unqualified critical inquiry and assessment did not exempt any given reality, authority, tradition, or institution. Knowledge is not a given but is a culturally and historically embodied language and therefore is always open to probing analysis and relentless criticism.

This scientific principle of the Enlightenment was institutionalized in the modern university as the empiricist paradigm of knowledge that gives primary import to evidence, data, and empirical inquiry, that is, to the "logic of facts." This modern logic relies on abstraction for the sake of rigor, evidence, and precision. At the same time this scientific principle has also engendered three major correctives that underscore the complexity, particularity, and corruption of reality.[19] (1) The esthetic corrective stresses experiential concreteness and intuitive imagination over rationalist abstraction; (2) the cultural corrective insists over and against the universalizing tendencies of the Enlightenment on cultural autonomy and on tradition as wisdom and heritage of a particular community; and (3) the political corrective asserts that there is no pure reason as instrument of knowledge that could lead to a just society. In the beginning was not pure reason but power. The institutions of so-called pure reason—

16. David Lyon, *Postmodernity* (Minneapolis: University of Minnesota Press, 1994), 21.

17. David Tracy, *Plurality and Ambiguity*, 31.

18. See also Jürgen Habermas, *Moral Consciousness and Communicative Action* (Cambridge, Mass.: MIT Press, 1995), 4: "Modernity is characterized by the rejection of substantive rationality typical of the religious and metaphysical world-views and by a belief in a procedural rationality and its ability to give credence to our views in the three areas of objective knowledge, moral-practical insight, and aesthetic judgment."

19. See my "Commitment and Critical Inquiry." *HTR* 82 (1989): 1–11.

the sciences, scholarship, and the university—hide from themselves their own complicity in societal agendas of power.[20]

These three correctives seek to move scholarly discourses beyond western modernity without relinquishing its emancipatory achievements. Most importantly, by critically demonstrating that the standard for the Enlightenment's claims about selfhood, reason, and universality was elite western man, feminist postmodern thinkers have shown that the rights and knowledge of the modern elite male subject were underwritten by the negation of such rights to his devalued others, such as wives, children, slaves, aliens, natives, and other disenfranchised wo/men. The accomplishments of the Enlightenment and its transformation of European society were achieved in the interest of the "Man of Reason"[21] and at the cost of his devalued others. At this crossing point postmodern emancipatory and postcolonial analyses meet in their critique of modernity, whose achievements have been bought at the price of colonialism.

However, the term *postcolonial* in the more commonplace sense does not connote the same thing as the expression *postmodern*.[22] The *American Heritage Dictionary* defines colonialism as a "policy by which a nation maintains or extends its control over foreign dependencies . . . [that are called] colonies." Although colonialism is mostly associated with European or American expansionism and imperialism, it is not restricted to the West, as a brief glance at the history of Korea indicates.

Does postcolonial mean that the global situation has moved "beyond" colonialism by building on and affirming colonialism? Does it mean that the First World extends its political rule and cultural control over the "others" devalued by the "Man of Reason" or over the Second or Third World beyond colonialism, thereby refining and enhancing it? Would this not be *neo*colonialism rather than *post*colonialism? Or does postcolonial mean that the global situation is no longer colonial and we have moved toward a utopian situation in which economic exploitation, cultural hegemony, and political domination are overcome and replaced by relationships of radical equality, independence, and well-being? Obviously, this is not the case!

A critical feminist sociopolitical analysis of domination as I have developed it understands western classical and modern society and biblical religions as determined by the tension between, on the one hand, kyriarchal—that is, lord/master/father/husband ruled—exploitative structures of domination and exclusion and, on the other hand, radical democratic visions of equality and well-being for all, which have been partially realized in history through emancipatory struggles and movements.[23] Such an analysis indicates that there are no postcolonial spaces that are free

20. See my "Commitment and Critical Inquiry," for documentation.

21. Genevieve Lloyd, *The Man of Reason: Male and Female in Western Philosophy* (Minneapolis: University of Minnesota Press, 1984).

22. See K. A. Appiah, "Is the 'Post' in 'Postmodernism' the 'Post' in 'Postcolonial'?" *Critical Inquiry* 17 (1991): 360–67.

23. For the development of such an analytic, see my books *Discipleship of Equals* and *But She Said*. For an analysis of the Japanese "kyriarchal" or emperor-system see Hisako Kinukawa, *Women and Jesus in Mark: A Japanese Feminist Perspective*, ed. Letty M. Russell (Maryknoll, N.Y.: Orbis Books, 1994).

of exploitation, domination, and dehumanization. The "post" must therefore be understood differently in postcolonial than in postmodern insofar as postmodernism, in certain instances, happily continues modern practices whereas postcolonialism must seek to break with all colonial structures. Postcoloniality therefore is best understood, I suggest, as "a condition that exists within, and thus contests and resists the colonial moment itself with its ideology of domination."[24] It must be understood as "contracoloniality."

The Bible and biblical studies are clearly associated with western colonialism. This is aptly expressed in the pithy saying ascribed to Bishop Tutu among others: "When the missionaries arrived they had the Bible and we had the land. Now we have the Bible and they have the land." Missionaries came to Asia or Africa not only in order to preach the gospel and to make converts but also in order to civilize and educate the heathens. As, for instance, the authors of *Sentimental Imperialists: The American Experience in East Asia* point out: Along with commerce a second persistent characterization of the American–East Asian relationship has been both evangelism bent on making converts and the export of western culture and learning. Missionaries, however, were also conscious agents of cultural change. They came to Asia to do something to Asia and Asians, to reshape foreign societies.[25] Moreover, missionaries played a crucial role in the shaping of American views of Asia. They provided "a model for later American governmental efforts to reshape developing societies on a world wide basis under secular auspices."[26]

Thus the form of biblical interpretation most closely associated with colonialism has been otherworldly evangelism and literalist fundamentalism that is oriented toward the salvation of the soul and professes an individualistic theology preaching the primacy of faith and personal loyalty to Scripture. In contrast, critical biblical studies at first glance seem not to be aligned explicitly with western colonialism because they allegedly are driven by scientific rationality and objectivity. Yet anyone studying the history of biblical interpretation from the perspective of emancipatory movements will recognize that biblical interpretation has been articulated for the most part not only by elite western educated clergymen but also in the interest of western culture and interests. Moreover, anyone joining a doctoral program in biblical studies soon will learn that the only legitimate questions to ask are those of the discipline which disciplines all its members[27] to adopt a modern doctrinal exclusivist or scientific allegedly value-free mindset that covertly functions in the interest of kyriarchal relations. This contradiction and collusion between fundamentalist and scientific uses of the Bible can best be clarified in and through paradigm criticism.

24. Francoise Lionnet, *Postcolonial Representations: Women, Literature, Identity* (Ithaca: Cornell University Press, 1995), 4.

25. James C. Thompson, Jr., Peter W. Stanley, and John Curtis Perry, *Sentimental Imperialists: The American Experience in East Asia* (New York: Harper Torchbooks, 1981), 44f.

26. Thompson et al., *Sentimental Imperialists*, 59.

27. See the article by W. H. Myers, "The Hermeneutical Dilemma of the African American Biblical Student," in *Stony the Road We Trod: African-American Biblical Interpretation*, ed. Cain H. Felder (Minneapolis: Fortress Press, 1991), 40–56.

Competing Paradigms in Biblical Studies

Thomas Kuhn's categories of scientific paradigm and heuristic model provide a theoretical framework[28] for comprehending theoretical and practical shifts in the self-understanding of biblical studies. A paradigm articulates a common ethos and constitutes a community of scholars formed by its institutions and systems of knowledge. However, a shift in scientific paradigm can take place only if and when the institutional conditions of knowledge production change. Moreover, paradigms are not necessarily exclusive of each other, but they can exist alongside and in corrective interaction with each other.

In the discipline of biblical studies one can chart today four such interpretive paradigms: the doctrinal-fundamentalist, the scientific-historical, the hermeneutic-(post)modern, and the rhetorical-emancipatory paradigms. Most recently Fernando Segovia also has advocated a critical reflection on the discourses of biblical studies in terms of paradigms.[29] While he agrees on the whole with my diagnosis of four disciplinary paradigms, he suggests a different nomenclature. He does so on grounds of a different analysis that distinguishes four disciplinary paradigms in terms of method rather than in terms of both methods and theoretical frameworks.

On grounds of method one can distinguish historical, literary, cultural criticism, and cultural studies paradigms as constituting the basic modes of biblical criticism. However, such a delineation of the field restricts biblical criticism to the academy and to "scientific" methods. This classification results in the eclipse of those biblical readings that are located in religious communities and have as their goal spiritual nourishment and motivation. Yet, such an eclipse of biblical interpretations is questionable not just in terms of feminist but also in terms of postcolonial emancipatory concerns, for both feminist and postcolonial studies derive their strength not primarily from the academy but from social-political movements for change. Since most biblical readers are not located in the university but in communities of faith, the religiously based paradigm of biblical studies must not be eclipsed.

While I agree that disciplinary paradigms are not hermetically closed off from but interact with each other on the level of method, I do not think that this is quite the case with respect to theoretical frameworks or perspectives. These are permeable but in the last analysis exclusive of each other. While one can and must deploy literary, archaeological, historical, cultural, sociological, anthropological, philological, and other methods in the process of interpretation, I do not think that one can "marry" theoretical frameworks such as religious dogmaticism, historical positivism, cul-

28. Thomas S. Kuhn, *The Structure of Scientific Revolutions* (Chicago: University of Chicago Press, 1962).

29. Fernando F. Segovia, "Introduction: 'And They Began to Speak in Other Tongues': Competing Modes of Discourse in Contemporary Biblical Criticism," in *Reading from This Place*, 1–32; see also his "Introduction: Pedagogical Discourses and Practices in Cultural Studies: Towards a Contextual Biblical Pedagogy," in *Teaching the Bible: The Discourses and Politics of Biblical Pedagogy*, ed. Fernando F. Segovia and Mary Ann Tolbert (Maryknoll, N.Y.: Orbis Books, 1998), 137–67.

tural relativism, and emancipatory theoretical commitment promiscuously with each other without losing one's theoretical and practical footing.

In addition, paradigms are not just theoretical but also institutional formations that develop not only distinct methodological approaches but also disciplinary languages and cultures. Practitioners are judged by professional criteria of excellence maintained by the hegemonic paradigm of biblical studies, and students are socialized into their disciplinary practices. For instance, whether a book is "scholarly" is still judged in terms of the dogmatic, historical, literary-cultural paradigms but not in terms of the emancipatory paradigm that would ask for competency in demystifying structures of domination. Alternatively, students who are coming from a religious, often biblicist, background to divinity schools or departments of religious or theological studies must not only learn to skillfully engage philological, historical, or literary academic methods, but also must be encouraged to explore the theoretical, often a-religious, self-alienating, and marginalizing underpinnings of these methods. Within the doctrinal paradigm, for instance, they learn to understand biblical authority in terms of kyriarchal obedience often without knowing that this paradigm also has understood biblical authority in terms of salvation. Or, within the historical and literary paradigms, students are socialized into accepting scientific "facticity" and disinterestedness as authoritative without ever reflecting on the kyriarchal tendencies of the scientific ethos to marginalize and objectify the "others" of elite white western men.

The Doctrinal-Fundamentalist Paradigm

For centuries the prevalent paradigm of Christian biblical interpretation has been the dogmatic or doctrinal paradigm, which understands the biblical record as sacred Scripture that is divinely revealed. But while the premodern hermeneutics of the dogmatic paradigm knows of a fourfold sense of Scripture, the modern articulation of this paradigm in conjunction with colonialism insists on a literalist reading of Scripture as factual truth. Thereby it declares its own cultural readings as divine revelation that may not be questioned. The place of this paradigm is institutional biblical religion.

Those who quote the Bible most often are neoconservative Christians who read the Bible in the context of proliferating fundamentalist movements[30] and their spiritualization of the global crisis of injustice. Many people in the world experience the impact of neocolonialism that results in the increasing globalization of inequality, and the complexity of their situation, not only as very confusing but also as very threatening. Growing job insecurity and economic impoverishment, erosion of traditional values and loss of a familiar world, steady news about ecological disasters, nuclear accidents, civil wars, starvation, refugees, daily murder, and the decay of

---

30. See Jerome Himmelstein, *To the Right: The Transformation of American Conservatism* (Berkeley: University of California Press, 1990); Martin E. Marty and R. Scott Appleby, eds, *Fundamentalisms Observed* (Chicago: University of Chicago Press, 1991).

neighborhoods fuel the desire for unambiguous solutions, eternal truth, and moral certainty.

Fundamentalist biblical discourses address this global postmodern anxiety by promising certainty in a sea of change, by delineating exclusivist group boundaries and clear-cut identities, and by fabricating emotional stability in an ever more complex and changing world. To that end they not only project a spiritualized vision of the world but also manipulate symbols of evil, stereotype the "others" as deviant, and rigidly defend "orthodox" tradition. By identifying "the enemy" and by scapegoating the deviant "others," they seek both to alleviate people's helplessness in a world that seems to be coming to an end and to promise salvation and success to those who have a claim to righteousness.

Although these modern fundamentalist movements are religiously and ethnically quite different, they share common traits: In an ever changing and conflictive world they promise religious security, certainty of faith, and a clear-cut identity. Whether fundamentalist Christians, Muslims, or ultra-orthodox Jews, they all maintain a literalist understanding of Scripture or tradition as the will of G*d and insist on the subordination of women[31] as natural and as ordained by G*d. At the same time they employ modern media technology in very sophisticated ways to advocate nationalist or religious exclusivism.

Christian colonialist fundamentalism claims either that the biblical message belongs to a totally different world and does not affect societal or political structures, or it insists that kyriarchal theocracy is the revealed order of society. According to the first claim, Christians who suffer in this world as Christ has suffered will receive their just reward in heaven. The "kingdom of G*d" is "not of this world." The second claim, in its more recent expressions, takes the form of a fundamentalist-colonialist rhetoric that constructs a religious world of righteousness and contrasts it with secularized, depraved, modern society. As the keeper and protector of traditional values, it stereotypes those who do not agree and scapegoats homosexuals, secular humanists, feminists, and liberals as enemies of the moral order.

Literalist fundamentalism vehemently rejects modern religious tolerance and pluralism but insists that the biblical message proclaims universal moral values and truth. Like modern science, it claims that this truth can be positively established and proven. Thus it promulgates philological, historical, or theological literalism that stresses verbal inspiration that understands the Bible as the direct, inerrant Word of G*d to be accepted by Christians without question. This emphasis on verbal inerrancy[32] asserts that the Bible and its interpretation transcend ideology and particularity. It obscures the interests at work in biblical texts and interpretations, and

---

31. For the Christian context, see Margaret Lamberts Bendroth, *Fundamentalism and Gender, 1875 to the Present* (New Haven: Yale University Press, 1993), and Betty DeBerg, *Ungodly Women: Gender and the First Wave of American Fundamentalism* (Minneapolis: Fortress Press, 1990).

32. For "inerrancy" as a modern reading strategy, see George Marsden, *Fundamentalism and American Culture. The Shaping of Twentieth-Century Evangelicalism, 1870–1925* (New York: Oxford University Press, 1980) 56–57.

reduces faith to intellectual assent rather than to a way of life. Such revelatory positivism promotes belief in the Bible rather than faith in G*d.

Biblicist fundamentalism not only reads the Bible through the theological lenses of individualized and privatized bourgeois religion, but also asserts militantly that its approach is the only legitimate Christian way to do so. It thereby obscures that different Christian communities and churches use the Bible differently and ignores that throughout the centuries different models of biblical interpretation have been and still are developed by Christians. Although such spiritualized biblicism berates mainline churches for succumbing to modernity and secularization, it itself has adopted a particular modern rationalist understanding of religion and the Bible as the only approach that is truly Christian. Even though colonialist biblicism stands in opposition to western modernity, it nevertheless shares some of its basic ideological structures. In spite of the fact that fundamentalism combats modern liberal religion, it is itself a modern phenomenon.[33] It seeks to recreate inside the religious world all that is no longer viable in the outside world. To that end it offers a modernist integrative meaning system and the certainty of revealed Truth in the process of increasing market globalization that dislocates traditional worldviews and meaning systems.

The "Scientific" Positivist Paradigm[34]

The increasing globalization of inequality and the colonialist fundamentalist response to it cries out for alternative liberating biblical visions. Are Christian theology and biblical scholarship able to step into the increasing vacuum of meaning and hope generated by the transnational globalization process? For those who subscribe to the "scientific" value-free modern (colonial) paradigm the resounding answer to this question is No.

Because the "scientific" ethos of biblical studies was shaped by the struggle of religious scholarship to free itself from dogmatic and ecclesiastical controls, it continues to insist on value-free inquiry and asserts a deep chasm between the past and the present. Hence biblical studies is not able to engage the question of meaning in a global situation of exploitation. The scientific paradigm strives to establish a single true meaning of the text in order to claim universality for its interpretations. It does so, however, not on theological but on methodological scientific grounds. Although it avows objectivity, disinterestedness, and value-neutrality in order to control what constitutes the legitimate scientifically established true meaning of the text, it is patently Eurocentric.

Just as European and American historiography as an academic discipline sought in the last quarter of the nineteenth century to prove itself as an objective science in analogy to the natural sciences, so also did biblical studies. Scientific historiography ostensibly sought to establish "facts" and "data" objectively, free from philosophical considerations or political interests. It was determined to hold strictly to facts and

33. Marty and Appleby, eds, *Fundamentalism Observed.*
34. See also chapter 6.

evidence, not to sermonize or to moralize but to tell the simple truth—in short, to narrate things as they really happened. Historical science is seen as a technique that applies critical methods to the evaluation of sources, which in turn are understood as data and evidence. The mandate to avoid theoretical considerations and normative concepts in the immediate encounter with the text is to assure that the resulting historical accounts would be accurate and objective, free from any ideology.

Since biblical scholarship developed in the political context of several heresy trials at the turn of the twentieth century,[35] its rhetoric of disinterested objectivity continues to reject all overt religious, sociopolitical, or theological engagement as unscientific. In this it joins the antitheological rhetoric of academic religious studies. The aspiration of biblical studies in particular and religious studies in general to "scientific" status in the academy and their claim to universal, unbiased modes of inquiry denies their hermeneutical-rhetorical character and masks their sociohistorical location as well as their sociopolitical or ecclesiastical interests.

Because they are rooted in the individualistic and relativistic discourses of modernity[36] and share with fundamentalism a positivist and technological ethos, liberal biblical and religious studies discourses are in no way equipped to address the crisis of justice and well-being brought about by the globalization of inequality. In spite of their critical posture, academic biblical studies are thus akin to fundamentalism insofar as they insist that scholars are able to produce a single scientific, true, reliable, and nonideological reading of the Bible. Scholars can achieve scientific certainty as long as they silence their own interests and abstract from their own sociopolitical situation.

Insofar as modern biblical scholarship insists that it is able to isolate the "facts" or the universal "truth" from the Bible's multivalent and often contradictory meanings, it denies its own particular Eurocentric perspectives and kyriarchal rhetorical aims, which are indebted to the European Enlightenment. By objectifying, antiquating, reifying, and privatizing biblical Scriptures, it is in danger of playing into the hands of fundamentalist biblicism, which also claims that it can identify with certainty the univocal Word of G*d in the Bible as a provable fact.

The (Post-)Modern Cultural Paradigm

Today this modern scientistic paradigm seems to be in the process of being decentered and replaced by a (post)modern hermeneutical or cultural paradigm. Whereas a decade ago the historical-positivist and literary-formalist paradigms of interpretation still were in ascendancy, today postmodern epistemological and hermeneutical discussions abound that are critical of the positivist scientific ethos of biblical studies. Their theoretical and practical force has destabilized the foundations of the field.

35. See Saunders, *Searching the Scriptures.*

36. For these characterizations of bourgeois biblical readings, see Johannes Thiele, "Bibelauslegung im gesellschaftlich-politischen Kontext," in *Handbuch der Bibelarbeit,* ed. Wolfgang Langer (Munich: Kösel Verlag, 1987), 106–14.

Even the critical theory of the Frankfurt school and ideological criticism have arrived on the program of biblical congresses. Critical theory, semiotics, reader response criticism, social world studies, and poststructuralist literary analyses, among others,[37] have engendered the recognition of the linguisticality of all interpretation and historiography, and generated postmodern elaborations of the undecidability of meaning and the pluralism of interpretive approaches.[38]

Such a postmodern hermeneutic does not assume that the text represents a given divine revelation or a window to historical reality, nor does it operate with a correspondence theory of truth. It does not understand historical sources as data and evidence but sees them as perspectival discourses constructing a range of symbolic universes.[39] Since alternative symbolic universes engender competing definitions of the world, they cannot be reduced to one single, definitive meaning. Therefore competing interpretations are not simply either right or wrong;[40] rather they constitute different ways of reading and constructing historical and religious meaning. Texts have a surplus of meaning that can never be fully mined.

In short, this third cultural-hermeneutical paradigm underscores the rhetoricity of historical knowledge,[41] symbolic power, and the multidimensional character of texts. It either ascribes personified status to the text in order to construe it as a dialogue partner or it sees the text as a multicolored tapestry of meaning. This paradigm likens the reading of the Bible to the reading of the "great books" or classics, whose greatness does not consist in their accuracy as records of facts, but depends chiefly on their symbolic power to transfigure human experience and symbolic systems of meaning.

Feminist and liberation theological interpretation have played a great part in the postmodern hermeneutical transformation of academic biblical scholarship. Nevertheless, even a cursory glance at the literature can show that the hermeneutical contributions of critical feminist scholarship are rarely recognized, and much less acknowledged, by malestream biblical studies. While the postmodern hermeneutical paradigm has successfully destabilized the certitude of the scientific objectivist paradigm in biblical studies, it still asserts its own scientific value-neutral and atheological character. Hence it tends to result in a playful proliferation of textual meanings and to reject any attempt to move from kyriocentric text to the sociohistorical situation of struggle that either has generated the text or determines its function today. Hence this third hermeneutical-postmodern paradigm of biblical

---

37. For bringing together the insights of this chapter, I have found the works of feminist literary and cultural criticism especially helpful. See, for example, Benhabib and Cornell, eds., *Feminism as Critique;* Spivak, *In Other Worlds;* de Lauretis, ed., *Feminist Studies/Critical Studies;* Flynn and Schweickart, eds., *Gender and Reading;* Greene and Kahn, eds., *Making a Difference;* Meese, *Crossing the Double Cross;* Newton and Rosenfelt, eds., *Feminist Criticism and Social Change;* Pryse and Spillers, eds., *Conjuring;* and Weedon, *Feminist Practice and Poststructuralist Theory.*

38. Amos N. Wilder articulated this literary-aesthetic paradigm as rhetorical. See his SBL presidential address, "Scholar, Theologians, and Ancient Rhetoric," and his book *Early Christian Rhetoric.*

39. See the discussion of scientific theory choice by Alcoff, "Justifying Feminist Social Science."

40. Mandelbaum, *Anatomy of Historical Knowledge,* 150.

41. See the preceding chapter.

studies also cannot address the increasing insecurities of globalized inequality nor accept the constraints that the ethical imperative of emancipatory movements places on the relativizing proliferation of meaning. Therefore, a fourth rhetorical-political paradigm needs to be acknowledged, one that inaugurates not just a hermeneutic-scientific but an ethical-political turn.

The Rhetorical-Emancipatory Paradigm

Since this fourth paradigm is still in the process of emerging and has not been able to create its own institutional structures, I have vacillated in giving it its proper name. I have, for instance, alternatively dubbed it the pastoral-theological, the liberationist-cultural, the rhetorical-ethical, or the rhetorical-political paradigm. In this chapter I have settled on the label *rhetorical-emancipatory* in order to articulate its method and goal. It deploys rhetorical analysis and the rhetoric of inquiry in order to assess the emancipatory implications and impact of biblical texts and contemporary interpretations of the Bible. Although, just like the expression *feminist,* the term *emancipation* is often used in a derogatory fashion—for instance, in Germany feminists are often labeled negatively *Emanzen*—emancipatory recalls the process of liberation from slavery. It is therefore an appropriate word for an interpretive approach that has as its goal overcoming structures of domination and achieving well-being for everyone.

Whatever its proper name will turn out to be, this fourth paradigm seeks to redefine the self-understanding of biblical scholarship in ethical, rhetorical, political, cultural, emancipatory terms and to understand the scholar in religion as a public, "transformative,"[42] connected, or integrated intellectual who is able to communicate with a variegated public with the goal of personal, social, and religious transformation for justice and well-being.

This fourth paradigm understands biblical texts as rhetorical discourses that must be investigated as to their persuasive power and argumentative functions in particular historical and cultural situations. It rejects the Enlightenment typecasting of rhetoric as stylistic ornament, technical skill, linguistic manipulation, or "mere words," and maintains not only "that rhetoric is epistemic but also that epistemology and ontology are themselves rhetorical."[43] At the heart of rhetoric is both the ethical and the political.

Hence this fourth paradigm utilizes both theories of rhetoric and the rhetoric of inquiry in order to display how, as political and religious discursive practices, biblical texts and their contemporary interpretations involve authorial aims and strategies, as well as audience perceptions and constructions. In this paradigm biblical

42. For the expression "transformative intellectual," see "Teaching and the Role of the Transformative Intellectual," in Stanley Aronowitz and Henry A. Giroux, *Education Still under Siege* (2d ed., Westport, Conn., and London: Bergin & Garvey, 1993).

43. Richard Harvey Brown, *Society as Text,* 85. See also, for example, Nelson et al., eds., *Rhetoric of the Human Sciences; White, Tropics of Discourse;* Nelson, "Political Theory as Political Rhetoric."

interpretation is not understood as doctrinal, scientific-positivist, or relativist but rather is seen in rhetorical-ethical terms. Such a critical rhetorical understanding of interpretation investigates and reconstructs the discursive arguments of a text, its socioreligious location, and its diverse interpretations in order to underscore the text's possible oppressive as well as liberative performative actions, values, and possibilities in ever changing historical-cultural situations. This approach understands the Bible and biblical interpretation as a site of struggle[44] over authority, values, and meaning.

Since the sociohistorical location of rhetoric is the public of the polis, the rhetorical-emancipatory paradigm shift seeks to situate biblical scholarship in such a way that its public character and political responsibility become an integral part of its contemporary readings and historical reconstructions. It insists on an ethical radical democratic imperative that compels biblical scholarship to contribute to the advent of a society and religion that are free from all forms of kyriarchal inequality and oppression. Hence biblical studies as critical public discourse has to be concerned not just with exploring the conditions and possibilities of understanding and using kyriocentric biblical texts but also with the problem of how, in the interest of wo/men's liberation, one can critically assess and dismantle their power of persuasion. Critical biblical scholarship must construct a theoretical model and epistemological framework that allows one to move toward the articulation of a critical ethics and rhetoric of inquiry.

Such a fourth paradigm of biblical interpretation is in the process of being articulated today all around the world, insofar as interaction with postmodern critical theory, emancipatory postcolonial, and feminist discourses have problematized the Enlightenment's notion of the universal transcendental subject as the disembodied voice of reason. They have done so in order to insist that the excluded others of elite western white man must be included.[45] These discourses have elaborated that the political-social and intellectual-ideological creation of the devalued "colonialized" others goes hand in hand with the creation of the "Man of Reason" as the rational subject outside of time and space.[46] He is the abstract knower and disembodied

---

44. John Louis Lucaites, Celeste Michelle Condit, "Introduction," in John Louis Lucaites, Celeste Michelle Condit, Sally Caudill, eds., *Contemporary Rhetorical Theory: A Reader* (New York: The Guilford Press, 1999), 11: "Disagreement is thus considered a rather 'natural' result of different social, political, and ethnic groups, with different resources. On this view, struggle, not consensus, is the defining characteristic of social life; accordingly, social discord is not a pathology to be cured but a condition to be productively managed."

45. Brian K. Blount, *Cultural Interpretation: Reorienting New Testament Criticism* (Minneapolis: Fortress Press, 1995), 3, correctly argues "that if one wants to achieve a non-ideological method of biblical interpretation, the perspectives of the societal marginal must be included." Such an inclusion will result in a multicolored rainbow of biblical interpretation. However, insofar as he positions his new approach as "cultural" interpretation, which has as its explicit goal the production of a nonideological reading, he remains within the third paradigm of biblical interpretation.

46. See my article, "The Politics of Otherness: Biblical Interpretation as a Critical Praxis for Liberation," in *The Future of Liberation Theology: In Honor of Gustavo Gutiérrez*, ed. Mark H. Ellis and Otto Maduro (Maryknoll, N.Y.: Orbis Books, 1989), 311–25.

speaker of Enlightenment science and knowledge who has arrogated to himself a "G*d's eye view" of the world.

In contrast to postmodern criticism, the voices from the margins of biblical studies insist that the colonialized others cannot afford to abandon the notion of the subject and the possibility of knowing the world differently. Rather, they insist that the subordinated others must engage in a political and theoretical process of constituting themselves as subjects of knowledge and history.[47] Those previously excluded from the academy have to use what they know about the world and about wo/men's lives for critiquing the dominant culture and for constructing a heterogeneous public that allows for the recognition of particular voices and fosters appreciation of difference.

In conclusion, although all four paradigms are situated within the university, three of them do not subscribe to the value-free disinterested ethos of biblical and religious studies in terms of positivist natural science. Whereas the first and last paradigm openly recognize their particular location and interests, the third paradigm seeks to engage biblical hermeneutics, but it often does so in terms of the second modernist paradigm that advocates a scientific value-neutral ethos of religious and biblical studies. The emerging fourth paradigm that conceptualizes biblical studies as public discourse utilizes together with traditional methods the analytical and practical methods of ideology critique and rhetorical inquiry. Since language not only creates a polysemy of meaning but also transmits values and re-inscribes social systems and semantic patterns of behavior, it calls for a critical sociopolitical interpretation of the Bible.

Emancipation and Interpretation

A Process of Emancipatory Interpretation

This fourth paradigm shift in biblical studies thus articulates a change in the aims and goals of critical exegesis and biblical interpretation. The task of interpretation is not just to understand biblical texts and traditions but to analyze their power of persuasion in order to change and transform western malestream epistemological frameworks, individualistic apolitical practices, and sociopolitical relations of cultural colonization. Thereby it seeks to engender a self-understanding of biblical scholarship as a critical communicative postcolonial praxis. Biblical interpretation, like all scholarly inquiry, is a communicative practice that involves interests, values, and visions.

Only in such a rhetorical-emancipatory paradigm of biblical studies will liberation theologies of all colors have the possibility of engaging the discourses of biblical studies on their own terms and on equal terms with Eurocentric malestream schol-

---

47. See, e.g., Elisabeth Schüssler Fiorenza and Shawn Copeland, eds., *Feminist Theologies in Different Contexts*; Elisabeth Schüssler Fiorenza, *The Power of Naming: A Concilium Reader in Feminist Christian Theology* (Maryknoll, N.Y.: Orbis Books, 1996); Ursula King, ed., *Feminist Theology from the Third World: A Reader* (Maryknoll, N.Y.: Orbis Books, 1994).

arship. By beginning with the religious experiences and articulations of the marginalized and colonized—of those wo/men traditionally excluded from interpreting the Bible, articulating theology, and shaping communal Christian self-understanding—they can change the starting point of traditional biblical interpretation.

Liberation theologies of all colors not only recognize the perspectival and contextual nature of theological knowledge and biblical interpretation but also assert that biblical scholarship and theology are—knowingly or not—always engaged for or against the oppressed. Intellectual neutrality is not possible in a historical world of exploitation and oppression. At the same time they must be careful not to romanticize the oppressed, the Minjung,[48] for—as the Brazilian educator Paolo Freire pointed out a long time ago—the oppressed have also internalized their own dehumanization and oppression as the will of G*d. Thus the Minjung are divided within and among themselves."The oppressed, having internalized the image of the oppressor and adopted his [sic] guidelines, are fearful of freedom. Freedom would require them to eject this image and replace it with autonomy and responsibility. Freedom . . . must be pursued constantly and responsibly."[49]

Since both the oppressed and their oppressors are "manifestations of dehumanization,"[50] the methodological starting point of such a rhetorical-emancipatory paradigm cannot simply be "commonsense" experience but rather must be systemically analyzed and critically reflected experience. Since wo/men have internalized and are shaped by kyriarchal "commonsense" mindsets and values, the hermeneutical starting point of feminist interpretation cannot simply be the experience of wo/men but must be experience that has been critically explored in the process of "conscientization."

Christian identity that is shaped by the Bible must in ever new readings be deconstructed and reconstructed in terms of a global praxis for the liberation of all wo/men. Equally, cultural identity that is shaped by biblical discourses must be critically interrogated and transformed. Hence one needs to reconceptualize the traditional spiritual practice of discerning the spirits as a critical ethical-political practice. As interpreting subjects, biblical readers must learn to claim their spiritual authority to assess both the oppressive as well as the liberating imagination of particular biblical texts and their interpretations.

By deconstructing the kyriarchal rhetorics and politics of inequality and subordination that are inscribed in the Bible, we are able to generate new possibilities for the ever new articulation of radical democratic religious identities and emancipatory practices. In order to do so, a critical ethical-political reading does not subscribe to

---

48. However, Kim Yong-Bok in *Messiah and Minjung: Christ's Solidarity with the People for New Life* (Hong Kong: Christian Conference of Asia, 1992), 8, claims that this "question often arises among those who despise and discriminate against the Minjung." In my experience any movement that idealizes its agents is bound to lose its emancipatory impetus whenever it realizes how much they are divided in and among themselves.

49. Paulo Freire, *Pedagogy of the Oppressed* (New York: Seabury Press, 1973), 31.

50. Ibid., 33.

one single reading strategy and interpretive method but employs a variety of exegetical and interpretive methods for understanding the Bible as public discourse.

Such an emancipatory process of biblical interpretation has as its "doubled" reference point the contemporary present and the biblical past. But whereas exegetical-historical methods are often restricted to the experts and not accessible to a general readership, a critical, rhetorical, ethical-political analysis must be accessible to anyone. For that reason, I have developed such a method of critical analysis and deliberation that engages seven interpretive strategies or moving turns in the process or "dance" of interpretation.

Strategies or Moving Turns of Emancipatory Interpretation

Feminists have used different rhetorical metaphors for naming such an emancipatory method, hermeneutical process of the rhetoric of inquiry. "Making visible," "hearing into speech," "finding one's voice," are just a few. I myself have favored metaphors of movement such as "turning," "dance," "ocean waves," or "struggle." Since Plato attacked rhetoric as "mere cookery," one could also think of biblical interpretation as cooking a stew and utilizing different herbs and spices that season the potatoes, meats, and carrots equally and when stirred together combine into a new and different flavor.

Whether one thinks of biblical interpretation as a "stew" or a "dance," crucial "spices" or "moves" in a critical process of interpretation and rhetorical analysis are conscientization, critical analysis of domination, suspicion, re-construction or re-membering, assessment and evaluation in terms of a scale of values, (re-)imagination, and transformation or action for change. These practices of an emancipatory ethics of interpretation, however, are not to be construed simply as successive independent steps of inquiry or simply as discrete methodological rules or recipes. Rather, they must be understood as interpretive moves or strategies of seasoning that interact with each other simultaneously in the process of reading a particular biblical or any other cultural text in light of the globalization of inequality.

These movements in the hermeneutical "dance" or "strategic flavorings" of a rhetoric of liberation work on two different levels of interpretation: on the level of the language-systems, ideological frameworks, and sociopolitical-religious locations of contemporary readers in kyriarchal systems of domination, on the one hand; and on the level of the linguistic and sociohistorical systems of biblical texts and their effective histories of interpretation, on the other. An ethics of interpretation strategically engages these hermeneutical "moves" or "seasonings" as rhetorical discursive practices on both levels in order to *displace* literalist doctrinal, positivist-scientific, and relativist free-for-all depoliticized academic as well as popular hegemonic practices of reading.

Such a complex interactive model of a critical interpretation for liberation challenges both the modern malestream ethos of biblical studies and its rhetorics of inquiry in order to transform them in the interest of all nonpersons struggling in neocolonial situations for human dignity, justice, and well-being. It seeks to recast interpretation not in positivist but in rhetorical terms. It does not deny but recognizes that religious texts are rhetorical texts, produced in and by particular historical debates and struggles.

This approach argues for the integrity and indivisibility of the interpretive process as well as for the primacy of the contemporary starting point of interpretation. This complex model of reading, which engages in a hermeneutical process of deconstruction and reconstruction, or of critique and retrieval, applies both to the level of text and to that of interpretation. Hence it seeks to overcome the hermeneutical splits between sense and meaning, between explanation and understanding, between critique and consent, between distancing and empathy, between reading "behind" and "in front of" the text,[51] between the present and the past, between interpretation and application,[52] between realism and imagination.

Since the fourth rhetorical-emancipatory paradigm understands biblical studies as public discourse, it requires a critical feminist-postcolonial conscientization and systemic ethical-political analysis. Its interpretive process or "hermeneutical dance" does not commence with placing malestream texts and traditions at the center of its attention. Rather, it begins with a *hermeneutics of experience and social location.*[53] It does, however, not simply ask for the experiences of wo/men with a particular text such as 1 Cor. 14 but also asks to reflect on how wo/men's social, cultural, and religious location has shaped their experience with and reaction to a particular biblical text or story.[54]

The goal in particular is to learn something about the struggles of wo/men at the bottom of the kyriarchal pyramid of domination and exploitation because their situation lays open the fulcrum of oppression and dehumanization threatening every wo/man. The victories in the struggles of multiply oppressed wo/men in turn reveal the liberatory presence of G*d in our midst. In short, a critical ethical-political emancipatory-rhetorical analysis does not simply begin with individualized and privatized experience.[55] Rather, it begins with a critical reflection on how experience with the biblical text is shaped by one's sociopolitical location. Equally, it will ask for the experiences of wo/men and their cultural locations inscribed in the biblical text. Hence a hermeneutics of experience critically problematizes the social-religious and

51. For such a hermeneutical reading, see Sandra Schneiders, *The Revelatory Text: Interpreting the New Testament as Sacred Scripture* (New York: HarperSanFrancisco, 1991).

52. Klaus Berger, *Hermeneutik des Neuen Testaments* (Gütersloh: Gütersloher Verlagshaus Gerd Mohn, 1988), insists on the distinction in order to safeguard the distanciating power of exegetical-historical interpretation and the freedom of selectivity in the application of texts in contemporary situations.

53. For a critical discussion of the category of experience in feminist thought see Joan W. Scott, "Experience," in *Feminists Theorize the Political*, ed. Judith Butler and Joan W. Scott (New York: Routledge, 1992), 22–40.

54. Ingrid Rosa Kitzberger, ed., *The Personal Voice in Biblical Interpretation* (New York: Routledge, 1998).

55. For an epistemological critique of experience see Judith Grant, "I Feel Therefore I Am: A Critique of Female Experience as the Basis for a Feminist Epistemology," in *Feminism and Epistemology: Approaches to Research in Women and Politics,* ed. Maria J. Falco (New York: Haworth Press, 1987), 99–114.

intellectual locations not only of biblical interpreters but also those of biblical texts in relation to global struggles for survival and well-being.

To that end it critically adopts an *analytic of domination* that insists on a systemic analysis that is able to disentangle the ideological (religious-theological) functions of religious texts for inculcating and legitimating the kyriarchal order. At the same time it seeks to underscore and explain their potential for fostering justice and liberation. I have detailed such a systemic analysis of kyriarchy and kyriocentrism in this book and elsewhere.[56] Such an analysis seeks to identify not only contemporary structures of domination but also those inscribed in biblical texts. It is justified to do so because its analytic is formulated in light of modern political structures as well as in light of the kyriarchal structures of antiquity.

Whatever systemic analysis one adapts will crucially determine one's interpretation. For instance, one will read the story of the wo/man with a hemorrhage differently depending on whether one utilizes a Lacanian, Thomistic, Aristotelian, capitalist, or anarchist analytic of domination. Analytic frames of interpretation cannot be liberative if they do not prioritize wo/men's struggles against multiplicative structures of oppression but privilege, for instance, cultural femininity, the religious text itself, or other malestream doctrinal, theological, spiritual, or theoretical frameworks.

After having utilized a critical systemic analysis for demystifying kyriarchal structures of domination and dehumanization, in a critical rhetorical-emancipatory paradigm one continues the process of interpretation with a *hermeneutics of suspicion*. A hermeneutics of suspicion seeks to demystify structures of domination that are inscribed in the text and in contemporary contexts of interpretation. To that end it scrutinizes both the presuppositions and interests of interpreters and those of biblical commentators as well as the androcentric strategies of the biblical text itself.

A hermeneutics of suspicion must not be misunderstood as uncovering a pre-given reality understood in essentialist terms. Rather, it is concerned with the distorted construction of the representations of wo/men's actual presences and practices in and through kyriocentric language and media. Such a hermeneutics of suspicion must not be mistaken for "a hermeneutics of discovery assuming that there is some order in the world . . . that can be discovered. . . . Truth is something discovered by employing a hermeneutics of suspicion, wherein one is suspicious of the various disguises one can use to cover up and distort reality."[57]

---

56. Although Anthony C. Thiselton, *New Horizons in Hermeneutics: The Theory and Practice of Transforming Biblical Reading* (London: HarperCollins, 1992), 449, in his discussion of my work claims that "what is at stake is hermeneutical theory," he does not bother to discuss *Bread Not Stone*, but rather focuses on a particular exegetical topic regarding women's witness to the resurrection discussed in *In Memory of Her*. The interests driving his misreading come to the fore in his emotionally laden comparison of my work with that of Susanne Heine. Although Heine's work has appeared later and is dependent on my work, albeit without acknowledging it, she finds Thiselton's favor because she attacks the work of other feminists. These interests also come to the fore in his repeated question as to how much a given tradition can undergo transformation before it ceases to be *this tradition*.

57. Bible and Culture Collective, *The Postmodern Bible*, 249.

Kyriocentric language, I have argued, does not cover up but constructs reality in a certain way and then mystifies its own constructions by naturalizing them. Kyriocentric texts, literary classics, visual art, works of science, anthropology, sociology, or theology do not cover up reality "as it is." Rather they are ideological-rhetorical constructs that produce the invisibility and marginality of wo/men as a given reality. To change them, such rhetorical-ideological practices must be exposed and dislodged from their contexts of domination.

Consequently, a hermeneutics of suspicion is best understood as a deconstructive practice of inquiry that denaturalizes and demystifies practices of domination rather than seen as working away at the layers upon layers of cultural sediments that hide or repress a "deeper truth." A hermeneutics of suspicion has the task to disentangle the ideological functions of kyriocentric text and commentary. It does not assume a kyriarchal conspiracy of the classics and their contemporary interpreters but insists that wo/men do not, in fact, know whether we are addressed or not by grammatically masculine generic texts.

A *hermeneutics of ethical and theological evaluation* assesses the rhetorics of texts and traditions as well as that of contemporary discourses. While a hermeneutics of consent, which is advocated by the doctrinal paradigm of interpretation, reads the Bible for guidance and edification and accepts its teachings on submission, a critical feminist hermeneutics of evaluation seeks both to make conscious the cultural-religious internalizations and legitimations of kyriarchy and to explore the values and visions that are inscribed as countercultural alternatives in biblical texts.

It also seeks to evaluate biblical texts and interpretations in terms of *a feminist scale of values* that may be inspired by, but is not necessarily derived from, the Bible. For instance, Sheila Redmond[58] has pointed out that the biblical values of suffering, forgiveness, purity, need for redemption, and obedience to authority figures prevent recovery from child sexual abuse and continue to disempower their victims. Hence a hermeneutics of evaluation seeks to adjudicate the oppressive tendencies as well as the liberatory possibilities inscribed in biblical texts along with their function in contemporary struggles for liberation.

Such a hermeneutics of evaluation does not reify texts and traditions in a dualistic fashion either as oppressive or as emancipatory. Rather, it seeks to adjudicate again and again how biblical texts function in particular situations. Its criterion or standard of evaluation, the well-being of every wo/man, must be established and reasoned out in terms of a systemic analysis of kyriarchal domination. For theological reasons it insists that biblical religions must cease to preach kyriarchal texts as the "word of G*d," since by doing so they proclaim G*d as legitimating kyriarchal oppression.

A *hermeneutics of remembrance and re-construction* works not only to increase the distance between ourselves and the time of the text, but also seeks an increase

---

58. Sheila Redmond, "Christian 'Virtues' and Recovery from Child Sexual Abuse," in *Christianity, Patriarchy, and Abuse: A Feminist Critique,* ed. Joanne Carlson Brown and Carole R. Bohn (New York: Pilgrim Press, 1989), 73–74.

in historical knowledge and solidarity. Hence it questions the historical "chasm" that historical positivism has constructed between contemporary readers and the biblical text. It seeks to displace the kyriocentric dynamic of the biblical text in its literary and historical contexts by recontextualizing the text in a sociopolitical-religious model of reconstruction that aims at making the subordinated and marginalized "others" visible again and their repressed arguments and silences "audible." It thereby attempts to recover wo/men's religious history and the memory of their victimization, struggle, and accomplishments as wo/men's heritage.

Such a hermeneutics of remembrance utilizes constructive methods of re-visioning insofar as it seeks not only for historical retrieval but also for a religious reconstitution of the world. It seeks to do so in and through a recovery of the forgotten past of wo/men's victimization and struggles for survival and well-being. With postmodern thinkers it is fully conscious of the rhetoricity of its own reconstructions but nevertheless insists that such work of historical remembrance is necessary in support of wo/men's struggles for survival and transformation today. If it is a sign of oppression when a people does not have a written history, then feminists and other subaltern scholars cannot afford to eschew such rhetorical and historical re-constructive work.

A rhetorical and historical method of reconstruction does not understand texts as windows to the world or as mirrors of the past and it does not read historical sources as objective data and evidence of how things really were. Neither does it understand historiography as a transcript and report of "what actually happened." Nor does it mistake its scientific models of reconstruction as describing reality. Rather, it remains conscious of the fact that all three phases of historiography—documentary research, explanation, and writing—must be rooted in a hermeneutics of suspicion and critical evaluation. Historical understanding depends on analogy. It is narrative laden and amounts to a remaking and retelling of reality, but it is not reality itself. History and memory of the past always imbricate imagination and are imbricated by it.

A hermeneutics of imagination therefore inspires and complements one of reconstruction. It seeks to generate utopian visions that have not yet been realized and to "dream" a different world of justice and well-being. For the space of the imagination is that of freedom, a space in which boundaries are crossed, possibilities are explored, and time becomes relativized. It is a space of memory and possibility where situations can be re-experienced and desires re-embodied. Because of our re-imaginative abilities, we can put ourselves into another person's position in order to relate to their feelings and participate in their deliberations and struggles.

Because of the imagination, we are able to conceive of change and how situations can be altered. Historical like all other imagination is absolutely necessary for any knowledge of biblical texts and worlds. Imagination enables us to fill in the gaps, empty spaces, and silences, and thereby to make sense out of the text. Usually we see the power of imagination embodied in art, music, literature, and dance, but not in science, since we generally assume that science works only with deductive, rational, logical arguments. However, such an assumption is incorrect insofar as science always works with hypotheses and models that depend on informed imagination. Imagination mines the unconscious as a store of feelings and experiences as well as a depository of commonsense practices and codes. These unconscious assumptions determine scientific thought and decide how we read texts, reconstruct history, and imagine the past.

A hermeneutics of imagination retells biblical stories, reshapes religious vision, and celebrates those who have brought about change. To that end it utilizes not only historical, literary, and ideology critical methods, which focus on the rhetoric of religious texts and their historical contexts. It also employs methods of storytelling, role-playing, bibliodrama, pictorial arts, dance, and ritual for creating a "different" religious imagination.

Imaginative role-playing establishes identity with the characters of the kyriocentric text and historicizes them. It also enacts "commonsense" understandings and brings to the fore repressed emotions and experiences that are culturally imbricated. Hence we need to scrutinize imaginative practices with a hermeneutics of suspicion, since our imagination and utopian visions *are always both informed and deformed by our present sociopolitical location.*

Finally, the critical interpretative process or "hermeneutical dance" has as its goal and climax a *hermeneutics of transformation* and action for change. It seeks to change relations of domination that are legitimated and inspired by kyriarchal biblical religions. To that end, it explores avenues and possibilities for changing and transforming relations of domination inscribed in texts, traditions, and everyday life. It stands accountable to those wo/men who struggle at the bottom of the kyriarchal pyramid of discriminations and dominations. It also seeks to articulate religious and biblical studies as a site of social, political, and religious transformation.

When seeking for future vision and transformation, we can only extrapolate from present experience that is always already determined by the past. Hence we need to analyze the present in order to articulate creative visions and transcending imaginations for a new humanity and religious community. Yet only if we want to work for a different future will imagination be able to transform the past and present limitations of our vision. As Toni Morrison so forcefully states in her novel *Beloved*: "She did not tell them to clean up their lives or to go and sin no more. She did not tell them they were the blessed of the earth, its inheriting meek or its glorybound pure. She told them that the only grace they could have was the grace they could imagine. That if they could not see it, they would not have it."[59]

The shared spiritual visions of biblical religions can evoke powerful emotions and responses and thereby create a sense of community necessary to sustain the struggles and visions for an alternative society and world. Biblical studies must, therefore, be refashioned in such a way that it can contribute to the formation of a Wisdom/Spirit-space of courage, hope, and vision in our variegated struggles for justice. The

---

59. Toni Morrison, *Beloved* (New York: New American Library; Plume, 1988), 88.

subdiscipline of biblical theology would have to be re-visioned in such a fashion that it could contribute to the articulation of a Spirit-center of global dimensions.

To sum up my explorations: a critical rhetorical-emancipatory process of interpretation challenges, practitioners of biblical studies and readers of the Bible to become more theo-ethically sophisticated readers by problematizing both the modernist ethos of biblical studies and their own sociopolitical locations and functions in global structures of domination. At the same time, it enables them to struggle for a more just and radical democratic *cosmopolitan* articulation of religion in the global polis.

In order to comprehend the contours of such a paradigm shift in the self-understanding of the discipline, one must move from a scientistic-academic to a critical public ethos of discourse that is fueled by the reflection on issues arising from wo/men's confrontation with injustice. Such a shift and transformation of biblical studies would be able skillfully to negotiate the Scylla of "what the text meant" and the Charybdis of "what the text means today" by focusing on ethical-theological biblical visions of justice and well-being for every wo/man on the globe.

A transformation of this kind gestures toward a biblical theology that is no longer dependent on modernist and positivist historicism for its criteria.[60] While biblical theology still would need to reason historically insofar as it still must read biblical texts as rhetorical texts in particular historical contexts, it nevertheless would be freed to ask the central ethical-political and theological question: What kind of values and visions do biblical texts and their contemporary interpretations advocate? Do they value theological visions that contribute to the well-being of everyone in the global *cosmopolis,* or do they reinforce the languages of domination and hate as theological?

A critical rhetorical method and hermeneutical process of interpretation for public theological deliberation and religious transformation is not restricted to Christian canonical texts but can be and has been explored successfully by scholars of traditions and Scriptures of other religions.[61] Moreover, it is not restricted to the biblical scholar as expert reader. Rather, it calls for transformative and engaged biblical readers who may or may not be professional interpreters. It has been used in graduate education, in parish discussions, in college classes, and in work with illiterate Andean women. The Swiss theologian Regula Strobel sums up her pastoral experience with people who, in parish Bible study groups, have engaged or "danced" the "dance" of interpretation:

> People who have worked with the hermeneutics of Elisabeth Schüssler Fiorenza changed in an impressive way. In the beginning they still sought the authority of the theologian, who was to decide how a biblical text is correctly understood and interpreted. Increasingly they learnt to understand themselves as subjects not only of biblical read-

---

60. Cf. the trenchant critique of A. K. M. Adam, "Biblical Theology and the Problem of Modernity: Von Wredestrasse to Sackgasse," *Horizons in Biblical Theology* 12 (1990): 1–18.

61. See Kwok Pui-Lan and Elisabeth Schüssler Fiorenza, eds., *Women's Sacred Scriptures,* Concilium 3 (Maryknoll. N.Y.: Orbis Books, 1998).

ings. On the basis of their experiences they have formulated what was liberatory and what was oppressive. They eschewed the pressure to derive all decisions from the [B]ible or the attitude of Jesus. For they experienced as meaningful and supportive as the criterion for decision and action everything that contributes to the liberation and life in fullness of wo/men and other disadvantaged persons. Thereby they could read even ambiguous [B]ible texts and be nourished by the liberating aspects without taking over the oppressive ones. [62]

In and through such a critical rhetorical process of interpretation and deliberation religious and biblical studies are constituted as public discourses that are sites of struggle and conscientization. The transformation of biblical studies into such a theo-ethics of interpretation calls for a rhetorical method of analysis that is able to articulate the power relations and radical democratic visions of well-being inscribed in biblical texts.

---

62. Regula Strobel, "Brot Nicht Steine: Elisabeth Schüssler Fiorenzas Hermeneutik in der Pfarrearbeit."

Chapter 3

Shifting the Focus:
The Politics of Biblical Studies

I have argued in the preceding chapter that the shift from a dogmatist, historical-scientistic or culturally relativist paradigm of interpretation to a critical rhetorical-emancipatory process paradigm challenges practitioners of biblical studies and readers of the Bible to become ethically more sophisticated readers. It invites them to problematize both the modernist ethos of biblical studies and their own sociopolitical locations and functions in global structures of domination. At the same time it enables biblical readers to struggle for a more just and radical democratic cosmopolitan articulation of religion in a global context. Hence such a rhetorical paradigm of interpretation is no longer directed just at the church or the academy as its publics of discourse. Rather, its audience is the public sphere of society, institutionalized biblical religions, and the academy—in other words, the public of the *ekklesia* of decision-making citizens.

Such a paradigm shift requires a reconceptualization of biblical studies in rhetorical-emancipatory terms. Rhetoric is best understood as epistemic because it reveals an ethical dimension of knowledge production as political practice. Since its goal is persuasion, the ethical knowledge rhetoric strives to achieve is that of commitment.

> Commitment and rhetoric stand in a reciprocal relationship: commitment generates rhetoric, and rhetoric generates commitment. . . . The justification of injury to others, especially when that injury is wide scale, finding expression in social and economic dominance or violence, is ordinarily rooted in the certainty of some commanding Truth taken as axiomatic. . . . If one may repair to standards of judgment that are fixed outside the individual conscience or even the interests of an immediate community, then one does not bear the burden of responsibility in making decisions. It is that relief from individual or communal responsibility that is the chief attraction of what is sometimes called, I believe mistakenly, "objective reality."[1]

It is not only popular[2] but also appropriate to mark such a paradigm shift in the

1. Robert L. Scott, "On Viewing Rhetoric as Epistemic: Ten Years Later," in *Methods of Rhetorical Criticism: A Twentieth-Century Perspective,* ed. Bernard L. Brock, Robert L. Scott, James W. Chesebro (3d rev. ed., Detroit: Wayne State University Press, 1989), 140–41.

2. For a historical location of this expression in philosophical discourse, see David R. Hiley, James F. Bohman, and Richard M. Shusterman, eds., *The Interpretive Turn: Philosophy, Science, Culture,* (Ithaca, N.Y.: Cornell University Press, 1991), 1–14.

self-understanding of the discipline as an intellectual turn because the expressions intellectual *turn* or *full-turn* invoke not only the metaphor of the dance, a figure for rhetoric that was already used by Quintillian, but also the *metanoia* of the Gospels: a radical turning around of one's mind and one's goals.

Critical Turns and Turnings in the Ethos of Biblical Scholarship

Four crucial intellectual "turns" in the contemporary dance of academic knowledge production make it possible to articulate the fourth emerging paradigm in biblical studies that challenges the scientific posture of disinterestedness and value-neutrality. Combining the force of these intellectual shifts, they could change biblical criticism from an academic discipline that is supposedly free from any ideological commitments to values and communal visions to one of politically engaged and publicly responsible scholarship.

These four intellectual turns, which are constitutive of a critical interdisciplinary rhetorical-emancipatory paradigm, also make possible a transformation in the ethos of biblical scholarship. They therefore provide the intellectual means for a change in the understanding of biblical scholars from the ethos of professionalized disinterested scientism to seeing ourselves as critically engaged public intellectuals who are working in rhetorical-political practices.

The Hermeneutical Turn

The notion of hermeneutics derives from the Greek word *hermeneuein* and means to interpret, exegete, explain, or translate. It owes its name to Hermes, the messenger of the Gods, who has the task to mediate the announcements, declarations, and messages of the Gods to mere mortals. His proclamation, however, is not a mere communication and mediation but is always also an explication of divine commands in such a way that he translates them into human language so that they can be comprehended and obeyed.

While hermeneutics can be understood with Derrida as a matter of the free play of signs[3] and with Rorty[4] as merely keeping the lines of communication open, according to Gadamer[5] hermeneutics has the task of translating meaning from one "world" into another.[6] Like Hermes, the messenger of the Gods, hermeneutics not

---

3. Jacques Derrida, "The Ends of Man," *Philosophy and Phenomenological Research* 30 (1969): 31–57.

4. Richard Rorty, *Philosophy and the Mirror of Nature* (Princeton: Princeton University Press, 1979), 315.

5. See Hans Georg Gadamer, *Truth and Method*, trans. Joel Weinsheimer and Donald G. Marshall (2d rev. ed., New York: Continuum, 1993) and *Philosophical Hermeneutics* (Berkeley: University of California Press, 1976).

6. See Richard Bernstein, "What Is the Difference That Makes a Difference? Gadamer, Habermas, and Rorty," in *Hermeneutics and Modern Philosophy*, ed. Brice R. Wachterhauser (Albany: State University of New York Press, 1986), 343–76.

only communicates knowledge but also instructs, directs, and enjoins. Hermeneutics thus has affinities to manticism and prophecy. It conveys revelation and interprets signs and oracles. It is a matter of practical understanding that involves the Aristotelian virtue of *phronesis*—practical judgment and adjudication that is secured not by an a priori method but only by the process of understanding.

As a discipline, philosophical hermeneutics has its roots in biblical interpretation. It is best understood as a theory and practice of interpretation that explores the conditions and possibilities for understanding not just texts but other practices[7] as well. As such, hermeneutics is less a disciplined scientific method and technique than an epistemological perspective and approach. It "represents not so much a highly honed, well-established theory of understanding or a long-standing, well-defined tradition of philosophy as it does a family of concerns and critical perspectives."[8]

Since Schleiermacher, Dilthey, and Gadamer,[9] hermeneutics has maintained over and against scientific positivism that understanding takes place as a process of engagement in the hermeneutical circle or spiral, which is characterized by the part-whole relation. It stresses that understanding is not possible without preunderstandings or prejudices and therefore that understanding is always contextually dependent. Hermeneutics does not ground intelligibility in the "pregiven, essentially changeless human subject, but in the public sphere of evolving, linguistically mediated practice."[10] Thus hermeneutics seeks to remain open for change and difference.

If we are part of a language and world that is not of our own making, we can never leave it behind even if we adopt a "disinterested" theoretical attitude. No presuppositionless understanding is possible.

> The languages we speak, the practices we unconsciously appropriate, the institutions we live out our lives in, the theoretical debates we inherit, and so forth, all form a loosely packed amalgam of meaningful relations that we can never entirely objectify and that we always presuppose in our thematic understanding of anything whatever.[11]

In short, our very ability to understand becomes defined by our preunderstandings, which we cannot simply cast off as we would a coat or a hat. Our presuppositions are not roadblocks that prohibit a true grasp of reality itself but rather a set of linguistically mediated preunderstandings we inherit, with which we gain the possibility of understanding the world.

Hermeneutics insists on the linguisticality of all knowledge, on its contextuality and its immersion in tradition. It stresses that human understanding can never take

---

7. Paul Ricoeur's theory of interpretation has argued that action may be regarded as a text. If an action, like a text, is a meaningful entity, then the "paradigm of reading" can also be applied to socio-religious practices. See Paul Ricoeur, *Hermeneutics and the Human Sciences*, ed. and trans. John B. Thompson (Cambridge and New York: Cambridge University Press, 1981), 197–221.

8. See Wachterhauser, *Hermeneutics and Modern Philosophy*, 5.

9. See Ricoeur, *Hermeneutics and the Human Sciences*, 43–62.

10. Wachterhauser, *Hermeneutics and Modern Philosophy*, 8.

11. Ibid., 21.

place without words and outside of time. Its key concepts are *empathy, historicity, linguisticality, tradition, preunderstanding, fusion of horizons,* and *the classic* with its notion of *effective history.* However, all seven aspects and theoretical emphases of hermeneutics are problematic from a critical feminist perspective because they do not take sufficiently into account relations of domination and power. Rather than conceiving of understanding as a fusion of horizons,[12] it is necessary, as Susan Shapiro has argued,[13] to articulate hermeneutics as rhetorics. Hermeneutics must become a critical inquiry into the rhetoricity of the structures of domination and goals of emancipation.

Feminist analyses have underscored that grammatically masculine, so-called generic language is a major cultural force in maintaining women's second-class status in culture and religion. If, according to Wittgenstein, the limits of our language are the limits of our world,[14] then grammatically masculine language that constructs the universe of women and men in androcentric or, better, kyriocentric terms, engenders a world in which wo/men are marginal or not present at all. Hence it does not suffice to understand the kyriocentric religious-cultural language, tradition, or classic. What is necessary is to change it.

A critical hermeneutics that is feminist and emancipatory, therefore, insists that we must analyze language as an instrument of power and ideology rather than as simply descriptive and communicative. Language is always rhetorical. Hence hermeneutical theory must be "braided" with rhetoric, for rhetorical discourse not only inscribes but also makes explicit the relation of language and power in a particular moment.[15] Utilizing this insight, a feminist hermeneutics insists that objective scholarship requires the critical articulation of one's kyriocentric preunderstandings. Yet, understanding the kyriocentric world of the text, whether behind or before the text, does not suffice. Scholarship must also recognize this world for what it is, a world of subordination and oppression. At this point it becomes evident that a critical hermeneutics that is feminist and emancipatory must move beyond hermeneutics to the critique of ideology that can lift into consciousness the distortions and rhetorical constructedness of this world.

If all language is rhetorical, if even objectivity is the product of a certain strategy, then discourses are no longer to be measured in terms of their adequacy to an objective standard (which Nietzsche's perspectivism exposes as a myth) but rather to be analyzed in terms of their strategic placement within a clash of competing forces themselves constituted in and through the very rhetorical dissimulations they employ.[16]

12. John Caputo, "Hermeneutics as the Recovery of Man," in *Hermeneutics and Modern Philosophy,* ed. Wachterhauser, 416–45, 424.

13. Susan Shapiro, "Rhetoric as Ideology Critique: The Gadamer-Habermas Debate Reinvented," *JAAR* 62, 1 (1994): 123–50.

14. On religious language and hermeneutics, see Dan R. Stiver, *The Philosophy of Religious Language: Sign, Symbol and Story* (Cambridge: Blackwell, 1996), 37–111.

15. See Lorraine Code, *Rhetorical Spaces: Essays on Gendered Locations* (New York: Routledge, 1995).

16. John Bender and David E. Wellbery, "Rhetoricality: On the Modernist Return of Rhetoric," in *The Ends of Rhetoric: History, Theory, Practice,* ed. John Bender and David E. Wellbery (Stanford: Stanford University Press, 1990), 27.

As a theory and practice of justice, critical rhetorical studies, however, cannot be limited to hermeneutical studies, which seek to understand, appreciate, and appropriate the texts and traditions of malestream culture and religion. Rather, a rhetoric of inquiry must draw on and braid together several approaches and reconfigure them in a critical feminist rhetorics of liberation.

The Political Turn

Hermeneutics has been severely criticized by modern theorists for harboring a conservative bias because of its focus on tradition and its neglect of power relations in the process of text production and interpretation. The critical "more" that the political turn brings to biblical studies is the insistence on the politics of interpretation and on the responsibility of the scholar as citizen. Politics has to do with the exercise of power in the act of interpretation. Obviously, I do not understand here *politics/political* in terms of partisan party politics. Rather, I understand it in the classical terms of the polis or in global contemporary terms of the *cosmopolis*.

The need for such a cosmopolitan political turn that would continue and correct the hermeneutical turn in biblical studies has been raised insistently not only by feminists but also by postcolonial scholars. Discussing the political climate in South Africa, Martin Prozesky writes in 1990:

> Amidst all this [political oppression] Religious Studies in our context will damn itself ... if it imagines that all it must do is document, analyze, interpret, and explain the reality of religions in South Africa, for the situation cries out for something more. It cries out for a new ethic of religions, a new creatively critical interrogation of religion in relation to both socio-personal liberation and oppression. ... [It] cannot now be credibly studied without prioritizing the problem of religions in the struggle for a more humane world order in general, and in the apartheid state in particular.[17]

In North American academic scholarship this political turn is brought about by social movements such as the civil rights, the postcolonial, and the feminist emancipatory movements. It implies a commitment to the principle of justice as that which grounds the demand for an end of discrimination not only against wo/men but against all those who in kyriarchal terms were defined not only as the "others" but as the "subordinate and inferior others" of the western elite "Man of Reason."

Since "voice," positionality, and heterogeneity are key categories in critical liberationist studies, feminist theory and theology always must insist that scholarship cannot be done from a disembodied value-neutral position. Research is always perspectival and sociopolitically situated. Thus the political turn encourages us to articulate biblical studies as *political criticism* that puts concern with the values,

---

17. Martin Prozesky, "South Africa's Contribution to Religious Studies," *Journal of Theology of Southern Africa* 70 (1990): 10–11.

18. S. P. Mohanti, "Us and Them: On the Philosophical Bases of Political Criticism," *Yale Journal of Criticism* 2, 2 (1998): 21.

texts, and cultures of the "others"[18] at its center. It calls for the articulation of a politics of interpretation that is conceptualized as a critical rhetorical activity practiced by citizens who in the *ekklesia* of the academy or the church/synagogue/mosque deliberate and decide the well-being of the *cosmopolis*.

However, it must not be forgotten that the rhetorical discourse of citizenship, *ekklesia,* and politics in antiquity and modernity has been constructed by relations of domination and exclusion. "Rhetoric always inscribes the relation of language and power at a particular moment (including who may speak, who may listen, who will agree to listen, and what can be said)."[19] Classical rhetoric has been aptly characterized by Cheryl Glenn as the tradition of "vocal men and muted women." It is well known that in antiquity wo/men were excluded from the rhetorical and political tradition, a tradition of elite educated and propertied men, i.e., of *kyrioi* (lords/masters/fathers/husbands). Political-rhetorical discourse in antiquity is not just heavily gendered but also subalterned, constructed in and through the exclusion of slaves, barbarians, and the others of the others.

Athenian *democratia* and *isonomia*—that is, equality before the law—were seen solely as the province of elite men who were heads of households.

> The egalitarianism of the Athenian ethos extended only to free citizen males. Women and slaves had carefully circumscribed rights and played a part in public life by facilitating the leisure of free males, and it was only under extraordinary circumstances that resident aliens might become Athenian citizens. Although their slaveholding and their exclusivity in extending the franchise to aliens were typical of ancient Greeks as a whole, the vehemence of their denial of women's value and capacity set Athenian men somewhat apart from other Hellenes.[20]

Ancient democracy was an elite male club that had been constituted in and through the exclusion of freeborn wo/men, slaves, resident aliens, and barbarians. This allowed freeborn male citizens to acknowledge each other and to ignore the remaining kyriarchal power relations within the democratic fraternity. The exclusion of wo/men and all the others of free citizens is the structuring principle that is constitutive for equality among male citizens. Plato and Aristotle laid out a stratified order in which status was rigidly defined and power was reserved for a few elite males.

In a similar fashion, rhetoric as political discourse was constructed as inferior to philosophy.[21] The philosophical discourse of Plato and Aristotle kept rhetoric in place as an imperfect system that separated the proofs *ethos* and *pathos* from that of *logos,* which was the domain of philosophy.

> The second wave of feminism beginning with de Beauvoir's *The Second Sex* has exposed this gendered discourse of privilege, a process Gayatri Spivak has called "the production of a discourse of man through a certain metaphor of woman" ("Displacement," 169). The

19. Cheryl Glenn, *Rhetoric Retold,* 1–2.

20. Jennifer Tolbert Roberts, *Athens on Trial: The Antidemocratic Tradition in Western Thought* (Princeton: Princeton University Press, 1994), 30.

21. Jane Sutton, "The Death of Rhetoric and Its Rebirth in Philosophy," *Rhetorica* 4 (1986): 203–26.

character projected onto the feminine as "other" shares with Plato's Sophists qualities of irrationality (or non-rationality), magical or hypnotic power, subjectivity, emotional sensitivity; all these are devalued in favor of their "masculine" or philosophic opposites— rationality, objectivity, detachment, and so on. . . . The devaluation of both the Sophists and wo/men operates as their reduction to a "style" devoid of substance.[22]

This kyriarchal constitution of political democratic discourse in and through the exclusion of the "other" together with the feminine typecasting[23] of rhetoric and its subordination to philosophy in and through the isolation of *logos* from *ethos* and *pathos* calls for a critical analysis of ideology. To recognize the kyriarchal deformation of notions such as citizenship, democracy, and justice does not mean that one must reject these discourses wholesale. It only means that they need to be thoroughly deconstructed in terms of a critical ideology analysis before they can be deployed with a difference.

The Ideology Critical Turn

The ideology critical turn[24] is closely connected with and engendered by the political turn, but it does not focus just on the political. With Jürgen Habermas, a representative of the Frankfurt School's critical theory, the ideology critical turn insists over and against the scientific as well as the hermeneutical program that the question of power is integral to understanding, linguisticality, tradition, and the classic. Habermas distinguishes

> three basic forms of our scientific interest in knowing about the world: the empirical-analytical, the hermeneutical-historical, and the critical-emancipatory. We seek to know in order to control social and natural realities (the empirical-analytic interest), to qualitatively understand and interpret such realities (the hermeneutical-historical interest), and to transform our individual and collective consciousness of reality in order to maximize the human potential for freedom and equality (the critical-emancipatory interest).[25]

Whereas the scientific study of the Bible is dedicated to analyzing the text as well as to describing its worlds, and hermeneutics is concerned with the surplus of meaning, critical theory focuses on the lack and distortion of meaning and method because of their determination by power relations of domination. Just as feminist analysis, so also critical theory stresses the distortion of language and tradition. The

---

22. Susan C. Jarratt, *Rereading the Sophists: Classical Rhetoric Refigured* (Carbondale: Southern Illinois University Press, 1991), 63.

23. Jane Sutton, "The Taming of Polos/Polis: Rhetoric as an Achievement Without Women," in *Contemporary Rhetorical Theory: A Reader*, ed. John Louis Lucaites, et al. (New York: Guilford Press, 1999), 101–27.

24. For biblical studies see David Jobling and Tina Pippin, eds., *Ideological Criticism of Biblical Texts*, Semeia 59 (Atlanta: Scholars Press, 1992).

25. Raymond A. Morrow with David D. Baron, *Critical Theory and Methodology* (Thousand Oaks, Calif.: Sage Publications, 1994), 146.

endurance of the classic, for instance, is due not just to its outstanding representation of meaning but much more to the persistence of kyriarchal power constellations that legitimate it and in turn are legitimated by it. Cultural and religious linguistic practices and traditions have been constituted within unequal power relationships. A feminist critical theory thus insists on and makes possible the concrete analysis of structures of power and domination. It engages in hermeneutics for the sake of ideology critique.

With the feminist theorist Michèle Barrett, I understand ideology as referring to a process of mystification or misrepresentation. Ideology is distorted communication rather than false consciousness. "The retrievable core of meaning of the term ideology is precisely this: discursive and significatory mechanisms that may occlude, legitimate, naturalise or universalise in a variety of different ways but can all be said to mystify."[26]

A fundamental assumption of critical theory holds that every form of social order entails some forms of domination and that critical emancipatory interests fuel the struggles to change these relations of domination and subordination. Such power relations engender forms of distorted communication that result in self-deception on the parts of agents with respect to their interests, needs, and perceptions of social and religious reality. Theologically speaking they are structural sin. "The notion of ideology must be situated with a theory of language that emphasizes the ways in which meaning is infused with forms of power. . . . To study ideology is not to analyze a particular type of discourse but rather to explore . . . the modes whereby meaningful expressions serve to sustain relations of domination."[27]

John B. Thompson has pointed to three major modes or strategies that are involved in how ideology operates: legitimization, dissimulation, and reification (literally: to make into a thing).[28] All three modes can be identified in the discourses of wo/men's silencing and censure. The first strategy is an appeal for legitimacy on traditional grounds, whereas the second conceals relations of domination in ways that are themselves often structurally excluded from thought. Or, as Jürgen Habermas puts it, ideology serves to "impede making the foundations of society [and, I would add, of religion] the object of thought and reflection."[29]

The third form of ideological operation is reification or naturalization, which represents a transitory, culturally, historically, and socially engendered state of affairs as if it were permanent, natural, outside of time, or directly revealed by G*d. This ideological strategy comes to the fore in the questionable theological arguments for wo/men's special nature. Ideology, moreover, contributes to the distorted self-understanding of oppressed people who have internalized belief in the legitimacy of their own subordination and innate status as inferior. Religious texts and traditions that represent and mystify kyriocentric cultural traditions and kyriarchal intellectual

26. Michèle Barrett, *The Politics of Truth: From Marx to Foucault* (Stanford: Stanford University Press, 1991), 177.

27. Morrow and Baron, *Critical Theory and Methodology*, 130–49.

28. John B. Thompson, *Studies in the Theory of Ideology* (Cambridge: Polity Press, 1984), 254.

29. Jürgen Habermas, "Ideology," in *Modern Interpretations of Marx,* ed. Tom Bottomore (Oxford: Blackwell, 1981), 166.

structures of domination as revealed truth call not only for an ideology critique but also for an ethics of interpretation.

The Ethical Turn

The intellectual turn to ethics[30] seems ubiquitous in the era of poststructuralism and postmodernism. It follows the "linguistic turn," which incorporated the insights of linguistics into the discourses of the human sciences. But whereas structuralism had as an organizing principle "language as the enabling condition of knowledge," French poststructuralists such as Derrida, Lacan, Levinas, Kristeva, and Foucault seem to share a concern about the ethical subject of discourse: "In the breach opened up by placing into question, or the deconstruction, if you will, of the traditional or humanist subject as a rational, willing agent, these thinkers in various ways have all been engaged to some extent in exploring what I will have been calling the ethical subject."[31]

In order to understand the ethical turn, it may be helpful to look at some terminological distinctions.[32] The term *ethics* generally is distinguished from morals and morality, but often these terms are used interchangeably. The word *moral(s)* is a synonym for custom, habit, practice, and encompasses norms and values that are expressed as laws and prohibitions. It pertains to and concerns itself with the principles or rules of right conduct or the distinction between right and wrong, with ethical (that is, moral) attitudes. The term expresses a tenet that is acknowledged as binding by the majority of a society or a specific group. The word *morality* means moral or virtuous conduct, a doctrine or system of morals, and the habit and conviction of wanting to do the good. Hence an action on the basis of morality can come into conflict with the de facto existing morals of a society or a group. An action is to be judged moral if it either follows a rule of the existing, hegemonic morality or if it is based on the morality of the moral agent.

According to the *Random House Dictionary*, the term *ethics* ("used with a sing. or pl. v.") designates a system of moral principles, as in "the ethics of a culture." It means both the rules of conduct recognized in respect to a particular class of human actions or a particular group, culture, and ("usually used with a sing. v.") a branch of philosophy that deals with values relating to human conduct, with respect to the rightness and wrongness of certain actions and to the goodness and badness of the motives and ends of such actions. Ethics as an academic discipline is distinct from morals in that it does not ask what must be done in a concrete instance but thematizes moral actions on a metalevel of reflection insofar as it asks for moral principles, norms, and criteria for judging an action as moral.[33]

30. Cf. Jane Adamson, Richard Freadman, and David Parke, eds., *Renegotiating Ethics in Literature, Philosophy, and Theory* (Cambridge: Cambridge University Press, 1998), who programmatically set out to explore the turn to ethics in the 1990s.

31. Peter Baker, *Deconstruction and the Ethical Turn* (Gainesville: University of Florida Press, 1995), 1.

32. Peter Singer, ed., *Ethics: An Oxford Reader* (New York: Oxford University Press, 1994), 1–15.

33. For delineation of the terms see also Annemarie Pieper, *Ethik und Moral: Eine Einführung in die praktische Philosophie* (Munich: Kösel, 1985), 10–43; and Gunhild Buse, *Macht-Moral-Weiblichkeit: Eine*

Ethics understood as a theory and vision of well-being or of the "good life," articulates the values and goals of human beings, of society on the whole, and of living nature. As such it belongs to the self-understanding of every human being.

> It is an understanding of what counts as highly valuable in personal encounters, in social relationships and in our ties to nature. It is a double vision, of what is and what ought to be, but if we have not already experienced it to some extent, and discovered it as a reality, we would never have been able to envision it as a goal. Conversely, if the good life had already totally realized itself, we would never have the need to speak about ethics. Thus ethics is first of all a vision which shapes us as human beings, as persons able to take our responsibilities for our life with others and with the whole living world.[34]

Disputes about the relationship between rhetoric and morality have been alive in rhetorical theory throughout its history. As Celeste Michelle Condit points out, however, most recently theorists have tended to use privatized and individualistic models of morality such as the conversational model of discourse, rather than to engage in public rhetoric "viewed as a process in which basic human desires are transformed into shared moral codes."[35] Such public morality is constructed, implemented, and enhanced through public argument. Conversely, if one looks at the rhetoric produced in particular situations, such as the civil rights struggle, one can come to understand the moral problem of racism in historical perspective.

Condit suggests that the best metaphor for the construction of morality is not private conversation or individualist intellectual quest but collective craft, since morality is constructed by citizens through public discourse. Such a rhetoric of morality "utilizes the capacity of discourse simultaneously to create, extend, and apply moral concepts," a process that is "bounded by an inductive historical objectivity."[36] Such a discourse of public morality is both intersubjective and political. It is made and unmade by rhetorical practices that are not to be seen as mirrors that reflect the world back to us. Participants in such moral discourse are active moral agents who deliberate, urge, validate, and argue meanings and actions with each other. Such an intersubjective democratic conceptualization of ethics has rhetoric at its center. Rhetoric as an intersubjective-democratic process "is doubly ethical: it is the result of a choice on the part of the rhetor as to the reality advocated and the method of doing so, and it urges choice rather than complete and necessary acceptance on the part of the audience. Truth which is rhetorically made encourages choice and awareness of alternative realities."[37]

---

feministisch-theologische Auseinandersetzung mit Carol Gilligan und Frigga Haug (Mainz: Grünewald, 1993).

34. Peter Kemp, "From Ethics to Bioethics," in Questioning Ethics: Contemporary Debates in Philosophy, ed. Richard Kierney and Mark Dooley (New York: Routledge, 1999), 283.

35. Celeste Michelle Condit, "Crafting Virtue: The Rhetorical Construction of Public Morality," in Contemporary Rhetorical Theory, ed. Lucaites et al., 311.

36. Condit, "Crafting Virtue," 320.

37. Barry Brummett, "Some Implications of 'Process' or 'Intersubjectivity' in Postmodern Rhetoric," in Contemporary Rhetorical Theory, ed. Lucaites et al., 166. However, a purely intersubjective conceptualization is still too privatized and individualist. Hence I have qualified it with democratic.

Such an intersubjective-democratic ethics must skillfully navigate on the one hand the Scylla of idealist ethics, which in Platonic fashion discovers the truth not by engaging in rhetoric but by the layered process of dialectic, and makes "objective reality" an obligation; and on the other hand the Charybdis of semanticist ethics, which views language as a map "with the implications that a good map will report a territory and not include mountains and rivers and valleys, where there are none."[38]

Whereas in semanticist ethics language matches a posited objective reality, in idealist ethics rhetoric is charged with discovering rather than constructing "the truth." Having "found the truth," the idealist cannot be held accountable for the consequences of actualizing and discovering "objective truth" or "reality"; s/he is not responsible for the truth found. In both cases, in the idealist[39] and the semanticist ethics, "the world," "the truth," or "reality" are understood as existing objectively outside of language, but they are not seen, as in an intersubjective-democratic ethics, as constructed rhetorically.

Since the "ethical turn" has driven home that morality and truth, vision and knowledge of the good life are constructed rhetorically, an ethics of interpretation is called for in biblical studies. An ethics of reading[40] that restricts itself to the interpretation of texts but does not critically analyze the rhetorical practices of the discipline is in danger of succumbing either to an idealist or a semanticist ethics of inquiry. Insofar as biblical studies continues to be governed either by idealist or semanticist ethics, it still needs to confront the ethical turn according to which morality and truth, the vision of the good life, are constructed through rhetorical practices. Biblical studies must therefore critically explore not only biblical texts and traditions but also the mores and customs of the discipline in terms of an intersubjective-democratic public ethics of interpretation.[41]

A (Feminist) Ethic of Inquiry

By an ethic of inquiry I mean a new evaluative form of cultural practice and critical investigation that is no longer circumscribed by the scientist objectivism, subjectivism, liberalism, and nationalism, or the masculine rationalism and European colonialism of modernity that have tended to relegate rhetoric to mere talk and to the dustbins of history. A rhetoric of inquiry is a second-order reflection that is able to critically explore not only the rhetoricality of biblical texts but also that of biblical studies discourses.

> Rhetoricality . . . is bound to no specific set of institutions. For this reason it allows for no explanatory metadiscourse that is not already rhetorical. Rhetoric is no longer the

38. Brummett, "Some Implications," in *Contemporary Rhetorical Theory*, ed. Lucaites et al., 164.

39. See especially the work of Rey Chow, *Ethics after Idealism: Theory-Culture-Ethnicity-Reading* (Bloomington: Indiana University Press, 1998), which argues that what must be examined critically is no longer identity politics but the "idealizing otherness" that lies at the heart of identity politics.

40. See Fewell and Phillips, eds., *Bible and Ethics of Reading*.

41. See D. J. Smit, "The Bible and Ethos in a New South Africa," *Scriptura* 37 (1991): 51–67.

title of a doctrine and a practice, nor a form of cultural memory; it becomes instead something like the condition of our existence. . . . Rhetoricality names the new conditions of discourse in the modern world and, thus, the fundamental category of every inquiry that seeks to describe the nature of discursive action and exchange.[42]

In an ethical research paradigm, which is scientific with a difference, objectivity[43] and method are also understood differently. Whereas in the scientific positivist paradigm research methods are understood as rules and regulations, they are seen in the ethical-rhetorical paradigm of study as modes of inquiry, as questions to be asked, and as perspectives to be clarified. Feminist critical theory has shown that malestream scientific methods and theoretical perspectives have been formulated and shaped in the context of kyriarchal (that is, lord/master/husband/father dominated) academic institutions, which until very recently have been exclusive of wo/men and other "inferior status" scholars.

Feminist scholars in religion, therefore, cannot simply assume that biblical or religious studies will produce knowledge that changes and transforms. Rather, they must evaluate all knowledge claims and not just analyze and thereby re-inscribe kyriarchal relations of domination, including gender relations. Hence an ethic of inquiry must insist that scholars have to submit their approaches, methods, and organizing frameworks to a critical process of rhetorical-ethical analysis and critical-evaluative reconfiguration, which braids or blends together various methods, if they are to serve liberatory goals. Such a braiding or hybridization of methods and approaches can be accomplished, I submit, only within a critical feminist framework of an ethic of inquiry that is aware of the rhetorical constructedness of its research and able to articulate its values and interest for public inspection and debate.

In short, by a differently scientific ethic of inquiry I do not mean primarily technical procedures and rules but rather modes of critical reflection and analysis. Such an ethic of inquiry does not need to draw exclusive interdisciplinary boundaries but rather must redraw and traverse such boundaries. It must seek to cultivate a rhetorical reflexivity that can explore what it means to do critical biblical studies and to articulate the scholarly ethos of the discipline differently.

Some will object that such a transformation of biblical scholarship in terms of critical feminist rhetorical studies amounts to an unscientific advocacy stance. As such it does not belong in the university, so it might be argued, but must remain the domain of theological schools or seminaries. The academic study of religion is allegedly committed to value-neutrality and to the study of the Bible "just for the sake of knowledge." It may not succumb to the biased and interested rhetoric of theology that speaks from within a particular religion and is committed to a particular religious community. Theology cannot be truly scientific, because it is no longer able to be free of value commitments and disinterestedness. Scholars

---

42. Bender and Wellbery, "Rhetoricality," in Bender and Wellbery, eds., *The Ends of Rhetoric*, 25–26.

43. For such a difference see, for instance, Bonnie G. Smith, "Gender, Objectivity, and the Rise of Scientific History," in *Objectivity and Its Other*, ed. Natter et al., 51–66; and, in the same volume, Samuel Weber, "Objectivity Otherwise," 33–47.

become missionaries who want to bring their audiences to commit themselves to a religious faith and community.

The academic study of religion, in turn, is said to be free from ideological commitments and to adopt a neutral scientific framework of research within which a particular kind of inquiry takes place for the sake of knowledge production. As a scientific discipline, the academic study of religion scrutinizes religious phenomena as empirical facts of history. The point of science is to limit itself to understanding the world "as it is" and to represent it as "accurately" as possible. Those who object that such an articulation of the claim reveals the scientific ethos as another form of ideology have not understood it. Its moral responsibility, according to Max Weber, is to limit itself simply "to teaching, research and writing," to the virtue of "plain intellectual activity." "The only rational action to which scholars, as scholars, are committed, the only moral action to which they are commanded and the only 'social responsibility' to which their *professional* position compels them, is to use their energies in order to explain in its full diversity as much as they can of the nature of the world in which they live."[44]

If scholars bring to their scientific discourses political interests—as feminist and other subaltern scholars are wont to do—they are seen as corrupting the "purity" of science. Their research allegedly is no longer ruled just by the demands of logic and their discourses supposedly no longer belong to the cognitive scientific domain alone, but promote cultural, political, or religious ends. Like theologians who, by wanting to bring students to subscribe to a particular religion, compromise the scientific character of their work, so also socially and politically engaged scholars corrupt the "purity" of science by wanting to be socially responsible citizens whose research is sustaining the myth of their culture.

Most recently, Donald Wiebe has set out again "to defend the academic study of religion as a discipline that is genuinely scientific." Under the heading "The Politics of Religious Studies" he points to

> the complex argument that academic students of religion must eschew politico-ideological interference of any kind even though the field of religious studies as a whole possesses an inevitably political quality. In essence, this argument deplores the importation of cultural, political, racial, ethnic, or other non-cognitive criteria (especially religious criteria) . . . in the adjudication of research in religious studies or in the assessment of competence for teaching in the field.[45]

Wiebe concedes that the establishment of the science of religion, which biblical criticism pioneered, constitutes a political act and produces a "politics of science." However, he insists that such a politics in the general sense is to be distinguished from the "politics of local concern," which includes, in his words, not only "party politics" but

---

44. Maurice Cowling, *The Nature and Limits of Political Science* (Cambridge: Cambridge University Press, 1963), 210.

45. Donald Wiebe, "The Politics of Religious Studies," *Bulletin of the Council of Societies for the Study of Religion* 27, 4 (1998): 95.

also "ideological commitment." Wiebe, however, overlooks that his own commitment and advocacy of the study of religion as "science" is ideological in the sense he defines it. "The discourse which establishes a science . . . is a discourse about methods for the attainment of a particular kind of conversation rather than a substantive discourse on behalf of a particular set of values. Such a discourse does not either explicitly or implicitly sanction the promulgation of a culturally specific world-view or ideology."[46]

Here universal scientific methods and particular culturally specific values and visions are pitted against each other. Such a scientistic rhetoric of disinterestedness, however, is not able to recognize biblical and religious studies as public discourses that analyze and promote culturally specific values and thereby function as ideology.

Wiebe seems to be blissfully unaware of or cavalierly to disregard the feminist and postcolonial critique of science as ideology. As Lorraine Code points out:

> Epistemic responsibility and the accountability it demands, move to the top of the agenda once one acknowledges the centrality of the question "Whose knowledge are we talking about?" to late twentieth-century feminism. These issues become still more urgent once one admits the extent to which such an acknowledgment politicizes epistemic inquiry. . . .[47]

By posing the "whose science" and "whose knowledge" questions, feminists refuse "to accept uncritically 'the world according to him,' despite the fact of having then to reconstruct, almost *ex nihilo* 'the world according to her.' "[48] Consequently, the central question for religious studies seems not what methods to use but who uses them and to what ends. The issue at stake in the dispute between theology and the scientific study of religion is not so much one of method but one of values and ideologies. This is driven home by an exchange between Katherine K. Young and Rita Gross. In her response to Young's charge that feminism turns the classroom "into a mission field" Gross points out:

> Perhaps Young teaches only elite or advanced classes which students enter already understanding and valuing neutrality and objectivity in the study of religion. But the undergraduate state university classroom in which I teach already is a mission field because of the values students *bring with them*. Many regard accurate factual knowledge of non-Christian religions or biblical history as "biased" because it does not support their previous religious training. . . . This happens because such suggestions challenge students to do things to which they are unaccustomed, with which many of them disagree, and which many of them refuse to do because of the beliefs and values they bring to this "mission field" in which the contested practices are *neutrality and objectivity*.[49]

---

46. Wiebe, "The Politics of Religious Studies," 96; see also Wiebe's book *The Politics of Religious Studies: The Continuing Conflict with Theology in the Academy* (London: Macmillan, 1999).

47. Code, *Rhetorical Spaces*, 17.

48. Sandra Lee Bartky, *Feminism and Domination: Studies in the Phenomenology of Oppression* (New York: Routledge, 1990), 111.

49. Rita M. Gross, "'A Rose by Any Other Name . . .': A Response to Katherine K. Young," *JAAR* 67, 1 (1999): 190.

Although she does not want to challenge the ethos of the discipline, Gross's reference to her own experience as a teacher makes it clear that value-neutrality is not a method but a disciplinary ideology endemic to a specific academic culture. Hence it is not science but ethics that is at the heart of the feminist debate with the scientific study of religion.

Reviewing Gross's book *Feminism and Religion,* Young chides Gross for opting for feminism rather than for women's studies. Feminism, in her view, is ideological, whereas women's studies conforms to the value-neutral disinterested ethos of the academy. She bemoans that Gross does not follow the ethos of the discipline that was "very self-consciously" developed by its pioneers "as a descriptive and interpretive discipline," whereas "theology and ethics were considered as evaluative and normative ones."[50] What is at stake here is the political character of religious studies. This comes to the fore in Young's concluding statement: "One way out of this conflict is to maintain Gross's initial distinction of women's studies and feminism, viewing the former as a proper domain of the university and the latter of the public square."[51]

Thus the longstanding dispute between religious studies and theological studies continues in feminist studies and also affects the articulation and self-understanding of biblical studies. Four areas in which feminists have challenged the "scientific" value-free understanding of religious studies are of special significance for an ethico-political rhetorical paradigm shift in biblical studies: *First,* the feminist challenge to a positivist understanding of religious studies; *second,* the feminist challenge to religious studies; *third,* the hermeneutical definition of religion; and *fourth,* the modern definition of religion in gender and colonialist terms.

The Feminist Challenge to a Positivist Understanding of Religious Studies

Although the positivist scientific ethos of value-neutral inquiry and objective impartiality has been assiduously critiqued not only by feminist theory but also by the discipline of hermeneutics, the Enlightenment construct of positivist scientific scholarship still fuels the debate between theology and religious studies.[52] Unlike theology, religious studies allegedly seeks to produce value-detached and objective knowledge. Whereas the academic study of religion is understood as feminist-friendly because it is situated within the university, theology is generally treated with suspicion by feminists because it is understood as a confessionally typed doctrinal practice that is beholden to the hegemonic interests of organized religion. In contrast to theological studies, which are believed to be biased and parochial, the academic study of religion is deemed to be scientific, ecumenical, and global. It supposedly

50. Katherine K. Young, "Having Your Cake and Eating It Too: Feminism and Religion," *JAAR* 67, 1 (1999): 169.
51. Ibid., 183.
52. See Jonathan Smith, "Religion, Religions, Religious," in *Critical Terms for Religious Studies,* ed. Taylor, 269–84.

describes and understands the religions of the world as objectively and with as little bias as possible without ranking them or identifying with any of them intellectually and spiritually. This positivist ethos of the discipline re-inscribes the modern dichotomy between religion and culture, between religious practice and the academic study of religion or the Bible.

In order to avoid the positivist fallacy, I suggest, one needs to understand religion or the Bible not simply as objects of study but as sites of struggle. Scholars always speak from within a communal religious tradition, even when they consciously have rejected it as their own religious heritage. However, by insisting that feminist studies speak from "within religion" or from "within biblical discourses," I do not mean to claim the interpretive and descriptive authority of the insider, as does Wilfred Cantwell Smith in his often quoted methodological rule, "no statement about religion is valid unless it can be acknowledged by that religion's believers."[53]

I do not want to imply that in order to understand religion one must refer primarily to the testimony of believers. Rather, I want to make a critical hermeneutical point: In order to study religion or any other subject matter, one always already has a pre-understanding of the subject matter that one seeks to understand. There is no value-neutral scholarship. Scholarship is always already localized—religiously, socially, culturally, and politically. Studies of biblical symbolic universes and historical practices are always already situated in biblical religions, insofar as they are shaped by their religious, intellectual, and communal traditions, even if they have rejected or claim to have surpassed them. Hence, like feminist theology, feminist studies in religion must become conscious of speaking from within a particular religious tradition or community to which they are both insider and outsider at the same time.

The Feminist Challenge to Religious Studies

Religion or the Bible as objects of study are often conceptualized in essentialist, unitarian, Tillichian,[54] or phenomenological terms.[55] Most recently, the notion of *sui generis* religion has been studied and critically evaluated by Russell T. McCutcheon. He argues that such a conceptualization has been used not only to constitute and institutionalize the field of religious studies but also to define its research object as an apolitical, fetishized, and sacrosanct area of study. It has created scholarly discourses that call for distinct and unique methods adequate to the interpretation of religious data and that insist on the institutional autonomy of the scientific study of religion. Religion as *sui generis* is widely conceived by scholars in the field as "autonomous, strictly personal, essential, unique, prior to, and ultimately distinct

53. Wilfred Cantwell Smith, "The Comparative Study of Religion: Whither and Why?" in *The History of Religions: Essays in Methodology*, ed. Mircea Eliade and Joseph Kitagawa (Chicago: University of Chicago Press, 1959), 42.

54. See Tracy Fessenden, "'Woman' and the 'Primitive' in Tillich's Life and Thought: Some Implications for the Study of Religion," *Journal of Feminist Studies in Religion* 14, 2 (1998): 45–76.

55. Ursula King, ed., *Religion and Gender* (Oxford: Oxford University Press, 1995), 4.

from, all other facets of human life and interaction. . . . In other words, the *sui generis* claim effectively brackets not only the datum but also the researcher as well from critical scrutiny."[56] Excluding or peripheralizing both the subject of inquiry and the social and political contents in defining what really counts as "religious" thus constitutes the "uniquely religious."

McCutcheon follows Rosalind Shaw, who has criticized the scientific *sui generis* notion of religion as decontextualized and depoliticized. According to her, three dominant perspectives of religious studies—religion as a reality *sui generis*, a primarily text-based view of religion, and a positivistic self-understanding as the science of religion—account for scholarship that renders religion decontextualized and ungendered. The uniquely religious is understood as the distinctively apolitical, insofar as excluding or marginalizing social and political contents and aspects constitutes it. The distinctly religious is understandable "only on its own terms." Hence studies of religion that engage in social-political rhetorical analysis are disqualified as "reductionist."

In short, malestream discourses on religion represent the "homo religiosus" or the "biblical hero" as a collective subject, which is undifferentiated by race, gender, class, ethnicity, or age. This view from "above" is underscored not only through the *sui generis* nature of religion but also through the emphasis given to religious texts and the privileging of scholarly elites. Wo/men who have been excluded from the articulation, proclamation, and interpretation of religious classics such as the Bible are thereby excluded from the higher levels of religious authority.

Since "religion" is a complex and ambiguous term, its study raises difficult methodological questions for feminist theory. If feminist studies in religion are concerned with all wo/men and not only with western white wo/men, they must unravel the gendered colonialist hermeneutic of essentializing and "othering" that permeates the study of religion, since the discourses of the history of religions have conceptualized religion in colonialist feminine terms. Hence feminists must redefine religion in liberationist terms and refuse to engage in its further colonization. In Shaw's words: "By re-conceptualizing power as integral to—as opposed to a detachable 'dimension of'—religion, feminist religious studies has the potential to generate conceptual change and renewal."[57]

Feminist studies in religion have greatly contributed to a different self-understanding of religion. They have not only challenged the androcentric character of religious studies but also insisted that both academic feminist studies and religious studies must remain accountable to social movements for change toward a radical democratic society. The Jewish feminist theologian Judith Plaskow has argued that academic women's studies in the United States have tended not to see feminist

56. Russell T. McCutcheon, *Manufacturing Religion: The Discourse on Sui Generis Religion and the Politics of Nostalgia* (New York: Oxford University Press, 1997), 26.
57. Rosalind Shaw, "Feminist Anthropology and the Gendering of Religious Studies," *Religion and Gender,* ed. King, 73.

studies in religion as a social-intellectual movement for change because they understand religion within a modernist frame. She points to the widespread suspicion in women's studies that anyone interested in religion must be either co-opted or reactionary and argues that such suspicion is not justified. However, religious studies does not have to be understood in such a modernist sense. Rather, the obligation of feminists to critically study and change oppressive ideologies is taken seriously by the powerful work done by feminists in religious studies. This general attitude of suspicion toward feminist studies in religion is regrettable for three major reasons.

1. Feminists need to study religion because it has played and still plays a key role in both women's oppression and liberation. Hence a central task of feminist studies consists in understanding the implication of religion in the continuing political exploitation of wo/men as well as its active participation in social movements for change. Plaskow asserts that an explicit connection between feminist critiques and social change has been made in feminist studies in religion from its very beginnings.

2. Feminist studies in religion is a variegated and vibrant field that has moved from analysis and critique of male texts toward reconstructing wo/men's heritage in and outside of hegemonic religious traditions, and most recently has focused on the constructive transformation of patriarchal traditions and the creation of new, feminist ones.

3. To a much greater extent than feminist scholars in other areas, feminists in religion have sustained strong connections to wo/men's communities outside the academy. Much work of feminist studies in religion has been generated and challenged by wo/men in and outside organized religions who search for a feminist spirituality and politics of meaning for their lives. Conversely, feminist scholars also are involved either in traditional religious feminist groups or in Goddess and spirituality movements that have critically challenged and enriched biblical articulations and religious formations.[58]

Since the institutional location of feminist studies in religion is that of malestream scholarship, it is necessary to construct a different intellectual discursive space. By conceptualizing feminist studies in religion as critical rhetorical-political practices for liberation, I argue, one can avoid the positivist or modernist snare. When one remains conscious of feminist studies' sociopolitical location in the academy, it becomes apparent what is at stake in the theoretical construction of such a discursive position. Feminists, who have been and still are "outsiders" or "aliens" in theology and academy, engage in religious and biblical studies in order to transform the kyriarchal discourses of institutionalized religion and the academy. However, they can do so only if they both become qualified residents and remain foreign speakers at one and the same time.[59]

58. Judith Plaskow, "We Are Also Your Sisters: The Development of Women's Studies in Religion," *Women's Studies Quarterly* 21, 1 (1993): 9–21.

59. See my book, *But She Said*.

The Modern Definition of Religion in Gender and Colonialist Terms

Feminist studies have contextualized this discourse on religion historically and politically. They have shown that in modernity religion has been feminized. Religion has been conceptualized as that over and against which progress, rationality, subjectivity, and modernity have been defined. Since the industrial revolution in Europe and America, institutionalized religions have been pushed out of the public realm and relegated to the private sphere of individualistic piety, charitable work, and the cultivation of home and family. Since theology was not considered to be a science and reason was defined in contradistinction to religion, like wo/men, religion had no public presence in the Enlightenment university. Nevertheless, both religion and women were crucial in maintaining public interest in the antithetical "other" and in shaping cultural self-identity.

In modernity "religion" was invented to operate within the limits of reason alone. It was feminized insofar as European Christianity was dislodged from its role as hegemonic and restricted to the private sphere, and religion was turned into a civilizing project of colonialism. In the process of religious privatization and cultural "feminization," the clergy and theology lost their privileged intellectual status and came to be treated like "women" in polite society. This feminization of religion has lead both to the emasculation of theology and clergy in society and to the reassertion of their masculine roles in theology, church, and the home.

Like the "White Lady," Christianity, the religious community from within which I speak, had the function of ameliorating the horrors of imperialism. Its task was to "civilize" the savages, who were understood as "untamed nature." The western discourses on femininity and female nature have their sociopolitical contexts in this colonial exercise of power. Both anthropology and comparative religious studies have their origin in such a colonial context. The study of religion turns religion into an object of the western colonialist kyriocratic gaze.

An explicit example of the power that the discourse of the history of religions exerts over the "other" can be found in the following journal entry of Mircea Eliade:

> I see the history of religions as a total discipline. I understand now that the encounters facilitated by depth psychology, with the stranger within, with that which is foreign, exotic, archaic in ourselves, on the one hand—and, on the other, the appearance of Asia and of the exotic or "primitive" groups in history—are cultural moments which find their ultimate meaning only from the perspective of the history of religions. The hermeneutic necessary for the revelation of the meanings and the message hidden in myth, rites, symbols, will also help us to understand . . . the historical age into which we are entering and in which we will be not only surrounded but also dominated by the "foreigner," the non-Occidentals.[60]

60. Mircea Eliade, *Journal II: 1957–1969* (Chicago: University of Chicago Press, 1989), 69–70.

In contrast to such an "othering" and controlling function of "the hermeneutics of the history of religions," which also has determined biblical studies, a critical ethical-political rhetoric sees religion and the Bible as sites of struggle over meaning, ethics, and theology. Insofar as it seeks to expose and to redress structures of subordination, exploitation, and oppression in society and religion, it breaks the structures of "othering," silencing, and exclusion inscribed in religion. Hence the ethos of biblical studies is transformed. It no longer can restrict itself to antiquarian science or parochial theological interests but must critically study and evaluate the Bible as a public discursive site of struggle over meaning and values.

The culture of silencing and exclusion that has marginalized all "the others" of elite "western man" has also configured the public location and social position of biblical studies. Only when one understands that wo/men's silencing has as its corollary a kyriarchally gendered scientific culture is one able to articulate the obstacles that prevent biblical scholarship from becoming an effective public discourse. Just as wo/man in modernity, so also religion has been relegated to the private sphere and has been made an "affair of the heart." Consequently, reading the Bible has become a private matter restricted to individual spiritual edification and ecclesiastical use.

Biblical scholarship in turn has sought to defend its "masculine" public persona by insisting on being a "hard discipline" espousing scientific value-neutrality, positivist factuality, and antiquarian irrelevancy immune to the concerns of the day. I remember quite vividly that a senior colleague took me aside when I started to teach thirty years ago and warned, "Elisabeth, never forget that you are a scholar whose duty it is not to cave in to the demands of students for discussing the relevance and significance of biblical texts." This advice was given at a time when most students— and they all were male—in my class on New Testament ethics were wrestling with the ethical and personal issues raised by the war in Vietnam.

Ironically, this value-free, factualistic, antiquarian ethos of irrelevancy and of spiritualized edification not only has made biblical scholarship extraneous to contemporary public discourses but, by seeking to safeguard its standing as a scientific discipline, has relegated it to an academic ghetto. By making the Bible a privatized book owned by institutionalized biblical religions, biblical scholarship has become embattled in a religionist parochial struggle over authority.

If biblical scholarship is to overcome the academic tendencies to "feminize" its public persona as a privatized religious practice, it needs to investigate the structural and ideological constraints that have prohibited not only wo/men but also religion from effectively speaking in public. At the same time it needs to break through the privatizing tendencies of academic studies that are part and parcel of its modernist scientific value-detached ethos of inquiry. However, we must not overlook that rhetorical criticism in biblical studies often has been either limited to the analysis of word sequences, stylistic patterns, word formations arranged in a certain way, or the form and genre of particular texts on the one hand, or functionalized for spiritual privatization on the other. While Dale Patrick and Allen Scult detail this literary reduction of rhetoric in biblical studies as not fully measuring up to Muilenburg's programmatic vision, which has decisively influenced the understanding of rhetorical criticism in biblical studies, they themselves are interested in a personal encounter with the text and outline an approach that is religiously full-bodied, yet critically rigorous: "Thus the norms of scholarly discourse provide a basis for managing the spiritual encounter with the text so that, in the hands of a sensitive scholar/interpreter, it yields historical insight as well as personal understanding, observation as well as testimony, judgment as well as conviction."[61]

In short, I argue, biblical studies still needs to develop an ethos of inquiry that is able to critically display and reflect on the rhetoricality of all knowledge, be it scientific or otherwise. Since biblical interpretation always must rely on probabilities rather than certainties, it is best understood in rhetorical terms. For the classical tradition of rhetoric "has emphasized the *public, persuasive, and contextual* characteristics of human discourse in situations governed by *contingency. Contingent* situations occur when decisions have to be made and acted upon but decision makers are forced to rely upon probabilities rather than certainties."[62]

However, whereas scholars always have been methodologically aware of the persuasive, contextual, and contingent character of biblical texts and interpretations, they have not sufficiently reflected on the public character of biblical scholarship. Understanding the biblical interpreter as a human scientist rather than as a public intellectual, the disciplinary ethos of biblical studies and its pedagogical practices of socialization have stressed technical skills and value-detached disinterestedness rather than public deliberation, interdisciplinary argument, and ethical adjudication of biblical texts, contexts, and values. Since rhetoric derives its impulses from the conditions of civic life, biblical studies understood in rhetorical terms would allow anyone to participate effectively in the rhetorical practices of invention and reflection. Moreover,

> because the rhetor is responsible for the truth that he/she advocates, he/she is less likely to make the extreme claims for it that irresponsibility encourages. Wheelis put this point very well when he wrote: "certainty leads us to attack evil; being less sure we would but resist it. The difference between attack and resistance is the difference between violence and argument, the thread on which our lives dangle." Knowledge of the possibility of other truth, that is to say, opposed shared meanings will reduce certainty of the truth the rhetor advocates. This awareness of other truths must stem from an ethic in which truth itself is rhetorically *made* by agreement not given or found absolutely. [63]

In order to bring about change in the ethos and ethics of the discipline, biblical studies, I argue, must develop a rhetoric of inquiry that is able to critically and systematically reflect on the discursive practices of biblical interpretation.

A rhetoric of inquiry illuminates these debates between the academic study of religion and theological studies understood in the narrow sense and shows that they

---

61. Dale Patrick and Allen Scult, *Rhetoric and Biblical Interpretation* (Sheffield: Almond Press, 1990), 24.

62. John Louis Lucaites and Celeste Michelle Condit, *Introduction to Contemporary Rhetorical Theory: A Reader*, ed. Lucaites et al., 2.

63. Brummett, "Some Implications," in *Contemporary Rhetorical Theory*, ed. Lucaites et al., 166.

are rhetorical constructs. These disciplinary discourses attempt to draw exclusive boundaries that must be negotiated by practitioners of the discipline. They are not so much opposed theoretical positions that exclude each other but rather rivaling discourses that compete with each other as to which scientific ethos should determine the discipline. What is at stake in this heated debate between disinterested academic scholarship on the one side and religiously and politically committed scholarship on the other is an outdated scientific ethos of the discipline and the scholars representing it.

According to Aristotle, the ethos or the character of the rhetor is a central means of persuasion. To inspire confidence in their scientific claims and authority, scholars must display the qualities that are held in high esteem by their audiences.[64] The scientific ethos binds both technically and morally. It is technically binding because it prescribes efficient procedures for securing the extension of certified knowledge. It is morally binding because it is believed to assert what is right and good.[65]

In his groundbreaking work on scientific ethos, the sociologist of science Robert K. Merton[66] identified the norms of good science as: (1) *universalism,* knowledge claims have to be subjected to pre-established, impersonal criteria; (2) *communality,* research is not a personal possession but must be made available to the community of scientists; (3) *disinterestedness,* scientists must strive to achieve their self-interest only through serving the interests of the scientific community; and (4) *organized skepticism,* scientists temporarily suspend judgment in order to scrutinize their materials critically against empirical and logical criteria of judgment.

However, subsequent research has shown that there exists in science an alternative set of norms or a set of counternorms.[67] These are: (1) *particularism,* for instance ability and experience of the author rather than the technical merits of the research claims; (2) *individualism,* scientists claim property rights to their own work; (3) *interestedness,* conduct that serves scientists' special communities of interest; (4) *organized dogmatism,* scholars assent fervently to their own interpretations while doubting the findings of colleagues. Whereas universality, disinterestedness, communality, and skepticism are seen as implying *emotional neutrality,* particularism, interestedness, individualism, and organized dogmatism suggest that *emotional commitment* to one's ideas is a desirable ingredient in science.

An ethic of inquiry understands these functional norms of science as rhetorical *topoi.* Scientific ethos is not a given fact, but it is constructed rhetorically in specific

64. Aristotle, *Rhetoric,* trans. W. Rhys Roberts (New York: Random House, 1954), 1356a5 and 1378a5–19.

65. Lawrence J. Prelli, "The Rhetorical Construction of Scientific Ethos," in *Rhetoric in the Human Sciences,* ed. Herbert W. Simons (Newbury Park, Calif.: Sage Publications, 1989), 48.

66. Robert K. Merton, in *The Sociology of Science: Theoretical and Empirical Investigations,* ed. Norman W. Storer (Chicago: University of Chicago Press, 1973), 267–78.

67. For example, Michael Mulkay, *Science and Sociology of Knowledge* (London: Allen, 1979).

rhetorical situations for engendering favorable or unfavorable perceptions of the field of science and its practitioners under discussion. These rhetorical *topoi* indicate the range of discursive strategies that are available and acceptable for making one's point.

> In science . . . we have a complex moral language which appears to focus on certain recurrent themes or issues; for instance on procedures of communication, the place of rationality, the importance of impartiality, and of commitment, and so on. But . . . no particular solutions to the problems raised by these issues for participants are firmly institutionalized. Instead the standardized verbal formulations to be found in the scientific community provide a repertoire or vocabulary which scientists can use flexibly to categorize professional actions differently in various social contexts.[68]

The ethic of inquiry also points out that the assertion of ethos bespeaks a conflictive situation and has a boundary-drawing or boundary-breaking function. Whereas the advocates of an academic scientific ethos in biblical studies insist on impartiality, disinterestedness, disciplinary norms, and universal claims, those advocating a scientific, political, and religious advocacy ethos stress interestedness, partiality, individual responsibility, as well as emotional engagement and commitment. But whereas the advocates of a purely academic ethos construct the rhetorical situation as determined and constrained by disputes over the professional standing of religious and biblical studies in the university, those advocating an academic ethos of responsibility construct a rhetorical situation determined by global political-religious disputes. The insight into the rhetorical character of these two opposing discourses on the ethos of biblical studies allows one to negotiate their claims not as scientific alternatives but as rhetorical-ethical options.

Conclusion

The theoretical inroads made by the hermeneutical, the critical, the political, and the ethical epistemological turns, I have argued, make it possible to construct a critical scientific rhetoric and to fashion a braided method of critical inquiry that is oriented toward justice, emancipation, and liberation. These intellectual turns and turnings have shown that scientific inquiry is not adequately understood if it is not conceptualized in rhetorical-ethical terms and scrutinized as to its political functions within structures of domination.

Raymie E. McKerrow has argued that all attempts to rescue rhetoric from its marginal status in the academy have been dispatched as universal statements of reason and thereby have kept rhetoric in its subordinate position to logic and dialectic.[69] The four intellectual turns affecting the ethos of biblical scholarship, however, make it

---

68. Mulkay, *Science and Sociology of Knowledge,* 71.

69. Rayme McKerrow, "Critical Rhetoric: Theory and Practice," in *Contemporary Rhetorical Theory,* ed. Lucaites et al., 441–63.

possible to accord to rhetoric its proper place. The task is not to rehabilitate rhetoric but to articulate it as a critical practice. As critical practice rhetoric is able to investigate the dimensions of domination and freedom in a cosmopolitan world.

> The critique of domination has an emancipatory purpose—a *telos* toward which it aims in the process of demystifying the conditions of domination. The critique of freedom, premised on Michel Foucault's treatment of power relations has as its *telos* the prospect of permanent criticism—a self-reflexive critique that turns back on itself even as it promotes a realignment in the forces of power that construct discourses of power. The aim is to understand the integration of power/knowledge in society—what possibilities for change the integration invites or inhibits and what intervention strategies might be considered appropriate to effect social change.[70]

If biblical studies were to be reconceptualized as a critical practice, it would need to subscribe to the following rhetorical principles and strategies.

1. *Ideologiekritik* must be understood as a practice in which description and evaluation are one. Critique always operates from a perspective or "orientation" that explores the possibilities of what will count as evidence for critical judgment.

2. All discourses are *material*. Nevertheless, although ideology is a property of the social world, agents always have the capability to interact with this world and to modify discourse. They do not come to the biblical text as a *tabula rasa* but always already with preunderstandings and ideological frameworks in place.

3. Rhetoric constitutes *doxastic* rather than epistemic knowledge. "Doxastic knowledge functions as the grounding of a critical rhetoric. Rather than focusing on questions of 'truth' or 'falsity,' a view of rhetoric as doxastic allows the focus to shift to how the symbols [biblical texts] come to possess power—what they do in society [and religion] as contrasted to what they are."[71]

4. *Naming* is the central symbolic act of a critical rhetorical practice. Whereas hermeneutic realism assumes the stability and determinacy of meaning because of constraints in the text, and hermeneutic idealism assumes the stability of meaning because of conventional constraints in readers' minds, a hermeneutic rhetoric sees meaning as constituted by rhetorical practices that are deployed in specific contexts.

5. *Influence does not equal causality.* As Celeste Michelle Condit has pointed out: "To say that something 'influences' a process, or has 'force,' eschews the determinism latent in the term 'cause.' An influence or force may be overridden or supplemented by other forces. It may even require the active participation of other forces (e.g., human choice) to become actualized."[72]

6. In understanding and evaluating *symbolic actions* such as biblical texts, to recognize what is absent is as important as what is present. Especially feminist histori-

---

70. Ibid., 441.

71. Ibid., 454.

72. Celeste Michelle Condit, "Democracy and Civil Rights: The Universalizing Influence of Public Argumentation," *Communication Monographs* 54 (1987): 2.

ans and rhetoricians have pointed out that the "unsaid of a situation" or "what has been left out" is as important as the "said," because the "non-said" reinforces what is said. Meaning is relational. Terms marked positively mean in relation to what is absent, unmarked, unspoken, or unsayable.

7. Interpretation is *polysemic* rather than monosemic. People who are differently located socially will activate the meaning of a text differently. A polysemic critique focuses on secondary or minority readings, which can contain the seeds of subversion of authority, whereas a primary or majority interpretation will tend to confirm the dominant cultural codes and religious norms.

8. Criticism is a performative activity within the context of certain social-political conditions. A rhetorical critic is therefore best understood as a "specific intellectual" (Foucault), a "connected" (Gramsci) or a "transformative" (Giroux) intellectual "whose radical work of transformation, whose fight against repression is carried on at the specific institutional site where he[she] finds himself [herself] and on the terms of his[her] own experience, on the terms inherent to his[her] own functioning as an intellectual."[73]

To become such public, connected, specific, and transformative intellectuals, I have argued, biblical scholars must position themselves both in the academy and in the public square of the *polis,* the *ekklesia.*

---

73. Frank Lentricchia, *Criticism and Social Change* (Chicago: University of Chicago Press, 1983), 6–7.

Chapter 4

Challenging the Rhetorical Half-Turn: Feminist and Rhetorical Biblical Criticism

At this particular critical juncture in its country's history,[1] South African biblical scholarship seems in a fortuitous position to make a significant contribution to biblical scholarship on the whole by engendering a "full rhetorical turn" in biblical studies.[2] Not only has significant work on the rhetoric and ethics of inquiry already been done here,[3] but the New South Africa in search of democratic forms of living together also seems to cry out for the articulation of an emancipatory rhetoric and politics of meaning. Hence it is my hope that this new situation will foster a rhetoric of inquiry that enables scholars to recognize the sociocultural location and religio-political functions of their discourses. The present rhetorical-historical situation of

---

1. This chapter has been published in Stanley E. Porter and Thomas H. Olbricht, eds., *Rhetoric, Scripture and Theology: Essays from the 1994 Pretoria Conference*, Part I, "Rhetorical Method and Interpretation" (Sheffield, England: Sheffield University Press, 1996), 28–53. Since this chapter was first conceptualized for a Congress on Rhetoric that met in 1994 in South Africa, it reflects the rhetorical situation that has engendered it. For rhetorical reasons I have not sought to delete this original setting.

2. I want to express my gratitude to the organizers of the Pretoria Congress on Rhetoric, Professors Johannes Vorster and Pieter Botha, who worked very hard to make my participation in this Congress possible and to organize lectures in different parts of the country. I deeply appreciate their hospitality and collegiality. I am especially grateful that they alerted me to the publication of the Congress papers on *Rhetoric and the New Testament: Essays from the Heidelberg Conference*. Reading the contributions in this volume has compelled me to change my original title, which spoke about the contributions of feminist theory to biblical rhetorical studies. This change indicates that I will focus on the problematic relationship between feminist and rhetorical criticism in biblical studies rather than put feminist criticism at the service of rhetorical criticism.

3. See the two articles by D. J. Smit, "The Ethics of Interpretation: New Voices from the USA," *Scriptura* 33 (1990), 16–28; idem, "The Ethics of Interpretation and South Africa" *Scriptura* 33 (1990) 29–43; and the various methodological contributions in P. J. Hartin and J. H. Petzer, *Text and Interpretation: New Approaches to the Criticism of the New Testament* (Leiden: Brill, 1991). It seems no accident that Wilhelm Wuellner wrote his foundational article "Hermeneutics and Rhetorics: From Truth and Method to Truth and Power" (*Scriptura S* 3 (1989): 1–54) in South Africa. See also Pere Frostin, *Liberation Theology in Tanzania and South Africa* (Lund: University Press, 1988); P. G. R. De Villiers, ed., *Liberation Theology and the Bible* (Pretoria: University of South Africa, 1987); Itumeleng J. Mosala, *Biblical Hermeneutics and Black Theology in South Africa* (Grand Rapids, Mich.: Eerdmans, 1989); Gerald West, *Biblical Hermeneutics of Liberation: Modes of Reading the Bible in the South African Context* (Pietermaritzburg: Cluster Publications, 1991); Jan Botha, "Creation of New Meaning: Rhetorical Situations and the Reception of Romans 13:1–7," *Journal of Theology for Southern Africa* 79 (1971): 24–37.

South Africa, which consists in a microcosm of global differences and struggles, challenges biblical studies, I suggest, to engage with feminist biblical studies[4] and feminist theory to create a theoretical space in which a radical democratic politics of meaning and a religious rhetoric of transformation can be articulated.

As the title of this chapter suggests, I will explore the rhetoric of inquiry in biblical studies by focusing attention on the contested notion of "feminist criticism."[5] I begin with the observation that biblical studies has become stuck in a "rhetorical half-turn." Although the past decade has seen the revival of rhetorical criticism,[6] I argue that biblical scholarship has not yet made the full epistemological turn to a rhetoric of inquiry insofar as it has barely recognized the contributions feminist and liberationist scholarship have made to the New Rhetoric.[7] Most recent malestream works on the reinvention of rhetoric or on new approaches in Christian Testament[8] studies barely take note of feminist and critical liberationist theories because they remain

---

4. For a review and analysis of the "field of feminist biblical studies," see Janice Capel Anderson, "Mapping Feminist Biblical Criticism," *Critical Review of Books in Religion* 2 (1991): 21–44; Schüssler Fiorenza, *But She Said*, 19–50; and Elizabeth A. Castelli, "Heteroglossia, Hermeneutics, and History: A Review Essay of Recent Feminist Studies of Early Christianity," *Journal of Feminist Studies in Religion* 10, 2 (1994): 73–98.

5. The term "feminism" is generally avoided as too political by those scholars who prefer to speak of wo/men's perspective or of women's and gender studies, or it is rejected by the academy as too ideological. In addition, feminist theory often is typed as white wo/men's theory that does not take into account class, race, or colonialism. Hence, one encounters a growing number of qualifiers or transmutations of feminist such as womanist, Asian, African, European, indigenous, or mujerista theology. Although there are many divergent forms and even contradictory articulations of feminism today so that it is appropriate to speak of feminisms in the plural, most feminists agree, nevertheless, that contemporary feminism is a political movement that is akin to other emancipatory movements. My preferred definition of feminism is: "Feminism is the radical notion that wo/men are people." This definition accentuates tongue in cheek that feminism is a radical concept and at the same time ironically underscores that in the twentieth century feminism is a commonsense notion. It asserts that wo/men are not ladies, wives, handmaids, seductresses, or beasts of burden, but that they are full citizens in academy and religion. Moreover, this definition positions the notion of feminism within democratic political discourses insofar as it alludes to the United States Declaration of Independence, which begins with "We the People." Such a contextualization evokes centuries of radical democratic struggles for equal citizenship.

6. See, for example, William A. Beardslee, "Theology and Rhetoric in the University," in *Theology and the University: Essays in Honor of John B. Cobb, Jr.*, ed. David Ray Griffin and Joseph C. Hough, Jr. (Albany: State University of New York Press, 1991), 185–200.

7. This expression was introduced by the translation of the work of Chaim Perelman and Luci Olbrechts-Tyteca, *The New Rhetoric: A Treatise on Argumentation*, trans. John Wilkinson and Purcell Weaver (Notre Dame, Ind.: Notre Dame University Press, 1969). Although this work has been co-authored, it is interesting to note that whenever the "seminal" importance of Perelman's rhetorical work is discussed in journals or books, Olbrechts-Tyteca is hardly mentioned—despite the fact that she has collaborated for ten years with Perelman in the study of rhetorical discourses. Yet in the historical accounts of the discipline her name is mentioned, at most, and her significant contributions are never elaborated. Thus Olbrechts-Tyteca is a good rhetorical example of how wo/men and their intellectual work are "written out" of history.

8. I use the expression *Christian Testament* in place of New Testament in order to avoid the rhetoric of Christian supersessionism.

caught up in the scientistic and objectivist ethos of the modern logic of identity.[9] I illustrate this contention with reference to Vernon Robbins's interpretation of the Markan anointing story. Next I sketch the salient points of a feminist critical rhetorical approach. In a third step I suggest that the "feminine" coding of religion and rhetoric keeps both of them in their ongoing captivity to positivist scientism. A concluding section discusses how the collaboration between a critical feminist rhetoric of liberation and a biblical or theological rhetoric of inquiry could be fruitfully configured. Here I reject the metaphorization of the relationship between feminist and rhetorical criticism as "wifely support," "sibling rivalry," or "corporate merger." Instead, I point to two metaphors that feminist criticism has favored for its practices of interpretation: the metaphor of vision and that of the dance. I go on to suggest that Annette Kolodny's now almost classic figuration of feminist criticism as "dancing through the minefield" must be complemented with Anna Julia Cooper's rhetorical figure of "the full circle of vision." Both metaphors, I argue, mark the rhetorical space in which feminist and rhetorical biblical criticism can engage each other for developing a religious rhetoric and spiritual vision in contemporary political struggles for the well-being of everybody in the global village and of our planet itself.

A Rhetoric of Inquiry

Since scholars use argument, persuasion, and perspectival discourse, they engage in rhetoric. The growing attention to epistemological questions that has problematized the reigning methods and scientistic frameworks of academic disciplines in general and of historical biblical criticism in particular has opened the door for the articulation of a rhetoric[10] of inquiry. By a critical rhetoric of inquiry, I mean a second-order reflection on the positivist practices, unacknowledged theoretical frameworks, and sociopolitical interests of scholarship that undergird its self-understandings as value-detached, objectivist science. Such a rhetoric of inquiry pays special attention to the argumentative discourses of scholarship and their theoretical presuppositions, social locations, investigative methods, and sociopolitical functions. Since the space of rhetorical discourse is the public and political realm, a rhetoric of inquiry does not need to suppress but is able to investigate the sociopolitical frameworks, cultural perspectives, and symbolic universes of cultural-religious texts and interpretations.

> Treating each other's claims as arguments rather than findings, scholars no longer need implausible doctrines of objectivism to defend their contributions to knowledge. At a

9. For a delineation of the "logic of identity" see for instance Teresa L. Ebert, "The 'Difference' of Postmodern Feminism," *College English* 53 (1991): 893: "any identity is always *divided within* by its other, which is not opposed to it but rather 'supplementary.' However, the logic of identity banishes this 'difference within' the privileged term by projecting its 'otherness' onto a secondary term seen as outside, thus representing the 'difference within' as an external dichotomy. In doing so, the phallogocentric logic is able to assert its primary (male) terms as seemingly coherent 'identities without differences,' as self-evident 'presences.'"

10. Wilhelm Wuellner has recommended that one distinguish between rhetoric as theory and rhetoric as practice. However, such a distinction dichotomizes theory and practice.

practical level, to stress rhetoric is to discount claims to neutrality. . . . Detailed attention to rhetoric can reveal underlying issues and better ways to consider them responsibly. At a theoretical level, to take rhetoric seriously is to dispute the spectator story of inquiry. To be sure, challenges to the received view of science are not unique to rhetoric. The spectator theory has suffered attacks for two centuries, though only recently has it lost decisive ground. The professed neutrality of social engineering has never been supported universally, though only recently has it attracted widespread scorn. Rhetoric of inquiry shows how such views fail to explain or improve the words and deeds of scholars. It also fosters more effective thinking, speaking and acting by their students and by audiences outside the academy.[11]

Biblical criticism, I argue, has remained in the captivity of empiricist-positivist science for far too long. Rhetorical biblical criticism shares in this captivity insofar as it has spent much of its energy in applying and re-inscribing to Christian Testament texts ancient rhetorical methods, disciplinary technology, terminological stylistics, and the scattered prescriptions of oratorical handbooks in antiquity. Margaret Mitchell's introduction to her study on *Paul and the Rhetoric of Reconciliation*[12] is an instructive case in point. Following in the footsteps of Hans Dieter Betz, she defends the antiquarian approach and technological method still prevalent in biblical rhetorical studies with a spirited attack on the practitioners of the so-called New Rhetoric. However, Mitchell does not recognize that her framework has much in common with the New Rhetoric insofar as the modern revival of rhetoric also has fallen prey to the conservative impulses of the rhetorical tradition and to the allure of technical Greek or Roman terms, which Samuel Butler has facetiously called the "hard words" of rhetoric. Mitchell also shows no awareness of the rhetorical impact of her methodological defense because she does not recognize that traditional techniques of rhetoric have been created and adapted to argue for existing power relations of domination.

More importantly, by reviving the technology of ancient rhetoric, rhetorical criticism in biblical studies has failed to make the full-turn to a political rhetoric of inquiry insofar as it has not developed critical epistemological discourses and a hermeneutics of suspicion. Instead, it has sought to validate its disciplinary practices in and through the logos of positivist or empiricist science that occludes its own rhetoricity.[13] Let me hasten to give an example in order to make my point. If I single out here Vernon K. Robbins's elaboration of his sociorhetorical method, I do so because his is one of the few Christian Testament studies that attempts to take rhetorical and feminist theoretical insights seriously. My discussion of his method in

11. John S. Nelson, Allan Megill, Donald N. McCloskey, "Rhetoric of Inquiry," in *The Rhetoric of Human Sciences: Language and Argument in Scholarship and Public Affairs* (Madison: University of Wisconsin Press, 1987), 4.

12. Margaret M. Mitchell, *Paul and the Rhetoric of Reconciliation: An Exegetical Investigation of the Language and Composition of 1 Corinthians* (Tübingen: J. C. B. Mohr, 1991), 1–19.

13. For the tension between "science" and "rhetoric" as two different modes of thinking, see Stanley Fish, "Rhetoric," in *Critical Terms for Literary Study,* ed. Frank Lentricchia and Thomas McLaughlin (Chicago: University of Chicago Press, 1990), 202–22.

action seeks to illustrate how even a sociorhetorical analysis that is aware of gender studies in the end resorts to a positivist social-scientific approach in order to validate its interpretation in terms of the logic of identity as the best reading and "reliable scientific" interpretation.

However, I do not single out for critical discussion Robbins's particular sociorhetorical reading of the Markan story about Jesus being anointed by an unnamed woman because I want to "prove" that my own reading is superior. Rather, I intend to show how a reading that postures as "scientific" reinforces the rhetoric of the text's grammatical gender system by contextualizing the story within the framework of a particular construction of the Mediterranean sociocultural sex/gender system. Such a reading then goes on to "naturalize" this constructed frame of reference as a scientific historical model that is said to accurately reflect the "commonplace" ethos of the Mediterranean in antiquity.[14]

In order to display the methodological operations of a sociorhetorical poetics, Robbins first reviews and appraises alternative methodological approaches to the interpretation of this Markan text. He discusses rhetorical, literary, social-scientific, and ideological approaches as separate methodological investigative procedures. By positing so-called ideological criticism as one method among others, rather than understanding it as a dimension of all interpretive methods and strategies, Robbins implies that only ideological criticism is concerned with and determined by ideology, insofar as it seeks to prevent that other approaches do not reproduce the ideological texture of the Markan account or their own preconstructed frames of meaning.

Not surprisingly, Robbins singles out Ched Myers's commentary on Mark[15] as well as my own interpretation of the anointing story in *In Memory of Her*[16] as examples of such "ideological criticism." He claims that I and subsequently Ched Myers have removed "the story from the social and cultural value and image systems that pervaded the Mediterranean world in late antiquity." He alleges that we both assume a biblical "ghetto culture" and therefore read Mark's text against a "story, one regularly studied in Bible study." After characterizing our interpretations in such a fashion, Robbins asks sarcastically, "Is a reader really to believe that the story of Samuel's anointing of Saul would be the primary semantic framework for understanding this story in the first century?"[17] This rhetorical question conveniently neglects to mention that the notion of a prophetic messianic anointed one was not as arcane for a Jewish audience in antiquity[18] as it may appear to Christian readers of the twentieth century.

14. For a critique of this method, see also Mary Ann Tolbert, "Social, Sociological, and Anthropological Methods," in *Searching the Scriptures*, vol. 1, ed. Schüssler Fiorenza, 255–71.

15. Ched Myers, *Binding the Strong Man: A Political Reading of Mark's Story* (Maryknoll, N.Y.: Orbis Books, 1988), 358–61.

16. Schüssler Fiorenza, *In Memory of Her*.

17. Vernon K. Robbins, "Using a Socio-Rhetorical Poetics to Develop a Unified Method: The Woman Who Anointed Jesus as a Test Case," *SBLSP* 31 (1992): 311.

18. See, for instance, the fresco at Dura Europos. Cf. Warren G. Moon, "Nudity and Narrative: Observations on the Frescoes from the Dura Synagogue," *JAAR* 40 (1992): 587–658.

More importantly, Robbins's restrictive understanding of sociorhetorical criticism in terms of formal literary criticism does not allow him to distinguish a long process of transmission nor to pay sufficient attention to the sociopolitical location and rhetorical situation of the story. Instead, he prefers to read the Markan text over and against the story of "the Mediterranean world," which functions as his scientific explanatory frame of reference or social model. Without problematizing the structuralist binary frame of inquiry or challenging the scientistic posture of those Christian Testament scholars who advocate the Mediterranean cultural model as a "fact," Robbins uncritically accepts a type of social scientific approach in biblical studies that is hermeneutically naive insofar as it still presents a structuralist notion of the Mediterranean as a "given scientific fact" and as an accurate descriptive and objective account of historical reality in the first century. In so doing, he does not mention that ethnologists have long pointed out that the "Mediterranean" is a scholarly construct. Since Robbins wants to argue that such a "scientific" account of the ancient world has more sociohistorical verisimilitude than the "Bible land" story of prophetic anointing, he does not critically reflect on and problematize that the "systems and cultural values of the Mediterranean" are a twentieth-century theoretical fabrication that needs to be seen as "story" rather than as "social scientific" objective description of reality.[19]

Finally, Robbins does not question his own reconstructive kyriocentric frame of reference, which makes it seem "common sense" that in "preparation for burial, it would be *appropriate for a woman* to anoint *every part of a man's body* with ointment"[20] (emphasis added). Although Robbins ostensibly wants to undermine traditional western male culture that shuns the body, he ends up by re-inscribing the malestream western sex/gender system that associates body and care for the living and the dead with women while attributing naming, defining, and leadership activities to men. He does so not only by eclipsing both historical wo/men's and contemporary feminists' signifying agency, but also by eliminating the methodological significance of a Jewish scriptural contextualization.

Again, let me repeat: I am not interested here in arguing for the superiority of my own interpretation of this text in *In Memory of Her*. Rather, I want to illustrate my contention that rhetorical criticism in biblical studies remains in captivity to an empiricist-positivist scientism, which it shares not only with literalist biblicism but also with its brother discipline, classics. Both biblical studies and classics were institutionalized as modern "gentlemen" disciplines dedicated to the study of philology,

---

19. See especially Michael Herzfeld's work, which argues that the ethnographic construct of the Mediterranean reflects a stereotypical notion of it. It should be investigated and problematized as a "social fact" and "ethnographic datum" but not deployed as an heuristic analytic frame of reference. See, for example, Michael Herzfeld, "'As in Your Own House': Hospitality, Ethnography and the Stereotype of Mediterranean Society," in *Honor and Shame and the Unity of the Mediterranean*, ed. David D. Gilmore, American Anthropological Association No. 22 (Washington, D.C.: American Anthropological Association, 1987), 75–89.

20. Herzfeld, "As in Your Own House," 313.

text, and history—pure and simple.[21] The resistance of biblical studies to a rhetoric of inquiry becomes even more intelligible when one considers that, beginning with Plato and Aristotle, not only logic but also rhetoric has had strong links with political conservatism and has legitimated relations of domination. As Susan Jarratt has observed:

> Never at ease with the democracy, he [Plato] laid out a stratified social order in which classes and roles were rigidly defined and power was reserved for the few.... For Plato rhetoric was the means of delivering truth through dialectic; whereas for the sophists, human perception and discourse were the only measure of truth, all of which are contingent.[22]

Although Aristotle developed an elaborate theory of rhetoric,[23] he kept it in place as an imperfect system, subordinate to science and reason in which freeborn wo/men had only a partial share and slave wo/men had no share at all.[24] In light of the logic of identity prevalent in western thought, one is justified in pointing out and asking:

> The art of rhetoric has always focused on the discourse of marketplace and forum, where the material power of contending factions holds more sway than academic notions of dispassionate and disinterested reason. When respectable academics come to rhetoric's abode, have they really abandoned their old faith in the mythical value-freedom of academic discourse? Or do they entertain a hope of transforming rhetoric into a practice that pious ex-positivists can embrace in good conscience, while they continue to devalue the passions and logic of the political [and religious] economy?[25]

Therefore, the literary scientific half-turn in which the New Rhetoric seems to be arrested can revolve into the full-turn of a rhetoric of inquiry only, I argue, if it owns its political roots and space. Such a rhetorical-political full-turn would enable biblical scholars to investigate the discursive arguments that perform particular kinds of actions in particular historical situations and at particular political sites. Such a political rhetoric of inquiry in biblical studies, I suggest, has its roots in the *ekklesia* as the public assembly of free and equal citizens in the power of the Spirit.[26] It

21. See especially the introduction and conclusion by Nancy Sorkin Rabinowitz and Amy Richlin, eds., *Feminist Theory and the Classics* (New York: Routledge, 1993).

22. Susan C. Jarratt, "The First Sophists and Feminism: Discourse of the 'Other,'" *Hypatia* 5 (1990): 28; see also her book *Rereading the Sophists*.

23. See A. H. M. Jones, *Athenian Democracy* (Baltimore: John Hopkins University Press, 1957); Susan Moller Okin, *Women in Western Political Thought* (Princeton: Princeton University Press, 1979), 73–98; Page duBois, *Centaurs and Amazons: Women and the Prehistory of the Great Chain of Being* (Ann Arbor: University of Michigan Press, 1982).

24. See Sutton, "The Taming of Polos/Polis," in Lucaites et al., eds., *Contemporary Rhetorical Theory*, 101–26.

25. Michael Calvin McGee and John R. Lyne, "What Are Nice Folks like You Doing in a Place like This?" in the *Rhetoric of the Human Sciences*, ed. Nelson et al., 382.

26. For such an argument see my book *Discipleship of Equals*.

could preserve the dream of a freely argumentative society [and church] as the means for formulating a critique of present styles of arguing and thinking. By looking backwards to those moments of free argumentation, which have briefly, unpredictably illuminated history, the critic can preserve the dream against the accusation that the realization of freedom is beyond the capacity of human nature. . . . Under these circumstances the revival of the old need not be purely nostalgic. It can convey a rhetoric which expresses hope, critique, and above all, argument. These may be backward looking but their aim is not to celebrate the past in a simple sense, but to "brush history against the grain."[27]

A Feminist Rhetoric

In the past two decades I have sought to contribute feminist theoretical insights to the fashioning of such a radical notion of democracy and political rhetoric of inquiry in biblical studies. I have done so in the belief that the "natural" allies of feminist biblical studies would be scholars who blaze the trail of the New Rhetoric. Yet, a cursory glance through recent volumes on the state of the disciplines of biblical and historical criticism can easily document that feminist critical models for literary-historical and political-rhetorical inquiry have yet to be fully recognized. The stories of the regeneration and revival of rhetorical criticism in biblical studies that recount the work of "seminal" figures in the field seem not even to be aware of the contributions that a feminist political rhetoric could bring to the table. Thus the identity-constituting biographies of the field[28] for the most part remain firmly positioned within the space of malestream "scientific" biblical criticism.

Surveys on the explosion of rhetorical criticism in the past decade or so and on the "rage of the rhetoricians"[29] in biblical studies may mention, for instance, my article on First Corinthians,[30] my SBL presidential address,[31] or my work on the Book of Revelation.[32] However, they do not refer to any publications that have "feminist"

27. Michael Billing, "Conservatism and the Rhetoric of Rhetoric," *Economy and Society* 18 (1989): 132–48; 146 f.

28. As far as I can see, the exception seems to be Wilhelm Wuellner, who at least refers to "feminist criticism" albeit only in passing. However, in his contribution "Rhetorical Criticism and Its Theory in Culture-Critical Perspective: The Narrative Rhetoric of John 11," in *Text and Interpretation*, ed. Hartin and Petzer, 177, Wuellner refers to Alter as his authority. In this most recent account on the history of rhetoric, he seems to have dropped even this gesturing toward a feminist rhetorical criticism in biblical studies. See his contribution to the Heidelberg Congress, "Biblical Exegesis in the Light of the History and Historicity of Rhetoric and the Nature of the Rhetoric of Religion," in *Rhetoric and the New Testament: Essays from the Heidelberg Conference*, ed. Stanley E. Porter and Thomas H. Olbricht (Sheffield: JSOT Press, 1993), 492–513.

29. See, for example, Steven Kraftschick, "Why Do The Rhetoricians Rage?" in *Text and Logos: The Humanistic Interpretation of the New Testament*, ed. Theodore W. Jennings (Atlanta: Scholars Press, 1990), 55–79.

30. Elisabeth Schüssler Fiorenza, "Rhetorical Situation and Historical Reconstruction in 1 Corinthians," *NTS* 33 (1987): 386–403 (reprinted as chapter 5).

31. Elisabeth Schüssler Fiorenza, "The Ethics of Biblical Interpretation: Decentering Biblical Scholarship." *JBL* 107, 1 (1988): 3–17 (reprinted as chapter 1).

32. Elisabeth Schüssler Fiorenza, *The Book of Revelation: Judgment and Justice* (1985; reprint, Minneapolis: Fortress Press, 1998); and *Revelation: Vision of a Just World*.

in the title,[33] probably because they do not understand feminist biblical criticism as an integral part of a rhetoric of inquiry but see it as a marginal area restricted to wo/men's issues. More importantly, mine is not an isolated experience. A recent book on *Rhetoric and Biblical Interpretation*, which places itself squarely in the tradition of the Muilenburg school of so-called Old Testament rhetorical criticism, for example, completely disregards Phyllis Trible's important work.[34] Further, the index of *Rhetoric and the New Testament*, the collection of the papers on Rhetorical Analysis and Biblical Documents given at the 1992 Heidelberg Congress, refers, for instance, neither to the books of Elizabeth Castelli[35] and Antoinette Wire[36] nor to feminist theory and feminist rhetorical criticism of the Bible in general. In short, scholarly discussions on rhetorical method and theory remain firmly anchored in the malestream of academic discourses that marginalize feminist work as ideological, if they mention it at all.[37]

If feminist criticism is mentioned in the self-portraying narratives of the discipline at all, the tendency seems to be to reduce it to "literary criticism" and then to contain it within "ideological criticism," rather than to credit feminist biblical criticism with having developed a complex critical rhetorical model of inquiry and biblical interpretation that does not restrict itself to ideological criticism. For instance, in his reflection on "Biblical Interpretation in an International Perspective," David J. Clines mentions the contribution of feminist literary criticism in passing but then goes on to argue:

> In my opinion "ideology" is going to be the catchword of the 1990s in biblical criticism, just as "the reader" was of the 1980s, "the text" was of the 1970s, and "the author" was

33. Elisabeth Schüssler Fiorenza, *Bread Not Stone;* "Text and Reality—Reality as Text: The Problem of a Feminist Historical and Social Reconstruction Based on Texts," *Studia Theologica* 40 (1989): 19–34; "The 'Quilting' of Women's History: Phoebe of Cenchreae," in *Embodied Love: Sensuality and Relationship as Feminist Values*, ed. Paula M. Cooey, Sharon A. Farmer, and Mary Ellen Ross (San Francisco: Harper & Row, 1987), 35–50; "The Rhetoricity of Historical Knowledge: Pauline Discourse and Its Contextualizations," in *Religious Propaganda and Missionary Competition in the New Testament World: Essays Honoring Dieter Georgi*, ed. Lukas Bormann, Kelly Del Tredici, and Angela Standhartinger (Leiden: Brill, 1994), 443–70 (reprinted as chapter 6).

34. Phyllis Trible, *God and the Rhetoric of Sexuality* (Philadelphia: Fortress Press, 1978); *Texts of Terror: Literary-Feminist Readings of Biblical Narratives* (Philadelphia: Fortress Press, 1984). For her response to this work, see her book *Rhetorical Criticism: Context, Method, and the Book of Jonah* (Minneapolis: Fortress Press, 1994).

35. Elizabeth A. Castelli, *Imitating Paul: A Discourse of Power* (Louisville: Westminster/John Knox Press, 1991).

36. Antoinette Clark Wire, *The Corinthian Women Prophets: A Reconstruction through Paul's Rhetoric* (Minneapolis: Fortress, 1990).

37. The "collaboration" between feminist and rhetorical criticism should also not be construed as that between feminism in general and biblical studies as a highly developed intellectual discipline in particular as it is done, for instance, by S. J. Nortje, who focuses on wo/men's experience as a hermeneutical tool and then goes on to read the Emmaus story in light of a woman's experience, thereby privatizing and individualizing the interpretation of the text. What is of interest here is not so much the author's textual reading as the editor's attempts to present it as a paradigmatic example of feminist criticism. This was done by adding "feminism" to the title of the article in the table of contents. See S. J. Nortje, "On the Road to Emmaus—A Woman's Experience," in *Text and Interpretation*, ed. Hartin and Petzer.

of previous decades of critical scholarship. When the partisan character of the biblical texts is more extensively uncovered—not just in its historical dimension, about which we know a lot already, but in the effect that its "interested" character has upon its "truth"—theology is going to have to come to terms with a Bible far different from the confessional document preserved by "believing communities" and then by the church, far different also from the charmingly antique (but essentially value-free and above all harmless) document lovingly restored by historical scholarship.[38]

Feminist biblical criticism is concerned, however, not only with the kyriocentric (elite male/master-centered) ideological inscriptions of the biblical text but also with those of the biblical discipline and its interpretive processes. African feminist scholars have pointed out, for instance, that white biblical interpretation is suffused with racism; Jewish feminists have underscored the anti-Jewish tendencies in Christian biblical interpretation; and Latin American feminists have pointed to the elite character of academic biblical interpretation. A critical feminist rhetoric of inquiry does not only recognize that the ethos and methods of biblical studies are ideologically scripted. It also underscores that wo/men, like men, are linguistic and historical subjects who can subvert and alter the cultural script of elite male/father/master domination (patri-kyriarchy). To that end, feminist readers must cultivate the habit of suspicion, especially when reading sacred kyriocentric (elite male, master-centered) texts. Such a hermeneutics of suspicion requires that feminist readers learn how to recognize and analyze biblical texts as rhetorical symbol systems.

Consequently, a critical feminist rhetoric of inquiry focuses especially on the ambiguity and instability of grammatically gendered language as rhetorical language and text. It does not subscribe to the logic of identity, assume linguistic determinism, strive for scientific certainty, or seek to establish one-to-one textual meanings because it does not understand language as a self-contained closed system. Rather, it conceives of language and text as cultural conventions or sociopolitical practices that enable speakers and hearers, writers and readers, to negotiate linguistic ambiguities and to create meaning in specific rhetorical contexts and sociopolitical locations. In this rhetorical understanding, language is not a straitjacket into which our thoughts must be forced or a "naturalized" closed gendered linguistic system but rather a medium that is shaped by its sociopolitical contexts and that changes in different sociopolitical locations. Such a rhetorical approach underscores that grammatically androcentric language can function either as gender specific or as generic inclusive language. In their interaction with androcentric or, better, kyriocentric texts, readers/hearers decide how to give meaning to them in their specific sociopolitical rhetorical situations and cultural-religious "ideological" contexts. How meaning is constructed depends not only on how one reads the social, cultural, and religious markers inscribed in the text but also on what kind of "intertexts," preconstructed "frames of meaning," commonsense understandings, and "reading paradigms" one utilizes when interpreting linguistic markers and textualized symbols.

---

38. See David J. A. Clines, "Biblical Interpretation in an International Perspective," *Biblical Interpretation* 1 (1993): 86.

In short, a critical feminist rhetoric of inquiry contributes four crucial insights that are important for biblical studies as rhetorical studies:[39]

1. Grammatically androcentric language is not reflective or descriptive of reality, but it is regulative and constructive. Androcentric or, better, kyriocentric language claims to be generic language while at the same time marginalizing or obliterating elite and multiply oppressed wo/men from hegemonic cultural-religious discourses altogether. Language is not reflective but performative. It creates and shapes the symbolic worlds it professes to evoke and describe.

2. Language is not just performative; it is political. Language shapes and is being shaped by preconstructed notions of kyriarchal reality, or of how the world really is. Kyriocentric language serves kyriarchal interests and kyriarchal interests shape kyriocentric texts. Language and texts are always dependent on their rhetorical situation and sociopolitical location.

3. Hence a critical intratextual analysis of the language and rhetoric of texts does not suffice. It must be complemented by a critical systemic analysis of sociopolitical and religious structures of domination and exclusion. The interpretation of rhetorical texts is determined by analytic frames of reference or theoretical lenses that presuppose but often do not articulate such a systemic analysis.

4. Language and knowledge of the world are rhetorical, that is, they are articulated in specific situations, by particular people, for a certain audience, and with certain articulated or suppressed goals and interests in mind. If all texts and knowledges are both rhetorical and political, then cultural mindsets and sacred texts can be changed. It does not suffice to know the world as it is; what is crucial is to transform and change it.

For that reason feminist studies in religion in general and feminist biblical studies in particular insist on a hermeneutics of suspicion with regard to biblical texts understood as rhetorical texts, their persuasive narrative worlds, and their ideological functions for inculcating the western kyriarchal order. Such a critical feminist rhetoric of inquiry pays special attention to the "preconstructed" frames of meaning[40] determining its readings. By making conscious the dominant symbolic frames of reference, it can empower readers to participate as subjects in the construction of biblical meanings while at the same time becoming conscious of such a construction. By showing how gender, race, class, or colonialism affect the way we read—or hear, for that matter—a feminist rhetoric of inquiry underscores the importance of the speaker/hearer's particular sociopolitical location. Reading and thinking in a kyrio-

39. On the question of language see Mary Vetterling-Braggin, ed., *Sexist Language: A Modern Philosophical Analysis* (Totowa, N.J.: Littlefield, Adams and Co., 1981); on the problem of "natural" versus "grammatical" gender, see Dennis Baron, *Grammar and Gender* (New Haven: Yale University Press, 1986). Similar observations can be made for race classifications; see Gloria A. Marshall, "Racial Classifications: Popular and Scientific," in *The "Racial" Economy of Science: Toward a Democratic Future*, ed. Sandra Harding (Bloomington: Indiana University Press, 1993), 116–27.

40. For the theoretical elaboration of this expression, see Rosemary Hennessy, *Materialist Feminism and the Politics of Discourse* (New York: Routledge, 1993); and my book *Jesus: Miriam's Child, Sophia's Prophet: Critical Issues in Feminist Christology* (New York: Continuum, 1994).

centric symbol system entices readers to identify not only with what is culturally-religious male but with what is elite male. Thus reading/hearing grammatically androcentric biblical texts intensifies one's internalization of a kyriarchal religious-political system whose values and worlds of vision are misogynist, racist, and western supremacist.

Still, the kyriocentric rhetoric of the biblical text derives not only its seductive but also its critical powers from its generic aspirations.[41] For instance, in the context of liberation struggles wo/men may read stories about Jesus, the Lord, without giving any significance to his maleness. Yet reading such stories in a religious-cultural con-textualization that underscores not only the maleness of Jesus but also his lordship reinforces wo/men's and subjugated peoples' cultural elite male identification and religiously founds Christian identity both as elite male and as antidemocratic. Focus-ing on the figure of Christ, the Lord and Son of the Father, doubles wo/men's self-alienation. In the act of reading or hearing, wo/men suffer not only from the alien-ating division of self against self, but also from the internalization that to be female is not to be Lord, not to be Son of G*d,[42] not to be divine. However, because of wo/men's conflicting positions in two contradictory discourses offered by society and biblical religions, such a cultural-religious elite male identification is not total. Wo/men and other nonpersons participate at one and the same time in the specifi-cally feminine discourse of submission, inadequacy, inferiority, dependency, and irrational intuition, on the one hand, and in the masculine "human" discourse of subjectivity, self-determination, freedom, justice, and equality, on the other.

Feminist literary critics have pointed out that readers do not engage texts in themselves. Rather, insofar as we have been taught how to read or how to listen, we activate reading paradigms.[43] Such reading paradigms consist of a set of discursive determinations that organize the practices of reading insofar as they relate texts, read-ers, and contexts to one another in specific ways. In short, biblical texts, readers, and contexts are not fixed once and for all in their interaction with each other, but they function differently within different reading formations. If reading paradigms estab-lish different relations between texts, readers, and contexts, then divergent rhetori-cal interpretations cannot be adjudicated in terms of the "true" meaning of the text itself. Rather, they must be assessed religiopolitically in terms of their implications for the struggles to end kyriarchal relations of dehumanization and to engender practices of democratic deliberation.

Consequently, feminist biblical criticism has focused on those biblical texts and traditions that have marginalized wo/men or silenced and erased them from our political-religious consciousness. As a critical feminist interpretation for liberation,

41. For this insight see, for example, Patrocinio P. Schweickart, "Reading Ourselves: Toward a Femi-nist Theory of Reading," in *Gender and Reading*, ed. Flynn and Schweickart, 31–62.

42. I spell G*d in this way in order to indicate that our language is incapable of expressing the divine.

43. Annette Kolodny, "Dancing through the Minefield: Some Observations on the Theory, Practice, and Politics of Feminist Literary Criticism," in *The New Feminist Criticism: Essays on Women, Literature, and Theory*, ed. Elaine Showalter (New York: Pantheon Books, 1985), 153.

it has sought not only to restore the radical egalitarian and democratic elements of the biblical tradition, which have never been fully realized, but also to call feminist critical work to the attention of a biblical public. To that end, it has consistently problematized and critiqued not only the scientistic empiricist and objectivist ethos of theological-historical biblical criticism but also the formalization and antiquarian stylistics of linguistic-rhetorical biblical criticism that cannot explore the political functions of language and its commonsense assumptions.

Since the revival of the antiquarian rhetorical tradition looks backward and that of the aesthetic rhetorical tradition fosters the marketing techniques of persuasive advertising and selling, some feminists rightly ask why bother to engage with a tradition[44] that is so strongly shaped by kyriarchal interests.[45] However, such an attitude neglects that all hegemonic traditions are imbued with kyriocentric ideology and function. If the goal of a critical feminist rhetoric of liberation is to change relations of domination and the knowledge that keeps them in place, then feminist scholars cannot but engage with discourses and traditions of exclusion and domination. As liberation theologians have consistently maintained, the critical rewriting and changing of cultural texts and intellectual traditions is always already also a rescuing of the subjugated and lost traditions of those marginalized, excluded, and dehumanized.

Moreover, I suggest there is a second reason why feminist biblical criticism must continue its engagement with a rhetoric of inquiry. Since feminist biblical criticism remains positioned within the margins of traditional theological schools or modern departments of religious studies, it is still forced to argue for its full citizenship in malestream discourses and institutions and to subject itself to the standard norms of objectivist-empiricist scientism and the father-authorities of the discipline. It is therefore in feminism's best interests to foster *a critical rhetoric of inquiry* in religious studies that challenges these authorities on epistemological grounds. A feminist criticism committed to the radical political-religious notion that wo/men are full citizens in academy and church needs to cultivate political rhetorical criticism not only in order to overcome its marginalization but also in order not to become co-opted and integrated into malestream discourses as "the same." If feminist scholars want to radically change discourses that deny the full citizenship of wo/men and other nonpersons, feminist studies cannot move to a special protected space but must remain bilingual, intellectually speaking the language of the academy and that of a political movement for change.[46]

44. For a short historical delineation of the history of rhetoric, see Brian Vickers, *In Defence of Rhetoric* (Oxford: Clarendon Press, 1988); and Thomas M. Conley, *Rhetoric in the European Tradition* (Chicago: University of Chicago Press, 1990).

45. See Edward P. J. Corbett, *Classical Rhetoric for the Modern Student* (3d ed.; New York: Oxford University Press, 1990), 577: "One of the reasons for the absence of women's names in the histories of rhetoric is that for most of the 2500-year history of rhetoric in the Western world, there have been very few, if any, women who could be called rhetoricians, either as theorists or as practitioners. And the reason for the lack of women rhetoricians is that for most of the 2500-year span, women were denied access to formal education and to the public arena. Rhetoric is one of the most patriarchal of all academic disciplines."

46. For the elaboration of this point, see my book *But She Said.*

Since a critical feminist rhetoric of liberation is committed to the emancipatory radical democratic struggles around the globe, it continues to invite biblical studies to articulate a politics of meaning and to foster a biblical imagination that can shape a more just future for the global village. Such a biblical imagination must be reconstructed as a historical imagination that is able to understand biblical texts not only as the memory of the suffering and victimization of all who have been considered nonpersons and noncitizens. It must be articulated also as the memory of those wo/men who in their struggles against patriarchal domination have shaped Christian history as religious interlocutors, agents of change, and survivors.[47] For that reason, a critical feminist rhetoric for liberation challenges biblical studies to reconstitute the religious-ethical rhetoric of the Bible and its liberating imagination of a more just world as a religious biblical politics of meaning. In short, biblical studies must engage feminist critical studies in order to become rhetorical-political studies.

The Feminine Coding of Rhetoric and Religion

This brings me to the third point of my argument. Rhetorical criticism in biblical studies, I contend, is limping along with the wobbling gait and one-sided hesitancy of a man with one eye, to use Anna Julia Cooper's metaphor.[48] The notion of "rhetorical half-turn," which my argument has utilized again and again, variegates the thesis of political philosopher Terrence Ball who has pointed out that the "linguistic turn" in political discourse is incomplete insofar as it has "largely ignored the twin issues of political conflict and conceptual change," although it has always insisted that "our language does not mirror an independently existing world, but is instead partly constitutive of it."[49] The deterministic and ahistorical view of language that has

47. In distinction to liberation and political theologies, a critical feminist theology insists that wo/men have not just been victims but also beneficiaries and collaborators in their own and other wo/men's oppression. "Solidarity with victims" does not suffice. The self-understanding of wo/men as historical and theological subjects is crucial for a feminist theological reconstruction.

48. The need for such a critical feminist rhetoric of liberation was eloquently expressed by the African American feminist thinker Anna Julia Cooper one hundred years ago. At the World Congress of Women, which took place in 1893 in Chicago, Cooper insisted that those who until now have been excluded from public speaking, from the articulation of knowledge, and from the exercise of political power must claim their rights to full world citizenship if the world is to have a more equitable and just future: "It is not the intelligent woman vs. the ignorant woman; nor the white woman vs. the black, the brown, and the red,—it is not even the cause of woman vs. man. Nay, it is woman's strongest vindication for speaking that the world needs to hear her voice. It would be subversive of every human interest that the cry of one half of the human family be stifled. Woman . . . daring to think and move and speak,—to undertake to help shape, mold, and direct the thought of her age, is merely completing the circle of the world's vision. Hers is every interest that has lacked an interpreter and a defender. Her cause is linked with that of every agony that has been dumb, every wrong that needs a voice. . . . The world has had to limp along with the wobbling gait and one-sided hesitancy of a man with one eye. Suddenly the bandage is removed from the other eye and the whole body is filled with light. It sees a circle where before it saw a segment. The darkened eye restored, every member rejoices with it." Anna Julia Cooper, *A Voice From the South, 1892,* Schomburg Library of Nineteenth-Century Black Women Writers (1892; reprint, New York: Oxford University Press, 1988).

been espoused by the "new criticism," functional structuralism, and some segments of postmodernism, assumes that language and texts are "autonomous" and operate independently of either author or audience.

However, if texts and discourses are studied without reference to human agency or sociohistorical situation, then language and texts become a closed system that takes on the character of "scientific law." Such a "linguistic half-turn" does not allow for a critical investigation into communicative processes as political processes that are best understood as the "action of speakers upon speakers about matters of public or common concern. . . . Disagreements about the scope and domain of the 'political' are themselves constitutive features of political discourse."[50] Such investigations into the rhetoric of scientific inquiry and theoretical knowledge, however, are not particular to political science. They have been made in the diverse disciplines not only of the humanities but also of natural science such as mathematics or biology. Feminist epistemological studies have greatly contributed to such a cross-disciplinary rhetoric of inquiry.[51]

The reluctance of rhetorical biblical criticism either to make a full rhetorical-political turn or to engage feminist criticism for doing so, I submit, is rooted in the unacknowledged and hence unreflected anxiety of the field that rhetorical biblical studies could be tainted with the negative reputation of rhetoric commonly understood as seductive persuasion, deceptive eloquence, and empty play with words. In popular understandings the word *rhetoric* often connotes empty verbiage, a clever way of telling lies, or a pseudoscientific posturing by using Greek and Latin terms for commonsense speech operations. When one considers the contested character of the field, it is not surprising that rhetorical criticism in biblical studies is not able or does not want to acknowledge its feminist and liberationist critical partners. The "fear" that it could be seen as "unscientific" prevents engagement with such critical political intellectual discourses.

This apprehension becomes even more understandable when one considers the negative "feminine" gendering of both rhetoric and religion in the antirhetorical discourses of philosophy and science. Like wo/men, religion and rhetoric figure as the excluded or idealized "other" in modern western discourses. Like wo/men, both religion and rhetoric are reduced by the modern rationalist tradition to emotion and passion, to style devoid of substance. They are identified with custom, fiction, or colorful ornament, likened to opium and pie in the sky, or associated with trickery and treachery.[52] In the last three centuries wo/men have had to struggle to overcome their actual exclusion from public speaking and academic institutions at the same time that the "feminine" has become a rhetorical figure of exclusion and subordination,

49. Terrence Ball, *Transforming Political Discourse: Political Theory and Critical Conceptual History* (Oxford: Blackwell, 1988), 5.

50. Ibid., 13.

51. See, for instance, the very uneven contributions in *The Rhetoric of the Human Sciences*, ed. Nelson, Megill, and McCloskey; Edmondson, *Rhetoric in Sociology*.

52. Jarratt, "The First Sophists and Feminism," 29.

which functions to contain religious and rhetorical discourses and their unruly sociopolitical possibilities.

Religion and theology as well as rhetoric have been coded as the "feminine other" of the masculine "hard" sciences.[53] Coded as feminine, they have been banished by the Enlightenment university to the margins of intellectual activity and public discourse. This marginalization and suppression of rhetoric has been achieved in part through its feminization. Consider the maxim, "facts are masculine, and words are feminine." Like wo/men, rhetoric is said to be about ornamentation and seduction. Rhetoric has been called "the harlot of the arts" who needs to be kept in place and under surveillance so that "she" would not corrupt the chaste mind of masculine science and inflict upon its adherents relativistic opinion in place of the certainty of scientific or religious truth. Like the proverbial "bad girl," rhetoric is said to play loose with scientific truth and objective fact, and like the virtuous wife, "good rhetoric" has been confined to college service courses and departments of preaching in theological schools.[54] Thus, metaphor, trope, and manner of speaking have been gendered in the antirhetorical western tradition and likened to the treacherousness of wo/men. False eloquence reminds one of the garrulousness and endless gossiping of wo/men, whereas decorum demands that an orator does not speak with a woman's small and shrill voice.[55]

Such a "feminine" coding of both biblical studies and rhetorical studies engenders "masculine" insecurity in biblical studies, which is compensated for by excluding actual wo/men from leadership of the clergy and the academy. Hence the admission of wo/men as equal partners in academy and religion threatens the scientific standing of both the discourses of rhetoric and of religion. Insofar as the discipline of biblical studies had to struggle not only for its freedom from doctrinal control but also against being lumped together with religion and theology as "unscientific," it expressly has developed its professional ethos as a "hard science." No wonder that the advocates of the New Rhetoric are hesitant to seriously engage feminist criticism and to learn from it.

In her fascinating study *Literary Fat Ladies: Rhetoric, Gender, Property,* which investigates the rhetoric at work "in specific texts and traditions of decorum, governance and disposition," Patricia Parker points to this interconnection between rhetoric, gender, and religion:

A term like "disposition" or orderly sequential placement, making it possible to "make

---

53. Karlyn Kohrs Campbell, "The Rhetoric of Women's Liberation. An Oxymoron," in Lucaites, Condit, and Caudill, eds., *Contemporary Rhetorical Theory*, 397–410, points out at 408, n. 22, that "the most explicit statement of the notion that audiences are 'feminine' and rhetors or orators are 'masculine' appears in the rhetorical theory of Adolf Hitler and the National Socialist Party in Germany." She refers to Kenneth Burke, "The Rhetoric of Hitler's 'Battle'," in *The Philosophy of Literary Form* (1941; reprint, New York: Vintage Books, 1957), 167.

54. For this characterization, see Michael Calvin McGee and John R. Lyne, "What Are Nice Folks like You Doing in a Place like This?" in *The Rhetoric of the Human Sciences*, ed. Nelson, et al., 381–83.

55. Patricia Parker, *Literary Fat Ladies: Rhetoric, Gender, Property* (London: Methuen, 1987), 109.

an Ende" appears equally in sixteenth century discussions of the divine distribution of the sequence of history, the institution of order in the civil state, the placement of words in sentences and logical propositions, and the disposition of the female and "the order of the household." But it is the handbooks—indices of the rise of rhetoric and its pedagogy in the early modern period—that reveal deliberately or not that what is presented in all these different contexts as ostensibly "natural" and necessary" is instead something both constructed and manipulable.[56]

In light of this interconnection between religion, state, language, and gender, it becomes comprehensible if not defensible why the regeneration of biblical rhetorical criticism is only capable of acknowledging its malestream patrimony but not its commonalities with sociopolitical theoretical discourses such as feminism. For that reason it has been arrested in mid-turn.

To complete the full-turn to a critical rhetoric of inquiry, biblical rhetorical studies, I argue, must recognize its "feminine" typing and cease to repress this insight by resorting to ancient technologies of rhetoric, which claim scientific value-neutrality and empiricist objectivism thereby denying its political situation and functions. Such a recognition does not suggest that biblical rhetorical criticism must become fractional, subjectivist, and blind to reason. Rather, it means that biblical critics must explicitly alert their audiences as to how and in what way their perspectives, interests, approaches, locations, assumptions, and conceptualizations of their investigations and interpretations have shaped their arguments. Moreover, such a biblical rhetoric of inquiry needs to alert its agents and audiences to the ways in which particular discourses constrain or empower not only biblical textual readings and historical reconstructions but also scholars themselves and their communities of discourse. Finally, it needs to acknowledge feminist theory and biblical criticism as significant partners in the "dance" of interpretation.

Critical Engagement

A critical engagement of rhetorical criticism with feminist theory, I propose, would engender such a full-turn of rhetorical criticism in biblical studies. However, it will do so only if such an engagement does not reproduce the rhetorical gendering of the discipline. Hence this concluding section explores in what manner an engagement and collaboration of feminist and rhetorical criticism should be conceptualized and put into practice. The expressions rhetorical "half-turn" or "full-turn" invoke the metaphor of the dance, a figure for rhetoric that was already used by Quintillian. Annette Kolodny's article "Dancing through the Minefield: Some Observations on the Theory, Practice and Politics of a Feminist Literary Criticism," which appeared almost fifteen years ago,[57] has become a classic rhetorical statement that uses the metaphor of the dance for problematizing the relationship between feminist critical theories and hegemonic disciplinary scholarship.

56. Ibid., 125.
57. *Feminist Studies* 6 (1980): 2–25, reprinted in *New Feminist Criticism*, ed. Showalter, 144–67.

Many feminist titles announce such an alliance by deploying the metaphor of dance partners. They do so by juxtaposing feminism with its respective partner and aligning both with a conjunctive "and," as, for instance, in "feminism and religion," "feminism and the church," "feminism and postmodernism," "feminism and the classics," "feminism and sociology," and, last but not least, "feminist criticism and rhetorical criticism." The late feminist philosopher Linda Singer has observed that this rhetorical construction of a relationship between often conflicting terms has heterosexual overtones. Focusing her analysis on "feminism and postmodernism," she argues that this terminology

> works dramatically against the grain of much of the writing, theory, and practice to which they are supposed to refer, since such terminological collection works to occlude, deny, or obscure the very differences, particularities and specificities upon which feminist and postmodern projects so much insist. The viability and credibility of paradigmatic designators like "feminism" and "postmodernism" depends on the production and circulation of some system or criteria of linkage, which establishes circuits of inclusion and exclusion.[58]

She then goes on to detail three of the dominant strategies for pursuing the linkage between feminism and postmodernism. The first strategy is "much like a proposal of marriage," which entails "romantic exclusivity," "loyal affiliation," or "marital fidelity" between feminism and postmodernism. However, as in any patriarchal marriage relationship, such an arrangement between feminism and postmodernism is unequal and in the final analysis obliterates the "wifely" contributions of feminism.

A second way to formulate the conjunction between feminism and postmodernism, according to Singer, has been that of "kinship and family resemblance."[59] Both can be seen as having their parentage in post-Hegelian critical theoretical traditions such as existentialism, psychoanalysis, and Marxism, and can be read as the offspring of the political practices of the 1960s. Both have inherited an ethos of resisting and challenging established forms of power. However, this coding also spells sibling rivalry over their patrimony. Whereas postmodernist discourses are rooted in canonical culture and tired of the games played in the "old boys' club," feminism starts with the recognition of exclusion from the same institutions. It cannot afford to focus on ends and death but, impelled by the impulse of beginnings, seeks to retrieve that of which it has been robbed.

A third way of figuring the relations between feminism and postmodernism is that of the corporate merger. This metaphor assumes diversity within and recognizes competition between the two entities to be merged for capitalist purposes. Ostensibly, the merger seeks to strengthen both operations and enhance their market value. However, as we well know, such mergers are often camouflaged "takeovers" in which one entity is subsumed and subjected to the demands of the other. There is no ques-

---

58. Linda Singer, "Feminism and Postmodernism," in *Feminists Theorize the Political*, ed. Butler and Scott, 464.

59. Ibid., 469.

tion of who the loser is in the academic marketplace. Singer concludes her argument with an allusion to the dance:

> The thematic and strategic interplay between these paradigms and their opposition tends to work against any mechanism of unification. The "and" therefore keeps open a site for strategic engagement. The "and" is a place holder which is to say, it holds a place open, free from being filled substantively or prescriptively. The "and" holds/preserves the difference between and amongst themselves. To try to fix that space by mapping it,—setting landmarks, establishing fixed points of conjunction-directionality—is precisely to miss the point of a conjunction which is also always already nothing.[60]

Singer's own figuration, however, also reveals its indebtedness to ludic postmodernism. It does not subvert the preconstructed gendered framework but instead re-inscribes its binary structure. In order to destabilize such a binary frame of reference I have favored the metaphor of the African American circle dance or the European folk dance for figuring the practices of a critical feminist biblical interpretation.[61] Such a figuration of a critical rhetoric as a circle dance forestalls binary genderization of feminist rhetorical biblical criticism. It suggests an image of interpretation as forward movement and spiraling repetition, stepping in place, turning over and changing of venue in which discrete methodological approaches become moving steps and artful patterns. Clumsy participants in this dance that figures the complex enterprise of biblical criticism may frequently step on each other's toes and interrupt each other's turns, but they can still dance together as long as they acknowledge each other as equals who are conscious of dancing through a political minefield. Such a dance can have many partners; it is neither heterosexually overdetermined nor an expression of competition and takeover. It does not need landmarks and fixed points, but its conjunctions need space and minimal rules of engagement.

Unlike Singer, I do not believe that the entity "feminism" is completely fluid and undetermined. Rather, with many others I have argued that feminism is a political movement for change. The "radical" notion of feminism that wo/men are people keeps alive its desire for change and inspires its struggles for liberation. Hence the conjunction *and* between feminist and rhetorical criticism in biblical studies cannot be "nothing" or remain an undetermined open space. Instead, it must be conceived of as a political space of struggle for change. The rhetorical space in which a critical feminist and a rhetorical biblical inquiry can engage each other fruitfully, I propose, is the political site of contemporary emancipatory struggles. Only if both rhetorical and feminist criticism remain firmly rooted in their original matrix of the political will they develop a religious rhetoric and spiritual vision for the well-being of all living beings on our planet. Only if rhetorical criticism makes the full-turn to a sociopolitical criticism and feminist biblical interpretation remains a critical practice of rhetorical inquiry, I argue, can they collaborate in the formation of a critical religious politics of meaning. If rhetorical criticism wants to accept the feminist invitation for

---

60. Ibid., 475.
61. Schüssler Fiorenza, *But She Said*, 2–14.

participating in the critical hermeneutical dance of biblical interpretation for liberation, it must reconsider its formalist technical preoccupation as well as its posture of scientistic certainty and antiquarian fixation. The only place where the mutual engagement of feminist and rhetorical biblical criticism can fruitfully take place is the radical democratic political space of the *ekklesia*,[62] which is inhabited by the heterogeneous struggles around the globe for change and transformation of religious, cultural, and political systems of oppression and dehumanization.

In 1991, a rhetorical event took place in Stockholm that brought together recipients of the Nobel prize to deliberate the future of the world. Since I saw only a television rebroadcast of this debate and have no transcript of it, I only recall its most salient point. One part of the panelists under the leadership of South African Bishop Tutu contended that humanity has the knowledge and the will to make a more humane future possible for the world. The other group of Nobel laureates, consisting mainly of natural scientists, argued to the contrary that modern knowledge and technology have brought our planet to the brink of destruction. The South African writer Nadine Gordimer summed up the rhetorical deadlock. In this debate, "knowledge" and "spiritual vision," she argued, are blindfolded and turned away from each other. Only when knowledge and spiritual vision embrace each other will we be able to create a livable future for all of humanity. If one engages Gordimer's insight for illuminating the problematic relation of so-called scientific-objectivist and rhetorical-political criticism in biblical studies, one comes to a similar diagnosis. To paraphrase Gordimer's statement: Biblical criticism and spiritual vision are blindfolded and turned away from each other. Only when feminist criticism and rhetorical criticism turn to each other in the attempt to change intellectual structures of dehumanization and domination will biblical studies be able to articulate a radical democratic vision and a liberating politics of biblical meaning that can foster a religious ethos of struggle for the well-being of all in the global *cosmopolis*. In the second part of the book I will therefore engage in a critical reading of some Pauline texts that explores the methodological contours and implications of biblical interpretation in the horizon of such a theo-ethics and rhetorics of inquiry.

---

62. For the theoretical and theological exploration of the term, see my book *Sharing Her Word*, 105–36.

Part Two

Rhetorical Practices

Chapter 5

Rhetorical Situation and Historical Reconstruction in 1 Corinthians

Although this chapter was developed and published more than ten years ago,[1] its basic assumptions and results have been confirmed through subsequent research. Let me highlight three of these here. The first is my contention that rhetorical analysis and especially the concept of "rhetorical situation" can integrate diverse methods such as literary, historical, hermeneutical, and social world studies.[2] In general, a rhetorical approach to 1 Corinthians has proven very fruitful and opened up new avenues of investigation.[3] Second, the technical study of Margaret Mitchell[4] has confirmed my thesis that 1 Corinthians is a letter of deliberative rhetoric. Third, although utilizing a somewhat different method, the careful study of the rhetoric of 1 Corinthians by Antoinette Clark Wire[5] has elaborated and confirmed the thesis of this essay that it is possible to reconstruct from Paul's letter the submerged alternative voices in the *ekklesia* of Corinth in and through an extensive rhetorical analysis of the letter.

In the past twenty-five years or so Christian Testament scholars have sought to balance the predominantly historical orientation of biblical studies with insights

1. This chapter is a slightly revised version of a paper first presented at the Forty-First General Meeting of SNTS in Atlanta, Georgia, on August 13, 1986, and subsequently published in *NTS* 33 (1987): 386–403.

2. See, for instance, Stephen M. Pogoloff, *Logos and Sophia: The Rhetorical Situation of 1 Corinthians,* SBLDS 134 (Atlanta: Scholars Press, 1992).

3. Cf. R. Dean Anderson, *Ancient Rhetorical Theory and Paul* (Kampen: Kok Pharos, 1996); C. J. Classen, "Paulus und die antike Rhetorik," *Zeitschrift für die neutestamentliche Wissenchaft* 82 (1991): 1–33; F. Gerald Downing, *Cynics, Paul, and the Pauline Churches* (New York: Routledge, 1998); Michael A. Bullmore, *St. Paul's Theology of Rhetorical Style: An Examination of 1 Corinthians 2.1–5 in Light of First-Century Greco-Roman Rhetorical Culture* (San Francisco: International Scholar Publications, 1995); Bruce W. Winter, *Philo and Paul Among the Sophists* (Cambridge: Cambridge University Press, 1997); Ralph Bruce Terry, *A Discourse Analysis of First Corinthians* (Arlington: University of Texas and Summer Institute of Linguistics, 1995); and Duane F. Watson and Alan J. Hauser, *Rhetorical Criticism of the Bible: A Comprehensive Bibliography with Notes on History and Method,* BIS 4 (Leiden: Brill, 1994); J. T. Reed, "Using Ancient Rhetorical Categories to Interpret Paul's Letter: A Question of Genre," in *Rhetoric and the New Testament: Essays from the Heidelberg Conference,* ed. Stanley E. Porter and Thomas H. Olbricht, JSNT Supp. Ser. 90 (Sheffield: JSOT Press, 1993), 292–324.

4. Mitchell, *Paul and the Rhetoric of Reconciliation.*

5. Clark Wire, *The Corinthian Women Prophets.*

6. Norman R. Peterson, *Literary Criticism for New Testament Critics* (Philadelphia: Fortress Press, 1978); Richard A. Spencer, *Orientation by Disorientation: Studies in Literary Criticism and Biblical Liter-*

and methods derived from literary studies and literary criticism.[6] In addition, discussions of hermeneutics[7] and pastoral "application" have attempted to replace the overall framework of meaning that has been eroded by the eclipse of biblical theology understood as salvation history.[8] Finally, the studies of the social world of early Christianity[9] have focused anew on the social-political situation and economic-cultural conditions of the Christian Testament writers and their communities. However, these discussions have not yet led to the formulation of a new integrative paradigm[10] in biblical interpretation. This chapter seeks to contribute to this three-pronged discussion by utilizing rhetorical criticism for the interpretation of Paul's first extant letter to the community of Corinth.[11] My main goal is thereby not to add a "new interpretation" to the many variant readings of 1 Corinthians but to explore the questions, methods, and strategies involved in the interpretation of the letter.

I have chosen rhetorical criticism for such an analysis because it is one of the oldest forms of both literary and political criticism that explores the particular his-

ary Criticism, Pittsburgh Theological Monograph Series 35 (Pittsburgh: Pickwick Press, 1980); L. J. White, "Historical and Literary Criticism: A Theological Response," *BTB* 13 (1983): 28–31.

7. For discussion of the literature see J. A. Sanders, "Hermeneutics," IDB Supp. (Nashville: Abingdon, 1976): 402–7; Peter Stuhlmacher, *Historical Criticism and Theological Interpretation of Scripture* (Philadelphia: Fortress Press, 1977); Anthony C. Thiselton, *The Two Horizons: New Testament Hermeneutics and Philosophical Description* (Grand Rapids: Eerdmans, 1980); Robert M. Grant and David Tracy, *A Short History of the Interpretation of the Bible* (2d ed., Philadelphia: Fortress Press, 1984); Elisabeth Schüssler Fiorenza, *Bread Not Stone: The Challenge of Feminist Biblical Interpretation* (Boston: Beacon Press, 1984); T. J. Keegan, *Interpreting the Bible: A Popular Introduction to Biblical Hermeneutics* (New York: Paulist Press, 1985); Letty M. Russell, ed., *Feminist Interpretation of the Bible* (Philadelphia: Westminster Press, 1985); Lynn M. Poland, *Literary Criticism and Biblical Hermeneutics* (Chicago: Scholars Press, 1985).

8. Cf. James Barr, "Biblical Theology," *IDB Suppl.,* 104–11; Stendahl, "Method in the Study of Biblical Theology," in *The Bible in Modern Scholarship: Papers Read at the 100th Meeting of the Society of Biblical Literature,* December 28–30, ed. J. Philip Hyatt (Nashville: Abingdon, 1965), 196–209; Gerhard F. Hasel, "Methodology as a Major Problem in the Current Crisis of Old Testament Theology," *BTB* 2 (1972): 177–98; Hendrickus Boers, *What Is New Testament Theology?* (Philadelphia: Fortress Press, 1979).

9. For a general review of the literature, cf. Carolyn Osiek, *What Are They Saying About the Social Setting of the New Testament?* (New York: Paulist Press, 1984); Wayne A. Meeks, *The First Urban Christians: The Social World of the Apostle Paul* (New Haven: Yale University Press, 1983), and his *The Moral World of the First Christians* (Philadelphia: Westminster Press, 1986); John E. Stambaugh and David L. Balch, *The New Testament in Its Social Environment* (Philadelphia: Westminster Press, 1986); E. V. Gallagher, "The Social World of Saint Paul," *Religion* 14 (1984): 91–99; Hans-Joseph Klauck, "Gemeindestrukturen im ersten Korintherbrief," *Bibel und Kirche* 40 (1985): 9–15; John H. Elliott, "Social-Scientific Criticism of the New Testament and Its Social World," *Semeia* 35 (Decatur: Scholars Press, 1986).

10. For the discussion of paradigm shifts in biblical interpretation, see my book *Bread Not Stone,* 117–49.

11. For the discussion of the Corinthian correspondence, cf. Victor P. Furnish, *II Corinthians,* Anchor Bible 32A (Garden City, N.Y.: Doubleday, 1984), 26–55.

12. Cf. George A. Kennedy, *Classical Rhetoric and Its Christian and Secular Tradition from Ancient to Modern Times* (Chapel Hill: University of North Carolina Press, 1980); Edwin Black, *Rhetorical Criticism: A Study in Method* (Madison: University of Wisconsin Press, 1978); W. J. Brandt, *The Rhetoric of Argumentation* (New York: Bobbs-Merrill, 1970); Terry Eagleton, *Walter Benjamin, or, Towards a Revolutionary Criticism* (London: Verso, 1981): 101–13.

torical uses of language in specific social political situations.[12] Such a choice seems to be appropriate not only because in antiquity the "science" of rhetoric was practically identical with advanced education and conceived of as public discourse, but also because the pioneering studies of Paul's rhetoric by Hans Dieter Betz[13] and Wilhelm Wuellner have demonstrated that Paul was well skilled in formal rhetoric, despite his claim to the contrary in 1 Corinthians. Moreover, discourse theory and reader-response criticism as well as the insight into the linguisticality and the rhetorical character of all historiography[14] represent a contemporary revival of ancient rhetorics. In the introduction to her anthology of reader-response criticism, Jane Tompkins points out that its view of language as a form of action and power is similar to that of the Greek rhetoricians:

> Relocating meaning first in the reader's self and then in the interpretive strategies that constitute it, [the reader-response critics] assert that meaning is a consequence of being in a particular situation in the world. The net result of this epistemological revolution is to repoliticise literature and literary criticism. When discourse is responsible for reality and not merely a reflection of it, then whose discourse prevails makes all the difference.[15]

I am not so much concerned in this paper to elaborate the rhetorical arrangements that were employed by Paul in writing the letter to the Corinthians as to explore the letter's rhetorical functions.[16] While Old Testament rhetorical criticism as practiced by J. Muilenburg and his students[17] shares in the formalism of the New Criticism, I would like to investigate whether a critical rhetorical interpretation of 1 Corinthians

13. Hans Dieter Betz, "The Literary Composition and Function of Paul's Letter to the Galatians," *NTS* 21 (1975): 353–59; idem, *Galatians: A Commentary on Paul's Letter to the Churches in Galatia*, Hermeneia (Philadelphia: Fortress Press, 1979).

14. See especially the work of Hayden White: "The Value of Narrativity in the Representation of Reality," *Critical Inquiry* 7 (1980): 5–28; "Historicism, History, and the Figurative Imagination," *History and Theory* 14 (1975): 43–67; "The Politics of Historical Interpretation: Discipline and De–sublimation," in *The Politics of Interpretation*, ed. W. J. T. Mitchell (Chicago: University of Chicago Press, 1983): 119–43; *Metahistory: The Historical Imagination in Nineteenth-Century Europe* (Baltimore: Johns Hopkins University Press, 1973); *Tropics of Discourse*. See, however, the critical discussion of G. G. Iggers, *New Directions in European Historiography* (rev. ed., Middletown, Conn.: Wesleyan University Press, 1984), 202–5.

15. Jane P. Tompkins, *Reader-Response Criticism: From Formalism to Post-Structuralism* (Baltimore: Johns Hopkins University Press, 1980), xxv. See also her historical overview (201–32) and her annotated bibliography. Cf. also Barbara Johnson, *The Critical Difference: Essays in the Contemporary Rhetoric of Reading* (Baltimore: Johns Hopkins University Press, 1980).

16. George Lyons, *Pauline Autobiography: Toward a New Understanding* (Atlanta: Scholars Press, 1985), 64, points out: "The freedom ancient writers exercised in the mixing of genres and in the organization of a discourse complicates rhetorical analysis making a measure of subjectivity unavoidable." He insists over against Betz that the "introduction and conclusion are particularly important for any determination of the genre and species of an oration, for here, if anywhere, the speaker makes his causa explicit" (26f.).

17. Jared J. Jackson and Martin Kessler, eds., *Rhetorical Criticism: Essays in Honor of James Muilenburg*, Pittsburgh Theological Monograph Series 1 (Pittsburgh: Pickwick Press, 1974); Trible, *God and the Rhetoric of Sexuality*; and idem, *Texts of Terror*.

is able to say something not only about the rhetorical techniques and narrative strategies of Paul's letter to the community in Corinth, but also about the actual rhetorical historical situation to which the letter is addressed.

In my work on the Book of Revelation[18] I have proposed that the concept of "rhetorical situation" developed in rhetorical criticism might help us to gain access to the historical communicative situation of Christian Testament writings. Forms of communication such as actual speeches, homilies, and letters are a direct response to a specific historical-political situation and problem. As Bitzer points out, they come into existence because of a specific condition or situation that invites utterance. The situation controls the rhetorical response in the same sense that the question controls the answer.[19] Rhetorical criticism focuses on the persuasive power and literary strategies of a text that have a communicative function in a concrete historical situation. Rhetorical discourse is generated by a specific condition or situation inviting a response. In a rhetorical situation, a person is or feels called to a response that has the possibility to affect the situation. Whereas the poetic work attempts to create and to organize imaginative experience, rhetoric seeks to persuade and to motivate people to *act rightly*. Rhetoric seeks to instigate a change of attitudes and motivations, and it strives to persuade, to teach, and to engage the hearer/reader by eliciting reactions, emotions, convictions, and identifications. The evaluative criterion for rhetoric is not aesthetics, but praxis.

According to Bitzer a rhetorical situation is characterized by an actual or potential exigence that can be completely or partially removed if discourse, introduced into the situation, can so constrain human decision or action as to bring about a significant modification of the exigence. In other words, a rhetorical situation is a situation in which one is motivated to a response that has the possibility for changing the situation. Such a response depends on the argumentative possibilities of the speaker as well as the possible expectations of her audience. Not only the exigence, but also these two types of constraints, which affect the audience decision or action and which are imposed on the author, constitute a rhetorical situation. Therefore the key question is not simply whether the speaker's/author's understanding of the audience is adequate, but whether her rhetoric meets the expectations of the audience. What is the overriding rhetorical problem the speaker/writer has to overcome in order to win the audience over to her point of view? Such a rhetorical problem is usually mentioned in the beginning of the discourse, and it may color the whole speech. In

18. Schüssler Fiorenza, *The Book of Revelation—Justice and Judgment* (Philadelphia: Fortress Press, 1985).

19. Lloyd F. Bitzer, "The Rhetorical Situation," *Philosophy and Rhetoric* 1 (1968): 1–14; see also S. Consigny, "Rhetoric and Its Situations," *Philosophy and Rhetoric* 7 (1974): 172–82; C. R. Miller, "Genre as Social Action," *Quarterly Journal of Speech* 63 (1984): 28–42; J. Patton, "Causation and Creativity in Rhetorical Situations: Distinctions and Implications," *Quarterly Journal of Speech* 65 (1979): 36–55; M. Garret and Xiaosui Xiao, "The Rhetorical Situation Revisited," *Rhetoric Society Quarterly* 23 (1993): 30–40; C. R. Smith and S. Lybarger, "Bitzer's Model Reconstructed," *Communication Quarterly* 44 (1996): 197–313; Barbara Biesecker, "Rethinking the Rhetorical Situation from within the Thematic of Différance," *Philosophy and Rhetoric* 22 (1989): 110–30.

short, in the rhetorical act the speaker/writer seeks both to convey an image of her- or himself as well as define the rhetorical problem and situation in such a way that these "fit" to each other so that the hearer/reader will be moved to the standpoint of the speaker/writer by participating in that construction of the world.[20]

How then can one utilize rhetorical criticism for reading a historical text in such a way that one moves from the "world of the text" of Paul to the possible worlds of the Corinthian community?[21] I would argue that in order to do so rhetorical criticism needs to distinguish between at least three levels of communication. Rhetorical criticism of the Bible must distinguish between the historical argumentative situation, the implied or inscribed rhetorical situation, and the rhetorical situation of contemporary interpretations, which again can be either actual or textualized. No longer can it read a letter of Paul in isolation but must work with the canonical collection and reception of Paul's letters.

I therefore propose that a rhetorical critical analysis has to move through at least four stages. It begins—as I have sketched above—by identifying the rhetorical interests, interpretive models, and social locations of contemporary interpretation; then it moves in a second step to delineate the rhetorical arrangement, interests, and modifications introduced by the author in order to elucidate and establish in a third step the rhetorical situation of the letter. Finally, it seeks to reconstruct the common historical situation and symbolic universe of the writer/speaker and the recipients/audience. True, such a rhetorical reconstruction of the social-historical situation and symbolic universe of a Pauline letter is still narrative-laden and can only be constituted as a "subtext" to Paul's text. Yet this subtext is not simply the story of Paul; it is, rather, the story of the Corinthian *ekklesia* to which Paul's rhetoric is to be understood as an active response.[22] Therefore, it becomes necessary to assess critically Paul's theological rhetoric in terms of its function for early Christian self-understanding and community. The nature of rhetoric as political discourse necessitates critical assessment and theological evaluation.[23]

In the following sections, I would like to engage these four levels of rhetorical critical analysis for the interpretation of the first letter of Paul to the Corinthians:

First, reader-response criticism distinguishes between the actual writer/reader and the implied writer/reader. The implied writer/reader encompasses the contemporary interpreter who in the process of reading constructs the inscribed author and

20. George A. Kennedy, *New Testament Interpretation through Rhetorical Criticism* (Chapel Hill: University of North Carolina Press, 1984), 34–36. Cf. also Perelman and Olbrechts-Tyteca, *The New Rhetoric*, 19–62.

21. For a discussion of this problem, cf. Bernard C. Lategan and Willem S. Vorster, *Text and Reality: Aspects of Reference in Biblical Texts*, Semeia Studies (Philadelphia: Fortress Press, 1985); Norman R. Petersen, *Rediscovering Paul: Philemon and the Sociology of Paul's Narrative World* (Philadelphia: Fortress Press, 1985), and Wayne A. Meeks, "Understanding Early Christian Ethics," *JBL* 105 (1986): 3–11.

22. Fredric R. Jameson, "The Symbolic Inference," in *Representing Kenneth Burke*, ed. Hayden White and Margaret Brose (Baltimore: Johns Hopkins University Press, 1982), 68–91.

23. Booth, "Freedom of Interpretation," has called for a revived ethical and political criticism in literary criticism. Cf. also *Making a Difference*, ed. Greene and Kahn; *Feminist Criticism and Social Change*, ed. Newton and Rosenfelt; and especially Meese, *Crossing the Double-Cross*, 133–50.

reader. Reader-response criticism has developed the notion of implied author and implied reader that can help us to elucidate Paul's rhetorical intention as it is constructed in the act of reading/interpretation today (reception hermeneutics[24]).

Second, the rhetorical arrangement or disposition of 1 Corinthians not only embodies the rhetorical strategies that Paul employs for persuading the Corinthian community to act according to his instructions, but also indicates the intended or inscribed audience of the letter.

Third, the "rhetorical situation" is constituted by the rhetorical occasion or exigency to which 1 Corinthians can be understood as a "fitting" response as well as by the rhetorical problem Paul had to overcome. Attention to both can help us to avoid reconstructing the historical situation of the Corinthian community simply as the story of Paul.

Fourth, since rhetoric also can be used negatively as propaganda or crafty calculation, ethical evaluation of the speaker and moral judgment of the rhetorical discourse in a concrete political situation is an essential part of philosophical discussions in ancient rhetoric. Christian Testament rhetorical criticism, therefore, cannot limit itself to a formalistic analysis of 1 Corinthians, nor to an elucidation of its historical-social context; rather it must develop a responsible ethical and evaluative theological criticism.

Contemporary Interpretations

In *The Rhetoric of Fiction*, Wayne Booth has distinguished between the actual author/reader and the implied author/reader. The implied author is not the real author, but rather the image or picture the reader will construct gradually in the process of reading the work. "The actual reader is involved in apprehending and building up the picture of the implied author (and implied reader); but in doing this the reader is assuming the role dictated by the author."[25] In other words, in the process of reading 1 Corinthians, the interpreter follows the directives of the inscribed author, who is not identical with the "real" Paul, as to how to understand the community of Corinth. That interpreters follow the directives of the implied author to understand the Corinthian Christians as "others" of Paul or as his "opponents" becomes obvious in all those interpretations that characterize the Corinthians as foolish, immature, arrogant, divisive, individualistic, unrealistic illusionists, libertine enthusiasts, or boasting spiritualists who misunderstood the preaching of Paul in terms of "realized eschatology."

---

24. For an overview, see Robert C. Holub, *Reception Theory: A Critical Introduction* (London: Methuen, 1984).

25. Edgar V. McKnight, *The Bible and the Reader: An Introduction to Literary Criticism* (Philadelphia: Fortress Press, 1985), 102; see, however, the incisive critique of the depoliticizing tendencies in reader-response criticism that do not take power relationships into account: M. L. Pratt, "Interpretative Strategies/Strategic Interpretations: On Anglo–American Reader Response Criticism," in *Postmodernism and Politics*, ed. Jonathan Arac, Theory and History of Literature 28 (Minneapolis: University of Minnesota Press, 1986), 26–54.

Since many things are presupposed, left out, or unexplained in a speech/letter, the audience must in the process of reading "supply" the missing information in line with the rhetorical directives of the speaker/writer. Historical critical scholars seek to "supply" such information generally in terms of the history of religions, including Judaism, while preachers and Bible-readers usually do so in terms of contemporary values, life, and psychology. Scholarship on 1 Corinthians tends to "supply" such information about Paul's "opponents"[26] either with reference to the symbolic universe of contemporary Judaism, of pagan religion, especially the mystery cults, philosophical schools, Hellenistic Judaism, or developing Gnosticism. The studies of the social setting or "social world" of Pauline Christianity, in turn, do not utilize ideological, doctrinal models of interpretation, but supply the missing information in terms of "social data" gleaned from the Pauline corpus, Acts, and other ancient sources, which themselves are organized in terms of sociological or anthropological models.

As diverse as are these interpretations and their implications for the understanding of the community in Corinth, they all follow Paul's dualistic rhetorical strategy without questioning or evaluating it. In short, a cursory look at scholarship on 1 Corinthians indicates that Paul is a skilled rhetorician, who throughout the centuries has reached his goal of persuading his audience that he is right and the "others" are wrong. The difference in interpretations is more a difference in degree than a difference in interpretational model. It depends on which directions encoded in the letter exegetes choose to amplify historically and theologically. Moreover, insofar as Christian Testament scholars read 1 Corinthians as a "canonical text," we often uncritically accept the implied author's claims to apostolic authority as historically valid and effective. However, we must ask whether the interpretation of 1 Corinthians would have developed different heuristic models if, for example, Paul was believed to be a Valentinian Gnostic or a Jewish rabbi writing against Christians.[27] In other words, does Paul's power of persuasion rest on his presumed authority or did it have the same effect in the historical situation in which such canonical authority cannot be presupposed?[28]

The Rhetorical Arrangement of 1 Corinthians

At first glance, the rhetorical strategies and situation of 1 Corinthians seem to be obvious. The Corinthians had written to Paul about certain issues and 1 Corinthi-

26. For a discussion of the problem, cf. Earl E. Ellis, "Paul and His Opponents: Trends in Research," in *Christianity, Judaism, and Other Greco-Roman Cults*, vol. 1, ed. Jacob Neusner (Leiden: Brill, 1975), 264–98, and especially Klaus Berger, "Die impliziten Gegner. Zur Methode der Erschliessung von Gegnern in neutestamentlichen Texten," in *Kirche*, ed. D. Lührmann and G. Strecker (Tübingen: Mohr, 1980), 373–400.

27. V. Hasler, "Das Evangelium des Paulus in Korinth: Erwägungen zur Hermeneutik," *NTS* 30 (1984): 109–29 points out that exegetes often succumb to the temptation to identify with Paul and to take over uncritically his theological interpretation.

28. For discussion and literature see Gerd Lüdemann, *Paulus*, vol. 2, *Antipaulinismus im frühen Christentum*, FRLANT 130 (Göttingen: Vandenhoeck & Ruprecht, 1983).

ans is a response to their inquiries or declarations. The letter form is a "fitting response" to the Corinthian correspondence. If that is the case, however, it must be explained why Paul's first reference to their correspondence is in chapter 7 and not in the beginning of the letter. If this ordering is an intended part of the rhetorical *dispositio,* then one must ask whether this indicates a different argumentative situation, since the rhetorical problem is usually articulated in the beginning of the discourse. In order to explore this question it becomes necessary to discuss the rhetorical genre of 1 Corinthians.

Ancient rhetoric distinguishes between "three types of oratory, the deliberative, the forensic, and the epideictic, which . . . corresponded respectively to an audience engaged in deliberating, an audience engaged in judging, an audience that is merely enjoying the orator's unfolding argument without having to reach a conclusion on the matter in question."[29] Forensic or judicial rhetoric has its *Sitz im Leben* in the courtroom. It seeks to accuse or to defend and to persuade the audience as the judge of its own assessment of the past. Deliberative rhetoric is at home in the forum, and it seeks to convince and move the audience to make the right decision for the future, whereas epideictic or demonstrative rhetoric is exercised in the marketplace or amphitheater, where the audience as spectators judge the oratory of the speaker in order to award praise or blame.

An exploration of rhetorical genre and its function can thus contribute to an understanding of the rhetorical situation insofar as arrangement and style reveal the speaker's perception of the audience and the ways chosen to influence it. Thus the audience is a construction of the speaker, but in a real life situation, as in the case of 1 Corinthians, care must be taken to form a concept of the audience as close as possible to reality if the speaker/writer wants to have any effect or influence on the actions of the hearers/readers.

1. In his article on "Greek Rhetoric and Pauline Argumentation," Wuellner has argued that 1 Corinthians represents epideictic or demonstrative discourse.[30] He thereby relies on the work of Perelman and Olbrechts-Tyteca, *The New Rhetoric,* that seeks to redefine the *genus demonstrativum* or epideictic genre. According to Lausberg, in antiquity demonstrative rhetoric was, in distinction to forensic and deliberative rhetoric, not so much concerned with the content or topic of the discourse as with the art of presentation or the rhetorical skills and eloquence speakers exhibited at festivals and in the amphitheater. Its primary function was praise in celebration of a person, community, or action.[31] Perelman and Olbrechts-Tyteca seek to redefine the *genus demonstrativum* not so much with reference to the speaker's performance, but rather with respect to the audience and its values.[32] Epideictic discourse, they argue,

29. Perelman and Olbrechts-Tyteca, *The New Rhetoric,* 21.

30. In *Early Christian Literature and the Classical Intellectual Tradition. In Honorem Robert Grant,* ed. William R. Schoedel and Robert L. Wilken. Théologie Historique 53 (Paris: Editions Beauchesne, 1979), 177–88.

31. Heinrich Lausberg, *Handbuch der literarischen Rhetorik: Eine Grundlegung der Literaturwissenschaft* (2d rev. ed., Munich: Max Huber Verlag, 1973), 55.

32. Perelman and Olbrechts-Tyteca, *The New Rhetoric,* 48f.

"sets out to increase the intensity of the audience's adherence to certain values which might not be contested when considered on their own but may nevertheless not prevail against other values that might come into conflict with them. In epideictic oratory the speaker turns educator."[33] Such discourse is less directed toward changing or modifying beliefs than toward strengthening the adherence to what is already accepted. It seeks to reinforce the sense of *communio* between the speaker and the audience by utilizing every means available to the orator.

Wuellner examines the phenomenon of Pauline digressions in 1 Corinthians in order to show that they are not careless style but rather examples of Paul's rhetorical skill for, in classical rhetoric, digressions are introduced for the purpose of elucidating the issue at hand. He identifies three major digressions: 1:19—3:21; 9:1—10:13; and 13:1-13. These digressions function *affectively* to intensify adherence. They belong to three argumentative units: 1:1—6:11; 6:12—11:1; and 11:2—14:40. He concludes: "The appeals to the audience to imitate the speaker . . . are an example, a paradigm, of the values lauded, with Paul seeking adherence to these values on the one hand, and on the other hand to strengthen disposition toward action."[34] He therefore rejects the thesis of Nils Dahl, who on the basis of a contentual but not formal analysis had argued that chapters 1–4 are best understood as an *apologia* because in these chapters Paul seeks to "reestablish his apostolic authority as the founder and spiritual father of the whole church in Corinth."[35]

2. However, Dahl's rhetorical understanding of chapters 1–4 as Pauline apology has received support from recent formal studies of Paul's rhetoric. In his study, *Briefformular und rhetorische Disposition im 1. Korintherbrief*, Michael Bünker has analyzed 1 Cor. 1:10—4:21 and 1 Corinthians 15 in terms of epistolary form and rhetorical arrangement. He shows that both sections have the rhetorical structure of forensic or judicial discourse. Although Paul claims that he did not speak in Corinth with "lofty words of wisdom," his distinction between *en peithoi sophias* and *en apodeixei pneumatos* indicates that he knew the rhetorical distinction between oratory as mere persuasion and speech as a process of forming one's opinion on the basis of arguments and proofs.[36]

Moreover, Bünker argues, according to rhetorical conventions, Paul's arrangement and disposition is artful and well planned but not obvious. This is the case especially in those sections in which Paul could not count on the agreement of the audience but rather expected attacks and counterarguments. Bünker, therefore, concludes that while Paul formally addresses the whole community in Corinth, in reality he is arguing with those few Corinthian Christians who are well educated and of high status. His rhetorical location of the implicit or intended reader thus confirms

---

33. Ibid., 51.

34. Wuellner, "Greek Rhetoric and Pauline Argumentation," 184.

35. Nils Alstrup Dahl, *Studies in Paul: Theology for the Early Christian Mission* (Minneapolis: Augsburg Publishing House, 1977), 329; cf. also J. Bradley Chance, "Paul's Apology to the Corinthians," *Perspectives in Religious Studies* 9 (1982): 144–55.

36. Michael Bünker, *Briefformular und rhetorische Disposition im 1. Korintherbrief*, Göttinger Theologische Arbeiten 28 (Göttingen: Vandenhoeck & Ruprecht, 1983), 48–76.

Theissen's social identification of the troublemakers in Corinth who have caused divisions and conflicts by competing with each other for the approval of different apostolic authorities.[37] Bünker's results, however, speak against Wuellner's thesis that Paul did not choose the epideictic genre in order to change the beliefs of the audience but rather in order to strengthen the Corinthians' adherence to values and beliefs which, although already accepted by many, were still contested by some.

In my opinion, Bünker's argument also has several weaknesses. He discusses the rhetorical disposition of chapters 1–4 and 15 only and not the rhetorical genre of the whole letter. Furthermore, his delineation of the intended or implicit audience is derived from considerations of general rhetorical practices that can be used in all kinds of rhetorical discourse. Finally, the ending of 1 Corinthians, in which Paul appeals to the Corinthians to acknowledge and accept the leadership of Stephanas and his coworkers, speaks against an identification of the intended audience whom Paul wishes to compel to act with those who cause the difficulties in the community. Since Stephanas is clearly one of the better-situated and educated members of the community, and since he belongs to those who are loyal to Paul, we have to conclude, to the contrary, that Paul relies on such persons for implementing his directives. Consequently, if Paul does not argue against but rather appeals to the social status group of Stephanas as the intended or the implicit readers, the overall genre of 1 Corinthians is not judicial or forensic. Rather, it appears that the genre of 1 Corinthians is best understood as "largely deliberative although it contains some judicial passages."[38]

3. The disposition or arrangement of deliberative rhetoric is closely related to that of the forensic genre. It consists basically of three sections. First, the exordium intends to secure the goodwill of the audience and states the desired goal of the speech. Second, in the main body or proofs the argument is advanced with reference to what is honorable, useful, and possible by appeal to ethos as a reflection of one's own good character (Paul's example), to pathos as a stirring appeal to the heart and the emotions, and to logos, that is, to reasoned argument. And third, the peroration restates with all possible force factors that are alluded to in the exordium and adduced or developed in the proofs.[39]

The major goal of deliberative rhetoric is to persuade the audience to take action for the future and to believe that this action is in its best interest. This goal is expressed in 1 Cor. 1:10 where Paul appeals to the Corinthians that they should all agree without dissensions and be united in the same mind and the same opinion.[40] It is also articulated in the peroration 16:15-18, where Paul urges the Corinthians to subject themselves and to give recognition to such persons as Stephanas and every

---

37. Bünker, *Briefformular,* 17 and 52f. Cf. also Gerd Theissen, *The Social Setting of Pauline Christianity: Essays on Corinth* (Philadelphia: Fortress Press, 1982), 56f.

38. Kennedy, *New Testament Interpretation,* 87.

39. See the literature cited by F. Forrester Church, "Rhetorical Structure and Design in Paul's Letter to Philemon," *HTR* 71 (1978): 17–31.

40. Hans Conzelmann's classification of this passage as "paraenetic" is too general. Cf. his commentary on *I Corinthians: A Commentary on the First Epistle to the Corinthians,* Hermeneia (Philadelphia: Fortress Press, 1975), 31.

coworker.[41] Bünker is thus correct in his suggestion that the inscribed or intended audience which is asked to decide the issues under discussion is composed of those who have either social or missionary status or both. The major issues that need to be settled are discussed in the main body of the letter: marriage and sexuality (chapters 5–7);[42] meat sacrificed to idols (8:1—11:1);[43] worship (11:2—14:40);[44] resurrection (15:12-37);[45] and the collection for the saints (16:1-4). In order to show that this delineation of 1 Corinthians as deliberative rhetoric is plausible, one has to test out whether it can be construed as a "fitting" response to the rhetorical situation.

Rhetorical Situation and Genre

At first glance the rhetorical situation of 1 Corinthians seems to support the understanding of the letter as epideictic rhetoric. The Corinthians had written to Paul about certain issues, and 1 Corinthians is a response to their request for advice and answers. If that were the case, however, it must be explained why Paul does not refer to the Corinthian letter before chapter 7. This observation suggests a different argumentative genre and situation. As we have seen, the "rhetorical situation" is constituted by the rhetorical occasion or exigency to which 1 Corinthians can be understood as a "fitting" response as well as by the rhetorical problem Paul had to overcome. Attention to both can help us to avoid reconstructing the historical situation of the Corinthian community simply as the story of Paul. Therefore it is necessary to define the argumentative situation in terms of the exigence and the rhetorical problem articulated in the beginning of 1 Corinthians.

According to the rhetorical handbooks, the basic issue of the case is usually discussed in the beginning of a discourse, but it needs to be restated also during the discourse. This seems to be the case in chapters 1:11—4:21; 9; 15:1-12; and 16:5-12. In 1 Corinthians stasis seems to be understood best as *status translationis* that is given

41. The emphatic expression *parakalo hymas* serves as rhetorical marker in 1:10, 4:16; and 16:15. For 4:16 see B. Sanders, "Imitating Paul: I Cor. 4:16," *HTR* 74 (1981): 353–63 but with a different emphasis in interpretation.

42. It is debated where the first part of 1 Corinthians ends and the second section begins. The traditional outline is chapters 1–6 (subjects raised with Paul orally) and 7–16 (subjects about which the Corinthians have written). Cf. William F. Orr and James Arthur Walther, *I Corinthians: A New Translation*, Anchor Bible 32 (New York: Doubleday, 1976), 120–22; K. E. Bailey, "The Structure of I Corinthians and Paul's Theological Method with Special Reference to 4:17," *NovT* 25 (1983): 152–81, argues that 4:17-21 are an introduction to chapters 5–7; the semiotic analysis of G. Claudel, "I Kor 6,12–7,40 neu gelesen," *Trierer Theologische Zeitschrift* 94 (1985): 20–36, argues for the unity of this section.

43. For bibliography cf. Wendell Lee Willis, *Idol Meat in Corinth: The Pauline Argument in I Corinthians 8 and 10*, SBLDS 68 (Chico, Calif.: Scholars Press, 1981); idem, "An Apostolic Apologia? The Form and Function of I Corinthians 9," *JSNT* 24 (1985): 33–48 argues that here Paul is not defending his conduct but rather argues on the basis of it.

44. Cf. Heinz-Dietrich Wendland, *Die Briefe an die Korinther*, NTD 7 (Göttingen: Vandenhoeck & Ruprecht, 1965), 80; cf. also my article, "Women in the Pre-Pauline and Pauline Churches," *Union Seminary Quarterly Review* 33 (1978): 153–66.

45. Cf. the careful structural analysis of W. Stenger, "Beobachtungen zur Argumentationsstruktur von I Cor 15," *Linguistica Biblica* 45 (1979): 71–128.

when the speaker's/writer's *auctoritas* or jurisdiction to address or settle the issue at hand is in doubt and needs to be established.[46]

"Those of Chloe" (or "Chloe's people—RSV) in 1:11 function as interlocutors who articulate such doubt as to the qualifications of Paul to settle the issues about which the Corinthians have written. It is generally assumed that Stephanas delivered the formal written questions or statements of the community,[47] whereas "those of Chloe" supplied the oral information, hearsay, and gossip to which Paul refers. Scholars such as J. Hurd, N. Dahl, or G. Theissen who seek to reconstruct the social-historical situation in Corinth from the information of the letter and not through outside information also make this distinction. For example, Dahl assumes that the official delegation of the church in Corinth headed by Stephanas "had not gossiped,"[48] whereas the people of Chloe had supplied the oral information referred to by Paul in 1:10—5 8; 5:13b—6:11; and 11:17-34. Theissen, on the other hand, argues that the "people of Chloe" who provided the information on party strife were slaves who looked at the problems in Corinth from "below," whereas the letter, which did not mention that problem, was probably written by people who possessed some degree of culture, some of the more prominent members of the community.[49] He concludes from this that Paul adopts the view "from below" and argues against the upper-class members who were responsible for the divisions in the church. However, we have no indication that Stephanas was the carrier of the letter sent by the Corinthians. It appears that he arrived later and gave Paul a more positive view of the situation at Corinth so that Paul could rely on him to present his response to the community and to see to it that his instructions were followed, for the community is told to subordinate itself to Stephanas and his coworkers.

"Those of Chloe" are usually understood to be either slaves or family members of the household of Chloe, a wo/man who might or might not have been a Christian. This prevalent interpretation overlooks, however, that here the Greek grammatical form (article with *genitivus possessivus*) is the same as the expression used for characterizing the followers of Paul, Apollos, Cephas, and Christ. It also overlooks that Paul uses a different grammatical expression (*tous ek ton,* gen. poss.), for instance, in Rom. 16:10 and 11, where he greets the members of the households of Aristobulos and of Narkissos.[50] It seems likely that the expression "those of Chloe" means "the people or followers of Chloe" in Corinth; therefore, I would suggest they were the official messengers of the community. They not only supplied Paul with oral background information, but they also presented the written communication of the community to him. Chloe's status in the community of Corinth was probably similar to that of Stephanas even though she and her followers did not belong

46. Lausberg, *Handbuch der literarischen Rhetorik,* 128f.
47. Ibid.
48. Dahl, *Studies in Paul,* 50.
49. Theissen, *The Social Setting of Pauline Christianity,* 57.
50. Cf. my article, "Missionaries, Apostles, Coworkers: Rom 16 and the Reconstruction of Women's Early Christian History," *Word and World* 6 (1986): 420–33.

to the converts of Paul because they obviously were not baptized by him. However, her social status and that of her followers are not clear.[51]

If the delegation traveled under the name of a wo/man, wo/men must have had influence and leadership in the Corinthian church not only in worship meetings but also in everyday life and the decision-making processes of the community. Against this assumption one cannot argue that Paul uses only "brothers" to address the members of the community, for androcentric language functioned in antiquity just as it does today as so-called generic, inclusive language.[52] Furthermore, this reading would explain the crucial place wo/men are given in the discussion of marriage in chapter 7[53] and especially in the ring-composition of chapters 11:2—14:40, a section beginning and ending with a discussion of women's role.[54]

In this section persuasive argument breaks down and is replaced with strong appeals to authority. After a *captatio benevolentiae* in 11:2 that the Corinthians have observed the traditions Paul preached to them, Paul in v. 3 emphatically ("but I want you to know") introduces a peculiar theological kyriarchal chain—God-Christ-man-wo/man [the head or source of every man is Christ, the head of woman is man, and the head of Christ is God][55]—which is restated in v. 7 as man "is the image and glory of God but woman is the glory of man." The argument in 11:2-16 is so convoluted that we can no longer say with certainty what kind of custom or style Paul advocates for wo/men prophets and liturgists. It is clear, however, that he does so because he wants them to know that the head or source of wo/man is man just as the head or source of Christ is God.[56]

Just as 11:2-16 ends with an authoritative assertion of the will of Paul, so does the argumentation in chapter 14 that demands silence, order, and subordination from speakers in tongues, interpreters of pneumatic speech, and prophets as well as from

51. It is debated whether Chloe's followers live in Corinth or have returned from Corinth to their residence in Ephesus. Meeks, *The First Urban Christians,* 59 argues that Chloe lived in Corinth because Paul expects that her name is recognized. However, he considers the people of Chloe to be her slaves or freedmen.

52. See my book *In Memory of Her,* 41–67.

53. Schüssler Fiorenza, *In Memory of Her,* 220–26.

54. 1 Cor. 11:2-16 and 14:33b-36 are both considered to be post-Pauline "pastoral" insertions by Winsome Munro, *Authority in Paul and Peter: The Identification of a Pastoral Stratum in the Pauline Corpus and I Peter,* Society of New Testament Studies Monograph Series 45 (Cambridge: University Press, 1983), 67–82; I consider not only 1 Cor. 11:2-16 but also 14:33b-36 as authentically Pauline since these verses cohere with the overall argument in chapter 14; cf. also the structural analysis of Wayne A. Grudem, *The Gift of Prophecy in I Corinthians* (Lanham, Md.: University Press of America, 1982), 231–55, however, with a different interpretational emphasis.

55. Paul may be alluding here to "the great chain of being" which was first formulated by Plato. See Alexander O. Lovejoy, *The Great Chain of Being: A Study of the History of an Idea* (1936; reprint, Cambridge, Mass.: Harvard University Press, 1976), 56: "The conception of the universe as a 'Great Chain of Being,' composed of an immense . . . number of links ranging in hierarchical order from the meagerest kind of existents, . . . up to the *ens perfectissimum* . . . every one of them differing from that immediately above and that immediately below it." This "chain of being" was formulated in the context of the polis in order to justify a hierarchical world of unchanging inequality.

56. For discussion of the literature and interpretation see *In Memory of Her,* 226–30.

wo/men or wives who participated in public discourse. "What, did the word of God originate with you. . . . If anyone believes that he or she is a prophet, or spiritual, he or she should acknowledge that what I am writing to you is a command of the Lord. If anyone does not recognize this, he or she is not recognized."[57] Did Paul fear that some of the Corinthian women prophets would not acknowledge what he was writing? Why does he need to appeal to a command of the Lord that is not known from anywhere else? Finally, it is interesting to note that only in the final greetings of Corinthians is Prisca mentioned after Aquila, a change that corresponds to patriarchal custom.

If, as I have argued, a reconstruction of the argumentative situation cannot assume without discussion that only oral information was communicated by Chloe and, conversely, also cannot demonstrate that the written information was entrusted to Stephanas as the head of the "official delegation," then the question must be raised anew: What was the rhetorical situation to which Paul's letter can be construed as a "fitting response"? Although the literature extensively debates whether there were four, three, or only two factions in Corinth,[58] it usually overlooks that the information of Chloe's followers about *erides* (pl.), that is, that debates, discussions, or competing claims among them, are reinterpreted by Paul (*lego de touto*) as party strife. It is Paul, and not the Corinthians, who understands their debates as party or school divisions.

Whereas Hurd has insisted that the Corinthians have not challenged Paul's authority as an apostle,[59] Dahl has argued that Paul had to establish himself as the apostle of the whole church. He construes the following situation: The quarrels in Corinth were the result of the Corinthians' debate about whom to consult for answers to some of their questions. Some might have suggested Cephas, because he was the foremost among the Twelve, whereas Paul's credentials were questionable; others might have voted for Apollos who, in contrast to Paul, was a wise and powerful teacher; many might have argued that they did not need to consult anyone since as a spirit-filled people, they were mature and competent enough to decide for themselves.

Since the letter was sent to Paul, those like Stephanas who thought that Paul was their best choice must have won out. While the official delegates, Dahl argues, rep-

---

57. D. W. Odell-Scott, "Let the Women Speak in Church: An Egalitarian Interpretation of I Cor. 14:33b–36," *BTB* 13 (1983) has argued that I Cor. 14:33b–36 represent a slogan of the Corinthian males against whom Paul argues. Cf. also Charles H. Talbert, "Paul's Understanding of the Holy Spirit," in Charles H. Talbert, ed., *Perspectives on the New Testament: Festschrift Stagg* (Macon: Mercer University Press, 1985), 95–108. However, in light of Paul's argument in 1 Cor. 11:3–4 such an interpretation is not convincing.

58. Cf. Philipp Vielhauer, "Paulus und die Kephaspartei in Korinth," *NTS* 21 (1975): 341–52; F. Lang, "Die Gruppen in Korinth nach 1. Korinther 1–4," *Theologische Beiträge* 14 (1983): 68–79; and especially the overview by John Coolidge Hurd, *The Origins of I Corinthians* (New York: Seabury Press, 1965), 95–107; Conzelmann, *I Corinthians*, 33–34 ("Excursus: The Parties"); and Hans-Joseph Klauck, *1. Korintherbrief* (Würzburg: EchterVerlag, 1984), 21–23.

59. Hurd, *The Origin of I Corinthians*, 111.

resented the Corinthians as loyal to Paul, the people of Chloe informed him of the quarrels and latent objections that broke into the open after the delegation had left. "As a consequence, Paul had to envisage the possibility that his letter containing his reply might easily make a bad situation worse. Quarrel and strife might develop into real divisions of the church, if his recommendations were enthusiastically received by one group and rejected by others."[60]

However, Paul's rhetoric of biting irony, and his attempt to shame, belittle, and undermine the Corinthian self-understanding is hardly designed to lessen tensions and to prevent divisions. Rather, just as in chapter 15, so also here the combative style of this section introduces dualistic categories and antagonistic alternatives.[61] Moreover, Hurd has observed that Paul's attitude toward the Corinthian community "contained a substantial measure of veiled hostility."[62] While I agree with Dahl that the rhetoric of 1 Corinthians clearly intends to *establish* "the authority of Paul as the founder and father of the entire church at Corinth," I would argue that it does not re-establish, but introduces, such unique authority claims. In other words, Paul does not defend his authority as an apostle among other apostles but rather argues for his authority as the *sole* founder and father of the Corinthian community.

Paul establishes a line of authority—God, Christ, Paul, Apollos, Timothy, Stephanas, and other local coworkers to which the Corinthians should subordinate themselves because they are "Christ's." Paul understands himself not only as Christ's steward and administrator, but he can also say that "in Christ he has begotten them through the gospel" (4:15). Moreover, the Corinthians not only owe their Christian existence to Paul's generative action, but they also are seen as passive objects (field, temple) of his missionary activity that establish his unique authority. This hierarchy of authority that extends from God down to the community seems to be paralleled by the one established in 11:2: God-Christ-man-woman. Just as the community is admonished to "subordinate" itself, so women/wives are not allowed to speak in the *ekklesia* but must subordinate themselves.

In 1 Corinthians Paul introduces the vertical line of kyriarchal subordination not only into the social relationships of the *ekklesia*, but into its symbolic universe as well by arrogating the authority of God, the "father," for himself. He does so in order to claim for his interpretation of divine power the authority of the singular father and founder of the community. He thereby seeks to change the understanding of persuasive-consensual authority based on pneumatic competence accessible to all into that of compulsory authority based on the symbolization of ultimate patri-kyriarchal power. It is Paul who introduces into the early Christian missionary movement "Christian patriarchalism which receives its coloration from the warmth of the ideal of love."[63]

60. Dahl, *Studies in Paul*, 49ff.

61. Stenger, "Beobachtungen zur Argumentationsstruktur," 85f.

62. Hurd, *The Origins of I Corinthians*, 113.

63. Ernst Troeltsch, *The Social Teaching of the Christian Churches*, vol. 1 (New York: Macmillan 1931), 78; cf. Gerd Theissen, *The Social Setting of Pauline Christianity*, 107.

Historical Reconstruction and Theological Assessment

The rhetorical situation to which 1 Corinthians can be understood as a "fitting" response might then be conceived as follows: The Corinthians had debates and discussions as to how their new self-understanding expressed in the pre-Pauline baptismal formula in Gal. 3:28 could and should be realized in the midst of a society rooted in the patriarchal status divisions between Greeks and Jews, slave and free, men and wo/men, rich and poor, wise and uneducated. Especially if the notion "no longer male *and* female" meant that patriarchal marriage was no longer constitutive for the new creation in the Spirit, this was bound to create difficult practical problems in everyday life. In light of it people might have raised questions such as: Did baptism abolish all previous marriage relationships? Could one, especially a wo/man, remain marriage-free even though this was against the law? If one remained married to a pagan, what about the children? Did it mean that one could live together without being married? Did it imply that one should live as a celibate and abstain from all sexual intercourse? Was marriage only a legal, and not also a religious affair? Did wo/men just like men have control over their own body and life?

In this situation of competing interpretations and conflicting practices[64] of what it meant to realize the "new life" in Christ, the Corinthian community decided to write to different missionaries for their advice since some of their differing interpretations most likely originated in different theological emphases of these missionaries and their preaching. Thus, the Corinthians and not Paul understood God's power of salvation in the sense that John Schütz has described as Paul's own understanding of power.

> Power is not a personal attribute because power is essentially an historical force. The central role of the gospel as an interpretation of this power stems from the fact that all Christians have access to power through the gospel. The apostle may preach the gospel, he may thereby make power available but he does not himself provide it or control it.[65]

Given this understanding, the consultation of missionaries did not mean that the community would accept and obey such advice without critical evaluation and judgment in terms of their own pneumatic self-understanding. Moreover, among those asked, Paul could have appeared—at least to some—as the least qualified in terms of pneumatic competence: He preaches on the elementary level and, as for actual pastoral experience, he has not shown up for a long time and does not live a lifestyle

---

64. DuBois, *Centaurs and Amazons*, points out that in order to define the polis as a "circle of equals," the other, the alien, women, and animals were set outside the circle and in its margins. "Equals were to exchange women: those outside the circle existed in an agonistic relationship to the body of citizens. In this model of the city, however, the position of women was gradually revealed as contradictory, since women were the objects of the culture-founding act of exchange. They were excluded from the city yet necessary for its reproduction. They came to represent a potentially dangerous, even poisonous force which was both within the city and outside of it" (5). However, I suggest that the word "women" needs to be qualified here with "freeborn," since not all women are meant.

65. John Howard Schütz, *Paul and the Anatomy of Apostolic Authority* (London: Cambridge University Press, 1975), 285.

appropriate to an apostle. Paul must somehow have learned that some of the Corinthians held his pneumatic as well as his practical competence in low esteem. In order to secure their acceptance of his interpretation, he had to argue why they should follow his instructions and not those of others if these turned out to be different from his own.

If Paul had only to assert that he shared access to divine power for building up the community with the Corinthians and other apostles, we could understand 1 Corinthians 1–4 as an apology for his apostleship and spirit-filled status. Yet Paul asserts more than this when he presents himself not only as the father of the community who, in analogy to God, the Father, has begotten or brought forth the community in Christ through the gospel, but also as the one who has the power to command and to punish,[66] although he ostentatiously chooses persuasion and love. Therefore, whenever, as in 1 Cor. 11:1-16 or 1 Cor. 14:33b-40, appeals and arguments break down, he resorts to commands and claims the authority of Christ and that of other churches.

Paul's rhetoric does not aim at fostering independence, freedom, and consensus, but stresses dependence on his model, order, and decency,[67] as well as subordination and silence. His theological reasoning and skillful rhetorical argument demonstrate, however, that the rhetorical situation required persuasion but did not admit of explicitly coercive authority.[68] Whom did Paul seek to persuade to accept his interpretation as "authoritative"? Following the lead of Theissen, Bünker has argued on grounds of a formal rhetorical analysis that the intended or inscribed audience against whom Paul argues are the few members of the community of high social status and considerable education who have caused the party-strife in Corinth. However, this claim that the intended readers are those who have caused the problems in Corinth can be maintained only if 1 Corinthians is classified as forensic or judicial discourse.

In deliberative discourse the author does not seek to pass judgment but to appeal to the audience so that they will make the right decision for the future just as an orator appeals to the *ekklesia*, that is, the voting assembly of freeborn men, to make the right political decisions for the common good of the polis. If my assessment of

---

66. Cf. Christopher Forbes, "Comparison, Self-Praise and Irony: Paul's Boasting and the Conventions of Hellenistic Rhetoric," *NTS* 32 (1986), 14, who suggests two alternative models: "those of a parent with children whose position is guaranteed by his paternity and of an ambassador, whose position is guaranteed by his sender." For a different understanding, compare Bengt Holmberg, *Paul and Power: The Structure of Authority in the Primitive Church as Reflected in the Pauline Epistles* (Philadelphia: Fortress Press, 1980), 188f. For the function of the father-title in Paul's symbolic universe, cf. Norman R. Petersen, *Rediscovering Paul,* 104–50.

67. Cf. also S. Barton, "Paul and the Cross: A Sociological Approach," *Theology* 85 (1982): 13–19. "Paul augments his authority by focusing attention on how he himself interprets 'Christ crucified,' thereby increasing dependence on himself as leader" (18).

68. For different understandings of authority in antiquity and today cf. Theodor Eschenburg, *Über Autorität* (Frankfurt: Suhrkamp, 1976); Richard Sennett, *Authority* (New York: Vintage Books, 1980); Dennis H. Wrong, *Power: Its Forms, Bases, and Abuses* (New York: Harper & Row, 1979).

1 Corinthians as deliberative discourse is correct, then Paul appeals to those who, like himself, are of higher social and educational status. They should make the ecclesial decisions that in his opinion are necessary in Corinth. His emphatic recommendation of Stephanas speaks for this understanding. His "veiled hostility" and appeal to authority in the so-called women's passages indicates, however, that he does not include women of high social and educational status in this appeal.

One could object to my thesis that Paul appeals to the well-to-do and knowledgeable male members of the community by pointing to 1 Cor. 1:26-29, in which he reminds the Corinthian community that not many of them—when called—were wise, powerful, and highborn according to worldly standards. Rather, God has chosen what is foolish, weak, low, despised, even what is nothing in the world.[69] This objection is not valid, however, because Paul does not say here that God has chosen the foolish, low, weak, and despised in order to make them wise, powerful, strong, and esteemed, a theology which the baptismal self-understanding of the Christians in Corinth seems to have asserted. Paul himself confirms this theological self-understanding of the Corinthian community in the proem in which he gives thanks that in Christ Jesus the Corinthians were made rich in everything, in all speech and in all knowledge, lacking in nothing. The whole letter documents this baptismal self-understanding of the many who were nothing in the eyes of the world before their call, but who now have freedom, knowledge, wisdom, riches, and power over their own bodies and life in their new kinship-community.

This pattern of reversal—the old life is contrasted with the new, weakness with power, foolishness with wisdom—also shapes Paul's own theological pattern of cross and resurrection. But he asserts it over against the baptismal self-understanding of the Corinthians for whom being in Christ, that is, in the church, meant living the "new creation" here and now. Paul also contrasts his former life with his new life in Christ, but he sees this new life as suffering, hardships, and cross, the marks of his apostleship for which he will be recompensed in the future. This different emphasis in theological interpretation must be rooted in Paul's own experience. If, as Hock and Bünker have argued, Paul himself was of relatively high social and educational status,[70] then his experience of becoming a follower of Jesus Christ was quite different from that of the majority of the Corinthians. While for them their call meant freedom and new possibilities not open to them as poor, slave, and even freeborn women in "the eyes of the world," for Paul and those of equal social status, their call implied relinquishment of authority and status; it entailed hardship, powerlessness, and foolishness "in the eyes of the world."

69. Cf. Luise Schottroff, "Nicht viele Mächtige: Annäherungen an eine Soziologie des Urchristentums," *Bibel und Kirche* 40 (1985): 2–8.

70. Ronald Hock, "Paul's Tentmaking and the Problem of His Social Class," *JBL* 97 (1978): 555–64; Bünker, *Briefformular,* 75; Christopher Forbes, "Comparison, Self-Praise, and Irony," *NTS* 32 (1986): 1–30.

A Critical Rhetorical Model of Analysis

I have found it helpful to present graphically the interpretive model of rhetorical analysis which has been articulated and developed in chapter 5. Since a critical rhetorical method is much more complex than a unitary literary or historical method of analysis, students have appreciated being able to visualize its operations, though such a visual model necessarily simplifies intricate intellectual relations.

I begin by diagramming the horizontal axis or vector of a basic *rhetorical* model of communication (Figure 1). This horizontal axis expresses the rhetorical force of an utterance, speech, or text. It understands language as a practice and event and hence is concerned with what a linguistic event or text can "do."

Rhetor ⟶ Speech ⟶ Audience

FIGURE 1: Rhetorical Model of Oral Communication

At a first level of application, which moves from speech to writing, this rhetorical model is changed insofar as, in the process of being read, the text is not just shaped by the author but is also affected by the response of the reader. If one understands the biblical process of communication as a literary process rather than an actual speech, this model is shown in Figure 2.

Author ⟶ Text ⟷ Recipients

FIGURE 2: Literary Model of Communication

On a second level of application the attention moves from the original text of the past to its contemporary interpretation. One can see most clearly on this level that not only is the text shaped by the interpreter but also shapes her or him. Moreover, readers are not passive recipients, but they also shape the text in and through the act of reading as meaning-making act. This observation applies also to the original historical recipients insofar as speakers or authors take their audiences into account when articulating a text. The diagram of rhetorical analysis that sketches the contemporary process of interpretation then is shown in Figure 3.

Interpreter ⟷ Text ⟷ Readers

FIGURE 3: Interpretive Model of Communication

Since the Bible is a historical text, the history of its interpretation and the history of its effects (*Wirkungsgeschichte*) must also be taken into account. Many interpreters and readers in variegated historical and contemporary situations have created and constituted an interpretive tradition of the text that is often neglected when the rhetorical model of author—text—reader is simply understood as the process of present biblical interpretation unmediated by past interpretations.

This simple rhetorical model needs to be theoretically complexified through both literary reader-response criticism, speech-act theory, and historical-social analysis. The *literary* distinction between the actual historical author (A) and the implied textual author (IA) as well as that between the actual historical audience (R) and the inscribed or textualized historical recipients (IR) must be sustained on both the original historical and the contemporary levels of interpretation. One must therefore also distinguish between interpreter (I) and textualized or inscribed interpreter (TI). This distinction applies equally to all the historical levels of interpretation between today and the biblical past. Figure 4 shows the expanded rhetorical model.

I-TI ◄───► A-IA ◄───► Text ◄───► IR-R ◄───► IR-R

FIGURE 4: Expanded Rhetorical Model of Communication

LEGEND: *A = actual historical author; IA = implied textual author; R= actual historical audience; IR = inscribed or textualized historical recipients; I= interpreter; TI = textualized or inscribed interpreter*

However, the horizontal-rhetorical process is only one dimension of interpretation. Since communication does not take place in a vacuum but within a "world," one must resort to a second axis. This "world" dimension is best diagrammed with a vertical vector or axis. This vertical axis of representation is concerned with what a text can say. Most modern historical and literary biblical criticism has been primarily concerned with this referential axis of communication.

Here again one must differentiate between the historical and symbolic worlds of interpreters, authors, recipients, and readers of a biblical text and their textualized inscriptions. In short, the historical-social dimension of the rhetorical process cannot be diagrammed simply with the horizontal rhetorical axis of communication but it also needs a vertical axis of representation that can visualize the historical and symbolic world dimensions inscribed in texts and communication. Figure 5 shows the model Paul Hernadi[71] has developed in terms of literary criticism, which is indebted to Roman Jacobson.

However, Hernadi himself points to a major problem with this model:

> Despite its obvious virtues of clarity and poise, such a map has at least one grave deficiency. It creates the impression that the literary work is suspended in a timeless net of relationships between author, reader, language, and what language is about. Written texts can indeed outlast the situation in which they were produced but the other four seemingly sturdy entities are subject to historical change.[72]

In order to avoid this impression, I suggest one needs to place the (social) world onto the map as the source of all linguistic and other events and understand language as circulating between all four poles of communication: author, text, reader, world as shown in Figure 6, my modification of Hernadi's model.

71. Paul Hernadi, "Literary Theory: A Compass for Critics," *Critical Inquiry* 3 (1976): 369–86.
72. Ibid., 370

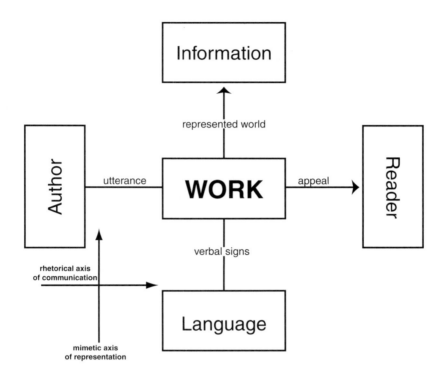

FIGURE 5: P. Hernadi's Literary Compass

Moreover, with respect to the axis of representation, one must differentiate between the actual rhetorical situation (S) and its inscription or textualization (IS) as well as between the actual ideological situation or symbolic universe (U) and the inscribed one (IU). If one does so, one can diagram the process or "dance" of interpretation as shown in Figure 7. This modified map must be seen as "doubled" since it applies to both the biblical and the contemporary levels of communication.

In short, in order to be able to distinguish between literary-rhetorical and historical-rhetorical levels of communication, a purely literary model does not suffice. Both axes of the rhetorical model of analysis, the communicative-horizontal as well as the representational-vertical one, are shaped by the "world" as reservoir of signs, as fields of action, as networks of power, and as constructions of symbolic universes. Rhetorical-textual transactions are never just linguistic-ideological but always also material practices. They do not just encompass the subject but also its world. Language is a part of the subject's world, shaped by it and shaping it.

Language may construct or imagine a different world, but it always must do so by operating and functioning in the "real" world. Consequently, neither a purely

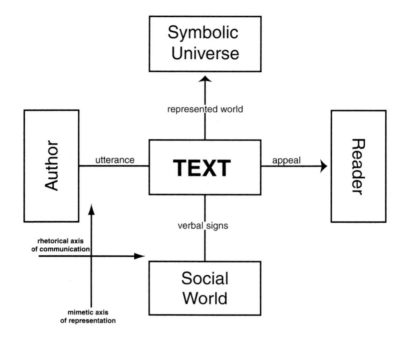

FIGURE 6: Rhetorical Revision of P. Hernadi's Literary Compass

literary nor a purely historical model or map of a biblical rhetoric of interpretation will suffice. Hence, in order to map such a model, I will again modify the map of reading that Paul Hernadi has worked out. For developing further Hernadi's model, which relies on speech act and semiotic theories, I will foreground a theory of rhetoric. Although his linguistic- and literary-based model adequately expresses rhetorical literary relations, in my view, it does not sufficiently take into account the rhetorical situation and its "world" dimension, which occasions the rhetorical speech act in the first place. I am interested here in mapping a rhetorical model in which "the world" or "reality" has a key place. Whereas Hernadi points to the "word" (*langue* and *parole*) as providing a reservoir of signs and language for the act of communication, I maintain instead that it is "the world" as "field of power" that primarily generates the significations, ideologies, and symbolic universes of the axis of representation. Figure 8 applies to both the biblical and the contemporary level of interpretation.

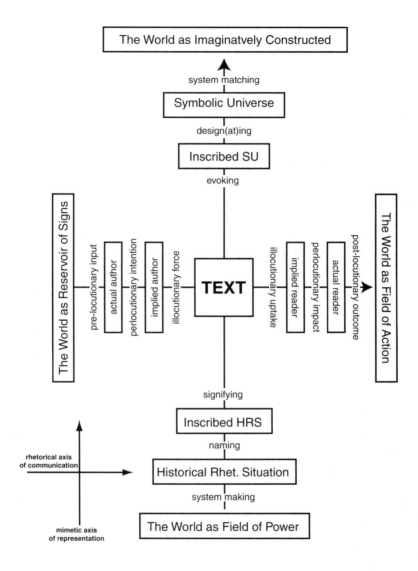

FIGURE 7: Expanded Rhetorical Compass

LEGEND: S = *actual historical situation; IS = inscription or textualization of historical situation; U = actual ideological situation or symbolic universe; IU = inscribed ideological situation or symbolic universe*

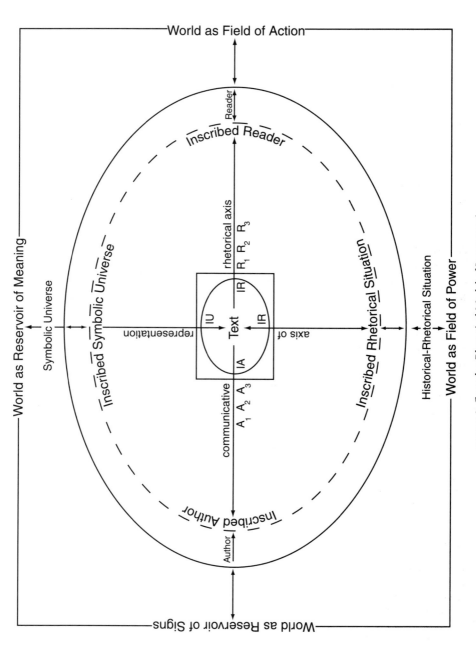

FIGURE 8: Complex Rhetorical Model of Interpretation

Chapter 6

The Rhetoricity of Historical Knowledge: Pauline Discourse and Its Contextualizations

Almost twenty years ago I had the opportunity to choose a topic for a graduate-level seminar on Jewish and Christian traditions sponsored by the Rosenstiel Foundation.[1] Hence I welcomed the opportunity to further explore the area of "religious propaganda" as an explanatory frame of meaning for interpreting Paul's correspondence and theology.[2] I invited Jewish and Christian scholars to address the problem of Greco-Roman, Jewish, and Christian religious propaganda in the first century C.E. Although during the early decades of this century considerable research had been done on the topic of religious propaganda in antiquity,[3] such research interests had almost disappeared in the intervening years, probably because of the negative political connotations of the term "propaganda." So I hoped that the subsequent publication of the invited papers would engender renewed discussion of religious propaganda among Jewish and Christian scholars.[4]

Judaism as well as Christianity had a period of great expansion at the beginning of our era. The spread of Hellenistic culture had torn down many ethnic barriers separating peoples from peoples, cultures from cultures, and religions from religions. The imperial imposition of the Pax Romana[5] made religious exchange, extensive

---

1. This chapter is a slightly revised version of "The Rhetoricity of Historical Discourse and Its Contextualizations," published in *Religious Propaganda & Missionary Competition in the New Testament World. Essays Honoring Dieter Georgi*, ed. Lukas Bormann, Kelly Del Tredici, and Angela Standhartinger (Leiden: E. J. Brill, 1994), 443–70.

2. See Dieter Georgi, *Die Gegner des Paulus im 2. Korintherbrief: Studien zur religiösen Propaganda in der Spätantike* (Neukirchen-Vluyn: Neukirchener Verlag, 1964), which was translated later as *The Opponents of Paul in Second Corinthians* (Philadelphia: Fortress Press, 1986).

3. See, e.g., M. Friedländer, *Geschichte der jüdischen Apologetik als Vorgeschichte des Christentums* (Zürich: Verlag Caesar Schmitt, 1903); K. Axenfeld, "Die jüdische Propaganda als Vorläuferin der urchristlichen Mission," *Missionswissenschaftliche Studien: Festschrift Warneck* (Berlin: Evangelische Missionsgesellschaft, 1904), 1–80; Paul Wendland, *Die hellenistisch-römische Kultur in ihren Beziehungen zu Judentum und Urchristentum* (Tübingen: J. C. B. Mohr, 1907); Frederick Milton Derwacter, *Preparing the Way for Paul: The Proselyte Movement in Later Judaism* (New York: Macmillan, 1930). See also the discussion of missionary activity in Georgi, *The Opponents*, 83–228, 358–89, 422–45.

4. Elisabeth Schüssler Fiorenza, ed., *Aspects of Religious Propaganda in Judaism and Early Christianity* (Notre Dame, Ind.: University of Notre Dame Press, 1976).

5. Cf. Klaus Wengst, *Pax Romana: Anspruch und Wirklichkeit* (Munich: Chr. Kaiser Verlag, 1986).

travel, and cultural alliances very easy. In appealing to audiences of the Greco-Roman world, Jews and Christians could utilize the means and methods of Greco-Roman rhetoric. The appropriation of such missionary propagandistic forms was indispensable if Jews and Christians were to succeed in competing with other religious associations or philosophical movements.

Centuries earlier Judaism had already confronted the task of communicating its ethos to a wider public, since over an extended period of time, Jewish faith-communities had been spreading throughout the Greco-Roman world. Still, this success of Jewish expansion also provoked anti-Semitic reactions and slanderous attacks. In order to counter such defamation, Jewish thinkers produced a body of sophisticated apologetic literature in Greek. This literature sought to convince both members of the Jewish community and gentile readers that such vilifying criticism of Judaism was not justified. Positively, Jewish writers wanted to persuade their diverse audiences of the truth, antiquity, and high moral standing of their own religion and community. In a similar fashion, early Christian writers intended to strengthen the identity of Christian audiences who shared the pluralistic ethos of the Greco-Roman world, although in many instances they were still members of Jewish communities.

In my introduction to *Aspects of Religious Propaganda* I attempted to highlight that early Christian writers engaged in rhetorical, persuasive discourses that were at home in the public political sphere.[6] Working within the methodological framework of redaction criticism, I attempted to show how the author of Acts shaped his narrative in such a way that it functioned as a persuasive argument within the context of Greco-Roman and Jewish religious propaganda. Other contributions to this volume did not concentrate on the function and form of rhetorical discourse. Instead, they circled around the Hellenistic figure of the "divine man"—a figure that was very much debated in the 1970s.[7]

In the intervening years scholarly interest in both rhetoric as a literary device and rhetoric as a cultural-religious discourse and public political practice has steadily increased in biblical studies.[8] This is due for the most part to epistemological discourses, which have rediscovered the significance of rhetoric in general, and to the theoretical discussions of historiography[9] that have underscored the rhetoricity of

6. Schüssler Fiorenza, "Miracles, Mission and Apologetics: An Introduction," in *Aspects of Religious Propaganda*, 1–26.

7. Cf. Dieter Georgi, "Socioeconomic Reasons for the 'Divine Man as a Propagandistic Pattern," in *Aspects of Religious Propaganda*, 27–42; and the discussion in his epilogue to the American edition of *The Opponents*, 390–415.

8. See, e.g., Kennedy, *Classical Rhetoric and Its Christian and Secular Tradition*, and *New Testament Interpretation;* Schüssler Fiorenza, *Bread Not Stone;* Duane F. Watson, "The New Testament and Greco-Roman Rhetoric: A Bibliography," *Journal of the Evangelical Theological Society* 31, 4 (1988): 465–72; Wuellner, "Hermeneutics and Rhetorics"; Burton L. Mack, *Rhetoric and the New Testament* (Minneapolis: Fortress, 1990).

9. Cf. Dominick Lacapra, *Rethinking Intellectual History: Texts, Contexts, Language* (Ithaca: Cornell University Press, 1983); Daniel Stempel, "History and Postmodern Literary Theory," in *Tracing Literary Theory,* ed. Joseph Natoli (Urbana: University of Illinois Press, 1987), 80–104; Pietro Rossi, ed., *Theorie der modernen Geschichtsschreibung* (Frankfurt: Suhrkamp, 1987); H. Aram Veeser, ed., *The New Historicism* (New York: Routledge, 1989).

historical texts and interpretations in particular. These theoretical explorations have shown that the choice of explanatory models, organizing images, or reconstructive paradigms depends on the sociopolitical location and communicative interests of those who produce historical knowledge.[10]

Generally, the label rhetoric/rhetorical masks persuasive speech as stylistic ornament, technical means, or linguistic manipulation, as discourse utilizing irrational, emotional devices that are contrary to critical thinking and reasoning. Academic and popular parlance continues to label those statements as "rhetoric/ rhetorical" that it wants to mark as "mere talk," stylistic figure, or deceptive propaganda. The revival of the understanding of "rhetoric" as not just a stylistic means but as persuasive discourse during the past decade or so,[11] aims at overcoming this modern academic and colloquial notion of rhetoric as deceitful and negative. Consequently, it seeks to revalorize rhetoric as a public form of discourse for the sake of liberating intellectual discourses from their captivity to so-called value-free objective "science." This understanding of rhetoric also allows for the recognition of the rhetoricity of biblical writings and contemporary historiography as well as for the articulation of a political ethos for the discipline of biblical studies.

Such a rhetorical approach will situate Paul's letters to the Corinthian community within the context of Greco-Roman political history and public discourse. Although the majority of critical scholars has constructed Paul's theology as "normative" over and against that of Paul's Gnostic (1 Corinthians) or propagandistic (2 Corinthians) *opponents,* I have tended to read the Pauline letters differently. In the hegemonic reading, Paul's remains the dominant "Christian" voice. In contrast I have sought to privilege the theological voices and visions of Paul's audience and to reconstruct Paul's theological voice as one among many.

In order to do so, I have argued in the previous chapter that a historical reading of Paul must differentiate between the textually inscribed *rhetorical situation* on the one hand and the *possible historical situation* that must be reconstructed from diverse extant sources on the other.[12]

In addition to the recovery of rhetoric as a critical discipline of inquiry, a second epistemological debate has been decisive for my own theological reading and historical reconstruction, which moves within a critical feminist framework of liberation.[13] In preparing the Rosenstiel seminar I became fascinated with the discovery—

10. See my SBL presidential address "The Ethics of Biblical Interpretation: Decentering Biblical Scholarship," *JBL* 107, 1 (1988): 3–17 (chapter 1); William A. Beardslee, "Ethics and Hermeneutics" in *Text and Logos: The Humanistic Interpretation of the New Testament,* ed. T. W. Jennings (Atlanta: Scholars Press, 1990), 15–32; D. J. Smit, "The Ethos of Interpretation."

11. For discussion of this development and relevant literature cf. Brian Vickers, ed., *Rhetoric Revalued* (Binghamton: New York University Press, 1982), and *In Defence of Rhetoric;* Beardslee, "Theology and Rhetoric in the University."

12. Schüssler Fiorenza, "Rhetorical Situation and Historical Reconstruction in 1 Corinthians," *NTS* 33 (1987): 386–403 (chapter 5); and my book *Revelation: Vision of a Just World.*

13. For the development of such a critical feminist liberationist framework see my book *Discipleship of Equals.*

mentioned in primary as well as secondary sources—that in antiquity Judaism was attacked as a "religion of wo/men" because it was believed to attract especially elite wo/men as converts.[14] The same charge is later also levied against Christian mission. Yet, since in 1973–74 feminist historical and biblical discourses were not yet available or only in the beginning stages, I did not quite know how to engage this observation and its theoretical importance for the reconstruction of early Judaism and Christianity; I lacked a theoretical framework to do so.[15] Hence I was not surprised that my colleagues also would or could not engage the question as to the participation and contribution of women to missionary propaganda.

In subsequent years the problem of how to write wo/men back into history— to use an expression of the feminist historian Joan Kelly[16]—has become one of the central questions in my own work. The question as to how one can responsibly reconstruct the participation and contribution of wo/men to early Jewish and Christian history continues to raise far-reaching methodological and hermeneutical issues. The privileging of wo/men in historical reading and scholarly discourse not only demands a different model for the sociopolitical reconstruction of women's history but also requires a critical reflection on historical scholarship and exegetical knowledge. It seeks to engender a theoretical paradigm shift in the self-understanding of biblical studies—a shift from a neopositivist "scientific" view to a rhetorical conceptualization of textual interpretation and historical reconstruction.[17]

Scientific Objectivist Frameworks

The twin epistemological problem of how to read the politics and rhetorics of ancient texts such as Paul's and of how to reconstruct Pauline history as that of the communities of wo/men and men to whom he writes, remains one of the foremost methodological problems in biblical studies. Since this problem is crucial for the theoretical debates and relations of malestream and feminist biblical scholarship, I will try to sketch its perameters and ramifications.

1. *Historical scientific criticism*[18] generally considers texts as archives, sources, and transcripts of historical facts. It reads texts in general and Pauline texts in particular

---

14. See the dissertation of Shelly Matthews, *Ladies First: The Function of Gentile Noble Women in Early Jewish and Christian Religious Propaganda,* forthcoming from Stanford University Press.

15. See Judith P. Zinsser, *History and Feminism: A Glass Half Full* (New York: Twayne Publishers, 1993), for a discussion of the historical development of feminist historiography in the United States; see Cheryl Johnson-Odim and Margaret Strobel, eds., *Expanding the Boundaries of Women's History: Essays on Women in the Third World* (Bloomington: Indiana University Press, 1992), for the history of feminism in the Third World; and Michele Perrot, ed., *Writing Women's History* (Cambridge: Blackwell, 1992), for the development of women's history in France.

16. Joan Kelly, "The Doubled Vision of Feminist Theory," in *Women, History, and Theory* (Chicago: University of Chicago Press, 1984), 51–64.

17. For a more fully developed argument and documentation, see my book *But She Said.*

18. For literature and discussion of this problem, see Archie L. Nations, "Historical Criticism and the Current Methodological Crisis," *Scottish Journal of Theology* 36 (1983): 59–71; W. S. Vorster, "The Historical Paradigm—Its Possibilities and Limitations," *Neotestamentica* 18 (1984): 104–23.

as windows on the world that give us accurate information and "data" about Pauline Christianity. Scientific descriptions of Pauline communities seek to create realistic historical accounts as though their historical narrative was an accurate transcription of how things really were. Disinterested and dispassionate scholarship is believed to enable biblical critics to step out of their own time, enter the minds and worlds of Paul's texts, and to study Pauline history or literature on its own terms, unencumbered by contemporary experiences, values, and interests.

In this research paradigm, variant scholarly accounts of the same historical information are contested with reference to *facts* rather than with reference to the rhetorical arguments that have transformed textual sources and historical events into data and facts. Positivist science does not require that the historian's narrative show *how* it is plotted, since it is supposed to be a faithful narration of what actually has happened. By asserting that a given interpretation of a Pauline text represents the objective "true" reading, scientific exegesis claims to comprehend the definitive meaning intended by the author, Paul. In privileging and legitimating one particular interpretation over other possible readings, one not only forecloses the text's multivalent meanings but also rules out alternative readings as illegitimate. If and when scholars admit that exegetical commentary is not free from rhetorical argument, they immediately assert that such argument must be restricted to showing how competing interpretations have misread the Pauline text.

Social scientific studies[19] in turn map Paul's rhetorical arguments and symbolic universe onto sociological or anthropological models of "Paul's" community and society. They maintain that their investigative research, critical methods, and explanatory models have scientific status because they are derived from the social sciences, especially from theoretical sociology and cultural anthropology. Hence anthropological and sociological biblical studies also understand their reconstructive work as an exercise in objective, social scientific criticism with universal truth claims. Consequently, they tend to take over sociological or cultural reconstructive models without problematizing their underlying theoretical frames and political implications.[20]

For instance, scholars have taken over Weber's and Troeltsch's concept of patriarchalism for describing Pauline Christianity without taking its feminist, sociological, political, or theological critiques into account. By adopting a Weberian or Durkheimian analysis,[21] scholars not only separate ideology or theology from

19. See, e.g., J. H. Elliott, "Social-Scientific Criticism of the New Testament: More on Methods and Models," *Semeia* 35 (1986): 1–34; Thomas Schmeller, *Brechungen: Urchristliche Wundercharismatiker im Prisma soziologisch orientierter Exegese* (Stuttgart: Verlag Kath. Bibelwerk, 1989), 16–49; P. F. Craffert, "Towards an Interdisciplinary Definition of the Social-Scientific Interpretation of the New Testament," *Neotestamentica* 25 (1991): 123–44.

20. For a similar critique from a different hermeneutical perspective see Mosala, *Biblical Hermeneutics of Black Theology in South Africa*, 55ff.

21. See Victoria Lee Erickson, *Where Silence Speaks: Feminism, Social Theory, and Religion* (Minneapolis: Fortress Press, 1992), for a feminist critique of Durkheim's and Weber's understanding of religion.

political and social struggles in the Roman empire but also treat the patriarchal institutionalization of some segments of early Christianity as a sociological law. Others adopt social science models such as Mary Douglas's group-grid construction, Wilson's typology of sects, or the system of honor and shame as scientific-objective givens and normative theoretical prescriptions.

Since social science models allegedly have been "tested" by the scientific disciplines of anthropology and sociology, biblical scholars claim that such scientific models enable them not only to avoid androcentrism and ethnocentrism but also to understand the cultures and peoples of the ancient Mediterranean world as they would have understood themselves. However, such a scientific reification or "naturalization" of sociological or anthropological theory overlooks that the disciplines of sociology, political theory, and cultural anthropology have also begun to reshape their "scientific" objectivist self-understandings into a rhetorical ethos.[22] Especially feminist theories have underlined the gendered character of theoretical concepts and scientific modes of investigation.[23]

The posture of scientific objectivism masks the extent to which the concept of objective science is itself a theoretical construct.[24] This rhetoric of disinterested science and presupposition-free exegesis silences reflection on the political interests and functions of biblical scholarship. Its claim to public scientific status both suppresses the rhetorical character of Paul's texts and their interpretations and obscures the power relations that constitute and shape Paul's rhetoric. Hence biblical scholarship that continues to subscribe to ostensibly value-neutral "scientific" theories not only surreptitiously advocates an apolitical reading of canonical texts, it also fails to articulate its theoretical assumptions or stand accountable for its political interests. Only when biblical studies begin to acknowledge their own social locations and interests, whether of confession, race, gender, nation, or class, will they become accountable to a wider audience.

Positivist "scientific" interpretation is conceptualized in kyriarchal (*Herr-schafts*) terms insofar as readers are compelled to submit and relinquish their own readings in favor of the seemingly unequivocal meaning of the "scientific" reading of Pauline texts. This objectivist politics of meaning obscures both the rhetoricity of the text and that of its own interpretation in its assertion to give a definite objective account of

---

22. Cf., e.g., Renato Rosaldo, *Culture and Truth: The Remaking of Social Analysis* (Boston: Beacon Press, 1989); Ball, *Transforming Political Discourse*.

23. Cf. Sandra Harding, *The Science Question in Feminism* (Ithaca: Cornell University Press, 1986); Terry R. Kandal, *The Woman Question in Classical Sociological Theory* (Miami: Florida University Press, 1988); Mary Lyndon Shanley and Carol Pateman, eds., *Feminist Interpretations and Political Theory* (University Park: Pennsylvania State University Press, 1991); Christine Farnham, ed., *The Impact of Feminist Research in the Academy* (Bloomington: Indiana University Press, 1987); Ruth A. Wallace, ed., *Feminism and Social Theory* (Newbury Park, Calif.: Sage Publications, 1989).

24. Sandra Harding, Sandra and Merrill B. Hintikka, eds., *Discovering Reality: Feminist Perspectives on Epistemology, Metaphysics, Methodology, and Philosophy* (Dordrecht, Netherlands: D. Reidel, 1983); Louise M. Antony and Charlotte Witt, eds., *A Mind of One's Own. Feminist Essays on Reason and Objectivity* (Boulder, Colo.: Westview Press, 1993).

Paul's meaning. Such a reifying politics of meaning also re-inscribes patriarchal relations by inviting identification with Paul and his arguments. In such a readerly identification with Paul's rhetoric, his insistence on his fatherly authority, for instance, allows ecclesial and academic "fathers" to claim Paul's authority for themselves.

By stressing the total chasm between the past and the present, between Paul and himself, the exegete obscures that Paul's meanings are present only in and through the words of his interpreters. Insofar as historical critical studies identify Pauline texts with Pauline reality, they obscure the *difference* between Paul's theological rhetoric and that of the early Christian communities, which Paul's text may misrepresent or silence. The scholarly rhetoric of radical differences between past and present thus serves to construct *sameness* between Paul, "his" communities, and his interpreters.[25] It does so either by identifying Paul's discourses with those of the communities to whom he writes and thereby suppressing and eradicating the historical voices and multiplex visions that are different from Paul's. Or it achieves its aim by claiming scientific authority for its own interpretations and by disqualifying those of others as biased, ideological, or as reading their own interests into the text. Finally, by understanding the "first" meaning of the Pauline text as a deposit of the definitive meaning of the author, historical biblical interpretation runs the risk of "shutting up" the "meaning" of the text in the past and turning it into an artifact of antiquity that is accessible only to the expert of biblical philology and history.

While serious scholars for the most part have abandoned extreme historical positivism, it is still widespread in popular culture. In popular discourses such "scientific" rhetoric functions to disqualify alternative critical voices as "unscientific." A sample from the article "Women and the Bible," which appeared in the popular magazine *The Atlantic Monthly* may illustrate my point:

> Scholarly work on women and the Bible faces certain inherent problems, certain inherent risks. In my talks with people in the field, the same worries were voiced by one scholar after another. A fundamental one has to do with the distinction between deriving an interpretation *from* a text and reading an interpretation *into* a text. It is one thing for a contemporary personal agenda—a desire, say to see women enjoy a position of full equality in religious institutions—to direct one's research focus. Agendas of one sort or another frequently drive scholarship. But can't they also get out of hand?[26]

Neither the scholars who "one after another" voiced their "worries," nor the writer who previously had published a similar article on Jesus in the same journal, mention here that not just feminist work but all interpretive historical scholarship faces the same risks. "Scientific" reconstructions of the Jesus of history, who is the central personification in early Christian writings, serve as a case in point. Claiming scientific accurateness and status for their own interpretations allows scholars and journalists both to remain silent about the ethico-political premises and interests of

---

25. For an exploration of sameness and difference in Pauline interpretation, see the intriguing work of Elizabeth Castelli, *Imitating Paul,* who utilizes Michel Foucault's theoretical framework for her analysis.
26. Cullen Murphy, "Women and the Bible," *The Atlantic Monthly* 272, 2 (August 1993), 64.

their own work and to stay oblivious to the ideological and disciplinary pressures of those scholarly or popular interpretive communities for whom they write.

2. *Postmodern literary and cultural criticism,*[27] in contrast to historical positivist criticism, underscore the impossibility of attaining objective historical knowledge from reading Paul's letters. Language and texts shape reality insofar as they not only transmit but also promote the values woven through the fabric of sociohistorical discourses and patriarchal societies. As texts the Pauline writings are not windows to the world but "doubled" mirrors that reflect back the image of Paul and his readers. Moreover, the social scientific language and texts of scholars are no exception. Social science texts and models are not one-dimensional and self-evident but rather perspectival, metaphorical, and constructive. If one gives a definite interpretation of a Pauline text or objective description—let's say, of Mediterranean society—one forcefully closes its meaning, insofar as texts are multilayered and engender endless possibilities of interpretation. If one gives a "definite" reading of a Pauline text one not only cuts off other possible meanings but also privileges one's own framework and model of reading as "true" over and against other interpretations.

Literary critics further argue that one commits the "referential fallacy"[28] if one assumes for instance that Paul's letters to the Corinthians reflect historical circumstances, events, or arguments as they actually took place. Formalist, deconstructivist, and rhetorical literary criticism insist that one cannot move beyond the Pauline text to the historical reality of Paul or of early Christian communities. Scientific literary analysis is only able to decipher and reconstruct the symbolic narrative world or the rhetorical strategies of the Pauline text, not the intention of its author and the arguments of its historical audience. Hence formalist literary or poststructuralist cultural theories contend that the past is *only* textual. History is only available in and through narratives and texts.

Historiography remains caught up in the undecidability of text and the multivocity of language. The rhetoricity of biblical texts and their interpretations is all that one can investigate. Historical reality is no longer accessible except as textual reality. In this view, the past is constituted as a domain of representation. "Facts" are created by the narrative acts of coding history and by the choice of narrative strategy, interpretive models, selection, plot, and closure.[29] Historians construct "scientific" historical discourse by choosing from a multiplicity of traces left by past events and by turning these symbolic traces into historical facts. Postmodern critical theory also challenges the modern progressivist dichotomy between historical reality and text,

---

27. For feminist studies see Carolyn J. Allen, "Feminist Criticism and Postmodernism," in *Tracing Literary Theory,* ed. Joseph Natoli (Urbana: University of Illinois Press, 1987), 278–305. For biblical studies, see especially Fred W. Burnett, "Postmodern Biblical Exegesis: The Eve of Historical Criticism," *Semeia* 51 (1990): 51–80, and Gary Phillips, "Exegesis as a Critical Praxis: Reclaiming History and Text from a Postmodern Perspective," *Semeia* 51 (1990): 7–50.

28. For feminist biblical studies, see, e.g., Janice Capel Anderson, "Matthew: Gender and Reading," *Semeia* 28 (1983): 3–28; Elizabeth Struthers Malbon, "Fallible Followers: Women and Men in the Gospel of Mark," *Semeia* 28 (1983): 29–48; Lone Fatum, "Women, Symbolic Universe, and Structures of Silence: Challenges and Possibilities in Androcentric Texts," *Studia Theologica* 43 (1989): 61–80.

29. White, *Tropics of Discourse.*

past and present. It insists that while ostensibly stressing the alien character of the text's world, historical narrative tells the story of ancient Greece or early Christianity by refracting the historical traces inscribed in the text into our own language and world. In the process of such a refracting, historians shape their materials by choosing a narrative frame, by selecting "data," by creating and valorizing time periods, and by ascribing significance to certain texts and methods of reading over and against others.[30] In short, historical reconstruction is linguistic re-presentation.

History is not only narrative-laden; it is also rhetorical. Scholars not only select their topics and materials but also utilize theoretical metaphors or models to organize them into a coherent argument. Models for historical reconstructions are metaphoric in the sense that metaphor is a way of describing something in terms of something else. For instance, the conception of history as seeking causal laws to explain objective facts has a mechanistic root-metaphor, whereas that of the evolution of history is based on an organic biological metaphor.[31] Moreover, historians create time-periods that reflect these root-metaphors and their politics of meaning. As a result historical periods such as Hellenism or early Christianity[32] are actually retrospective symbolic constructions that were unavailable to those historical persons living at the time.

Over and against the modern self-understanding of biblical scholarship as "scientific, objective, and disinterested," a critical postmodern paradigm of interpretation recognizes that all historical narrative is informed by our own historical-cultural position, interwoven with the values and practices of our own time, and shaped by our historical-cultural location as well as by the ways we are implicated in power relations. By underscoring the fact that all cultural forms of representation are ideologically grounded and that access to reality is always mediated through language, one can problematize and denaturalize rhetorical assertions of what is real.

To sum up, malestream and feminist biblical discourses theorize the relationship between text and reality, between historical representation and history as event, between past and present, and between the ancient and the contemporary reader either in terms of radical difference or in terms of radical identity. Those Pauline scholars who subscribe to historical criticism tend to emphasize the radical difference between contemporary interpreter and text, between our and Paul's world. Those

---

30. Feminist historians have specifically questioned the valuations of periodization. See, e.g., Joan Kelly, "Did Women Have a Renaissance?" reprinted in her *Women, History, and Theory,* 19–50.

31. See Brown, *Society as Text,* 97–112.

32. Georgi's arguments against using the marker "Christian" for the emerging communities of the Jesus movement in the Mediterranean world have their place here. I concur with him that one should abandon the exclusivist differentiation between the Jesus movement in rural Palestine and the early Christian missionary movement in the Greco-Roman urban centers, a distinction I had taken over from Social World Studies in my book *In Memory of Her.* Nevertheless, insofar as scholarly discourses have the function to classify and to order, they cannot but re-inscribe such classifications and distinctions from their location in the present. The replacement of Christian community with Jesus community does not overcome the historical split, acrimony, and violence of Christianity toward Judaism, since the name of Jesus has authorized Christian anti-Jewish practices.

who adopt literary formalism, stylistic rhetorical analysis, or poststructuralist criticism stress the impossibility of moving from text to reality, underscore the linguisticality of all knowledge, and maintain the inextricable entanglement of present interpretation and knowledge of the past.

Kyriocentric Rhetoricity and Historical Reality

A feminist sociocritical rhetoric concurs with postmodern discourse analysis that all texts, interpretations, and historical reconstructions are relative and perspectival. If what one sees depends on where one stands, social-ideological location and rhetorical context are as decisive as text for how one re-constructs historical reality or interprets biblical texts. The sociopolitical locations and interests of interpreters determine historical knowledge production. Historical reconstructions are not value-free, objective descriptions of what actually happened, but are rhetorical insofar as they rest on the theoretical models and metaphors of reality that they employ. Historical writings such as the Pauline letters do not reflect historical reality; as prescriptive and persuasive texts they construct it. Paul's texts do not just respond to the rhetorical situation but also create it.

This insight into the rhetoricity of historical knowledge, however, does not persuade a critical feminist liberationist theory either to succumb to nihilism or to advocate a value-free relativist pluralism. Rather, it compels liberationist feminists to produce a *different* knowledge and history from their perspective as insiders/outsiders or resident aliens in kyriocentric culture and academy.[33] In contrast to "ludic" postmodern[34] textualism and relativism, a critical feminist rhetoric of liberation does not abandon the modern critical interest in reconstructing the history of freedom as the past of those who have struggled for freedom, human dignity, and equality. Although we can know the past today only in and through texts and discourses, persons and events of the past are not just fictions of historical imagination.

All women and subjected men shape and have shaped culture and religion, even though classic androcentric records do not mention our existence and work.[35] Rec-

---

33. For the notion of "insider/outsider," see Patricia Hill Collins, *Black Feminist Thought: Knowledge, Consciousness, and the Politics of Empowerment* (Boston: Unwin Hyman, 1990), and for that of "resident alien," see my *But She Said.*

34. Hennessy, *Materialist Feminism and the Politics of Discourse,* proposes this distinction: "Whereas ludic postmodernism signals an emphasis on the mechanics of signification, with language understood as a formal system of differences, resistance postmodernism is concerned with the politics of the production and maintenance of subjectivities, that is, with language as a social practice" (3).

35. For instance, neither Jürgen Becker, ed., *Die Anfänge des Christentums: Alte Welt und neue Hoffnung* (Stuttgart: Kohlhammer, 1987) nor Howard C. Kee, "Sociology of the New Testament," *Harper's Bible Dictionary* (San Francisco: Harper & Row), 961–68, mentions my book *In Memory of Her* or other feminist historical works alongside, e.g., those of Judge, Meeks, or Theissen. According to such hegemonic "scientific" historical records, feminist historical work still does not exist! Yet the eclipse of feminist work by androcentric scholarly records, does not mean that in actuality such work does not exist. It only means that historians of the twenty-second century will have to consult other sources to reconstruct the history of feminist biblical scholarship.

ognizing that the past is only known to us in and through textual traces is not "the same as saying that the past is only textual as the semiotic idealism of some forms of poststructuralism seems to assert."[36] Rather, the experience and analysis of patriarchal colonization tells us that all women and subjugated men are today—and always have been—historical subjects and agents. Historical narrative representation gives not *existence* but only *meaning* to the past. Feminist liberationist scholars therefore claim the hermeneutical privilege of the oppressed for their theoretical work:

> The "master position" in any set of dominating social relations tends to produce distorted visions of the real regularities and causal tendencies in social relations. . . . The feminist standpoint epistemologies argue that because men are in the "master position" vis-à-vis women, women's social experience—conceptualized through the lenses of feminist theory—can provide the grounds for a less distorted understanding of the world around us.[37]

A postmodern symbolic criticism that eschews all historical diachronic reconstruction and rejects any attempt to give a "truer," more adequate account of the historical world[38] in which Paul and his audience lived cannot but remain ensconced in the rhetorical world projected by the kyriocentric text which seeks to maintain the status quo. If there is no possibility of reconstructing a historical world *different* from the kyriocentric world construction of the text, or if it is impossible to take a reading position different from that engineered by the text, then historical interpretation is doomed to re-inscribe the kyriarchal reality constructed by the grammatically masculine text. Consequently, a critical liberationist rhetoric maintains that one can break the hold of the androcentric text over the religious and historical imagination of its readers if one recognizes the agency of interpreters in reading texts as well as in reconstructing their sociohistorical contexts.

1. *Feminist sociocritical deconstructive readings*[39] investigate and display how, for instance, Paul's textual strategies and their subsequent interpretations are political and religious discursive practices. Communicative aims, points of view, narrative strategies, persuasive means, and authorial closure as well as audience perceptions and constructions are rhetorical practices that have determined not only the production of the Bible but also its subsequent interpretations. By interpreting the Pauline text from a particular sociotheological location, readers engage not just in a hermeneutical but also in a rhetorical practice. By carefully examining the rhetori-

---

36. Linda Hutcheon, *The Politics of Postmodernism* (London: Routledge, 1989), 81. See also Weedon, *Feminist Practice and Poststructuralist Theory.*

37. Harding, *The Science Question in Feminism,* 191. For a similar position but different accentuation, see Nancy C. M. Hartsock, *Money, Sex and Power: Toward a Feminist Historical Materialism* (New York: Longman, 1983).

38. For the discussion of this position see Judith Newton, "History as Usual? Feminism and the New Historicism," *Cultural Critique* 9 (1988): 87–121, 98.

39. Irene Harvey, "The Wellsprings of Deconstruction," in Natoli, *Tracing Literary Theory,* 127–47, and Mary Poovey, "Feminism and Deconstruction," *Feminist Studies* 14 (1988): 51–66, give an excellent introduction to the strengths and limits of deconstructive reading.

cal strategies of the androcentric Pauline text and its symbolic universes, one is able to explore not only *what* the text excludes, but also to investigate *how* the text constructs what it includes.[40]

Although feminist theory has underscored the ideological rhetoricity of grammar and language, biblical studies have not yet sufficiently theorized the far-reaching implications of a pragmatic understanding of language for reading historical source-texts. Rather, literary biblical studies have tended to adopt a framework of linguistic and symbolic determinism.[41] However, only a pragmatic understanding of language can break through the ideological strategies of androcentric language and grammar. Androcentric texts marginalize all wo/men and subordinated men, subsume them under generic elite male terms, and through kyriocentric inscriptions eradicate altogether the historical presence of those marginalized. Thus, androcentric, grammatically masculine texts are not simply descriptive reflections of reality. Rather, as kyriocentric texts they produce linguistically the marginality and absence of all wo/men from public historical consciousness. How one reads the "silences" of the unmarked grammatically masculine Pauline text and how one fills in its "blank spaces" depends on how one contextualizes one's reading in specific historical political experience.[42]

If readers understand language not as a closed linguistic system but as a social convention and communicative tool, they can become accountable for their own readings, which they negotiate and create in specific contexts and situations. For instance, in their interaction with a Pauline textual convention such as the masculine address "brothers," readers must decide how to read this androcentric appellation. Whether they read this expression in a generic or in a gender-specific way depends both on their judgment of Paul's specific linguistic and social contexts and on their own social experience and ideological interests. If language is not a straitjacket into which our thoughts must be forced, that is, if it is not a naturalized closed system but rather a medium which is affected by social conditions and which changes in response to social changes, then writing, translation, and interpretation become the sites of struggle for change.[43]

"Scientific" interpretation that does not critically undermine but continues to "naturalize" the rhetorical strategies of the kyriocentric text cannot but reproduce its historical perspective and symbolic universe. It is bound to deepen the historical silence about wo/men and all those whom patriarchal and kyriarchal historical texts marginalize or erase them from historical consciousness. Only if one reads the kyri-

---

40. Adrienne Munich, "Notorious Signs: Feminist Criticism and Literary Tradition," in *Making a Difference,* ed. Greene and Kahn, 256.

41. For such a distinction see Deborah Cameron, *Feminism and Linguistic Theory* (London: Macmillan, 1985).

42. Karen Dugger, "Social Location and Gender-Role Attitudes: A Comparison of Black and White Women," *Gender and Society* 2 (1988): 425–48; Carole Ann Taylor, "Positioning Subjects and Objects: Agency, Narration, Rationality," *Hypatia* 8 (1993): 55–80.

43. For a similar stress on the reader's agency and the possibility of change, see, e.g., Fowler, "Postmodern Biblical Criticism."

ocentric text against its androcentric grain and makes those whom the text marginalizes or does not mention at all central to historical reconstruction is one able to break the text's ideological hold over its readers. If Pauline texts construct at one and the same time both the reality that brought them forth and the reality to which they respond, then this reality is accessible to us not only in the world that they display but also in all that they repress or marginalize. Hence one cannot simply follow the directives for reading that are inscribed in the surface of the Pauline text. Rather, one must interrogate the power-knowledge relations structuring both Pauline texts and the discourses of Pauline studies.

One can do so because androcentric language and male-authored texts presuppose all wo/men's and subjected men's historical presence and agency although for the most part they do not articulate it. True, the relationship between kyriocentric text and historical reality cannot be construed as a window or a mirror-image. Nevertheless, it can be decoded as a complex ideological construction.[44] Consequently, the kyriocentric text's rhetorical silences, contradictions, arguments, prescriptions, and projections, its discourses on gender, race, class, culture, or religion can be exposed as the ideological inscriptions that they are.

2. *A critical feminist historiography* seeks both to break the hold of the kyriocentric Pauline text over historical imagination and to explore the textual exclusions and "scientific" choices that constitute the historical knowledge of early Jewish and Christian discourses in the Greco-Roman world. In so doing, it aims to make present the different voices inscribed both in the text and in its ancient and contemporary contexts. To that end it exploits the contradictions and silences inscribed in the text for reconstructing not only the symbolic "world of the biblical text," but also the sociohistorical worlds that have made possible the particular world construction of the text.

As a rhetorical communicative practice, a sociocritical feminist historiography does not seek to sunder text and reality, whether in an antiquarian or in a formalist fashion. Rather, its "texts" seek to re-construct and to construct a *different* sociohistorical reality. By analyzing the sociopolitical functions of Pauline texts as well as by articulating adequate models for historical reconstruction, it seeks to displace the dualistic inscriptions of the andro- and kyriocentric text. It does not deny but recognizes that Pauline texts are rhetorical texts, produced in and by particular historical debates and struggles. Andro- and kyriocentric texts tell communal stories, narrate social worlds, and construct symbolic universes that mythologize, reverse, absolutize, and idealize patriarchal differences. In so doing, such texts obliterate or marginalize the historical presence of the devalued "others." For

---

44. Rosemary Hennessy, "Women's Lives/Feminist Knowledge: Feminist Standpoint as Ideology Critique," *Hypatia* 8 (1993): 14–34. Hence, it is inappropriate either to restrict ideological criticism to feminist and sociohistorical readings or to assume that social science interpretation provides "intertextual data" about the Mediterranean world for a socio-rhetorical reading as if social-scientific readings were not also perspectival and ideological. For such an argument, see Robbins, "Using a Socio-Rhetorical Poetics to Develop a Unified Method."

instance, if scholars read the prescriptive texts of the Pauline tradition that advocate patriarchal submission as descriptive of the patriarchal institutionalization process in early Christianity, they valorize this kyriarchal rhetorics by re-inscribing it as early Christian history.

A feminist sociocritical rhetoric argues that an emancipatory reconstruction of early Judaism and Christianity in the Greco-Roman world becomes possible if one interfaces the kyriocentric text with a reconstructive historical model that can bring to the fore the contributions of those marginalized or silenced by the classical or sacred text. Pauline rhetorical discourses create a world in which those whose arguments they oppose either become the "deviant others" or are no longer heard at all. On the one hand an inclusive reconstructive historical model allows one to interrogate the persuasive strategies of the canonical or classic text and its author as well as to focus on the subjugated knowledges and submerged voices inscribed in their discourses. On the other hand such a model enables one to dislodge texts from their androcentric or kyriocentric frame of reference (*Herr-schaftsrahmen*) and to reassemble and recontextualize them in a different frame of meaning.

Such a "doubled" process of historical interpretation could be likened to the quilting of a patchwork or to the creating of a mosaic. The image of quilting[45] rather than that of reporting is an apt metaphor for a postmodern liberationist understanding of the historian's task. This process of the displacement of androcentric source-texts that have generated the politics of submission and rhetorics of otherness and of their reorganization together with all other available information in an emancipatory historical model, reconstructs historical-social "reality" not as a "given fact" but as a plausible "subtext" to the kyriocentric text. Such a reconstructive historical model of early Jewish and Christian struggles and arguments about the "politics and rhetorics of patriarchal submission" allows one to understand the cultural dependencies and effects generated by these debates and struggles. The validity and adequacy of this as of all historical reconstruction must be judged on whether it can make centrally present as historical agents and speaking subjects those whom the kyriocentric text marginalizes or excludes.[46]

"Religious Propaganda" in a "Doubled" Process of Interpretation

Such a "doubled" mode of sociocritical rhetorical analysis also can shed light on the debate on religious propaganda in antiquity. If one contextualizes both the inter-

45. A fuller elaboration of this organizing metaphor can be found in my article "'Quilting' Women's History: Phoebe of Cenchreae," originally published in *Lessons from Women's Lives*, ed. Judith Long (Syracuse, N.Y.: Syracuse University Maxwell School of Citizenship and Public Affairs, 1984): 22–29; reprinted in *Embodied Love: Sensuality and Relationship as Feminist Values*, ed. Paula M. Cooey, Sharon A. Farmer, and Mary Ellen Ross (San Francisco: Harper & Row, 1987), 35–50.

46. See also my article "Text and Reality—Reality as Text," and the proposal of Joan W. Scott, "Deconstructing Equality-Versus-Difference: Or the Uses of Poststructuralist Theory for Feminism," *Feminist Studies* 14 (1988) 33–50.

pretations of Paul's correspondence to the Corinthians and the discussions on early Jewish and early Christian propaganda in the ancient world within a reconstructive emancipatory framework, one is struck by the dualistic conceptualizations of both. Exegetical discourses continue to understand the writings of the Christian Testament[47] either theologically as documents of inner-Christian struggles between different parties, groups, and theologies. Or they read them sociologically as records of opposing sectarian groups that are defined in contrast to the institutionalized church. In both instances, scholars understand early Christian canonical writings as products of doctrinal, especially christological controversy and sectarian strife rather than as cultural religious rhetorical practices.

Moreover, scholars tend to conceptualize not only the literature but also the history of early Christianity in terms of dualistic oppositions and exclusivist dichotomies. Thus they fail to reconstruct the history of early Christian literatures and communities as the history of communicative persuasion, emancipatory struggles, and common visions. This failure is compounded by the inclination to rend early Christianity from early Judaism, to split mission from apologetics, and to delineate strict boundaries between inside and outside, between Mediterranean culture and ours. In so doing, scholars disregard that the self-understanding of religious communities is intertwined with their cultural-religious environment and overlook that communication or historical reconstruction is only possible if and when one can assume some kind of common language and symbolic universe.

As I have argued above, this research situation invites a "doubled" critical strategy of exploration. It invites a deconstructive reading that interrogates the pervasive kyriocentric dualisms on one hand and on the other a historical-political reconstructive rhetoric that reassembles available information and retells ancient history within the framework of an emancipatory democratic paradigm.

1. *A deconstructive reading* has three key moments: (a) it investigates key organizing models and structuring images of scholarship;[48] (b) it scrutinizes tacit assumptions and unconscious premises; and (c) it suspects the historical critical discourses' interestedness in coherence, univocity, and symbolic totality.

(a) As we have seen, the discourses on Paul's theology and ancient propaganda construct a series of dualistic religious, cultural, and political oppositions such as orthodoxy-heresy, community-market, honor-shame, mission-propaganda, and apologetics-rhetorics, rather than underscoring democratic values such as differences, pluriformity, equality, and deliberation. This series of dualisms privileges the

---

47. Since the designations Old Testament and New Testament as parts of the Christian Bible suggest anti-Jewish supersessionism, I generally attempt to replace the appellation *New Testament* with *Christian Testament,* a designation that points to the Christian authorship and ownership of first-century canonical writings. Other scholars use *First and Second Testament* to underscore the secondary character of the New Testament. Yet a widely accepted solution is not likely to emerge as long as popular and academic Christian discourses maintain the kind of theological supersessionist anti-Jewish rhetoric associated with the appellation *New Testament.*

48. See my early article "Women in the Pre–Pauline and Pauline Churches," *Union Seminary Quarterly Review* 33 (1978): 153–66.

first term of the opposition by claiming it either for Paul, orthodoxy, Christianity, Judaism, or hegemonic patriarchal culture, and constructing the second term as "other" by attributing it to, for example, the opponents, Hellenistic propagandists, Jewish legalists, and so on. Such interpretive dualistic oppositions obfuscate the third linking series of terms such as "audience, community, assembly" by subsuming it under either pole of the opposition. The most telling dualistic construct is that of gender, which is already inscribed in the Pauline letters insofar as Paul understands himself as the "father" of the Corinthian community who presents the community "as a pure bride to her one husband," Christ (2 Cor. 11:2-3). This genderization of the community has negative overtones since it is connected with a reference to the seduction of Eve. The symbolic construct of gender dualism at once coheres in and undermines the other oppositions insofar as it casts all speaking subjects (Paul, the serpent, the opponents, the interpreters, etc.) as *masculine* and construes their audience (the Corinthian community, early Judaism, the Greco-Roman world, the readers, etc.) in *feminine* terms as passive, immature, and gullible.

(b) The tacit assumption underlying such dualistic constructions is the supposition that the actual rhetorical situation and its historical power relations are identical to and correspond with the rhetorical situation inscribed in the Pauline correspondence[49] or in other textual sources. In other words, such dualistic oppositions presuppose the "scientific" theoretical understanding of texts either as windows or as mirrors and thereby mystify the rhetoricity of text and language. Such a premise privileges the "masculine" hegemonic voice inscribed in kyriarchal Pauline or other ancient source-texts rather than particularizing and relativizing this voice by reconstructing a varied assembly of voices.[50] Such a reconstruction of a pluriform congregation of fully responsible "adult" voices who have equal standing becomes possible only if one deconstructs the gendered conceptualization of dualistic oppositions. It would require that one re-construct a radical democratic historical model that can comprehend the disputes in the Corinthian *ekklesia* in terms of *parresia*—the free speech of citizens—rather than cast them in terms of confessional internecine altercations or imperial market competition.

(c) A postmodern deconstructive reading must name the drive to coherence, unity, and identity as the motivating ideological force in Pauline studies, a drive that engenders the oppositional models and rhetorical assumptions of the prevalent gendered discourses on Pauline theology and religious propaganda. This drive comes to the fore, for instance, in the attempts of Pauline scholarship to declare texts such as 1 Cor. 11:2-16 and 14:34-36 as later interpolations because they do not cohere with the reigning scholarly appreciation of Paul's theology. Or scholars rearrange the extant text and reconstruct the rhetorical situation of the diverse fragments of Paul's Corinthian correspondence in such a way that the symbolic coherence of Paul's theological argument is safeguarded. Feminist theorists have unmasked this drive to

---

49. Cf. Elizabeth Castelli, "Interpretations of Power in 1 Corinthians," *Semeia* 54 (1992): 159–96.

50. Cf., e.g., my article "Missionaries, Coworkers, and Apostles," and Clark Wire, *The Corinthian Women Prophets*.

coherent reading, univocity, and symbolic totality as the western "logic of identity" and "politics of otherness."[51] This "politics and rhetorics of othering" establishes identity either by declaring the difference of the other as the same or by vilifying and idealizing difference as otherness.[52] It justifies relationships of ruling[53] by obfuscating structures of domination and subordination as "naturalized" differences. Ancient and modern philosophy have developed the ideological "politics and rhetorics of otherness" in the attempt to legitimate that not all but only certain people can claim the rights of citizens, participate in democratic government, or deliberate in public debate.[54]

2. *A postmodern emancipatory historiography*, however, does not cease with a deconstructive reading. Rather, it seeks to displace the politics and rhetorics of subordination and otherness with a politics and rhetorics of equality and multivocity. My interpretive work has sought to develop such a reconstructive historical model that valorizes difference, plurivocity, and democratic participation. It conceives of early Christian writings as taking sides in the emancipatory struggles of antiquity and conceptualizes early Christian community as a democratic assembly (*ekklesia*) of differing voices and sociorhetorical practices. The differences and contradictions in the rhetoric of early Christian sources point to sociopolitical conflicts and religiocultural tensions between Hellenistic, Jewish, or early Christian "egalitarian" movements and their dominant patriarchal Greco-Roman, Jewish, and emerging Christian sociopolitical contexts.

These differing and contradictory sociorhetorical practices also point to sociopolitical conflicts *within* early Christian communities. Such rhetorical tensions can be traced between those who advocate both the ethos of the *ekklesia* as a "basileia discipleship of equals" and as "a community of freedom in the Spirit" on the one hand, and those hegemonic discourses once more emerging within segments of the Christian community that advocate patriarchal leadership and organization on the other hand. The latter arguments for a politics and rhetorics of submission seek to reintroduce the patriarchal division between the public and private spheres, between those who speak and those who are silent, between women and men, between slaves and free, between Jews and Greeks in the *ekklesia*. They argue for relegating (elite) married women to the private sphere, for restricting their activity to proper "feminine" behavior, and for limiting women's leadership. Their arguments for the "ethics and politics of submission" not only engender restrictions against women's

51. For discussion and literature on the "politics of otherness," see Schüssler Fiorenza, "The Politics of Otherness."

52. Cf. Bartky, *Femininity and Domination*.

53. For this expression, see Dorothy E. Smith, *The Conceptual Practices of Power: A Feminist Sociology of Knowledge* (Boston: Northeastern University Press, 1990).

54. For the development of the "political philosophy of otherness" as legitimizing patriarchal societal structures of domination in antiquity, see Moller Okin, *Women in Western Political Thought*, 15–98; Elizabeth V. Spelman, *Inessential Woman: Problems of Exclusion in Feminist Thought* (Boston: Beacon Press, 1988), 19–56; and especially duBois, *Centaurs and Amazons*.

leadership but also promote acceptance of slave women's sufferings as well as advocate the adaptation of the whole community to hegemonic kyriarchal structures.[55]

Pluralistic reconstructive historical models like this one enable readers to displace the "scientific" dualistic paradigm of sectarian conflicts and exclusions and to recontextualize early Christian debates within Greco-Roman and Jewish public democratic discourses. In such a new contextualization early Christian writings can be read as public arguments that seek to persuade and convince "citizens" who share the same religious and cultural worlds. Rather than mapping religious propaganda in a negative dualistic way and dividing it into two discrete areas, mission and apologetics, a rhetorical democratic model of analysis can understand missionary and apologetic discourses as the two sides of one and the same rhetorical "coin."

A sociocritical rhetorical model of historical reconstruction must distinguish, however, between "imperial" kyriarchal and emancipatory "egalitarian" forms of propagandistic functions, aspirations, and institutions and may not consolidate them as oppositional discrete formations. Rather it should seek to reconceptualize "religious propaganda" as a site of interacting rhetorical-political and cultural-religious practices. In so doing it may not privilege the authorial voice of the canonical or classic text but must position itself on the side of the historical victims and their subjugated knowledges.

Such a sociocritical rhetorical model could be likened to a nesting doll. Just like the Russian doll in which smaller dolls fit inside ever bigger ones, so a feminist liberationist reconstruction of the historical tensions and struggles between imperial patriarchy and self-determining *ekklesia* in Greco-Roman society, early Judaism, and early Christianity seeks to situate the religious history of women within early Christian history, within Jewish history, within Greco-Roman history, and within the history of western society, rather than playing one of these against the other. However, such a conflictive model of historical reconstruction would be misapprehended if it were read either in terms of linear development or in terms of rapid and uncontested decline from *ekklesia* as the discipleship of equals to *ekklesia* as the patriarchal household of God.

But such a historical-emancipatory conceptualization of the politics of *ekklesia* in terms of ongoing struggles to change structures of domination should not be misread in a positivist sense as descriptive of "how it actually was." Rather, it must be understood as a critical rhetorical and hermeneutical proposal. Although I have sought to defend against its misreading in terms of "pristine origins," scholars continue to misapprehend the feminist reconstruction of early Christian beginnings that I have proposed in *In Memory of Her* as constituting a "golden age" that then allegedly functions in a theological way as a "canon within the canon."

This insistence of some colleagues that the book has to be understood as a historical "golden age" account that provides a hermeneutical-theological *discrimen*

---

55. For the fuller development of such an emancipatory reconstructive argument, see my article "A Discipleship of Equals: Ekklesial Democracy and Patriarchy in Biblical Perspective," in *A Democratic Catholic Church*, ed. Eugene C. Bianchi and Rosemary Radford Ruether (New York: Crossroad, 1992).

persists. That it does so over and against my repeated protests against such a mis-reading is odd to say the least. One is therefore compelled to ask: What is at stake in this debate? I want to explore this question here with reference to one of my attentive readers and sophisticated critics.

Wayne Meeks most recently has raised again the issue of the "golden age" character of *In Memory of Her*. In a discussion on the hermeneutical problem of the biblical slavery texts,[56] he cites my historical reading of the household code rather than my hermeneutical discussion of it in *Bread Not Stone*. Yet he does not ask what makes his book, *The First Urban Christians,* a historical account of the social world of the apostle Paul rather than a "golden age" account although both of our works adopt a similar approach of "social world criticism," albeit in quite different ways. Is it because his book is more historically positivist and less hermeneutically explicit? He, like many others, seems not to understand the shift in perspective required by a critical feminist interpretation. To ask for the possibility of wo/men's historical agency is not to ask for "pristine beginnings" or to look for a "golden age" in order to justify Christianity. To ask for wo/men's early Christian heritage is *not* to ask for a canonical *discrimen* that would allow one to assert theologically a "canon within the canon." Rather, it asks for a paradigm shift from a kyriarchal to a feminist historiography.

In addition, it is regrettable that Meeks conveniently overlooks (or does not know any of my hermeneutical discussions, since he does not refer to them) that I myself have raised all the objections against such a "golden age" and "canon within the canon" hermeneutic that he alleges I advance. Whether intended or not, such a stereotyping of my position relegates it to a naïve foundationalism that bespeaks feminist ideological zeal. If Meeks had looked at my hermeneutical work, however, he could have seen that the following hermeneutical proposal he advocates at the end of his article comes very close to the hermeneutical position I have advanced, for instance, in *But She Said* and revisited in the chapters of this book.

> Moral argument is a matter of persuasion and consensus always grounded in a particular historical situation. The job of hermeneutics is to set the rules for a fair argument. One job of Christian moral formation is to create practices and occasions that will nurture "the daily habit of fellow feeling" so as to shape a moral intuition appropriate to the gospel. . . . At least one rule of thumb then emerges for ethical use of the Bible: whenever the Christian community seeks to reform itself, it must take steps to make sure that among the voices interpreting the tradition are those of the ones who have experienced harm from that tradition.[57]

I could not agree more. However, I would add that such a hermeneutical rule should apply not only to the churches but also to the academy and its scholarly

---

56. Wayne A. Meeks, "The 'Haustafeln' and American Slavery: A Hermeneutical Challenge," in *Theology and Ethics in Paul and His Interpreters: Essays in Honor of Victor Paul Furnish,* ed. Eugene H. Lovering Jr., and Jerry L. Sumney (Nashville: Abingdon Press, 1996), 232–53.

57. Ibid., 252f.

discourses. If that were the case, then those who are genuinely interested in such a rule of thumb would need to hear more accurately the voices from the margins rather than trying to put their "new wine into old wineskins."

In sum, a feminist historical reconstruction and evaluative interpretation for liberation seeks to recover the biblical past as shaped by women and men for the sake of the present and the future. It does not simply "apply" or translate the solutions of the past to the problems of the present, but its historical imagination seeks to reconstruct the socio-ecclesial world of biblical writings in order to open them up for critical inquiry and theological reflection. Studying the biblical past in order to name the destructive aspects of its language and symbolic universe as well as to recover its unfulfilled historical possibilities becomes a primary task for biblical scholarship.

Instead, this model seeks to conceptualize early Christianities and their struggles as a pluriform movement of wo/men and men engaged in an ongoing debate over equality and full "citizenship." If the exegetical reconstruction of Pauline debates is interfaced with an intercultural and interreligious reconstructive historical model, one can show that such emancipatory rhetorical practices and sociopolitical religious struggles for freedom[58] and the right of "citizenship" began long before the Christian movements emerged on the scene. They have continued throughout western history and still go on today. The recognition of the rhetoricity of Pauline discourses allows scholars to position their research within the ongoing history of such struggles.

---

58. Orlando Patterson, *Freedom*, vol. 1, *Freedom in the Making of Western Culture* (New York: HarperCollins Publishers, 1991) claims to be the first such emancipatory history of freedom. It seems not accidental that his historical reconstruction of the struggles for freedom in antiquity recognizes wo/men's crucial participation in and contribution to these struggles.

Chapter 7

Ideology, Power, and Interpretation: Galatians 3:28

It is only appropriate to explore the topic ideology, power, and interpretation[1] with reference to the interpretation of Gal. 3:28: There is neither Jew nor Greek, there is neither slave nor free, there is neither male and female.[2] This passage always has been a bone of contention in both biblical exegesis and the scriptural articulation of equality, which has inspired Christian liberation movements throughout the centuries. Whereas those struggling for change have cited Gal. 3:28 as the Magna Carta of freedom, equality, and equivalence, malestream exegesis has sought to explain away Gal. 3:28's radical theological claim to equality or to evaporate it eschatologically. Nevertheless, in more recent feminist work this text is also controverted. Hence, I will focus on recent feminist interpretations of it that stand in tension with my own egalitarian reading, in order to explore the difference a critical feminist theoretical lens can bring to the interpretation of this passage.

Ideology, Power, and Interpretation

Feminist literary critics have pointed out that readers do not engage texts "in themselves." Rather, insofar as readers have been taught *how* to read, they activate reading paradigms.[3] Reading paradigms determine the selection of methods and provide the interpretive frameworks and theoretical perspectives of reading. They organize the practice of reading insofar as they relate texts, readers, and contexts to one another in specific ways. Both professional and nonprofessional readers draw on the "frame of meaning"[4] and the contextualization provided by the symbolic-religious constructions of social-cultural worlds, which they usually share, of the texts they read. Hence scholars must become conscious of and explicate the

---

1. This chapter was prepared for a conference "Ideology, Power, and Interpretation" that took place in August 1997 at Selly Oaks College in Birmingham, England. Parts of it also appear in a different form in *Berliner Theologische Zeitschrift* (Berlin: Wichern-Verlag, 1999).

2. οὐκ ἔνι Ἰουδαῖος οὐδὲ Ἕλλην, ουκ ἔνι δοῦλς οὐδὲ ελεύθερος, οὐκ ἔνι ἄρσεν και θῆλυ: πάντες γὰρ ὑμεῖς ἕις ἔστε.

3. Kolodny, "Dancing through the Minefield," in *Feminist Criticism,* ed. Showalter, 153.

4. For the expression "frame of meaning," cf. Anthony Giddens, *New Rules of Sociological Methods: A Positive Critique of Interpretative Sociologists* (New York: Basic Books, 1976), 64.

reading frameworks, "lenses," or "eyeglasses" with which they approach biblical texts.[5] Therefore I have affirmed throughout this book that my own lens is that of a critical feminist hermeneutic and rhetoric of liberation. Such a feminist perspective is radically egalitarian in the original sense of the word, if one understands radical as "complete, thorough, without compromise, totally, from the ground up."

Ideology Critique

Although feminist theory and hermeneutics has understood itself from its very inception as ideology critique, even progressive voices in biblical studies do not acknowledge this. Instead, they prefer to speak of cultural criticism and ideology critique as a pluralistic disciplinary umbrella paradigm under which feminist, postcolonialist, and liberation theological hermeneutics can be subsumed. Such a choice of cultural criticism as the umbrella paradigm for diverse methodological approaches in biblical studies fits into the liberal ethos of the university because cultural studies tend not to explicitly thematize and critique oppressive sociopolitical power relations.

Feminist theory and theology have articulated a fourfold critique of ideology and power. This critique is not only a critique of reason and rationality, of science and knowledge production, of academic disciplines and language, but it is also especially a critique of the sex/gender system understood as oppressive power relation and ideology. Since gender assumptions determine the intellectual frameworks of interpretation or the lenses with which scholars read Gal. 3:28, I will explore the kyriarchal ideology that multiplicates racism, class exploitation, colonialism, and gender as basic structures of oppression and marginalization.

Feminist theory and theology primarily have problematized the ideological construct of polarized gender relations. With Michèle Barrett, however, feminist studies understand ideology no longer simply as "false consciousness" but as a "generic term for the processes by which meaning is produced, challenged, reproduced, and transformed."[6] A critical feminist hermeneutics of liberation does not define the category of sex/gender in dualistic anthropological terms but conceptualizes it as a political-cultural-religious category that funds western societies as heterosexual. The modern ideology of the two-gender system that counts as commonsense knowledge reduces the manifold differences between humans to a naturally given, metaphysically determined, or divinely ordained essential difference. It does not see, however, that this difference is a social construct of oppressive power relations. Exegesis of Gal. 3:26-29 employs such a pre-critical gender concept whenever it argues that the pre-Pauline

5. In light of new developments in the field, I have reformulated the last two categories of the typology of the four hegemonic reading paradigms in biblical studies that I elaborated in *Bread Not Stone* (see note 20) so that I would now map the following four: the doctrinal-theological, the scientific-literary/historical, the cultural-postmodern, and the emancipatory-feminist/postcolonial paradigm. Such methodological paradigms must be distinguished although they are interfaced with different feminist theoretical paradigms to map the field of feminist biblical studies. (See chapter 2.)

6. Michèle Barrett, *Women's Oppression Today: Problems in Marxist Feminist Analysis* (London: NLB, 1980), 97.

baptismal formula sabotages the "order of creation" because it envisions the abolition of gender duality and propagates allegedly Gnostic androgyny or transvestism.

Instead, I argue, gender must be understood as a historical construct.[7] Thomas Laqueur, for instance, has shown that a decisive shift took place in modernity from the ancient one-sex model to the present dichotomous two-sex model.[8] For thousands of years it was considered commonsense knowledge that wo/men had the same sex and genitals as men except that they were inside wo/men's bodies whereas men's were outside. The vagina was understood as an interior penis, the labia as foreskin, the uterus as scrotum, and the ovaries as testicles.

Not sex but gender as a cultural category was primary and part of the order of things. What it meant to be a man or a woman was determined by social rank and by one's place in society, not by sexual organs. As man or woman one had to perform a cultural role according to one's social status rather than be organically one of two incommensurable sexes. Not sex but the social status of the elite propertied male heads of household determined superior gender status. The ancients did not need the facts of sexual difference to support the claim that women were inferior to men and therefore subordinate beings.

Beginning with the Enlightenment the two-sex model, the notion that there are two stable, incommensurable, opposite sexes, emerges. Now it is held that the economic, political, and cultural lives of women and men, their gender roles, are based on these two different sexes that are biologically given. Just as in antiquity the body was seen as reflecting the cosmic order, so in modernity the body and sexuality were seen as representing and legitimating the social-political order. Social and political changes wrought by the Enlightenment produced the change from the one-sex to the two-sex model. Since the universalistic claims for human liberty and equality did not include freeborn wo/men, arguments had to be fashioned if men were to justify their dominance of the public domain, whose difference to the private world of wo/men was figured in terms of sexual difference.

Moreover, the promise of democracy that wo/men and disenfranchised men could achieve civic and personal liberties generated a new kind of antifeminist argument on the basis of nature, physiology, and science. Those who opposed the democratic participation of freeborn wo/men, for instance, generated evidence for wo/men's mental and physical unsuitability for the public sphere and argued that their bodies and biology made them unfit for it. The doctrine of separate spheres for men and wo/men thus has engendered the dual-sex model. It also has modified the notion of a hierarchy or, better, kyriarchy of men. In antifeminist and feminist discourses "woman" is no longer construed as *lesser man* but as totally different from man, as a being of a "purer race," as an "angelic species" less affected by sexual drives and desires. Since wo/men have to be excluded from the new civil society because

7. See my article "Gender," in *The Encyclopedia of Politics and Religion* (Washington, D.C.: Congressional Quarterly Books, 1998), 290–94.

8. Thomas Laqueur, *Making Sex: Body and Gender from the Greeks to Freud* (Cambridge, Mass.: Harvard University Press, 1990).

of their biology, catalogues of physical and moral differences seek to insure that woman and man ought not to resemble each other in mind any more than in looks. Two incommensurable sexes are the result of these discursive exclusionary practices.

Similar arguments were put forward to exclude the so-called darker races and uncivilized savages from assuming civic responsibilities and powers. The distinction between biological sex and cultural gender as well as between race and ethnicity that has become common sense even in feminist discourses is an ideological product and process of antifeminist as well as emancipatory Enlightenment discourses that have located differences within the dualistic framework of the modern sex-gender system.

Among the variegated feminist theories of ideology, it is Rosemary Hennessy's work I have found most helpful for critically reflecting on and reformulating the notions of "woman" and gender. Hennessy has theorized feminism as a critical practice for bringing about change in the lives and status of wo/men by elaborating Althusser's notion of ideology and Gramsci's concept of hegemony. She begins by positioning her own materialist feminist theory between two feminist discourses in the West and asks how so-called French feminist theory and North American standpoint theory construct the basic analytic feminist category "*woman.*" Whereas postmodern French feminism focuses on the "priority of systems of signification, takes the unconscious as a privileged area of exploration, and in some versions, contends that wo/men have no position in the symbolic order from which to speak," North American feminism tends to "treat woman as a 'self'" and language as a "transparent communication." Hennessy critically evaluates both feminist discourses and assesses them as unsatisfactory if one understands feminism both as a political movement and as a theory that can "make sense" out of a world marked by oppression and dehumanization.

By reading so-called French feminist and North American standpoint theories in conjunction with and critically against each other, Hennessy seeks to develop an "analytic" that extends postmodern and feminist critiques of the centered subject without giving up a belief in and a commitment to the possibility of transformative social change.[9] To that end she critically problematizes Althusser's notion of ideology and especially his concept of interpellation as too subversive of agency.[10] She finds his theory of language helpful, however, because it understands language as "social action" and as the means through which subjects are fashioned. Ideology produces discourses that can be seen, heard, spoken, proclaimed, printed, believed, valued—in other words, all that counts as socially determined reality. "To say that ideology is a material force in that it (re)produces what counts as reality suggests that other material forces, both economic and political, are not merely reflected in ideology but that they too are at least in part shaped by ideology."[11]

9. See Hennessy, *Materialist Feminism and the Politics of Discourse,* 33–36.

10. Louis Althusser, *Essays on Ideology* (London: Verso, 1984), 36–45. According to Althusser, "an ideology represents the imaginary relationship of individuals to their real conditions of existence."

11. Hennessy, *Materialist Feminism,* 75.

Such a concept of ideology seeks to correct empiricist-positivist understandings of "reality" as outside of discourse. It does so by including "the discursive within the materiality" out of which the social is produced. Hence one must distinguish between the "raw material," the real object (that is, the actual world) on the one hand and the discursively elaborated real as the object of knowledge on the other. The clear implication for feminist biblical discourses consists not only in the insight that "reality," whether that of the Pauline communities or that of women's experience, is always already an ideological construct shaped by the cultural languages and theoretical frameworks of particular historical moments. It also means that such ideological discourses as Gal. 3:28 construct the reality about which they speak.

Hennessy then goes on to elaborate this notion of ideology in terms of the concept of hegemony Gramsci has developed. In Gramsci's theory hegemony is understood and defined as a process whereby a ruling group comes to dominate by establishing the cultural "common sense." Cultural power is not simply exercised from the top down, but rather is negotiated and contested in a process of discursive articulation.[12] The assumption of "natural" sex/gender differences, for instance, informs everyday experience and turns it into so-called commonsense knowledge that makes gender or racial differences appear to be "commonplace" and "G*d given." It serves as a preconstructed frame of meaning for biblical and theological readings that understand the modern sex/gender system of masculine and feminine differences in positivistic terms either as a natural-historical fact or as a metaphysical essence that is given or revealed rather than socially constructed.

By presenting the sex/gender system as universal and "common sense," this preconstructed ideological frame of meaning obscures and mystifies the reality that the very notion of two sexes is a sociocultural construct formulated for maintaining kyriarchal domination rather than a biological "given" or innate essence. It makes us forget that not so long ago racial and national differences were, and still are considered by some today, as natural biological facts, as ontological difference, or as ordained by G*d. In order to get hold of the complex nature of oppression, feminist ideology critique cannot limit itself to the category of sex/gender but must always also include an analysis of race, class, and colonialism because wo/men *as wo/men* are determined by these power structures and ideologies. Consequently, Gal. 3:28 is best understood as espousing a counterideology to that of kyriarchy. It does not just announce the invalidity of kyriarchal gender ideology but also of ethnic, religious, and status differences.

Most of the interpretations of Gal. 3:28c work with the ideological framework of so-called natural gender differences that have been produced by and institutionalized in and through patriarchal marriage. The "hidden" frame of meaning that governs malestream as well as feminist interpretation is that of the modern kyriarchal sex/gender system. This western sex/gender ideology operates simultaneously on four discursive levels: first, on the *sociopolitical* level; second, on the *ethical-symbolic*

---

12. Hennessy, *Materialist Feminism*, 76.

level; third, on the *biological-natural* level; and finally, on the *linguistic-grammatical* level. These levels are interactive and mutually reinforce each other. Different feminist approaches enter their critical analyses at different nodal points of these interlocking discursive levels and hence emphasize different aspects of the sex/gender system. Neither "male nor female" in v. 28c seems to advocate an equality that abolishes all gender differences in the messianic corporation which is grammatically signified as masculine.

The Discursive Construction of Gal. 3:28

It is therefore not surprising that the meaning of Gal. 3:28 is still very much controverted not only in malestream but also in feminist biblical interpretation. But whereas malestream exegesis has debated whether the text means social-ecclesial equality or speaks of a spiritual eschatological or transcendent reality, feminist and postmodern interpretations ask whether this text can be considered to be liberating or whether it must be judged to promote patriarchal ideology that takes maleness and sonship as its theological standard. This dispute also centers on the question as to whether the text constitutes the theological climax of Paul's theology, which he then explicates in the whole letter, or whether it is a pre-Pauline liturgical tradition that Paul corrects and modifies. It remains further controverted whether this text speaks of egalitarian sociopolitical and cultural-religious status differences or whether "male" and "female" in Gal. 3:28c alludes to the myth of primordial androgyny.

Form critical analyses converge in the delineation and classification of Gal. 3:26-28 as a baptismal formula that is quoted by Paul.

1.	3:26a	For you are all children of God
2.	3:27a	For as many as were baptized into Christ
	b	have put on Christ
3.	3:28a	There is [valid] neither Jew nor Greek
	b	There is neither slave nor free
	c	There is no male and female
4.	3:28d	For you are all one[13]

Though scholars differ on the delineation of the individual lines, they agree that the core of the traditional formula is Gal. 3:28abc. The three parallel statements of v. 28 express the self-understanding of the newly baptized. Because of the oppositional pair Jew/Greek, exegetes assume that this text was formulated in a Jewish-Hellenistic community. Therefore it seems reasonable to attribute this baptismal confession to the pre-Pauline missionary movement, which probably centered

---

13. ²⁶Πάντες γὰρ υἱοὶ θεοῦ ἐστε διὰ τῆς πίστεως ἐν Χριστῷ Ἰησοῦ.
    ²⁷ὅσοι γὰρ εἰς Χριστὸν ἐβαπτίσθητε, Χριστὸν ἐνεδύσασθε·
    ²⁸οὐκ ἔνι Ἰουδαῖος οὐδὲ Ἕλλην,
       οὐκ ἔνι δοῦλος οὐδὲ ἐλεύθερος,
       οὐκ ἔνι ἄρσεν καὶ θῆλυ·
    πάντες γὰρ ὑμεις εἷς ἐστε ἐν Χριστῷ Ἰησοῦ. (NA²⁶)

around Antioch, and to see it as an integral part of this movement's theology of the Spirit rather than as a theological "peak formulation" of Paul.

Hans Dieter Betz has acknowledged that commentaries on Galatians "have consistently denied that Paul's statements have political implications." Such commentaries are prepared in Betz's view to state the opposite of what Paul actually says in order to preserve a "purely religious" interpretation. In doing so, they tend to emphasize the reality of equality before God sacramentally and at the same time to "deny that any conclusions can be drawn from this in regard to the ecclesiastical offices [*sic*] and the political order."[14]

Others argue that Gal. 3:28 does not yet reflect the same notion of anthropological unification and androcentric perspective that has determined the understanding of equality found in later Gnostic and patristic writings. According to various Gnostic and patristic texts, becoming a disciple means for a woman becoming "male" and "like man," because the male principle stands for the heavenly, angelic, divine realm, whereas the female principle represents either human weakness or evil. While patristic and Gnostic writers could express the equality of Christian women with men only as "manliness" or as vilification of wo/men's sexuality, Gal. 3:28 extols not ontological maleness but the social oneness of the messianic community in which social, cultural, religious, national, and biological gender divisions and status differences are no longer valid. On this reading the pre-Pauline formula Gal. 3:28 rejects all structures of domination. Not the love patriarchalism of the post-Pauline school, but this egalitarian ethos of "equality in the Spirit" expresses the vision and praxis of the Early Christian missionary movement.

The Ideological Function of Kyriocentric Language

Feminist ideological suspicion is first of all directed toward andro-kyriocentric, that is, grammatically masculine languages and symbol-systems of domination. Western languages including Hebrew, Greek, and Latin are androcentric or, better, kyriocentric languages that claim to function as generic languages that include wo/men. They mention wo/men only if they are the exceptions to the rule, if they cause problems, or in cases of direct address, or in order to inculcate feminine behavior. Normally they subsume wo/men under grammatically masculine terms, whose inclusive or exclusive meaning must be established with reference to their literary and historical contexts. The ambiguity of kyriocentric language that engenders the epistemological problem of how to understand historical sources and their interpretations has until now not received sufficient attention in biblical scholarship. It has been discussed as the problem of liturgical language but not as an epistemological-hermeneutical problem that requires new research.

In order to understand and translate Gal. 3:26-29, one needs to ask, for instance, whether the expressions "Jew/Greek, slave/free" mean only men or whether they include wo/men so that wo/men as a matter of course belong to these

---

14. Betz, *Galatians*, 189.

groups. However, if the first pairs include both men and women, then the question arises as to how the third pair "male and female" (ἄρσεν καὶ θῆλυ) is to be understood. For it would be redundant to add "men and wo/men" to the other two pairs. As Krister Stendahl pointed out a long time ago, "male and female" seems to allude to Gen. 1:27, a text that relates sex/gender to procreation and was understood as referring to marriage.

The androcentric language of Gal. 3:28 must be translated, I suggest, as generic language to mean: "neither Jewish nor Greek wo/men, neither slave nor freeborn wo/men, neither husband and wife." Such a translation does not suppress the notion that the first two pairs of the baptismal proclamation, Jews and Greeks, slaves and free are gendered. It also underscores that patriarchal marriage is at the root of the kyriarchal sociopolitical status system that reproduces kyriarchy and is produced by it. In short, gender is overdetermined by kyriarchal structures and differently constructed for freeborn wo/men or slave wo/men, for Jewish or Gentile wo/men, for Roman or Asian wo/men.

One must ask whether Paul masculinizes the generic language of the baptismal formula or whether he still understands it in generic terms as to include wo/men, since the baptismal formula Gal. 3:28 is framed in v. 26 and v. 29 by the kyriocentric Pauline statements that the baptized are sons of G*d, Abraham's offspring, and heirs according to the promise. Gal. 4:1-7 explicates the meaning of "sons of G*d" in Gal. 3:26-29. Paul applies a legal metaphor (vv. 1-2) to the present situation of the Galatians (v.3) and explicates it in vv. 4-6 with traditional christological formulae and legal concepts. Verse 7 draws the conclusion in terms of the pronouncements in 3:26 and 29: "Therefore you are no longer a slave but a son, and if a son then also an heir through G*d."

The observation of andro- and kyriocentric language also makes it clear why Paul did not add this phrase in 1 Cor. 12:13,[15] since he addresses problems in 1 Corinthians 7 that relate to sexuality and marriage. The same applies to the enumeration in Col. 3:11,[16] which is followed in 3:18 by so-called *Haustafela* (household code), the rules for the household, which begin with the exhortation of wives to subordinate themselves to their husbands.

In a careful analysis of the extant materials on circumcision, Judith Lieu[17] has pointed out that—as far as we can tell from written and inscriptional[18] evidence— no clear ritualization and theological understanding of wo/men's conversion to Judaism existed in the first century. However, at the turn from the first to the second century, a clarification of the status of proselytes and an explication of the understanding and rite of conversion seems to have occurred. Shaye Cohen has argued, for

15. καὶ γὰρ ἐν ἑνὶ πνεύματι ἡμεῖς πάντες εἰς ἓν σῶμα ἐβαπτίσθημεν, εἴτε Ἰουδαῖοι εἴτε Ἕλληνες, εἴτε δοῦλοι εἴτε ἐλεύθεροι, καὶ πάντες ἓν πνεῦμα ἐποτίσθημεν. (NA²⁶)

16. ὅπου οὐκ ἔνι Ἕλλην καὶ Ἰουδαῖος, περιτομὴ καὶ ἀκροβυστία, βάρβαρος Σκύθης, δοῦλος, ἐλεύθερος, ἀλλα τα πάντα και ἓν πᾶσιν Χριστός. (NA²⁶)

17. Judith Lieu, "Circumcision, Women, and Salvation," *NTS* 40 (1994): 358–70.

18. See Bernadette Brooten, *Women Leaders in the Ancient Synagogue* (Chico, Calif.: Scholars Press, 1982).

instance, that one of the factors in developing a structured ritual may have been the needs of wo/men converts.[19] Hence one may assume that this discussion was already developing in the first century. Accordingly, Lieu reads the exchange between Justin, the Christian, and Trypho, the Jew, as part of this ongoing debate.

Against the Jew Trypho, who insisted that the provisions of the Torah regarding sabbath observance, circumcision, new moons, and purity were eternal, Justin argues that they were late and temporary. He cites Abraham, Isaac, Jacob, Noah, and Job as having failed to observe them, and then adds: "I might also cite Sarah, the wife of Abraham, Rebecca, the wife of Isaac, Rachel, the wife of Jacob and Leah, and all the other such women up to the Mother of Moses, the faithful servant, who observed none of these—do you think they will be saved?" (Dial. 46.3)

Interestingly, this argument lists the foremothers in terms of their family status as wives and mothers. If, as in Greco-Roman religion,[20] a tradition existed in Judaism that defined the membership of wo/men in terms of their affiliation as wives and mothers, then the declaration in Gal. 3:28c could be understood as standing over and against this tradition.[21]

Earlier in the debate Justin had sought to refute Trypho's argument that circumcision was already enjoined upon Abraham by making reference to the biblical wo/men. Justin argues that wo/men are part of the people of God, they predate the giving of the commandment of circumcision to Abraham and his sons, but are excluded from circumcision by their very nature of not having a penis.

> Furthermore, that the female sex is unable to receive fleshly circumcision demonstrates that this circumcision was given as a sign and not as a work of righteousness. For God made women equally able to observe all that is right and virtuous. We see that in physical form male and female have been made differently, but we are confident that neither is righteous or unrighteous on this basis but only on the basis of piety and righteousness. (*Dial. Sav.* 23.5)

This argument fits with the tenor of the pre-Pauline baptismal formula. It also underscores that Paul's argument is contrary to it.

---

19. See Shaye Cohen's articles: "The Rabbinic Conversion Ceremony," *Journal of Jewish Studies* 41 (1990): 177–203; "Crossing the Boundaries and Becoming a Jew," *HTR* 82 (1989): 13–33; "The Origins of the Matrilineal Principle in Rabbinic Law," *AJSR* 10 (1985): 19–53.

20. See my discussion of the household-code trajectory in *In Memory of Her* and *Bread Not Stone.* See also Clarice Martin, "The Haustafeln," in *Stony the Road We Trod,* ed. Felder, 206–31.

21. Lieu, "Circumcision, Women, and Salvation," 369, cites my statement, "If it was no longer circumcision but baptism which was the primary rite of initiation, then women became full members of the people of God with the same rights and duties" (*In Memory of Her,* 210). Granted that this statement is ambiguous, I still would want to insist that the baptismal formula asserted the full membership of women—independently of male family affiliation—with the full rights and duties of "citizenship" in the *ekklesia*. With this assertion I did not and do not want to suggest that women were not full members in Judaism. However, in light of my analysis above, I would no longer follow the lead of Paul and connect this assertion with his debate on circumcision.

Equality and Difference

Such an interpretation of Gal. 3:28 in terms of radical social-religious equality has become contentious in recent years, however, because in postmodern discourses equality is understood as sameness and univocity that negates difference. Gal. 3:26-29 seems to express an ethos of domination that negates differences and aims for standardization. This is the case if the text is read in such a way that it does declare all differences between Jews and Greeks, slave and free, male and female as abolished. Moreover, the text seems not only to take as its standard and *tertium comparationis* the Messiah, the One, for articulating the equality of the baptized, it also declares that they all have become "sons" and a single one (εἷς not ἐν). Equality seems to be understood here as uniformity that does not admit of differences. If such a notion of equality is connected with the claim to orthodoxy, religious differences will no longer be positively acknowledged but seen as a sign of unorthodox syncretism.

The classic concept of equality goes back to Aristotle, who demands that equals should be treated the same but unequals should be dealt with differently.[22] Equals are to be considered as equal, unequals as unequal. This Aristotelian definition of equality has produced considerable inequalities because its standard and *tertium comparationis* for being human has been—and still is—the elite propertied educated man, the lord, master, father of the household. He is the measure for what it means to be human; he defines who or what is equal and who therefore can expect equal rights, and who or what is unequal and hence must be treated differently.[23]

This classic concept of equality does not admit of differences. Since it measures equality with a single criterion, it cannot but negate difference and see it as something to be overcome and eradicated. This leveling notion of equality functions as an oppressive concept insofar as it legitimates inequalities in the name of uniformity. Either you are like a white, educated, propertied man, and you can expect that you will be treated in the same way, or you are not like such an elite man and will then be treated differently from him and hence as unequal.

It was—and still is today—the elite western educated propertied Christian "Man of Reason" who has either defined the others as deficient in comparison to himself or who has idealized them in a romantic fashion. Kyriarchal equality, that is, equality that takes as its standard the lord/master/husband/father, has propagated colonialist Eurocentrism, which under the cover of equality and democracy has co-opted or exploited other peoples and cultures. Its rhetorics of equality, understood as uniformity and sameness, has engendered and perpetuated racist theories and practices that needed to prove that certain people could not be treated as equals because they were different. Postmodern theorists argue, therefore, that striving for emancipation, equality, and liberation always also engenders forms of domination and dehumanization. But whereas Christian universalism has legitimated the negation

22. Lisa Schmuckli, *Differenzen und Dissonanzen: Zugänge zu feministischen Erkenntnistheorien in der Postmoderne* (Königstein/Taunus: Ulrike Helmer Verlag, 1996), 346ff.

23. Birgit Rommelpacher, *Dominanzkultur: Texte zu Fremdheit und Macht* (Berlin: Orlanda Frauenverlag, 1995), 346.

of differences with reference to monotheism or biblical texts such as Gal. 3:28, Enlightenment philosophy, in the name of reason, has connected the ideal of equality of all human beings with the politics of inequality.[24]

However, the recognition of the problematic sense of equality does not mean that one should abandon the term. It means only that equality must be defined differently. Over and against some postmodern theories, it must be stressed that inequalities are not engendered by emancipatory movements and theories of equality, which seek to overcome such unequal otherness. Rather, they are produced by the institutional structures of heterosexism, racism, class prejudice, and colonialism that continue to reinforce differences as inequalities.

Such an understanding of equality as kyriocentric uniformity, however, does not sufficiently scrutinize the notion of difference that it seeks to rehabilitate. One could argue that it is not equality but the interests of domination that manufacture difference and dissimilarity as inequality. Kyriarchal differences manifest themselves as inequalities that are re-inscribed through structures of socialization and domination. Racism, colonialism, anti-Judaism, poverty, and heterosexism turn most people not just into totally others but into deficient others.

In contrast, difference can also be understood as multiplicity, pluriformity, and variety that is not constituted in and through kyriarchal exclusions but in and through self-determination and responsibility, as the claiming of one's own possibilities and potentials. Oppressed and marginalized groups of people derive their notion of equality from the self-understanding that they have achieved in liberation struggles.

From a feminist liberationist perspective difference can mean both: (a) structures of oppression and ideologies that determine the life of wo/men according to kyriarchal standards; and (b) societal-ecclesial structures of potentiality, cultural-religious visions, and emancipatory heritage. Both meanings—difference as kyriarchal inequality and difference as cultural-religious diversity, as rich heterogeneity of power and possibilities—constitute the complex problematic of "equality and difference." This is the theoretical horizon within which, today, the interpretation of Gal. 3:28 and the discussion of its ideological language necessarily must move.

Galatians 3:28 as a Focal Point of Feminist Debate

Recent feminist interpretations of Gal. 3:28 utilize gender as their interpretive framework to interrupt or perpetuate kyriarchal relations of domination and dehumanization. They understand language "as a social action" in and through which subjects are constituted. In constrast to malestream exegetes, I am not so much interested to establish and defend here a single, "correct" interpretation of Gal. 3:28, which is

24. Rommelspacher, *Dominanzkultur,* 19: John Locke and Thomas Hobbes for instance justify British colonialism with the argument that people who behave *irrationally* should not be treated as human beings but more like animals or machines. If rationality constitutes humanness, then according to their logic, only rational persons can expect to be treated with respect as humans.

usually one's own. Rather, I am concerned to investigate the ideological implications of the text for Christian identity formation and to scrutinize the contemporary frameworks of interpretation with which it is read.

Male Texts and the Community of Men

The Danish feminist Lone Fatum has forcefully protested against an inclusive reading of Gal. 3:28 and its reconstructive intentions. She herself argues on the basis of a textual and historical understanding that masculine grammatical texts must be understood literally as meaning what they state. If Paul, for instance, says "brothers," then he means brothers. The Pauline communities were male clubs that allowed women only marginal membership under male conditions.

From such a positivistic feminist point of view no normative value can be ascribed to Gal. 3:28. It is not at all the case that in Christ equality has been achieved as a historical fact and that the difference between men and women has been abolished in principle. The opposite is the case. Therefore she argues that injunctions to subordination like those in 1 Cor. 11:2-16 must be given the same weight hermeneutically as Gal. 3:28. At the same time it is necessary to interpret the whole text of Gal. 3:26-29 and not just v. 28. However, Fatum herself does not read Galatians 3 and 1 Corinthians 11 dialectically against each other but understands Gal. 3:28c in terms of 1 Cor. 11:2-3.

Moreover, Fatum's approach relies heavily on the opposition Jew-Greek when she presupposes that Paul has formulated the notions of equality and unity in antithesis to the Jewish law. According to her

> the concepts of unity and equality in the Christian fellowship of life are so independent of the law—and should thus also be applied by the brothers independently of the law—as to include woman on the terms of man in exactly the same way as the Greek is included on the terms of the Jew and the slave on those of the freeborn.[25]

In Fatum's view, Paul discusses the conflict in Galatia from the perspective of the freeborn Jewish male and addresses only the brothers in Galatia. His insistence on freedom from the law produces the "either-or" quality of his argumentation. Freedom from the law and the same opportunities on the grounds of faith are promised, however, only to the sons of G*d.

Fatum understands the expression "male and female" of Gal. 3:28c with reference to Gen. 1:27 in an anthropological rather than a sociological way. She interprets it in the sense that sexuality and gender differentiation are abolished in Christ.

> [V]. 28c does not relate to social categories. Man and woman are not considered here as social modes or types in relation to each other, but male and female are viewed

---

25. Fatum, "Image of God and Glory of Man: Women in Pauline Congregations," in *Image of God and Gender Models in Judeo-Christian Tradition,* Kari Elisabeth Børresen, ed. (Oslo: Solum Forlag, 1991), 64; see also Fatum, "Women, Symbolic Universe, and Structures of Silence: Challenges and Possibilities in Androcentric Texts," *Studia Theologica* 43 (1989): 56–137; and "1Thessalonians," in *Searching the Scriptures,* vol. 2, ed. Schüssler Fiorenza, 2:250–62.

together as one comprehensive expression of human sexuality. An annulment of sexuality is tantamount to an annulment of gender differentiation.[26]

Hence one is hermeneutically not permitted to draw social consequences from verse 28c. Asexuality allows a woman to be seen as a full human being, but she can understand herself only as male, son, or brother before God.[27]

> The freedom and equality of asexuality as the consequence of baptism thus implies that in Christ the woman is no longer at one with her sexuality and her reproductive functions but on the contrary, as a son of God she has become like a man in God's image. She is no longer female in relation to male; she is male.[28]

It becomes clear here that Fatum works with a modern naturalized gender concept that identifies gender with sexuality and understands sexuality itself as a natural given, not social-cultural construct. Fatum also does not consider that the notion of *son* in Galatians does not need to be understood in a naturalized biological sense. Rather, it could also be read as referring to the legal language of Roman inheritance law according to which only the son but not the daughter could become legally a fully responsible adult.

In 4:1-2 Paul likens the status of a minor heir to that of a slave. Although he is potentially the legal owner, he is under the supervision and control of a legal guardian (*epitropos*) and of the administrator of the household. Both exercise the *patria potestas* until the time when, according to the testament of the father, the heir becomes emancipated and is given free access to the inheritance. The metaphor in 4:1-2 is drawn from Roman family law according to which the *pater familias* held the *patria potestas*—the power over the children—and the *dominica potestas*—the ownership of the household. The Roman *familia* or household included not only children and relatives legally dependent on the head of the family but also slaves. Adoption made one a full member of the *familia*, subject to the *patria potestas* and entitled to inheritance.[29] According to Francis Lyal it is birth or adoption and not the death of the father that made children heirs.[30] On the death of the *pater familias* adult male heirs are not seen to receive his property but to acquire control over it.

Daughters remained under the *patria potestas* even after their father's death and often also after they got married. The *pater familias* decided whether at marriage his

---

26. Fatum, "Image of God and Glory of Man," 66.

27. Ibid., 65.

28. Ibid., 70.

29. The power of the Roman *pater familias* was without parallel in Greek law. It extended to the determination of life and death over all the members of the household. The *pater familias* had control over persons, personal relationships, income, assets, and possessions of all the members of the *familia* who had not been emancipated legally. He had not only the benefit of their acquisitions and transactions but was also liable for them. This was true for children and relatives as well as for slaves. Sons of any age with their offspring remained subject to the authority of the *pater familias*, but they were emancipated upon his death or at a time chosen by him. Minors were given a legal guardian who had extensive powers of control not only over property but also over personal conduct, which paralleled those of the *patria potestas*.

30. Francis Lyall, *Slaves, Citizens, Sons: Legal Metaphors in the Epistles* (Grand Rapids, Mich.: Zondervan, 1984).

daughter would remain in his power or would be emancipated from it into the power of her husband or of a legal guardian. Only if the marriage was contracted with *manus* (subjection to the "hand" of the husband) was the daughter transferred from the authority of her father to the power of her husband. Upon the death of the *pater familias* the custody of all daughters, not only of minors, as in the case of sons, would pass to the next male relative unless the father had designated another guardian in his will.[31] Only a very few women, such as the vestals or those freeborn and freed who had borne three or four children, were exempt in the first century from guardianship. Although practically guardianship had often become a formality, legally women remained minors under the tutelage of a guardian all their lives.

In Gal. 4:3 Paul applies this legal metaphor to all the baptized whether they were Jewish or Gentile in origin. In their pre-Christian situation they all had the status of minors or slaves. Gentiles were enslaved to cosmic powers, whereas Jews had the Law as a pedagogue or master over them which had the function to curb or prevent transgression during their bondage to sin (cf. Gal. 3:19-25). However, G*d has sent the son Jesus Christ who was born as a Jew, to free those under the supervision of the guardian so that the baptized could be adopted as sons and receive the spirit of G*d's son. Therefore the Galatians are no longer slaves but "sons" and, as "sons," heirs.

It is obvious that here Paul does not employ the legal metaphor of the patriarchal Roman *familia* in order to exclude wo/men or to legitimate patriarchal relationships of control and dependence. Rather, the opposite is the case. The text uses this metaphor in order to profile the freedom, inheritance, and independence of the new status of baptized persons as "sons." The Pauline letters are full of symbols and metaphors derived from the social universe of the patriarchal *familia,* which integrates the kinship and master-slave systems.[32] These symbols probably have shaped not only Christian religious but also social self-understanding, since the distinction between the sociopolitical and the religious-cultural is a modern distinction. Although Galatians applies the concepts of fatherhood and lordship to G*d and Christ, it does not understand them in terms of either the *patria potestas* (power of the father) or the *dominica potestas* (power of the Lord). Since the text acknowledges the status of Christians as legally free and adult "sons" who are emancipated from any guardianship and control, and thus are full members of the *ekklesia,* its aim is freedom and responsibility rather than kyriarchal dependence and enslavement.

Such a status of freedom, political-religious independence, and responsibility in the *ekklesia,* however, could not be signified with the symbol *daughter* since according to Roman law daughters had the legal status of "minors." Not masculinity or sexuality but the legal status of the emancipated adult "son" and full citizen seems to have determined the choice of "son" as a preferred early Christian symbol for characterizing the status of the members of the *ekklesia.* It is not the dependence and obedience of children, who as minors were like slaves under the power and control

---

31. However, if adult women did not receive the approval of their guardians, they could appeal to the magistrates or have a different guardian appointed.

32. For this distinction, see Petersen, *Rediscovering Paul.*

of the *pater familias,* but the freedom, authority, and responsibility of adults that characterize the status of the baptized in the *familia* of G*d. If one does not "naturalize" and "biologize" androcentric language and text, as Fatum does, one can understand "son" as an inclusive concept and translate it in such a way that it is not restricted to males only.

Subversion of Phallocentrism

Brigitte Kahl has accepted the theoretical challenge of Fatum, who understands Galatians as a letter addressed to males only. She consequently seeks to investigate the letter as to whether it advocates phallocentrism.

> One would be justified to call Paul's letter to the Galatians the most "phallocentric" document of the New Testament. Nowhere else is pure maleness so much underscored as the center of a deeply theological and highly emotional debate: foreskin, circumcision, sperm, castration— to name only some of the relevant terms. Paul even links the gospel to male anatomy coining the unique terms "gospel of the foreskin" and "gospel of circumcision" (2:7). For most translations this seems too much exhibitionism. They prefer more discrete, less compromising terms such as "gospel for the Gentiles" and "gospel for the Jews" or at the most "gospel for the circumcised/uncircumcised."[33]

With such a provocative link between male body and gospel Paul seeks to address the central problem of Galatians, why non-Jews who have become full members of the messianic community of Jesus are not allowed to become circumcised. At the center of the dispute are questions of the Galatian men such as "Who are we? What rules of behavior are still valid? Are we uncircumcised men not really men, but a third gender? Is not being circumcised and belonging to Israel an identity definition of women?"

Moreover, in Kahl's view the matrix of Galatians is the Genesis story, the core narrative of the peoplehood of Israel. Paul uses the Genesis story in order to develop, so to speak, a messianic spermat(he)ology that defines Jewish monotheism in an antihierarchical and inclusive-universal sense. Through the faith gene *pi* (= *pistis*), all the faithful become in principle offspring and heirs of Abraham. Only being the offspring of G*d *the* Father and the nonbiological father Abraham counts any longer.

However, Kahl's positive reading does not problematize that Paul's theological nomenclature re-inscribes patriarchal genealogical relationships though he spiritualizes and metaphorizes them. Whereas the baptismal formula Gal. 3:28 attempts to eliminate every "normal" genealogical, social, and political hierarchy, Paul reintegrates this egalitarian vision into a patriarchal framework.

---

33. Brigitte Kahl, "Der Brief an die Gemeinden in Galatien: Vom Unbehagen der Geschlechter und anderen Problemen des Andersseins," in *Kompendium feministischer Bibelauslegung,* ed. Luise Schottroff and Marie-Therese Wacker (Gütersloh: Chr. Kaiser Gütersloher Verlagshaus, 1998), 604. See also Kahl's paper "No Longer Male: Masculinity Struggles behind Gal 3:28?" presented at the SBL Panel on Gal. 3:28, Orlando, Florida, 1998.

Kahl agrees that Gal. 3:28 seeks to denaturalize masculine and feminine images and to liberate from biologically fixated role expectations, gender stereotypes, and patriarchal marriage ideals. However, she attributes this ideology and critical achievement to Paul rather than to the *ekklesia* in which Paul participated. She concedes that Paul uses for his argumentation patriarchally defined language and that he does not mention real wo/men even once. But she does not utilize a hermeneutics of suspicion for exploring this insight further. Rather, she looks for positive elements in Paul's androcentric discourse. Hence she stresses that in chapter 4 "the mothers"— the mother of Jesus (4:4), the mother Jerusalem (4:25f.), the mother Hagar (4:24f.31), the mother Sarah (4:31), and the "mother" Paul (4:19)—are central figures. Although the androcentric language of the letter does not address wo/men in the community, they are not totally absent. Rather, they surface again in the images of Hagar and Sarah, the slave and the freeborn wo/man.

Yet, as Sheila Briggs has pointed out, the allegory of Gal. 4:21-31 depends on metaphors taken from the institution of slavery and the sexual use of wo/men in slavery. "One may argue that Paul's use of the language of slavery in figurative speech did not constitute an endorsement of slavery in the social realm; however, one cannot simply sever the rhetorical strategy from the content of discourse."[34]

This allegory re-inscribes not only the social division between freeborn and slave women in absolute and metaphysical terms but also constructs wo/men in terms of the cultural formation of motherhood. It does so in order to underscore the cultural-religious "status difference" between Jews and Greeks.

> All identity markers and perhaps also combat terms of an exclusivist-separatist Judaism, which rejects from a superior position the Pauline praxis of mission as a betrayal of Jewishness . . . are positioned on the wrong side of the equation: Sinai covenant, biological fatherhood of Abraham (national identity), contemporary Jerusalem are listed in the same rubric with slavery, Non-Israel (Arabia/Hagar), flesh. On the opposite side of the Spirit appear Israel and Non-Israel together (we/you 4:28.31) under the motherhood of Sarah, the heavenly Jerusalem, as (biologically) fatherless children of Abraham in virtue of the promise.[35]

Whereas the metaphor of the "taskmaster" who disciplines children and that of the son as free mature adult citizen could be read in a "developmental fashion" as saying, "you have been immature children, but now you are free adults," in the context of the "two mother" metaphor—the climax of the whole argument in chapters 3 and 4—it must be read as exclusive: The children of the slave wo/man have a totally different status than those of the freeborn wo/man.

Thus Paul uses these metaphors from the Scriptures in order to rewrite Gal. 3:28. First, he displaces "Greeks" (a political cultural term) with the religiously determined term "Gentile." He thus rewrites the first pair of the baptismal formula, which asserted that no sociopolitical or cultural-religious status difference between Jews and Greeks any longer exists or is valid, to mean that there is an absolute status difference

---

34. Sheila Briggs, "Galatians," in *Searching the Scriptures*, ed. Elisabeth Schüssler Fiorenza, 2:224.
35. Kahl, "Der Brief an die Gemeinden in Galatien," 608.

between Jews and Gentiles. Judaism has not only been displaced but also replaced by Christianism. This rewriting of Gal. 3:28, which is at the center of the letter, is funded by the rewriting of the second and third pairs of the baptismal formula in terms of the absolute sociocultural and religious division between slaves and freeborn wo/men and the reaffirmation of maternity and paternity as the identity-producing metaphors in the discussion on the offspring of Abraham. Paul's praise of freedom is thus purchased not only with the violent displacement of Judaism but also with the deployment of "woman" as a figure of speech at the expense of historical wo/men as members of the community.

Since Kahl wants to argue that the Sarah-Hagar allegory undermines all polar oppositions and dichotomies, her argument needs at least certain segments of Judaism as a negative foil. Who then are those whom Paul attacks with very strong words (anathema, drive them out)? Definitely not "the Jews" in general but "orthodox" (or maybe, better, fundamentalist) Jewish opponents who used violence against any dissidents and insist on sameness—for example, on circumcision of the Gentile converts.

It seems thus that a literalist as well as a metaphorical reading of androcentric language that eschews a hermeneutics of suspicion not only marginalizes wo/men but also must indict at least a segment of Judaism. Kahl's brilliant feminist reading that is appreciative of Paul's theology in Galatians stands in tension with the feminist critique of Paul as it has been articulated for instance by Elizabeth Castelli,[36] Sheila Briggs,[37] Antoinette Clark Wire,[38] and myself. Yet it is in agreement with the empathic understanding of Paul as developed and defended by Luise Schottroff,[39] for example, and some evangelical feminists.[40] Whereas a feminist deconstructive re-reading of Gal. 3:28 seeks to recover and bring to the fore the voices of wo/men who were silenced, feminist empathic reading appears to want to save the liberating voice of Paul.

Paul's Eradication of Gender and Race

Most recently Daniel Boyarin's book, *A Radical Jew: Paul and the Politics of Identity*, has provided another feminist reading of the baptismal formula Gal. 3:28 and Paul's reception of it. Boyarin characterizes his hermeneutical perspective as that of "a talmudist and postmodern Jewish critic," that is, "as a practicing Jewish-non-Christian,

---

36. Castelli, *Imitating Paul.*

37. Briggs, "Galatians," 2:218–36.

38. Clark Wire, *The Corinthian Women Prophets.*

39. Luise Schottroff, "Wie berechtigt ist die feministische Kritik an Paulus? Paulus und die Frauen in den ersten christlichen Gemeinden im Römischen Reich," in *Einwürfe* (Munich, 1985), 2:107.

40. See, e.g., J. M. Gundry-Volf, "Male and Female in Creation and New Creation: Interpretations of Galatians 3:28C in 1 Corinthians 7," in *To Tell the Mystery: Essays on New Testament Eschatology in Honor of Robert H. Gundry,* ed. Thomas E. Schmidt and Moisés Silva (Sheffield: Sheffield Academic Press, 1994), 95–121; and Alvera Mickelsen, ed., *Women, Authority, and the Bible* (Downers Grove, Ill.: InterVarsity Press, 1986).

critical but sympathetic reader of Paul."[41] Since he explicitly introduces his reading as "feminist," his reading of Gal. 3:28 does not so much exemplify the difference between a nonfeminist and feminist interpretation, as one between two different feminist interpretations and reading methods from different socioreligious locations.

Although Boyarin recognizes that Paul utilizes in Gal. 3:28 a prebaptismal liturgical formula, he nevertheless does not read Paul's text over and against this traditional "performative utterance" but, like Kahl and McDonald, he understands it as a part of Pauline theology. Boyarin accepts Wayne Meeks's interpretive concept of "androgyny" as it has been further elaborated by Dennis McDonald.[42] For this concept Meeks refers especially to the "'new man' symbolized by the clothing who is 'renewed after the image of his creator'" of Col. 3:10 (cf. Eph. 4:24), whereas McDonald emphasizes its Gnostic origin. Within this framework Meeks understands "neither male and female" in Gal. 3:28 in terms of the "eschatological restoration of man's original, divine, androgynous image."[43] Yet while Meeks claims that this performative utterance effects "an objective change in reality which fundamentally modifies social roles,"[44] Boyarin reinterprets the baptismal formula with reference to the context of Galatians to mean "that a reading of the entire context of the passage in Galatians leads rather to the conclusion that what is being referred to is an ecstatic experience, in which are modified *not social roles but ontological categories* [emphasis added] in the pneumatic moment of initiation."[45]

In Boyarin's view, Gal. 3:28c speaks about the "eradication of gender," an accomplishment he attributes to Paul rather than to the pre-Pauline baptismal formula. Although in 1 Corinthians Paul clearly expresses his own preference for the marriage-free state, Boyarin claims that Paul was unwilling "as some of his more radical followers [were] to disallow or to disparage marriage."[46] While Paul could envision the freedom of slaves and passionately desired the erasure of the boundaries between Jews and Gentiles, he could not condone the abolition of marriage and hence the gendered status of "wife." Boyarin concurs here with the interpretation I have proposed in *In Memory of Her*. However, he feels compelled to defend Paul.

> In arguing that "no male and female" did not and could not mean a fundamental change in the status of wives, I am not arguing that he was inconsistent (nor being inconsistent myself) in the preservation of male privilege but rather I am suggesting

41. Daniel Boyarin, *A Radical Jew: Paul and the Politics of Identity* (Berkeley: University of California Press, 1994), 1. His thesis is that rabbinic Judaism and Pauline Christianity are "two different hermeneutic systems for reading the Bible" that "generate two diametrically opposed, but mirror-like forms of racism—and also two dialectical possibilities of anti–racism," 233.

42. Dennis McDonald, *There Is No Male and Female: The Fate of a Dominical Saying in Paul and Gnosticism* (Philadelphia: Fortress Press, 1987); idem, "Corinthian Veils and Gnostic Androgynes," in *Images of the Feminine in Gnosticism*, ed. Karen L. King (Philadelphia: Fortress Press, 1988), 276–92.

43. See Wayne A. Meeks, "The Image of the Androgyne: Some Uses of a Symbol in Earliest Christianity," *History of Religions* 13 (1974): 165–208.

44. Meeks, "The Image of the Androgyne, 182.

45. Boyarin, *A Radical Jew*, 186.

46. Ibid., 190.

that Paul held that *wives are/were slaves* and that their liberation would have meant an end to marriage. Jews and Greeks need ultimately to cease being Jews and Greeks; slaves need to cease ultimately to be slaves, and the equivalent is that husbands and wives need ultimately to cease being husbands and wives, but Paul feels that the last is unrealistic for most people, even Christians.[47]

Understanding "neither male and female" also in terms of status based on marriage, I have argued to the contrary that the *ekklesia* envisioned and attempted to practice such a marriage-free ethos and that Paul seeks to modify this praxis. Boyarin does not reason why Paul "feels" that the abolition of status based on marriage is "unrealistic" if some seem to have lived it. Although he is aware of the conservative implications of his own interpretation, he insists that it "should not be taken as a totalizing statement denying wives (either in Christianity or in rabbinic Judaism) all freedom and subjectivity."[48] In order to make his point he refers again to my work as having shown that wives had "partial leadership in the Pauline churches." Yet I have argued to the opposite: Because of Gal. 3:28 wives could have leading roles in the early Christian movements. They were among those who initiated and shaped those movements, and it was Paul who, in defense of patriarchal marriage, sought to curb their work.

The Ideological Reproduction of Early Christian Identity

If ideology is the means through which subjects are fashioned, then it is important to critically assess these different interpretive discourses of Gal. 3:28. It would be tempting to appeal here to the scientific exegesis of the text for establishing a true nonideological reading as the correct one. However, for methodological and epistemological reasons, it is no longer possible to resort to such a procedure and to maintain that texts have a definite single meaning. Instead, one must explore the basic hermeneutical difference between the different feminist readings of Gal. 3:28c and underscore their ideological implications that reproduce and construct reality:

1. Unlike Fatum's and Boyarin's my interpretation does not work with an ontological, essentializing understanding of gender that tends to "naturalize" socially constructed gender differences as "divinely ordained," as "given," or as inscribed in the "body." Rather, I understand gender and body as culturally, religiously, politically, and socially constructed and "normalized," as "commonsense" knowledge that "reproduces what counts as reality" in the interest of kyriarchy. That I do not misconstrue

47. Ibid., 200. At two points of this argument Boyarin refers to my interpretation of Gal. 3:28 in *In Memory of Her.* The following statement indicates that his interpretation draws on my own but immediately distances itself from it: "Rather than 'resting on the assumed natural differences between the sexes institutionalized in patriarchal marriage,' as Fiorenza [*sic*] puts it, I would imprudently suggest that patriarchal marriage—that is at least until now—*produces* such naturalized gender differences (Fiorenza, 1983, 207 [*sic!*])," 199. Yet, this is not an imprudent new assertion but rather a restating of my own thesis in different words since kyriarchal discourses always are shaped by and shape gender ideology. Obviously, gender dualism is produced by patriarchal marriage relations and produces them.

48. Ibid., 322, note 52.

this basic difference in interpretive frameworks comes to the fore in the following statement of Boyarin that in variations runs through the book like an underground river.

> With regard to women and gay people, there is some "objective reality," some somatic referent, about which to even ask the question of essence. At least ostensibly the category of women is defined by something they are in their bodies, and gay and lesbian people by something they do with their bodies. There is, in both cases, as I have said, something about which to ask the question regarding essence, although I have argued that it is a different question in each of these cases. But what about Jews? In what sense does this category exist—even as a nominalist category? I suggest that only genealogy can fill that function for Jews.[49]

Since Boyarin senses that his emphasis on circumcision could lead to a misunderstanding of Judaism in terms of masculine overdetermination, he argues that circumcision marks the male Jew both as G*d's covenant partner and as "woman" or as feminine in relation to G*d.[50] His midrashic reading of the male Israelites in Song of Songs 3:11 as "daughters of Zion" allows him to construe the male Jew in terms of androgyny, a conceptualization that has been shown to retain the male as the defining element while arrogating "feminine" traits to himself.[51] This analogization of women and Jews allows Boyarin to insist again and again that circumcision as a mark on the male flesh is the site of difference between Judaism and Christianity. However, this argument overlooks that women are Jews and Jews are women.[52] If they are ontologically different as wo/men, then this ontological difference constitutes them also as ontologically different from Jews whose identity is constituted in and through circumcision. If circumcision as mark in the flesh constitutes Jewish identity and is the site of difference between Judaism and Christianity, then Jewish wo/men can only be seen as full members of the covenant people if they are not construed as ontologically different from Jewish men.

Rather than to understand wo/men as ontologically different from men, one must recognize that they are defined as "woman" ideologically by the structures of kyriarchal oppression that crisscross their identities. Hence the "feminist we," which seeks to effect change must be articulated in critical interaction with wo/men's struggles for equality and equity, particularly with the struggle of those suffering from multiple oppressions and working to survive and change kyriarchal relations of

---

49. Ibid., 239.

50. Ibid., 128–30.

51. For a critical discussion of the notion of androgyny, see, e.g., Mary Vetterling-Braggin, ed., "*Femininity,*" "*Masculinity,*" *and "Androgyny": A Modern Philosophical Discussion* (Totowa: Rowman and Littlefield, 1982).

52. Boyarin goes so far as to say that the same cultural dynamics that produced allegoresis—as a primary European reading strategy—also produced the universal subject as a Christian male. The difference between allegorical and midrashic readings, between midrashic reading focused on a particular body and an allegorical reading focused on a disembodied universality, are the crux of the matter. "The crucial issue dividing Judaism from Christianity is the relation to the body, in general as a signifier of corporeal existence in all of its manifestations, and here in particular as a signifier of a particular kin-group."

domination. Like race, class, or ethnicity, gender is not an ontological property or essence but is produced historically and therefore can be changed.

2. Therefore, in difference to Boyarin, McDonald, and Fatum, I have not adopted a dualistic gender framework or one of androgyny, but have proposed a reconstructive theoretical model of contradiction and struggle: between hegemonic political-cultural kyriarchy (that is, the domination of elite, propertied, educated Greco-Roman men, or the rule of the lord, master, father as head of household) on the one hand; and on the other the practice and the vision in the *ekklesia,* that is, the democratic assembly of full citizens, of the radical equality of those considered to be second-class citizens, religio-culturally inferior, and socially subordinated, such as slave wo/men, freeborn wo/men, resident aliens, and barbarians. Read within this reconstructive framework, the baptismal formula can be understood as emphasizing that all status-differences are abolished in Christ, in the messianic corporation. This entailed for elite men (that is, for those who were lords/masters/fathers/husbands) a relinquishment of their sociocultural and religious status privileges in the interest of equality.

If one reads the baptismal formula of Gal. 3:28 in the context of hegemonic structures of domination, then it becomes clear that kyriarchal status and power differences have produced and perpetuate gender, race, class, or religious differences as inequality. In Christ as the messianic corporation or in the democratic *ekklesia,* such status inequalities are no longer valid. Positively speaking, sociopolitical and cultural-religious differences are to be understood as multiplex difference in the power of the Spirit.

3. A basic difference consists in method. Boyarin as well as Fatum and Kahl read Paul's universalistic argument as drawing out the implications of the baptismal formula and understand it as basically in line with Paul's overall theology. Because he follows the lead of McDonald, Boyarin tends to emphasize the dangers of those gnosticizing discourses in which the baptismal formula shares. This allows him to read Pauline and rabbinic Judaism in conjunction and in comparison with each other, so that rabbinic Judaism can be understood as representing post-Pauline Judaism. Kahl's metaphorical reading in turn tends to see Gal. 3:28 as a radical egalitarian expression of Pauline theology but in doing so re-inscribes the dualistic argument of Paul.

In contrast, I have sought to read the baptismal formula as an articulation of the emancipatory vision of a broad-based egalitarian Jewish movement whose language Paul shares but which he seeks to control. If one does not foreclose but consciously sets out to read Paul's text "against the grain," one can trace how Paul rewrites the baptismal formula in Galatians. Rather than take the kyriocentric text at face value, one must read its silences and occlusions in order to make visible what they repress and marginalize. In other words, one must assume that Jewish wo/men were those who shaped the emerging Christian movements and their discourses. Methodologically one must read Gal. 3:28 as the tip of the iceberg that indicates what Paul's text submerges. The circumference of this "iceberg" is to be measured and located in a pre-Pauline context, probably in that of Antiochene theology. This theology, which is connected with figures such as Barnabas, Apollos, the Syrophoenician woman, and the so-called Hellenists of Acts, remains for the most part shrouded in historical silence. Instead of reading Paul's kyriocentric text in a literalist fashion, as Fatum does, or to displace it metaphorically, as Kahl does, one must try to comprehend its ambiguities, gaps, and contradictions in order to make visible again the struggles the rhetoric of the text mystifies or marginalizes.

Pauline rhetoric and theology, I contend, are rooted in pre-Pauline soil and sharpened in the struggles around the realization of the baptismal confession. Both Paul and his conversation partners in the communities refer back to the same theological ground and the same symbolic world but interpret them differently, drawing different, often contradictory conclusions from this pre-Pauline heritage. Methodologically one must therefore read the extant historical texts and sources as interactions with and responses to wo/men's historical presence and agency.[53] In other words, one must assume that Jewish and Greco-Roman wo/men were those who have shaped the emerging Christian movements and their discourses. Antoinette Clark Wire's detailed analysis of 1 Corinthians has elaborated such a methodological approach and convincingly shown that the Corinthian wo/men prophets had a different theological perspective and ecclesial praxis than Paul. Thus a feminist ideology-critical reading has the task neither to defend nor to condemn Paul; rather, it has the task to hear anew the voices, debates, and practices of our foresisters that have been historically silenced and marginalized and to place them into the center of attention.

The Pauline exhortations and the household-code tradition within the New Testament still speak to these tensions and conflicts. Their injunctions, which demand the subordination of slaves, women, and children, may express the interests of the "owner and patron class," as Judge has suggested—as well as reflect the interests of husbands and masters, the heads of families, who felt that their prerogatives were being undermined. Of course, it is difficult for us to decide whether or not such motivations played a role in the modifications of the Christian baptismal self-understanding, that is, which admonitions to subordination were due to a genuine concern for the Christian group's embattled situation and which arose from a defense of kyriarchal dominance couched in theological terms, since the theological counterarguments, for instance of slave wo/men, have not survived in history.

To assume such resentment is historically plausible, to the extent that the baptismal declaration of Gal. 3:28 runs counter to the general acceptance of male religious privilege among Greeks, Romans, Persians, and also Jews of the first century C.E. As I have pointed out in *In Memory of Her*, the baptismal utterance can be understood as challenging deeply ingrained elite male status prerogatives when read over and against a widespread rhetorical commonplace that Greco-Roman men (including Jews) were grateful that they were fortunate enough not to be born as

53. Taking up this line of thought, Judith Plaskow, in her classic work *Standing Again at Sinai: Judaism from a Feminist Perspective* (San Francisco: Harper & Row, 1990), has developed a similar argument for Judaism.

beasts, barbarians, boors, slaves, or wo/men (Jews would add Gentiles to this list).[54] For elite men—especially for those who were also wealthy slave owners—baptism into Christ entailed a radical break with their former social and religious self-understandings.

4. Such a radically egalitarian reconstructive historical and interpretive model is difficult to comprehend today even for feminists because our imagination and experience are still kyriarchally determined. Since this radical egalitarian view of early Christian beginnings still contradicts the commonsense understanding of reality today, it is difficult to imagine and to accept. The full impact that this "commonsense" assumption retains today has been perceptively articulated by the well-known philosopher Richard Rorty:

> For to be a full-fledged person in a given society is a matter of double negation: it is not to think of oneself as belonging to a group which powerful people in that society thank God they do not belong to.
>
> In our society straight white males of my generation—even earnestly egalitarian straight white males—cannot easily stop themselves from being grateful that they were not born mentally retarded or schizophrenic. This is in part because of a calculation of the obvious socio-economic disadvantages of being so born, but not entirely. It is also the sort of instinctive and ineffable horror which noble children used to feel at the thought of having been born to non-noble parents, even very rich non-noble parents.
>
> At some future point in the development of our society, guilty relief over not having been born a woman may not cross the minds of males, any more than the question "noble or base-born?" now crosses their minds. That would be the point at which both males and females had *forgotten* the traditional androcentric language, just as we have all forgotten about the discussion between base and noble ancestry.[55]

It has been my contention that in the beginnings of Christianity such a vision and praxis of equality already existed. This does not mean that such an egalitarian consciousness and practice only existed among the messianic Jews who soon were called Christians nor that it was realized by everyone. The contrary seems to be the case. A close rereading of the arguments of Paul in Galatians can show that Paul displaces the "sign" of circumcision and re-inscribes its significance in a different way as Christian superiority.

What is at stake in this debate over the interpretation of Gal. 3:28 can be stated differently and perhaps be seen more clearly when one considers the debate that ensued in 1933 on the *Arier Paragraph* in the Lutheran church of Germany. This legislation excluded from the ministry of the church all persons who were of non-

---

54. This cultural self–understanding seems to have been adopted by Judaism in the first or second century c.e. and found its way into the synagogue liturgy. Three times a day an orthodox Jewish man still thanks G*d that he did not create him a gentile, a slave, or a woman. This must not be understood as a misogynist prayer but as an expression of gratitude. Although it is difficult to say whether this prayer was already known in the first half of the first century, its assumption of religious male privilege was widespread in the Greco-Roman world.

55. Richard Rorty, "Feminism and Pragmatism," *Michigan Quarterly Review* 30, 2 (1991), 248.

Aryan descent or who were married to such persons. If an Aryan pastor subsequently married a non-Aryan, he also would be dismissed.

A group of delegates to the annual Synod of Hesse requested a theological evaluation of this church-sponsored legislation, and the theological faculties of Marburg and Erlangen responded. The Erlangen faculty under the leadership of Paul Althaus and Werner Elert stressed in defense of the *Arier Paragraph* "the order of creation" according to which family and nation were divinely instituted. Although they asserted that "there is no distinction between Jew and Gentile" in the "order of salvation," they immediately insisted that the equality of the baptized as children of G*d in no way abolished natural biological and sociological status differences. Quoting 1 Cor. 7:20, the Erlangen faculty argued that the structures of the "order of creation" bind persons to the conditions and prerogatives with which they were born. Oneness in Christ pertains to faith and has nothing to do with ecclesial organization. Those who are ordained must be in line with their particular communities; that is, they must be members of the German people. Since Jews are a "different" and an "alien" people, they cannot serve the church of the German people. Just as the church excludes wo/men from ordination on grounds of the "order of creation," so it must exclude Jews because of their race from church office.

The Marburg faculty under the leadership of Rudolph Bultmann and Hans von Soden argued on the other side that the new law was contrary to the essence of the church because it reduced non-Aryan Christians to second-class membership. Historically the church has viewed Jews religiously rather than racially. Jewish Christian communities in antiquity were not racially based. Rather, the unity of the body of Christ does not allow Christians to claim that race and nationality should be respected by the church as the "order of creation." Those who do not acknowledge the full equality of Jewish and non-Jewish Christians act against the Bible as the Word of G*d. The *Arier Paragraph* contradicts the truth of the church of Christ.

In response to the Marburg statement, a Göttingen theologian by the name of Georg Wobbermin insisted that the basic issue was race.[56] The *Arier Paragraph* does not deal with the church but with the human sphere, which has only some significance for the order of the church:

> The apostle Paul, to be sure, wrote in Galatians that there is neither Jew nor Greek, slave nor free, male nor female because all are one in Jesus Christ. This position, however, did not prevent him from distinguishing between men and women with respect to church order. Women, he prescribed, were to keep silent in the church. Thus there also may be distinctions in church order between Jew and Greek or Aryan and non-Aryan. Today we must honor this distinction in order to protect the unity of the German spiritual life.[57]

56. Georg Wobbermin, "Zwei theologische Gutachten in Sachen des Arier-Paragraphen-kritisch beleuchtet," *Theologische Blätter* 12 (December 1933): 356–59.

57. As summarized by H. Jackson Forstman, "A Chapter in Theological Resistance to Racism: Rudolph Bultmann and the Beginning of the Third Reich," in *Justice and the Holy: Essays in Honor of Walter Harrelson*, ed. Douglas A. Knight and Peter J. Paris (Atlanta: Scholars Press, 1989), 257–70, on whose information I rely for the above argument; 267.

Bultmann, to the contrary, maintained that one cannot affirm theologically or ethically that persons are fated by birth for certain positions and groups since the human being is not just an animal and one's being and status are very much determined by historical conditions: "Only a rationalism blind to reality can isolate a natural order like biological determination as significant for human intercourse. One's race as a pure given carries with it no clear direction for acting, for it is given only in a definite historical situation."[58]

Nevertheless, Bultmann affirmed the "order of creation" doctrine because humans in his view were not persons abstractly but concretely. But in so doing he identifies gender and race as structures of domination with creation and insists that our relation to the created order of sex, family, nationality is first of all a positive one. Aware of this danger, he goes on to emphasize that this does not mean that the creator G*d can be understood simply as immanent in any "order" because nothing in the word is unambiguously divine or sacred.

Hence the task of the theologian is a critical one because G*d is both creator and judge of the world.[59] Although Bultmann saw the historical conditionedness of gender, family, race, and nation, he does not apply his critical theology to them. Hence, he does not reject them as unjust social structures but rather affirms them as the "order of creation." Consequently, his critical protest could be made only in ecclesiological terms but not in terms of social justice.

In sum, the vision of radical equality enunciated in Gal. 3:28 was controverted in its very beginnings and has remained so throughout the centuries, but cannot be eradicated. It is not a "peak sentence of Paul, nor a sporadic Christian spark." It is also not a *utopia* because it is historically not without a place. Rather, the vision of radical equality articulated in Gal. 3:28 announces a claim that must still be realized today in societal as well as ekklesial everyday praxis.

---

58. Rudolf Bultmann, "Der Arier Paragraph im Raum der Kirche," *Theologische Blätter* 12 (December 1933): 364.

59. Rudolf Bultmann, "Die Aufgabe der Theologie in der gegenwärtigen Situation," *Theologische Blätter* 12 (June 1933) 161–66.

Chapter 8

Pauline Theology
and the Politics of Meaning

Whether and how to construct or articulate a biblical or even just a Christian Testament theology[1] has been controverted for quite some time.[2] The emergence of a diversity of methods in textual, historical, literary, psychological, or ideological criticism—a diversity which is now generally accepted, at least in the North American academy—has challenged traditional theological inquiry, but it has not yet fashioned a new, commonly accepted understanding of biblical theology. After the demise of the word-study approach, the existential demythologization hermeneutics, and the salvation-history paradigm, the nature and rhetoric of biblical theology continue to be questioned. Traditionally, interpreters have separated hermeneutically the historical-critical approach as descriptive from the theological approach as normative. Since they have understood biblical theology as the re-statement of key doctrinal concepts, e.g., "G*d[3] acting in history" or the "divinity of Christ," they have sought to locate these concepts in the text and to use biblical texts as proof-texts for dogmatic beliefs.

Biblical Theology as a Theological Rhetoric of Inquiry

With the arrival of form- and redaction-critical methods, scholars increasingly have attempted to synthesize individual biblical writings in theological terms. Whole volumes—for example, on "the theology of Paul" or "the theology of Q"— have been published. More recently scholars have used narrative criticism to derive biblical theology from the textual articulation of the characters or the perspective of the narrator, whereas reader-response critics have located theological meaning in the interaction between reader and text. Social world studies in turn have taken over basic insights from the sociology of knowledge and assumed that the social arrangements portrayed by the text and the symbolic arrangements inscribed in it are correlated. Norman Petersen, for instance, distinguishes between symbolic universe

---

1. In its embryonic form this chapter was prepared for the Consultation on a Political Interpretation of Paul chaired by Richard Horsley and presented at the annual meeting of the Society of Biblical Literature in 1996.

2. See Boers, *What Is New Testament Theology?*

3. In this way I seek to indicate the brokenness, ambiguity, and indeterminacy of human G*d language.

and theology. Whereas the symbolic universe is the world of the text "as it is viewed," according to him, theology is the systematic reflection on that universe. The social roles in the "world as it is viewed" are correlated with the social roles in society.[4]

Traditionally, theology has been understood as the explication of dogmatic tenets and the elaboration of the symbols of Christian faith. It also has been conceptualized as "faith seeking understanding." On this latter definition theology has a hermeneutical purpose and goal. However, I want to propose here a third approach to the conceptualization of theology. *Theology* in the original sense of the Greek word (*theo-legein*) means either speaking about G*d or "G*d speaking." *Theo-legein* is a rhetorical activity.[5] The subject in the traditional understanding of theology is "faith," whereas in the rhetorical understanding of theology it is the interpreter.

If theology is defined as the speaking activity of G*d and understood as the "Word of G*d," then the meaning of theology approaches that of prophecy. Theology and prophecy become almost equivalent. Whereas the understanding of theology as G*d speaking or as divine revelation obfuscates the human mediation of the biblical word, prophecy clearly signifies that mediation by maintaining that G*d speaks through the mouth of the prophet. In light of biblical criticism, therefore, biblical writings as canonical Scriptures are strictly speaking not theology but prophecy. Whereas divine revelation calls for obedience, prophecy calls for critical theological reflection[6] or for the discernment of the Spirit, since biblical writers know well that not all spirits are "from G*d."[7]

If biblical writings are the prophetically *mediated* words of and about G*d rather than a codification of the *direct* words of G*d, of G*d speaking right to us, then theology must be understood primarily in the sense of speaking *about* G*d. Consequently, the task of a biblical theology becomes to critically explore all human speaking about G*d. Doing theology calls for critical deliberation and accountability. In my view, therefore, theology is best understood not as a system but as a rhetorical practice that does not conceive of language merely as signification and transmission, but rather as a form of action and power that affects actual people and situations.[8]

4. Petersen, *Rediscovering Paul*, 29–30.

5. In her discussion of the SBL Pauline Theology Group's work, Jouette M. Bassler "Paul's Theology: Whence and Whither?" in *Pauline Theology*, vol. 2, *1 and 2 Corinthians*, ed. David M. Hay [Minneapolis: Fortress Press, 1991], 3–17), points out that no agreement exists as to what is meant by theology and that the term is given a whole range of connotations. Rather than to understand theology in terms of system, core, or coherence, Bassler defines theology as "*activity*." See also Steven J. Kraftschick, "Seeking a More Fluid Model: A Response to Jouette M. Bassler," *Pauline Theology*, 18–34.

6. Compare also the definition of theology by Victor Furnish, "Paul the Theologian," in *The Conversation Continues: Studies in Paul and John in Honor of J. Louis Martyn*, ed. Robert T. Fortna and Beverly Gaventa (Nashville: Abingdon, 1990), 25. According to him, theology is a "critical reflection on the beliefs, rites, and social structures in which an experience of ultimate reality has found expression." My own definition is more specific.

7. For the exploration of early Christian prophecy, see my *The Book of Revelation: Justice and Judgment*, 2d ed. 133–56, and my article "The Words of Prophecy: Reading the Apocalypse Theologically," to appear in *Jahrbuch für biblische Theologie*, 1999.

8. See Jane P. Tompkins, "The Reader in History: The Changing Shape of Literary Response," in *Reader-Response Criticism*, ed. Jane P. Tompkins, 201–32.

As a consequence of such a redefinition of theology, the subdiscipline of biblical theology must be reconceptualized in rhetorical terms. If, however, theological language is best understood in the classical sense of rhetoric as speech that constructs and shapes reality, rather than reflecting it, then an ethics of interpretation is called for.[9] Its task is to critically analyze and evaluate both how biblical scholars in general and biblical authors in particular speak about the divine. Biblical theology therefore must not be relegated to being just a confessional religious undertaking that is restricted to members of biblical communities. Rather, it must be understood also as a social-political and cultural public responsibility insofar as the Bible has shaped and still shapes the cultural-political self-understanding of the West.

In a very perceptive article A. K. M. Adam has explored the impact of modernity on the self-understanding of biblical studies, an impact that has led to the diagnosis of biblical theology as moribund and, in many cases, to its demise. Adam argues that biblical scholars must abandon the modern attempt "to construct a biblical theology on a historical foundation."[10] Yet Adam is careful to stress that this does not mean the passing away of historical analysis. Instead of constructing biblical theology on historical foundations and modern rationality, Adam proposes that

> a biblical theology will have to do with theology, with theological topics and concerns. Not the religion of Israel; not the religion of the first Christians; with theology as we know it and as we care about it (including topics like Creation, the Trinity, soteriology, ecclesiology, and so on) which are usually excluded from biblical theology on the ground that they reflect the theologian's interest, rather than an interest which inheres to the text.[11]

What makes biblical theology theological according to this view is a traditional understanding of theology as dogmatic systematics. Proper "theological terms" are traditional dogmatic categories. Although Adam believes that the margins are a promising place to search for a biblical theology, he overlooks an important difference between the understanding of theology done in the margins and that practiced in the center that is significant for the understanding of biblical theology.

As Blount[12] and Segovia[13] have pointed out, two fundamental differences distinguish the perspective of the margins from that of the Eurocentric center of biblical studies. The first is that the center stresses christology and the question of *religious* salvation (soteriology), whereas the margins are concerned with social inequity and injustice. The second is that, whereas the center underscores the conceptual and formal issues of biblical texts as documents of the past and advocates their spiritual, purely religious, individualistic appropriation, the margins emphasize the interper-

---

9. See my article, "The Ethics of Interpretation: Decentering Biblical Scholarship. SBL Presidential Address," *JBL* 107, 1 (1988): 3–17, reprinted here as chapter 1.

10. Adam, "Biblical Theology and the Problem of Modernity," 1.

11. Ibid., 12.

12. Blount, *Cultural Interpretation,* 1–23 and 175–94.

13. Segovia, "Introduction: Pedagogical Discourses and Practices in Biblical Criticism," 1–28.

sonal interaction between readers and text as well as the significance of social-religious location for biblical readings for today.

It is therefore instructive to note that Adam defines the difference in the understanding of biblical theology as one between center and margin, one that reflects the theologian's interest, rather than an interest that inheres in the text. Hence the difference between margin and center that Adam announces is not the difference he actually inscribes as constitutive for biblical theology. Rather, he falls back on the old difference that has plagued the discussion of biblical theology in modernity, which is the difference between dogmatic and historical biblical studies. How then would Adam conceptualize the heart of biblical theology differently if he were to observe the difference between center and margins diagnosed by Blount and Segovia?

In order to negotiate the Scylla of a purely rational-historical understanding of biblical theology and the Charybdis of dogmatic definition, I suggest, one needs to reconceptualize biblical theology as a critical theo-ethical rhetoric. With liberation theologians I argue that the central theological question today is not the modern question of whether G*d exists but the ethical question of what kind of G*d religious communities and their Scriptures proclaim. Is it a G*d legitimating exploitation, injustice, and oppression, or is it a G*d inspiring liberation and well-being?

To that end one needs to develop a multifaceted theological analysis and engender a critical hermeneutical process that is able to investigate the rhetoric of a text or tradition[14] in terms of an ethics of liberation. One has to do so in order to be able to adjudicate how biblical writings that claim to be the word of G*d actually speak about the divine. Such a critical mapping and evaluation of biblical texts and their G*d-rhetorics can explore their theological values and visions, as long as it does not presuppose that the Bible is the unmediated word of G*d. Rather, it must understand that G*d's speaking is mediated in and through human, mostly elite male, language and text.[15]

If theology in general has the task to engage in a critical delineation, reflection, and evaluation of the "rhetoric of G*d";[16] or on how Scriptures, traditions, and believers speak about their G*d; and how their practices of *theo-legein* shape their self-understanding, worldviews, and social-political relations; then biblical theology in particular has the task of critically mapping and reflecting on how the Scriptures speak of the divine. In chapter 4 I have identified and elaborated seven rhetorical strategies and hermeneutical methods—a hermeneutics of experience, of systemic analysis, of suspicion, of evaluation, of remembrance, of imagination, and of trans-

14. For a fuller development of a rhetorical approach, see my book *Revelation: Vision of a Just World*. This approach seems to gain ground in more recent research on Revelation. Compare, e.g., Robert M. Royalty, Jr., "The Rhetoric of Revelation," in *SBL 1997 Seminar Papers* (Atlanta: Scholars Press, 1997), 596–617; Pete Antonysamy Abir, *The Cosmic Conflict of the Church: An Exegetico-Theological Study of Revelation 12, 7–12* (Frankfurt: Peter Lang, 1995), 250–309.

15. Terence E. Fretheim, "Is the Biblical Portrayal of God Always Trustworthy?" in *The Bible as Word of God in a Postmodern Age*, ed. Terence E. Fretheim and Karlfried Fröhlich (Minneapolis: Fortress, 1998), 97–112.

16. See my forthcoming article "G*d—The Many Named": Without Place and Proper Name," in Herman Haering, ed., *Geloof in God*.

formation—as crucial for such a critical biblical theological approach. These methodological strategies are critical hermeneutical tools that must be deployed on every level of textual investigation and interpretation.

Biblical Theology as a Politics of Meaning

In the past decades liberation theologians and critical theorists have brought to public consciousness that all discourses depend on their sociohistorical location[17] and represent political interests. This focus on a critical emancipatory politics of interpretation, I have argued, is able to decenter the master-discourses of both apologetic theological and objectivist so-called scientific biblical scholarship as well as biblical writers such as Paul. It can demystify ideologies of domination and subordination inscribed in biblical texts and scholarship and work to unravel the western logic of identity that has served to legitimate structures of domination, that is, of *kyriarchy*, understood as the rule of the lord/master/father/husband.

Therefore, one must inquire not only as to how the Scriptures construct theological meaning and speak about the living G*d, but also as to how biblical interpreters construct the theology of biblical writings. Do they speak about an all-powerful monarch who demands obedience and submission or about a G*d fostering justice, love, and well-being (salvation)? Such a process of critical theo-ethical reflection is not concerned with (re)producing the theology of a biblical book or writer once and for all. Instead, it is interested in an ongoing critical-constructive process of "doing" theology as a critical rhetorics of liberation.[18]

However, even those who have attempted to seriously engage an ethic and rhetoric of theological interpretation have tended to construe such an exploration in either scientific-objectivist, individualist-privatized, or dogmatic-confessional rather than in systemic sociopolitical terms. In so doing they have tended, for instance, to re-inscribe and legitimate the master-voice of Paul as that of hegemonic scientific biblical scholarship. Such biblical-theological discourses that remain either unconscious of their rhetorical functions or abstracted from their political context are in danger of re-inscribing the malestream discourses of value-free scientism and/or apologetic theological fundamentalism against which they argue.

Only a focus on a critical emancipatory politics of meaning, I submit, is able to decenter the master-discourses of apologetic-dogmatic and objectivist "scientific" conceptualizations of biblical theology that encompass both the scholarly discourses on the Bible as well as those of biblical writers themselves, such as Paul. A biblical theology that is conceptualized as a rhetoric of divine justice and well-being, I argue, is able to demystify ideologies of domination and subordination inscribed in biblical texts and scholarship. It also is able to unravel the western logic of identity

---

17. See the collection of essays collected by Segovia and Tolbert, eds., *Reading from This Place.*

18. See my books *But She Said; Jesus: Miriam's Child, Sophia's Prophet;* and *Sharing Her Word* for the elaboration of this approach.

that has served to legitimate structures of domination—that is, of kyriarchy—for much too long.

The Hegemonic Politics of Meaning

The difference this understanding of biblical theology would make comes to the fore when one engages a rhetoric of inquiry for examining the politics of hegemonic biblical theology. Constitutive elements of such a rhetoric and politics of inquiry are: (1) the politics of otherness and its tendencies of marginalization and vilification; (2) the politics and logics of identity; and (3) the politics of identification and of inspiration.

The Politics of "Othering"

The hegemonic politics of theological interpretation engenders a politics and rhetorics of "othering" that establishes identity either by declaring the difference of the other as the same or by vilifying and idealizing difference as otherness.[19] It justifies relationships of ruling[20] by obfuscating structures of domination and subordination as "naturalized" differences. Hence this politics of otherness can be changed only when it is understood not as a universal transcultural binary structure but as a historical political practice.

Such a theological politics of othering and vilification permeates all our scholarly discourses as well as the discourses of Paul himself.[21] Its relentless othering engenders the strategies of marginalization and silencing inscribed in the biblical text and in contemporary scholarship. For instance, my own work has sought to theorize a paradigm shift in the discourses of the discipline in terms of critical feminist emancipatory studies and has consistently argued that a critical feminist interpretation re-inscribes the marginalizing and excluding tendencies of the grammatically androcentric text if it focuses just on the study of wo/men in the Bible. Nevertheless, just as other critical feminist work, so my own is persistently misread as speaking about wo/men in early Christianity, because for many feminism and wo/man is still one and the same.

Hence the hegemonic politics of interpretation continues to relegate the contributions of feminist biblical studies to the marginal topic "wo/men," on the one hand, and authoritative theory to the domain of "great men," on the other. It thereby continues the politics of othering already inscribed in the Pauline letters. Not just religious studies but all modern theories of political and moral life are shot through with ideologies of sexism, colonialism, and racism, the systems and discourses of marginalization, vilification, and dehumanization. This politics of othering is indebted to the classic antidemocratic discourses of Plato and Aristotle as well as

---

19. Cf. Bartky, *Femininity and Domination*.

20. For this expression, see Dorothy E. Smith, *The Conceptual Practices of Power*.

21. For instance, one needs only to read the invectives of Paul against those with whom he disagrees in Galatians or Philippians.

those of modern democratic philosophers such as Locke, Hobbes, Rousseau, and Hegel, which position the "civic public" and the "impartial and universal point of view of normative reason" as opposite to the private realm that encompasses the family as the domain of wo/men, "the body, affectivity and desire."[22]

Ancient and modern western philosophies have developed this "politics and rhetorics of otherness"[23] in the attempt to legitimate that not all members of the polis but only certain men can claim the rights of citizen, participate in democratic government, or deliberate in public. In its classical form this politics of otherness is rooted in the practices of the androsocial Greek polis, its political-philosophical subtext is democracy, and its social formation is patriarchy or, better, kyriarchy, the governing dominance or supremacy of elite propertied men. The exclusion from democratic government of freeborn propertied wo/men, poor wo/men, slave wo/men, as well as barbarian wo/men required ideological justifications. It needed to be argued why only freeborn propertied Greek male heads of households could be full citizens if, as the Sophists maintained, all are equal by nature.[24]

The articulation of dualisms such as human-animal, male-female, slave-free, native-alien, and the assertion of the "natural" inferiority of freeborn women as well as slave wo/men are ideological constructs that reproduce the politics of otherness in the various historical mutations of western capitalist kyriarchy. They were reproduced in the discourses of political philosophy at the emergence of modern democracy, which advocated the Enlightenment construction of the "Man of Reason,"[25] and in colonialist rationalizations of racism. This western political and philosophical rhetorics of otherness marks the oppressive relations of domination and exclusion in systemic patri-kyriarchy. However, it must be recognized that this politics of interpretation does not elaborate generic man but rather the imperial Sovereign-Father or in black idiom, the Boss-Man, as the universal subject. Its totalizing discourse of male-female dualism masks the complex interstructuring of systems of exploitation and dehumanization in the kyriarchal domination of western societies and religions.

The western "politics of identity and rhetorics of othering" establishes identity either by comparison to the other as an inferior "same" or by emphasizing and stereotyping difference as the otherness of the other.[26] Such differences are established as "relationships of ruling,"[27] in which structures of domination and subordination are mystified as "naturalized" differences. This politics of otherness has

22. Iris Marion Young, "Impartiality and the Civic Public: Some Implications of the Feminist Critiques of Moral and Political Theory," in *Feminism as Critique,* ed. Benhabib and Cornell, 59. Kathleen Jones, *Compassionate Authority: Democracy and the Representation of Women* (New York: Routledge, 1993).

23. For the development of the "political philosophy of otherness" as legitimizing patriarchal societal structures of domination in antiquity, cf. Moller Okin, *Women in Western Political Thought,* 15–98; Spelman, *Inessential Woman,* 19–56; and especially duBois, *Centaurs and Amazons.*

24. DuBois, *Centaurs and Amazons.*

25. Lloyd, *The Man of Reason.*

26. Cf. Bartky, *Femininity and Domination.*

27. For this expression, see Smith, *The Conceptual Practices of Power.*

found its way into the canon of Christian Scriptures and permeates theological discourse on the whole as well as biblical writings and their contemporary theological interpretations.

It is no accident, therefore, that the majority of scholars have constructed Paul's arguments as "normative" over and against Paul's so-called Gnostic, libertine, or Jewish legalistic "opponents." Exegetical discourses continue to understand the Pauline writings either theologically as documents of intra-Christian struggles between orthodoxy and heresy or they read them sociologically as records of opposing sectarian groups that are defined in contrast to the orthodox church. In both instances, scholars understand canonical voices as right and true but vilify their submerged alternative arguments as false and heretical.

In other words, the scholarly discourses on Paul's theology construct a series of dualistic religious, cultural, and political oppositions such as orthodoxy-heresy, apostle-community, honor-shame, mission-propaganda, and theology of the cross-libertine enthusiasm, rather than underscoring that they are theological arguments over meaning and interpretation. This series of dualisms privileges the first terms of the oppositions by reserving them either for Paul, orthodoxy, or Christianity on the whole, and constructs the second terms as negative "other" by attributing them either to the opponents, to Hellenistic propagandists, to Jewish legalists, or to other outsider groups. Such interpretive dualistic oppositions muddle and play down the linking and connecting terms (such as "audience," "community," "gospel") by subsuming them under either pole of the opposition rather than seeing in them a possibility for overcoming the argumentative dualism constructed by Paul.

The most telling dualistic construct is that of gender, which is already inscribed in the Pauline letters insofar as Paul understands himself as the "father" of the Corinthian community who is to present the community "as a pure bride to her one husband," Christ (2 Cor 11:2-3). This gendering of the community has negative overtones since it is connected with a reference to the seduction of Eve. Such a symbolic construct of gender dualism at once coheres in and undermines the other oppositions insofar as it casts all speaking subjects (Paul, the opponents, contemporary interpreters, and so on) as *masculine* and construes their audience (the Corinthian community, Judaism, or contemporary readers, etc.) in *feminine* terms as passive, immature, and gullible.

The Politics of Identity

The politics of othering, with its series of dualisms that mystify and occlude relations of domination, bespeaks the logic and politics of identity. The logic of identity "consists in an unrelenting urge to think things together, in a unity," to formulate "an essence that brings concrete particulars into unity."[28] I would suggest that this drive to coherence, unity, and identity is the motivating methodological and ideological

---

28. Young, "Impartiality," 61.

force in Pauline studies. It is expressed in the positivistic ethos of "scientific" exegesis as well as in the essentializing tendencies of Pauline theology.

In the modern scientific paradigm of theological interpretation, scholarship expresses the impartial, objective, abstract point of view of reason that stands apart from any interests and desires. This requires the construction of the impartial and universal moral reasoner abstracted from any historical context or political commitment. Feminist and postmodern theorists have unmasked this drive to coherent reading elaborating the master-voice of the text, its univocity, and symbolic totality as the western "logic and politics of identity."[29]

Disinterested and dispassionate scholarship is believed to enable biblical critics to enter the minds and worlds of Paul's texts, to step out of their own time, and to study Pauline history or literature on its own terms, unencumbered by contemporary experiences, values, and interests. By asserting that a given interpretation of a Pauline text represents the only objective and "true" reading, "scientific" exegesis claims to comprehend the definitive meaning intended by the author or inscribed in the text. In privileging and legitimating one particular interpretation over other possible readings, it not only closes the text's multivalent meanings but also rules out alternative multiple readings as illegitimate.

Insofar as "scientific" interpretation insists on "the logic of identity" as establishing an unequivocal single truth, it has to reason why only its own interpretation of the text is the true and "correct" interpretation. If and when, however, scholars admit that exegetical commentary is not free from rhetorical argument and socio-political-religious interests, they immediately assert that such argument and interest must be restricted to showing why and how competing interpretations have misread the Pauline text. In order to produce such unity of meaning as historical fact, social scientific studies[30] intensify these essentializing reifications and mystifications of the text by mapping Paul's rhetorical arguments and symbolic universes onto positivistic-functionalist sociological or anthropological models of interpretation.

The posture of scientific objectivism hides the extent to which the concept of objective science is itself a theoretical construct that serves a hegemonic politics of meaning.[31] This rhetoric of disinterested science and presupposition-free exegesis silences reflection on the political interests and functions of biblical texts and scholarship. Its claim to public scientific status suppresses the rhetorical character of Paul's texts and their interpretations while obscuring the power relations that constitute and shape Paul's own rhetoric and that of his modern interpreters.

The drive to coherence, unity, and identity also is the motivating ideological force in the construction of a Pauline theology. In its search for a "canon within the canon" or the "unity" of Scripture, biblical theological interpretation enacts this

---

29. For discussion and literature on the "politics of otherness," see Schüssler Fiorenza, "The Politics of Otherness," in *The Future of Liberation Theology,* ed. Ellis and Maduro, 311–25.

30. See, e.g., Elliott, "Social-Scientific Criticism of the New Testament"; Schmeller, *Brechungen,* 16–49; Craffert, "Towards an Interdisciplinary Definition."

31. Harding and Hintikka, eds., *Discovering Reality;* Antony and Witt, eds., *A Mind of One's Own.*

"logic of identity" that eliminates both the irreducible difference of Paul's arguments to those of other early Christians and the difference between Paul and his contemporary interpreter. This drive also comes to the fore in the attempts of Pauline scholarship to rearrange the extant text and to splinter it into discrete rhetorical fragments in such a way that the symbolic coherence of Paul's theological argument—as scholars have reconstructed it—is safeguarded. It is at work in the attempts of scholars to declare texts such as 1 Thess. 2:14-16; 1 Cor. 11:2-16; and 14: 34-36; or Rom. 13:1-7 as later interpolations because they do not cohere with their own reading of Paul's theology. Still other scholars rearrange the extant text and reconstruct the rhetorical situation of the diverse fragments of Paul's Corinthian or Philippian correspondence in a way that safeguards the symbolic coherence of Paul's theological argument for "radical obedience."[32]

Such a "logic of identity" with its drive to univocality energizes, for instance, J. Christian Beker's reconstructive model of coherence and contingency in Pauline theology. After discussing the essentializing tendencies in the reconstruction of Paul's theology, he concludes:

> [Paul's] ability to focus in the midst of the early churches' *variety* of theological expressions on the one central core of "Christ crucified and risen" together with his ability to allow that focus to light up and interact with every conceivable *variety and particularity* of human existence is a feat which—with perhaps the exception of Luther—no other apostle or theologian in the church has achieved.[33]

Although Beker is concerned with the *fluidity* of Paul's hermeneutic interactions, he nevertheless asserts that Paul articulated the "abiding truth" of the gospel and thereby gave to the church "the beginnings of a doctrinal 'orthodox' structure."[34] Although Beker's coherence-contingency hermeneutical model intends to be a *via media* between the "extremes of sociological analysis"—which he calls the sociological captivity of Paul—and the dogmatist imposition of a specific center on Paul's thought, he himself does not avoid speaking about such an essentialized core.

As Paul Achtemeier has observed, the concepts of core or center in biblical theology "are not easily jettisoned for the sake of convenience in meeting the objections of one's critics."[35] In order to differentiate and evaluate the postulated circular relationship between coherence and contingency or to know what Paul himself believed to be peripheral to the coherent core of his theology, Achtemeier argues, one needs to be able to locate and articulate the center, essence, or core of the coherence of Paul's thought. Although Beker names as the site of the interaction between coher-

32. Cynthia Briggs Kittredge, *Community and Authority: The Rhetoric of Obedience in the Pauline Tradition.* HTS (Harrisburg, Penn. Trinity Press International, 1998).

33. *Union Seminary Quarterly* (1978): 150. See also J. Christian Beker, "The Method of Recasting Pauline Theology: The Coherence-Contingency Theme as Interpretive Model," in *SBL 1986 Seminar Papers*, ed. Kent H. Richards (Atlanta: Scholars Press, 1986), 597.

34. Ibid., 599.

35. Paul J. Achtemeier, "Finding the Way to Paul's Theology," in *Pauline Theology*, vol. 1: *Thessalonians, Philippians, Galatians, Philemon*, ed. Jouette M. Bassler (Minneapolis: Fortress Press, 1994), 25–36, at 29.

ence and contingency the Holy Spirit and speaks of a "pneumatic democracy," his concern with safeguarding the theological master-voice of Paul forces him again and again to resort to the logic of identity that must speak of a center, core, or essence. At stake in such an essentializing logics and rhetorics of identity is not just the theological authority of the master-voice of Paul but also the "orthodoxy" of the church.

The Politics of Identification

Such an essentializing politics of inspiration, I suggest, also re-inscribes malestream relations of privilege and orthodox relations of exclusion by inviting readerly identification with Paul and his arguments. Such an identification with Paul's theological rhetoric—for instance, that of his fatherly authority—allows ecclesial and academic "fathers" to claim Paul's authority for themselves. Moreover, by stressing an unbridgeable gulf between the past and the present, between Paul and himself, the exegete occludes the fact that Paul's meanings are present only in and through the words of interpreters. Thereby he—and it is still mostly a he—surreptitiously claims Paul's theological authority for his own interpretation. Such a rhetoric of identification achieves its aim by both claiming scientific authority for its own interpretations and by disqualifying the others as biased, ideological, or as reading their own interests into the text.

Moreover, the rhetoric of radical differences between past and present complements the rhetoric of identification insofar as it serves to construct *sameness* between Paul and "his" communities.[36] It does so either by identifying Paul's discourses with those of the communities to whom he writes and thereby suppressing and eradicating the historical voices and multiplex visions that differ from Paul's. Or insofar as historical-critical studies see Pauline texts and their arguments—that is, the rhetorical situation construed by Paul—as identical with the actual historical-rhetorical situation, they not only obscure the *difference* between Paul's theological rhetoric and that of his contemporary interpreters but also between that of the early Christian communities Paul's text may misrepresent or silence.

For scholars who argue within the doctrinal and theological historical paradigm of interpretation, even more is at stake. By identifying their own interpretation with the meaning intended by Paul, as well as by invoking the inspiration and the authority of revelation, scholars can then claim divine authority for their own interpretation. Hence the politics of identification with Paul and that of inspiration are two sides of the same coin. The famous debate between Bultmann and Barth on *Sachkritik* (subject matter criticism) speaks to this problem.[37]

Bultmann criticized Barth for having seen the necessity of *Sachkritik* but nevertheless having stopped with philological historical criticism because of the dogma of

---

36. For an exploration of sameness and difference in Pauline interpretation, see the intriguing work of Elizabeth Castelli, *Imitating Paul*, which uses Michel Foucault's theoretical framework for its analysis.

37. For the whole argument, see Bernd Jaspert, "Sachkritik und Widerstand: Das Beispiel Rudolf Bultmanns," *Theologische Literaturzeitung* 115 (1990): 161–82.

inspiration that Bultmann believed underwrote Barth's work. This dogma of inspiration does not help to clarify "*die Sache*" (the subject matter). The spirit of the Bible consists of many different spirits, and the Spirit of Christ does not speak directly to us in any text. Hence the text of the Bible is only the indirect but not the direct word of G*d. Nobody, not even Paul, is able to express completely the subject matter of the gospel. Because the revelation given in Scripture is always veiled and the word of G*d is always obscured, exegetical critique must always be *Sachkritik*.

In Bultmann's view *Sachkritik* can never be radical enough, since its task is to discern the heterogeneous spirits at the roots (Latin *radix*) in order to find behind the words of Scripture G*d's Word, which is the *Sache* of the gospel. However, I would suggest that Bultmann himself does not go far enough in his radical *Sachkritik* insofar as he also begs the question by maintaining that *Sachkritik* is able to identify Jesus Christ, the Word of G*d himself, as the central subject matter of the *kerygma*, the only important matter in life and death, and the ultimate criterion of all human existence. Barth's response to Bultmann that the Word of G*d must be discerned in, through, and against "the voices of those other spirits" in turn begs the question how this can be done. Both Bultmann and Barth remain beholden to the dogmatic rhetoric of inspiration, although Bultmann shifts his accentuation from the Spirit to Christ. His christological bottleneck of biblical hermeneutics cancels the radical potential of *Sachkritik* and plays into the hands of a politics of identification.

The politics of identification, however, works not only on a theological but also on a historical level. Insofar as scholars tend to understand Paul as having the authority of the gospel to compel, control, and censure the persons or communities to whom he writes, they tend to read Paul's letters as authoritative rather than as argumentative interventions in the theological discourses of his audience. They thereby fail to understand that "Pauline Christianity" is a misnomer for the early Christian communities to whom Paul writes. These communities existed independently of Paul although we know about them only in and through the letters of Paul.

The failure to see early Christian communities in their own right is compounded by the inclination of scholars to rend early Christianity from early Judaism and to draw inflexible boundaries between inside and outside, or to postulate a deep historical gulf between Mediterranean culture and ours. In so doing, scholars disregard that the self-understanding of religious communities is intertwined with their cultural-religious environment. They also overlook that historical and theological understanding is only possible if and when one can assume some kind of common language and shared symbolic universe.

In his article on "History and Rhetoric," Paul Ricoeur has underscored this aspect of historical understanding. He argues that historical interpretation is a "historical activity" that has a "complex relation to the people of the past who themselves 'made history.'" Historical interpretation and historiography are possible not only because of a single "tempo-spatial framework" but also because of

> a single field of praxis, evidenced by the historian's dependence on the "making of real historical actors" for his own "history making." Before presenting themselves as mas-

ter craftsmen of stories made out of the past, historians must first stand as heirs of the past. . . . Before even forming the idea of re-presenting the past, we are in debt to the men and women of the past who contributed to making us what we are. Before we can represent the past we must live as beings affected by the past.[38]

Although Ricoeur speaks of the men and wo/men of the past, he does not critically reflect on his gendered assumption that interpreters and historians are "master craftsmen" who can present the past because they stand in the same "tempo-spatial frame" and "field of praxis." This analysis sheds light on why at least since Robbin Scroggs's article on "Paul and the Eschatological Woman," which appeared in 1972,[39] Pauline scholars have been so persistent in their "defense of Paul against his feminist critics."

For example, although he details the atrocities of the history of Pauline texts such as Romans 13, 1 Thessalonians 2, or especially 1 Corinthians 11 and 14, even a liberationist scholar like Neil Elliott argues that these texts are later additions to the genuine Pauline letters. His desire to liberate Paul from his post-Pauline domestications and to read his theology as liberating compels him to jettison feminist objections to such a reading and to insist that "heard rightly, Paul's message could not be more appropriate for some of us, Christians in the first world, who [if we are honest] find ourselves in the place of the Corinthian elite."[40] Yet to place middle-class North Americans in the position of the Corinthian elite does not justify Paul's politics of vilifying othering.

The tacit context of such malestream defenses of Paul because of their unconscious, taken-for-granted identification with Paul rather than, let's say, with the Corinthian women prophets, as Antoinette Clark Wire suggests,[41] is a politics and rhetorics of interpretation that surmises that the actual rhetorical situation of the Pauline letters and its historical power relations are identical to and correspond with the rhetorical situation Paul inscribed in his correspondence.[42] In other words, such a politics of interpretation presupposes both the "scientific" theoretical understanding of texts either as windows or as mirrors and the essentializing tendencies of orthodox theology. By mystifying and occluding the rhetoricity of Pauline language and text, it is able to privilege the "masculine" hegemonic voice inscribed in kyriarchal Pauline or other ancient source-texts rather than to particularize and relativize this voice by reconstructing a varied assembly of voices and arguments.[43]

In short, all three strategies of the hegemonic politics of meaning seek to reinscribe the kyriarchal politics of subordination that is inscribed in past and present biblical discourses by valorizing the voice of the canonical Paul. In contrast,

38. Paul Ricoeur, "History and Rhetoric," *Diogenes* 168 (1994): 23.

39. Reprinted in Robin Scroggs, *The Text and the Times: New Testament Essays for Today* (Minneapolis: Fortress Press, 1993), 69–95.

40. Neil Elliott, *Liberating Paul: The Justice of God and the Politics of the Apostle* (Maryknoll, N.Y.: Orbis Books, 1994), 229; see also notes on 282–87 for his critical discussion of Antoinette Clark Wire's work.

41. Clark Wire, *The Corinthian Women Prophets.*

42. Cf. Castelli, "Interpretations of Power in 1 Corinthians."

43. Cf., e.g., my article "Missionaries, Coworkers, and Apostles."

the critical emancipatory politics of meaning for which I have argued in this book would be able to displace the hegemonic politics of meaning and to replace it with a radical democratic politics of emancipation.

Biblical Theology as the Rhetoric of *Ekklesia*

To undercut the hegemonic politics of meaning one must conceptualize not only early Christian communities but also contemporary reading practices as sites of communicative persuasion, emancipatory struggles, and theological visions that are shared by all the participants. Such a re-conceptualization of *ekklesia* as a pluriform congregation of fully responsible "adult" voices who have equal standing becomes possible, I suggest, only if one deconstructs the gendered identification between Paul and his interpreters that underwrites the authority claims of biblical scholars. This would require that one replace the politics of theological identification with a radical democratic politics of *ekklesia* that can comprehend the disputes in the early Christian *ekklesia* in terms of *parresia*—the free speech of citizens—rather than cast them in terms of confessional internecine altercations or imperial market competition.[44]

My own work has sought to develop such a reconstructive historical politics of interpretation that valorizes difference, plurivocity, argument, persuasion, and the democratic participation of all those excluded from or subordinated by theological discourses. In her dissertation, Cynthia Briggs Kittredge has examined the rhetoric of obedience in the letters attributed to Paul and in particular has focused on the rhetoric of Philippians and Ephesians. By distinguishing between the inscribed rhetorical and the possible historical situation, her work is able to trace in these letters the struggle between a rhetoric of *ekklesia* and one of kyriarchal submission. "In both Philippians and Ephesians, the authors use the language of obedience to respond to alternative languages and symbolic universes within early Christian communities. Evidence of these visions survives in the early Christian traditions that Paul and the Pauline author employ in their arguments."[45]

Biblical theology that understands itself as a politics of *ekklesia* attempts to trace and revalorize the early Christian egalitarian traditions. At the same time it seeks to displace the politics and rhetorics of subordination and otherness that is inscribed in the "Pauline" correspondence with a politics and rhetorics of equality and responsibility. It conceives of early Christian writings as taking sides in the emancipatory struggles of antiquity and conceptualizes early Christian community as a radical democratic assembly (*ekklesia*) of differing theological voices and sociorhetorical practices.

Such a radical egalitarian politics of *ekklesia* requires the articulation of a theology of divine *politeuma* as its theological grounds and theoretical frame for

44. See Dieter Georgi, *Theocracy in Paul's Praxis and Theology* (Minneapolis: Fortress Press, 1991), for this expression.
45. Briggs Kittredge, *Community and Authority*, 178.

which it can draw on biblical resources. Christian Testament writings such as Philippians or 1 Peter express the self-understanding of the early Christians as foreigners and resident aliens whose citizenship is elsewhere. For instance, in Phil. 3:20 Paul asserts in dualistic terms that Christian "citizenship" or "commonwealth" (*politeuma*) is "in heaven and it is from there that we are expecting a savior." As Carolyn Osiek points out:

> This is the second time in the letter that Paul draws upon the language of the city-state (see 1:27) to imply that all Christians, male and female, have the responsibility of full participation in the commonwealth in which they belong most appropriately. This is the basis for any vision of a discipleship of equals in the Pauline churches. In a world of social inequalities, Christians are to live in the consciousness of their heavenly equal citizenship here and now.[46]

The "*politeuma* in heaven" has usually been understood in dualistic terms as "pie in the sky" or as otherworldly spiritualized reality that has nothing to do with the reality and politics of the earthly *politeuma*. However, if one understands heaven not as opposite to earth but as the site of G*d's justice and well-being that is traditionally called "salvation," then one can conceptualize the divine *politeuma* as the theological location from where a radical critique of oppressive "earthly" structures becomes possible.[47]

Such a theoretization of the "*politeuma* in heaven" would allow for the placing of biblical theology as the rhetoric of the *ekklesia* under the radical horizon of G*d's alternative world,[48] which I have called here *cosmopolis*. Such a hermeneutical-theological horizon can acknowledge the kyriarchal deformations of the biblical text. It does not need to justify or explain away such kyriarchal scriptural formations but can sustain a hermeneutics of suspicion with respect to all biblical texts and theological traditions. It can theologically explore the contradictions and conflicts inscribed in biblical texts and their interpretations.

Such differences and contradictions in the rhetoric of early Christian sources point to sociopolitical conflicts and religiocultural tensions *between* "egalitarian" movements—be they Hellenistic, Jewish or early Christian—and their dominant

---

46. Carolyn Osiek, "Philippians," in *Searching the Scriptures*, ed. Schüssler Fiorenza, 2:246.

47. Ronald F. Thiemann, *Religion in Public Life: A Dilemma for Democracy* (Washington, D.C.: Georgetown University Press, 1996), 169, suggests a similar but different argument when he argues: "The engagement of the religious citizen with a democratic regime is perhaps best captured under the notion of 'pilgrim citizenship.' Recognizing the penultimate character of the public realm, believers will not seek their final resting place in this sphere of power and persuasion." I would add that the "heavenly" *politeuma* of believers must be re-visioned as a sphere of democratic power and persuasion if religious utopia should fulfill its critical function.

48. In his lectures on the political theology of Paul, the Jewish philosopher Jacob Taubes has argued that the "people of G*d" are to be envisioned as a historical community free of domination. The explosive power of the political theology of Israel consists in the fact that in it the people replace the king as the representative of G*d. However, in the horizon of Jewish thought, the institutions of domination of people by people cannot and may not represent the Messiah. The messianic must not legitimate the political order but can only relativize and ultimately replace it. See Jacob Taubes, *Die politische Theologie des Paulus*, ed. Aleida Assmann and Jan Assmann (Munich: Wilhelm Fink Verlag, 1993), 178–80.

kyriarchal sociopolitical-religious contexts. These differing and contradictory socio-rhetorical formations also point to sociopolitical conflicts *within* early Christian communities that understood themselves as a "pneumatic democracy." Such rhetorical tensions can be traced between those who advocate the ethos of *ekklesia* both as a "*basileia* discipleship of equals" and as "a community of freedom in the Spirit" on the one hand, and those that advocate the kyriarchal leadership of elite male power and the kyriarchal institutionalization of the *ekklesia* on the other hand.

The kyriocentric arguments of a politics and rhetorics of submission seek to reintroduce into the *ekklesia* the dualistic split between the public and private spheres, between those who speak and those who are silent, between women and men, between slaves and free, between Jews and Greeks, between humans and nature. For instance, they insist on relegating (elite) married women to the private sphere, on restricting their activity to proper "feminine" behavior, and on limiting women to leadership over other women. These arguments for the "ethics and politics of submission" not only place restrictions on women's leadership in the *ekklesia* but also promote acceptance of slave women's sufferings and advocate the adaptation of the whole Christian community to hegemonic kyriarchal structures of superordination and subordination.[49]

In contrast, the politics of *ekklesia* enables readers to displace both the "scientific" paradigm, which reconstructs early Christianity in terms of sectarian conflict and exclusions, and the doctrinal paradigm, which defines it in terms of orthodoxy-heresy. It can do so by recontextualizing early Christian debates within Greco-Roman and Jewish radical democratic discourses and by ceasing to articulate an unbridgeable gulf between past and present.

In such a new contextualization Pauline writings can be read as public arguments that seek to persuade and convince "citizens" who share common cultural worlds and religious visions of equality and freedom. Rather than to map the rhetorical situation of Paul in terms of the logic of identity and politics of otherness, a rhetorical radical democratic politics of meaning can understand Pauline discourses and their suppressed alternative voices as two sides of one and the same rhetorical "coin." Hence such a politics of meaning is able to reconceptualize the Pauline text as the site of rhetorical-political struggle and an arena of competing cultural-religious practices.

Such a biblical theology defined as the politics of *ekklesia* no longer needs to privilege the authorial master-voice of Paul or that of any other canonical writer, but can position its own inquiry on the side of the historical victims whose subjugated knowledges have left traces in the canonical text. However, such a conflictive egalitarian politics of interpretation would be misapprehended if its re-visioning of early Christian life were read in dualistic terms either as linear development or as rapid and uncontested decline from *ekklesia* as the discipleship of equals to *ekklesia* as the kyriarchal household of God.

---

49. For the fuller development of such an emancipatory reconstructive argument, see my article "A Discipleship of Equals: Ekklesial Democracy and Patriarchy in Biblical Perspective," in *A Democratic Catholic Church*, ed. Eugene C. Bianch and Rosemary Radford Ruether (New York: Crossroad, 1992).

Instead, this model seeks to conceptualize the struggles of "Pauline" Christianity as a pluriform movement of wo/men engaged in an ongoing theological debate over equality, freedom, dignity, and full "citizenship" in the *ekklesia*. If such a historical-theological reconstruction of the debates in the pneumatic *ekklesia* is interfaced with an intercultural and interreligious reconstructive historical model of reading, one can show that such emancipatory rhetorical practices and sociopolitical religious struggles for freedom[50] and for the right of "citizenship" are not restricted to early Christianity but began long before the Christian movements emerged on the scene, and are still going on today. They have continued throughout western history, although a kyriarchal politics of interpretation has failed to write this ongoing history of struggle. The recognition of the rhetoricity rather than the authority of biblical discourses would allow scholars to position their research within this ongoing history of such struggles and their politics of interpretation.

To sum up my argument: If scholars would understand biblical theology as public deliberative discourse of the *ekklesia,* then they could re-vision it as both a critical reflection on the religious-communal and social-political practices encoded in Scripture and as a critical rhetoric of inquiry that is able to explore the rhetorical function of biblical texts and contemporary interpretations. The task of biblical theology would then not only be descriptive-analytic utilizing all the critical methods of exegetical, historical, and literary scholarship but also hermeneutic, ideology critical, evaluative, and theological ones.

Such an approach to biblical theology as a rhetoric of inquiry would then not only open up the rhetorical practices of the Bible to the critical scrutiny of other academic disciplines but also enable students to participate in an intellectual community of critical discourse. The professional education of both ministerial and doctoral students in biblical studies would need to be rethought in light of this. Students would need to acquire not only philological, textual, and historical skills but also adeptness at critical theological reflection and ideological assessment. Finally, questions of ideology critique raised especially by feminist biblical scholars, liberation theologians, Third World or postcolonial critics, cultural studies, and other interpretive approaches that are presently peripheral to the exegetical enterprise could become central for such a biblical theology. In short, the ramifications of a rhetorical reconceptualization of the method and task of biblical theology would be far-reaching and compelling not only for theological education but also for public discourses involving the Bible.

As I have argued throughout this book, unlike a hermeneutic-aesthetic inquiry that strives for textual understanding, appreciation, application, and consent, a critical feminist rhetorics is concerned not just with exploring the conditions and possibilities of understanding and with tracing kyriocentric texts and traditions but also

---

50. Patterson, *Freedom in the Making of Western Culture,* claims to be the first such emancipatory history of freedom. It seems not accidental that his historical reconstruction of the struggles for freedom in antiquity recognizes women's crucial participation and contribution to these struggles.

with the problem of how one can critically assess and, if need be, dismantle their power of persuasion. It also searches for those liberating visions inscribed in biblical texts that have not yet been historically realized. To that end it constructs a critical theoretical framework that can move toward the articulation of a critical rhetoric of inquiry. Finally, biblical theology as a critical rhetoric of inquiry calls for a redefinition of the notion of truth in the emancipatory terms of Wisdom-Sophia.

Examining ancient Greek legal, philosophical, and literary texts on torture, the feminist scholar Page duBois has argued that classical Greek philosophy has developed a "logic of identity" that elaborates truth as something hidden, to be excavated or extracted by the torture of slaves. "This logic demands a closed circle, an other, an outside, and creates such an other. And in the case of the Greek city, the democracy itself used torture to establish this boundary, to mark the line between slave and free, and to locate truth outside."[51]

Consequently, western philosophy on the whole understands truth as something that is not known, but buried, secreted in the earth, in the body, in the woman, in the slave, in the totally "other": something that must be extricated through torture or sexual violence. In a similar fashion, biblical revelation has been understood in traditional theology as an uncovering of a hidden mystery that is located in the unknown and in the beyond. It is directly known only to a select few, and it can be extracted only through arduous labor or stringent asceticism. The "canon within the canon" approach, for instance, seeks to uncover, to distill, or to abstract a universal truth or authoritative norm from the multilayered meanings of biblical texts and the often contradictory writings collected in the canon.

According to Page duBois, this kyriarchal understanding of "truth" in the "logic of identity" is articulated in reaction to the "logic of democracy." Whereas the logic of identity relies on strategies of "othering" and subordination, the logic of democracy is determined by the notion of equal power among members of a society. Such a logic of democracy requires a radical redistribution of wealth as well as the elimination of social and political hierarchies. For some ancient thinkers, according to duBois, even slavery itself was eventually called into question.

Such a recontextualization of biblical theology in the paradigm of radical democracy produces a different notion of theological truth. It does not understand the truth of the sacred or of the Bible as a metaphysical given buried in the "other" but seeks to comprehend the truth of the divine *politeuma* in and through the interactive deliberation of a multiple, polyvalent assembly of voices in the *ekklesia*. Truth is not, as in the logic of identity, a process of discovering the hidden or forcing into the open a divine that is buried. Rather, truth is a historical process of public deliberation for the creation of radical democratic equality for every wo/man in the global village. The truth of biblical theology is produced in radical democratic struggles and debates between equals as an alternative discourse to torture and inquisition. In such a radical logic of democracy, the truth or the sacred is best understood as a moment in an interpretive political process, a progressive extension of rights and equality to all res-

---

51. Page duBois, *Torture and Truth: The New Ancient World* (New York: Routledge, 1991).

idents of our expanding world community. The truth of the *ekklesia* is *multivoiced and cosmopolitan.* A conception of "truth" in this sense comes close to the biblical notion of "doing the truth," a truth that "will set you free."

By deconstructing the biblical rhetorics and politics of subordination, a critical feminist rhetoric of *ekklesia* is able to generate new possibilities for the communicative construction of religious identities and emancipatory practices. To that end a critical biblical theology that is positioned in the radical democratic space of *ekklesia* interrogates religious texts, traditions, and institutional practices for religious visions that foster equality, justice, and the logic of the *ekklesia,* rather than that of kyriarchal domination. Yet only when biblical theology radically throws into question the kyriarchal discourses of exclusion inscribed in the Bible and biblical traditions, I submit, will it be able to identify the radical democratic discourses inscribed in Scripture.

A critical hermeneutical integration of notions of liberty, equality, and democracy with the radical egalitarian religious vision of *ekklesia,* I argue, can engender critical biblical-theological discourses of possibility for a different understanding of human well-being. The task of biblical theological studies is to articulate and envision the divine *politeuma* as a radical democratic Wisdom-Spirit-center of global dimensions.

In Place of a Conclusion

To reformulate biblical theology as a critical rhetoric and politics of meaning that is positioned in the public square of *ekklesia* would allow biblical studies to articulate a biblical rhetoric and spiritual vision that could critically address public political discourses and individual questions seeking for a world of justice and well-being. Such a critical biblical theology could do the work of Divine Wisdom.[52] "Wisdom-Sophia has sent out Her women servants to call from the highest places in the town, 'Come eat of my bread and drink of the wine I have mixed.' Leave immaturity and live and walk in the way of Wisdom-Sophia" (Prov. 9:3-6).

Instead of concluding, I continue to turn and to move, beginning at the end, circling back to the beginning. Like the tides of the ocean, Divine Wisdom-Sophia always moves and returns, but with a difference. If biblical studies moves and changes in the direction of the divine *politeuma,* it might glimpse a vision of Her all-embracing justice and enveloping well-being. As Karen Baker-Fletcher has seen Her ceaseless motion:

> When I watch the wind tease and urge into dance the waves of the ocean, when I feel the moon's pull on the waters and on the cycles of my own body, I often think of the deep powerful waters of the ocean dancing with the spirit of God. . . . Creation is born out of a loving, creative dance between Spirit and the elements of the cosmos. We

52. See my book *Sharing Her Word* and the perceptive discussion of my proposal of a Wisdom–theo/alogy by Martin Hailer, *Theologie als Weisheit: Sapientiale Konzeptionen in der Fundamentaltheologie des 20. Jahrhunderts* (Neukirchen: Neukirchener Verlag, 1997).

humans are *adam* (which means "earth creature" in Hebrew), dependent on all the elements of water, earth, air, sun. Our own nativity and the birth of our children's children is dependent on this power of life.[53]

If the Scriptures were likened to the "deep powerful waters of the ocean dancing with the Spirit of G*d," biblical theology could then be understood as articulating and participating in "the creative dance between the Spirit and the elements" of the biblical traditions. In the critical deliberations of such an emancipatory-rhetorical paradigm of interpretation, biblical discourses could become Divine Wisdom-Sophia's power for life again.

---

53. Karen Baker-Fletcher, *Sisters of Dust, Sisters of Spirit: Womanist Wordings on God and Creation* (Minneapolis: Fortress Press, 1998), 27.

Appendix 1

The Ethics of Interpretation: Thirteen Theses[1]

I. As an intellectual discipline the ethics of interpretation must be distinguished from the ethics of a text, for example the ethics of Paul or of the Christian (New) Testament. In my view a Christian Testament ethics investigates and systematizes the ethical or moral contents of Christian Testament writings. The ethics of interpretation in turn is a second-order methodological reflection on the ethos and morals of biblical studies.

II. "Ethics" is understood here in the general sense as "morality rendered self-conscious" whereby morality names a "pervasive and often only partly conscious set of value-laden dispositions, inclinations, attitudes and habits."[2] Thus "ethics" is best conceptualized as a critical scientific metatheory. Hence I introduce the ethics of interpretation as a new interdisciplinary area of critical reflexivity and research that studies the "pervasive and often only partly conscious set of value-laden dispositions, inclinations, attitudes, and habits" of biblical studies as an academic discipline. Such a critical exploration of the ethos and morality of biblical scholarship, or of what it means to work scientifically and ethically, has as its goal scholarly responsibility and accountability as an integral part of the research process. In other words, the ethics of interpretation seeks to articulate a professional ethics for biblical studies.

III. To propose the ethics of interpretation as a new interdisciplinary area in biblical studies means to overcome the assumed dichotomy between engaged scholarship (such as feminist, postcolonial, African American, queer, and other subdisciplines) and scientific (malestream) interpretation. Whereas the former

1. These theses were formulated at the conclusion of an advanced seminar on "Neutestamentliche Ethik und die Ethik der Interpretation" at the University of Heidelberg, which Prof. Dr. Gerd Theissen and I chaired in the summer semester 1999. I want to thank professor Theissen and the other members of the seminar, especially Annette Merz, Friedericke Wendt, Gunnar Garleff, Ulrike Bruinings, Bettina Nicklas, Andrea Pistor, Andre Urbanczyk, Thomas Sülzle, Michio Hamano, Bärbel Ganster, Simone Sinn, Monica Minor, and Walter Kallenback for the lively and substantive discussions we had.

2. Wayne A. Meeks, *The Origins of Christian Morality: The First Two Centuries* (New Haven: Yale University Press, 1993), 4.

is allegedly utilizing ethical criteria, the latter is said to live up to a scientific ethos that gives precedence to cognitive criteria. Instead, I would argue that a scientific ethos demands *both* ethical and cognitive criteria that must be reasoned out in terms of standard knowledge and at the same time intersubjectively understandable and communicable. To split off rationality from ethics opens the door for irresponsible scholarship that can nevertheless from a subjective point of view be quite ethical.

IV.   The subdiscipline ethics of interpretation consists of the following areas of investigation:
1. The *ethics of reading* or of the exegesis of texts
2. The *ethics of interpretive practices,* that is, of the scientific production of scholarship
3. The *ethics of scholarship,* that is, the ethos, attitudes, habits, dispositions, and inclinations of biblical scholarship and its communication
4. The *ethics of scientific valuation and judgment,* that is, the ethical-moral norms, values, visions, and ideals as well as the criteria of discernment and evaluation

V.   The *ethics of reading* pertains to the text and the methods used to interpret it. It investigates not only the values, norms, principles, and visions of the text but also the value-laden assumptions and theoretical frameworks that are introduced through the chosen methods of reading.

VI.   The *ethics of reading* understands
1. *Language* not as descriptive and reflective, as window to reality, but as polysemic, constructive-performative, rhetorical-communicative, and as ideological misrepresentation, as marginalizing and repressive.
2. *Text* as rhetorical, as inscribed communicative practices, as product of communications, as determined by rhetorical situations, arguments, persuasive goals, and visions. Texts are multivoiced and tensive-conflictive.
3. *Context* as produced rhetorically through selection, classification, and valuation. Social contexts are produced through selection of materials, models, images, and reconstruction of the social world through analogy, contrast, and imagination.
4. *Interpretation* as determined by the effective history of a text as well as the communities of reading and their norms.

VII.   The *ethics of interpretive practices* or scientific production has the task to critically research the process of how interpretation is produced, authorized, communicated, and used. For instance, it investigates
1. The area of questions and problem formulation
2. The "commonsense" assumptions and unarticulated presuppositions
3. The lenses of reading, patterns of interpretation, categories of analysis
4. The reconstructive models, analogies, and images

5. The theoretical frameworks, worldviews, and points of reference
6. How the discourse of interpretations is constructed, which authorities are appealed to, or which references are missing
7. The rhetoric, that is, logos, ethos, and pathos of scientific discourses
8. Which boundaries and limits are constructed and maintained by a scholarly discourse, which questions are not admitted, which arguments are silenced
9. What the critical reflexivity and comprehensiveness of a discourse is (for instance, emancipatory interpretations are bound to be more complex and critically reflexive because they need to take both the hegemonic and the marginal discourses into account)

VIII. The *ethics of scholarship* investigates the ethos, social location, and positionality of biblical interpretations. Who are its subjects? How are they socially located, what is their standpoint and perspective? What are the social and political values of a certain interpretation? In order to approach this question, it is necessary to develop or articulate a social-societal systemic analysis. The investigation of the unarticulated interests and goals of an interpretation is absolutely necessary in order to adjudicate its sociopolitical and religious functions and effects. Rhetorics, politics, and ethics are epistemologically as well as historically intertwined.

IX. The *ethics of scientific valuation and judgment* explores what kind of knowledge is produced: Is it technological, hermeneutic, emancipatory? Scholarship, current and past, is always produced by and for people with certain experiences, values, and goals. Hence one must investigate the implicit interests and unarticulated goals of scholarship, its degree of conscious responsibility, and its accountability.

X. The *ethics of scientific valuation and judgment* examines the norms, values, interests, visions, or ideals implicit or explicit in biblical interpretations as well as the criteria of discernment and evaluation. If texts are polysemous and have an oppressive history of effects, their interpretation always requires judgment and evaluation. Interpretation is intrinsically interested and value-laden. Hence the criteria for adjudicating between different readings cannot be only cognitive but are always also evaluative.

XI. To that end, the *ethics of communication* assesses interpretive practices as to whether they do justice not only to the text and its interpretations but also to contemporary readers, especially to those biblical readers who are affected by biblical texts today. It analyzes scholarly interpretations as to their interests, values, and visions in order to show that not only so-called engaged but also scientific supposedly value-free or value-neutral scholarship is an ideologically, theologically, or ethically motivated communication.

XII. The *ethics of communication* inspects biblical scholarship as an assembly of divergent communicative scientific practices. Interpretation and communication can be distinguished, but they must not be dualistically separated or split off from each other as two different procedures, as interpretation and application. One can distinguish, for instance, between different forms or modes of communication, between scientific-technical communication (university lecture), journalistic communication (through the diverse media), everyday communication (recipes for cooking), artistic communication, or ideologically interested communication (preaching) of an interpretation, but not between communication that is "scientific" and communication that is "applied," since the rhetorical process of interpretation is always already communicative. It intervenes in a specific communicative situation and discourse. The institutional division between scientific exegesis and ecclesial application derives from the historical-critical positivistic discourse of biblical studies as a hard science, which understood itself as "pure" objective and antiquarian exegesis free from dogmatic-ecclesiastical controls.

XIII. In short, the ethics of interpretation must reconceptualize both biblical studies as a discipline and biblical education as socialization into the ethos of "pure," value-detached, positivistic scientism. To that end, it must foster an ethos of critical reflexivity, democratic debate, intellectual, multilingual, and multidisciplinary competence. It takes as its goal publicly accountable scholarship and the responsible production and communication of such scholarship.

Appendix 2

The Rhetoric of Interpretation: Analytic Compass

Suggested questions of investigation have as their double reference point the rhetoric of interpretation in the present and the rhetoric of interpretation in the past.

1. Subject of Interpretation
      Social-cultural-religious location
      Gender, race, class, religious, ethnic, sexual, bodily determination
      Viewpoint: perspective, standpoint, pathos
      Theoretical-theological-ideological frameworks and perspectives
      Community of interpretation: arguments from authority and communities of accountability

2. (Unreflected) Presuppositions
      Worldview, belief systems, experience, unconscious assumptions
      Power relations, status differences, ideologies
      Values, prejudices, emotions
      Convictions, beliefs, goals, and dreams

3. Intellectual Frameworks and Models
      Understandings of scholarship, scientific investigation, interpretation, history, or theology
      Anthropological understanding, social theory, understanding of reality
      Theory of language, representation, interdisciplinary reasoning
      Understanding of objectivity, critique, hermeneutics, ethics

4. Methods and Methodology
      Control of scientific methods
      Ways and rules of investigation
      Selection, use, and combination of methods: for example, text and source-critical, archaeological historical-critical, literary, sociological, anthropological, semiotic, intertextual, sociohistorical, rhetorical discourse analysis, ideology-critical methods, reader-response criticism, structuralist and poststructuralist analysis, bibliodrama, spiritual and theological methods
      Critical methodological reflexivity

5. Area of Research

> Selection, delineation, translation, and categorization of texts
>
> Knowledge, selection, evaluation of source materials pertaining to their contexts
>
> Utilization of scholarly resources, supportive materials, and commentaries
>
> Delineation of areas of research, exclusions, and claims to comprehensiveness
>
> Periodization, classification, accentuation, authentication

6. Basic Questions and Interpretive Metaphors

> Key questions and arguments
>
> Key images, models, analogies, metaphors of representation
>
> Rhetorical means; logos, pathos, ethos
>
> Principles of organization, narration, and representation
>
> Central theories and argumentation

7. Values, Goals, and Visions

> Interpretation for whom and in which context
>
> Whose history: the history of men, wo/men, hierarchy, orthodoxy, or marginal groups?
>
> Which and whose perspectives and interests are taken for granted, are seen as important or are rejected?
>
> What and who is marginalized, trivialized, not mentioned?
>
> Which claims to universal truth and validity are made for a particular interpretation?
>
> Who has the power to authorize interpretations? How is this accomplished rhetorically?
>
> What appeals to authority are made and which ideals, utopias, and visions are appealed to?

Selected Bibliography

Compiled by Lyn Miller

Abir, Pete Antonysamy. *The Cosmic Conflict of the Church: An Exegetico-Theological Study of Revelation 12, 7–12*. Frankfurt: Peter Lang, 1995.

Adam, A. K. M. "Biblical Theology and the Problem of Modernity: Von Wredestrasse zu Sackgasse." *Horizons in Biblical Theology* 12 (1990): 1–18.

Adamson, Jane, Richard Freadman, and David Parke, eds. *Renegotiating Ethics in Literature, Philosophy, and Theory*. Cambridge: Cambridge University Press, 1998.

Alcoff, Linda. "Justifying Feminist Social Science." *Hypatia* 2 (1987): 107–27.

Althusser, Louis. *Essays on Ideology*. London: Verso, 1984.

Anderson, R. Dean. *Ancient Rhetorical Theory and Paul*. Kampen, Netherlands: Kok Pharos, 1996.

Andrews, William L. *Sisters of the Spirit: Three Black Women's Autobiographies of the Nineteenth Century*. Bloomington: Indiana University Press, 1986.

Antony, Louise M., and Charlotte Witt, eds. *A Mind of One's Own: Feminist Essays on Reason and Objectivity*. Boulder, Colo.: Westview Press, 1993.

Appiah, K. Anthony "Is the 'Post' in 'Postmodernism' the 'Post' in 'Postcolonial'?" *Critical Inquiry* 17 (1991): 360–67.

Aristotle. *Rhetoric*. Translated by W. Rhys Roberts. New York: Random House, 1954.

Aronowitz, Stanley, and Henry A. Giroux. "Teaching and the Role of the Transformative Intellectual." In *Education under Siege: The Conservative, Liberal, and Radical Debate over Schooling*, edited by Stanley Aronowitz and Henry A. Giroux, 23–46. South Hadley, Mass.: Bergin & Garvey, 1985.

Bailey, K. E. "The Structure of I Corinthians and Paul's Theological Method with Special Reference to 4:17." *Novum Testamentum* 25 (1983): 152–81.

Baker, Peter. *Deconstruction and the Ethical Turn*. Gainesville: University of Florida Press, 1995.

Baker-Fletcher, Karen. *Sisters of Dust, Sisters of Spirit: Womanist Wordings on God and Creation*. Minneapolis: Fortress Press, 1998.

Ball, Terrence. *Transforming Political Discourse: Political Theory and Critical Conceptual History*. Oxford: Blackwell, 1988.

Barkun, Michael. *Religion and the Racist Right: The Origins of the Christian Identity Movement*. Chapel Hill: University of North Carolina Press, 1994.

Baron, Dennis. *Grammar and Gender*. New Haven: Yale University Press, 1986.

Barr, James. "Biblical Theology." In supplemental volume to *The Interpreter's Dictionary of the Bible: An Illustrated Encyclopedia*, 104–11. Nashville: Abingdon, 1976.

Barrett, Michèlle. *The Politics of Truth: From Marx to Foucault*. Stanford: Stanford University Press, 1991.

Bartky, Sandra Lee. *Femininity and Domination: Studies in the Phenomenology of Oppression*. New York: Routledge, 1990.

Barton, S. "Paul and the Cross: A Sociological Approach." *Theology* 85 (1982): 13–19.

Bass, Dorothy C. "Women's Studies and Biblical Studies: An Historical Perspective." *Journal for the Study of the Old Testament* 22 (1982): 6–12.

Beardslee, William A. "Theology and Rhetoric in the University." In *Theology and the University: Essays in Honor of John B. Cobb, Jr.*, edited by David Ray Griffin and Joseph C. Hough, Jr., 185–200. Albany: State University of New York Press, 1991.

Becker, Jürgen, ed. *Die Anfänge des Christentums: Alte Welt und Neue Hoffnung.* Stuttgart: Kohlhammer, 1987.

Beker, J. Christian. "The Method of Recasting Pauline Theology: The Coherence-Contingency Theme as Interpretive Model." In *SBL 1986 Seminar Papers*, edited by Kent H. Richards, 596–602. Atlanta: Scholars Press, 1986.

Benhabib, Seyla, and Drucilla Cornell, eds. *Feminism as Critique: On the Politics of Gender.* Minneapolis: University of Minnesota Press, 1987.

Bender, John, and David E. Wellbery. "Rhetoricality: On the Modernist Return of Rhetoric." In *The Ends of Rhetoric: History, Theory, Practice*, edited by John Bender and David E. Wellbery, 3–39. Stanford: Stanford University Press, 1990.

Berger, Klaus. "Die impliziten Gegner: Zur Methode der Erschliessung von Gegnern in neutestamentlichen Texten." In *Kirche*, edited by D. Lührmann and G. Strecker, 373–400. Tübingen: Mohr, 1980.

———. *Hermeneutik des Neuen Testaments.* Gütersloh: Gütersloher Verlagshaus Gerd Mohn, 1988.

Betz, Hans Dieter. "The Literary Composition and Function of Paul's Letter to the Galatians." *New Testament Studies* 21 (1975): 353-59.

———. *Galatians: A Commentary on Paul's Letter to the Churches in Galatia.* Hermeneia. Philadelphia: Fortress Press, 1979.

Bible and Culture Collective. *The Postmodern Bible.* New Haven: Yale University Press, 1995.

Biesecker, Barbara. "Rethinking the Rhetorical Situation from within the Thematic of Différance." *Philosophy and Rhetoric* 22 (1989): 110–30.

Billing, Michael. "Conservatism and the Rhetoric of Rhetoric." *Economy and Society* 18 (1989): 132–48.

Bitzer, Lloyd F. "The Rhetorical Situation." *Philosophy and Rhetoric* 1 (1968): 1–14.

Black, Edwin. *Rhetorical Criticism: A Study in Method.* Madison: University of Wisconsin Press, 1978.

Blount, Brian K. *Cultural Interpretation: Reorienting New Testament Criticism.* Minneapolis: Fortress Press, 1995.

Boers, Hendrickus. *What Is New Testament Theology? The Rise of Criticism and the Problem of a Theology of the New Testament.* Philadelphia: Fortress Press, 1979.

Booth, Wayne C. "Freedom of Interpretation: Bakhtin and the Challenge of Feminist Criticism." In *The Politics of Interpretation*, edited by W. J. T. Mitchell, 51–82. Chicago: University of Chicago Press, 1983.

Børresen, Kari Elisabeth, ed. *Image of God and Gender Models in Judeo-Christian Tradition.* Oslo: Solum Forlag; [Atlantic Highlands,] N.J.: Distributed in the United States by Humanities Press, 1991.

Botha, Jan. "Creation of New Meaning: Rhetorical Situations and the Reception of Romans 13:1–7." *Journal of Theology for Southern Africa* 79 (1971): 24–37.

Brackenbury Crook, Margaret. *Women and Religion*. Boston: Beacon, 1964.

Brandt, W. J. *The Rhetoric of Argumentation*. New York: Bobbs-Merrill, 1970.

Briggs Kittredge, Cynthia. *Community and Authority: The Rhetoric of Obedience in the Pauline Tradition*. Harvard Theological Studies. Harrisburg: Trinity Press International, 1998.

Brock, Bernard L., Robert L. Scott, and James W. Chesebro, eds. *Methods of Rhetorical Criticism: A Twentieth Century Perspective*. 3d rev. ed. Detroit: Wayne State University Press, 1989.

Brodribb, Somer. *Nothing Mat(t)ers: A Feminist Critique of Postmodernism*. Melbourne: Spinifex Press, 1992.

Brooten, Bernadette. *Women Leaders in the Ancient Synagogue*. Chico, Calif.: Scholars Press, 1982.

Brown, Richard Harvey. *Society as Text: Essays on Rhetoric, Reason, and Reality*. Chicago: University of Chicago Press, 1987.

Brown Zikmund, Barbara. "Biblical Arguments and Women's Place in the Church." In *The Bible and Social Reform*, edited by Ernest R. Sandeen, 85–104. Philadelphia: Fortress Press, 1982.

Buker, Eloise A. "Feminist Social Theory and Hermeneutics: An Empowering Dialectic." *Social Epistemology* 4 (1990): 23–39.

Bullmore, Michael A. *St. Paul's Theology of Rhetorical Style: An Examination of 1 Corinthians 2:1-5 in Light of First-Century Greco-Roman Rhetorical Culture*. San Francisco: International Scholar Publications, 1995.

Bultmann, Rudolf. "Die Aufgabe der Theologie in der gegenwärtigen Situation." *Theologische Blätter* 12 (June 1933): 161–66.

———. "Der Arier Paragraph im Raum der Kirche." *Theologische Blätter* 12 (December 1933): 359–70.

Bünker, Michael. *Briefformular und rhetorische Disposition im 1. Korintherbrief*. Göttinger Theologische Arbeiten 28. Göttingen: Vandenhoeck & Ruprecht, 1983.

Burke, Kenneth. "The Rhetoric of Hitler's 'Battle.'" In *The Philosophy of Literary Form*. 1941. Reprint. New York: Vintage Books, 1957.

Burnett, Fred W. "Postmodern Biblical Exegesis: The Eve of Historical Criticism." *Semeia* 51 (1990): 51–80.

Buse, Gunhild. *Macht-Moral-Weiblichkeit: Eine feministisch-theologische Auseinandersetzung mit Carol Gilligan und Frigga Haug*. Mainz: Grünewald, 1993.

Bushnell, Katherine C. *God's Word to Women: One Hundred Bible Studies on Woman's Place in the Divine Economy*. Reprint, North Collins, N.Y.: Ray Munson, 1923. First published as *God's Word for Women: The Women's Correspondence Bible Class*. London 1912.

Butler, Judith, and Joan W. Scott, eds. *Feminists Theorize the Political*. New York: Routledge, 1992.

Cadbury, Henry J. "Motives of Biblical Scholarship." *Journal of Biblical Literature* 56 (1937): 1–16.

Cady Stanton, Elizabeth, ed. *The Original Feminist Attack on the Bible: The Woman's Bible.* 1895, 1898. Facsimile ed. New York: Arno, 1974.

Cameron, Deborah, ed. *The Feminist Critique of Language: A Reader.* New York: Routledge, 1998.

Cannon, Katie G. *Black Womanist Ethics.* Atlanta: Scholars Press, 1988.

Capel Anderson, Janice. "Mapping Feminist Biblical Criticism." *Critical Review of Books in Religion* 2 (1991): 21–44.

Capps, Walter H. *The New Religious Right: Piety, Patriotism and Politics.* Columbia: University of South Carolina Press, 1990.

Castelli, Elizabeth A. *Imitating Paul: A Discourse of Power.* Louisville: Westminster/ John Knox Press, 1991.

———. "Interpretations of Power in 1 Corinthians," *Semeia* 54 (1992): 159–96.

———. "Heteroglossia, Hermeneutics, and History: A Review Essay of Recent Feminist Studies of Early Christianity." *The Journal of Feminist Studies in Religion* 10, 2 (1994): 73–78.

Chance, J. Bradley. "Paul's Apology to the Corinthians." *Perspectives in Religious Studies* 9 (1982): 144–55.

Chow, Rey. *Ethics after Idealism: Theory-Culture-Ethnicity-Reading.* Bloomington: Indiana University Press, 1998.

Church, F. Forrester. "Rhetorical Structure and Design in Paul's Letter to Philemon." *Harvard Theological Review* 71 (1978): 17–31.

Clark Wire, Antoinette. *The Corinthian Women Prophets: A Reconstruction through Paul's Rhetoric.* Minneapolis: Fortress Press, 1990.

Classen, C. J. "Paulus und die antike Rhetorik." *Zeitschrift für die neutestamentliche Wissenschaft* 82 (1991): 1–33.

Claudel, G. "I Kor 6,12—7,40 neu gelesen." *Trierer Theologische Zeitschrift* 94 (1985): 20–36.

Clines, David J. A. "Biblical Interpretation in an International Perspective." *Biblical Interpretation* 1 (1993): 67–87.

Code, Lorraine. *Rhetorical Spaces: Essays on Gendered Locations.* New York: Routledge, 1995.

Condit, Celeste Michelle. "Democracy and Civil Rights: The Universalizing Influence of Public Argumentation." *Communication Monographs* 54 (1987): 1–18.

Conley, Thomas M. *Rhetoric in the European Tradition.* Chicago: The University of Chicago Press, 1990.

Consigny, S. "Rhetoric and Its Situations." *Philosophy and Rhetoric* 7 (1974): 172–82.

Conzelmann, Hans. *I Corinthians: A Commentary on the First Epistle to the Corinthians.* Hermeneia. Philadelphia: Fortress Press, 1975.

Cooey, Paula M., Sharon A. Farmer, and Mary Ellen Ross, eds. *Embodied Love: Sensuality and Relationship as Feminist Values.* San Francisco: Harper & Row, 1987.

Cooper, Anna Julia. *A Voice from the South.* 1892. Reprint, Schomburg Library of Nineteenth-Century Black Women Writers, New York: Oxford University Press, 1988.

Corbett, Edward P. J. *Classical Rhetoric for the Modern Student.* 3d ed. New York: Oxford University Press, 1990.

Cowling, Maurice. *The Nature and Limits of Political Science*. Cambridge: Cambridge University Press, 1963.

Craffert, P. F., "Towards an Interdisciplinary Definition of the Social-Scientific Interpretation of the New Testament." *Neotestamentica* 25 (1991): 123–44.

Dahl, Nils Alstrup. *Studies in Paul: Theology for the Early Christian Mission*. Minneapolis: Augsburg Publishing House, 1977.

DeBerg, Betty. *Ungodly Women: Gender and the First Wave of American Fundamentalism*. Minneapolis: Fortress Press, 1990.

De Lauretis, Teresa, ed. *Feminist Studies/Critical Studies*. Bloomington: University of Indiana Press, 1986.

Derrida, Jacques. "The Ends of Man." *Philosophy and Phenomenological Research* 30 (1969): 31–57.

De Swarte Gifford, Carolyn. "American Women and the Bible: The Nature of Woman as a Hermeneutical Issue." In *Feminist Perspectives on Biblical Scholarship*, edited by Adela Yarbro Collins, 11–33. Chico, Calif.: Scholars Press, 1985.

De Villiers, P. G. R., ed. *Liberation Theology and the Bible*. Pretoria: University of South Africa, 1987.

Derwacter, Frederick Milton. *Preparing the Way for Paul: The Proselyte Movement in Later Judaism*. New York: Macmillan, 1930.

Diamond, Sara. *Spiritual Warfare: The Politics of the Christian Right*. Boston: South End Press, 1989.

Dirlik, Arif. "Culturalism as Hegemonic Ideology and Liberating Practice." In *The Nature and Context of Minority Discourse*, edited by Abdul R. JanMohamed and David Lloyd, 394–431. New York: Oxford University Press, 1993.

———, ed. *The Postcolonial Aura: Third World Criticism in the Age of Global Capitalism*. New York: Westview Press, 1997.

Downing, F. Gerald. *Cynics, Paul and the Pauline Churches*. New York: Routledge, 1998.

duBois, Page. *Centaurs and Amazons: Women and the Prehistory of the Great Chain of Being*. Ann Arbor: University of Michigan Press, 1982.

———. *Torture and Truth: The New Ancient World*. New York: Routledge, 1990.

Dugger, Karen. "Social Location and Gender-Role Attitudes: A Comparison of Black and White Women." *Gender and Society* 2 (1988): 425–48.

Eagleton Terry. *Walter Benjamin, or, Towards a Revolutionary Criticism*. London: Verso, 1981.

Ebert, Teresa L. "The 'Difference' of Postmodern Feminism." *College English* 53 (1991): 886–904.

Edmondson, Ricca. *Rhetoric in Sociology*. New York: Cambridge University Press, 1985.

Eliade, Mircea. *Journal II: 1957–1969*. Chicago: University of Chicago Press, 1989.

Elliott, J. H. "Social-Scientific Criticism of the New Testament: More on Methods and Models." *Semeia* 35 (1986): 1–34.

Elliott, Neil. *Liberating Paul: The Justice of God and the Politics of the Apostle*. Maryknoll, N.Y.: Orbis Books, 1994.

Ellis, Earl E. "Paul and His Opponents: Trends in Research." In *Christianity, Judaism, and Other Greco-Roman Cults,* edited by Jacob Neusner, 1:264–98. Leiden: Brill, 1975.

Enslin, Morton S. "The Future of Biblical Studies." *Journal of Biblical Literature* 65 (1946): 1–12.

Erickson, Victoria Lee. *Where Silence Speaks: Feminism, Social Theory, and Religion.* Minneapolis: Fortress Press, 1992.

Eschenburg, Theodor. *Über Autorität.* Frankfurt: Suhrkamp, 1976.

Farnham, Christine, ed. *The Impact of Feminist Research in the Academy.* Bloomington: Indiana University Press, 1987.

Fatum, Lone. "Women, Symbolic Universe, and Structures of Silence: Challenges and Possibilities in Androcentric Texts." *Studia Theologica* 43 (1989): 61–80.

Felder, Cain Hope, ed. *Stony the Road We Trod: African-American Biblical Interpretation.* Minneapolis: Fortress Press, 1991.

Fessenden, Tracy. "'Woman' and the 'Primitive' in Tillich's Life and Thought: Some Implications for the Study of Religion." *JFSR* 14, 2 (1998): 45–76.

Fewell, Danna Nolan, and Gary A. Phillips, eds. *Bible and Ethics of Reading.* Semeia 77. Atlanta: Scholars Press, 1997.

Fiorenza, Francis Schüssler. "Theory and Practice: Theological Education as a Reconstructive, Hermeneutical, and Practical Task." *Theological Education* 23 (1987): 113–41.

———. "Religious or Theological Studies: The Contest of the Faculties." In *Shifting Boundaries: Contextual Approaches to the Structure of Theological Education,* edited by Barbara Wheeler and Edward Farley, 119–49. Louisville: Westminster/John Knox Press, 1991.

———. "Theology in the University." *Bulletin of the Council of Societies for the Study of Religion* 22 (April 1993): 34–39.

———. "Response to Wiebe." *Bulletin of the Council of Societies for the Study of Religion* 23 (April 1994): 6–10.

Fish, Stanley. "Rhetoric." In *Critical Terms for Literary Study,* edited by Frank Lentricchia and Thomas McLaughlin, 202–22. Chicago: University of Chicago Press, 1990.

Flynn Elizabeth A., and Patrocinio P. Schweickart, eds. *Gender and Reading: Essays on Readers, Texts, and Contexts.* Baltimore: Johns Hopkins University Press, 1986.

Forbes Christopher. "Comparison, Self-Praise, and Irony." *New Testament Studies* 32 (1986): 1–30.

Forstman, H. Jackson. "A Chapter in Theological Resistance to Racism: Rudolph Bultmann and the Beginning of the Third Reich." In *Justice and the Holy: Essays in Honor of Walter Harrelson,* edited by Douglas A. Knight and Peter J. Paris, 257–70. Atlanta: Scholars Press, 1989.

Fowler, Robert M. "Postmodern Biblical Criticism." *Foundations and Facets Forum* 5, 3 (1989): 3–31.

Freire, Paulo. *Pedagogy of the Oppressed.* New York: Seabury Press, 1973.

Fretheim, Terence E. "Is the Biblical Portrayal of God Always Trustworthy?" In *The Bible as Word of God in a Postmodern Age*, edited by Terence E. Fretheim and Karlfried Fröhlich, 97–112. Minneapolis: Fortress Press, 1998.

Frostin, Pere. *Liberation Theology in Tanzania and South Africa*. Lund, Sweden: Lund University Press, 1988.

Funk, Robert W. "The Watershed of the American Biblical Tradition: The Chicago School, First Phase, 1892–1920." *Journal of Biblical Literature* 95 (1976): 4–22.

Furnish, Victor P. *II Corinthians*. Anchor Bible 32A. Garden City, N.Y.: Doubleday, 1984.

———. "Paul the Theologian." In *The Conversation Continues: Studies in Paul and John in Honor of J. Louis Martyn*, edited by Robert T. Fortna and Beverly Gaventa, 19–34. Nashville: Abingdon, 1990.

Gadamer, Hans Georg. *Philosophical Hermeneutics*. Berkeley: University of California Press, 1976.

———. *Truth and Method*. Translated by Joel Weinsheimer and Donald G. Marshall. 2d rev. ed. New York: Continuum, 1993.

Gallagher, E. V. "The Social World of Saint Paul." *Religion* 14 (1984): 91–99.

Garret, M., and Xiaosui Xiao. "The Rhetorical Situation Revisited." *Rhetoric Society Quarterly* 23 (1993): 30–40.

Georgi, Dieter. "Rudolf Bultmann's Theology of the New Testament Revisited." In *Bultmann: Retrospect and Prospect. The Centenary Symposium at Wellesley*, edited by E. C. Hobbs, 75–87. Harvard Theological Studies 35. Philadelphia: Fortress Press, 1985.

———. *The Opponents of Paul in Second Corinthians: A Study of Religious Propaganda in Late Antiquity*. Philadelphia: Fortress Press, 1986. Originally published as *Die Gegner des Paulus im 2. Korintherbrief: Studien zur religiösen Propaganda in der Spätantike*. Neukirchen-Vlyn: Neukirchener Verlag, 1964.

———. *Theocracy in Paul's Praxis and Theology*. Minneapolis: Fortress Press, 1991.

Glenn, Cheryl. *Rhetoric Retold: Regendering the Tradition from Antiquity through the Renaissance*. Carbondale: Southern Illinois University Press, 1997.

Good, James, and Irving Velody, eds. *The Politics of Postmodernity*. Cambridge: Cambridge University Press, 1998.

Grant, Judith. "I Feel Therefore I Am: A Critique of Female Experience as the Basis for a Feminist Epistemology." In *Feminism and Epistemology: Approaches to Research in Women and Politics*, edited by Maria J. Falco, 99–114. New York: Haworth Press, 1987.

Grant, Robert M., and Tracy, David. *A Short History of the Interpretation of the Bible*. 2d ed. Philadelphia: Fortress Press, 1984.

Greene, Gayle, and Coppélia Kahn, eds. *Making a Difference: Feminist Literary Criticism*. New York: Methuen, 1985.

Gross, Rita M. "'A Rose by Any Other Name . . .': A Response to Katherine K. Young." *Journal of the American Academy of Religion* 67, 1 (1999): 185–94.

Grossberg, Lawrence. *We Gotta Get Out of This Place: Popular Conservatism and Postmodern Culture*. New York: Routledge, 1992.

Grudem, Wayne A. *The Gift of Prophecy in I Corinthians*. Washington, D.C.: University Press of America, 1982.

Gundry-Volf, Judith M. "Male and Female in Creation and New Creation: Interpretations of Galatians 3:28c in 1 Corinthians 7." In *To Tell the Mystery: Essays on New Testament Eschatology in Honor of Robert H. Gundry*, edited by Thomas E. Schmidt and Moisés Silva, 95–121. Sheffield: Sheffield Academic Press, 1994.

Habermas, Jürgen. "Ideology." In *Modern Interpretations of Marx*, edited by Tom Bottomore, 155–69. Oxford: Blackwell, 1981.

———. *Moral Consciousness and Communicative Action*. Cambridge, Mass.: MIT Press, 1995.

Hailer, Martin. *Theologie als Weisheit: Sapientiale Konzeptionen in der Fundamentaltheologie des 20. Jahrhunderts*. Neukirchen: Neukirchener Verlag, 1997.

Harding, Sandra, and Merrill B. Hintikka, eds. *Discovering Reality: Feminist Perspectives on Epistemology, Metaphysics, Methodology, and Philosophy*. Dordrecht, Netherlands: D. Reidel, 1983.

Hartin, P. J., and Petzer, J. H. *Text and Interpretation: New Approaches to the Criticism of the New Testament*. Leiden: Brill, 1991.

Hasel, Gerhard. F. "Methodology as a Major Problem in the Current Crisis of Old Testament Theology." *Biblical Theology Bulletin* 2 (1972): 177–98.

Hasler, V. "Das Evangelium des Paulus in Korinth: Erwägungen zur Hermeneutik." *New Testament Studies* 30 (1984): 109–29.

Hay, David M., ed. *Pauline Theology*. 2 vols. Minneapolis: Fortress Press, 1991.

Hennessy, Rosemary. *Materialist Feminism and the Politics of Discourse*. New York: Routledge, 1993.

Hernadi, Paul. "Literary Theory: A Compass for Critics." *Critical Inquiry* 3 (1976): 369–86.

Herzfeld, Michael. "As in Your Own House: Hospitality, Ethnography and the Stereotype of Mediterranean Society." In *Honor and Shame and the Unity of the Mediterranean*, edited by David D. Gilmore, 75–89. American Anthropological Association No. 22. Washington, D.C.: American Anthropological Association, 1987.

Hiley, David R., James F. Bohman, and Richard M. Shusterman, eds. *The Interpretive Turn: Philosophy, Science, Culture*. Ithaca: Cornell University Press, 1991.

Hill Collins, Patricia. *Black Feminist Thought: Knowledge, Consciousness, and the Politics of Empowerment*. Boston: Unwin Hyman, 1990.

Himmelstein, Jerome. *To the Right: The Transformation of American Conservatism*. Berkeley: University of California Press, 1990.

Hock, Ronald. "Paul's Tentmaking and the Problem of His Social Class." *Journal of Biblical Literature* 97 (1978): 555–64.

Holmberg, Bengt. *Paul and Power: The Structure of Authority in the Primitive Church as Reflected in the Pauline Epistles*. Philadelphia: Fortress Press, 1980.

Holub, Robert C. *Reception Theory: A Critical Introduction*. London: Methuen, 1984.

hooks, bell. *Ain't I a Woman: Black Women and Feminism*. Boston: South End Press, 1984.

Huber, Elaine C. "They Weren't Prepared to Hear: A Closer Look at *The Woman's Bible*." *Andover Newton Quarterly* 16 (1976): 271–76.

Hunter, James Davison. *Culture Wars: The Struggle to Define America.* New York: Basic Books, 1991.

Hurd, John Coolidge. *The Origins of I Corinthians.* New York: Seabury Press, 1965.

Hutcheon, Linda. *The Politics of Postmodernism.* London: Routledge, 1989.

Iggers, George G. *The German Conception of History: The National Tradition of Historical Thought from Herder to the Present.* Rev. ed. Middletown, Conn.: Wesleyan University Press, 1983.

————. *New Directions in European Historiography.* Rev. ed. Middletown, Conn.: Wesleyan University Press, 1984.

Jackson, Jared J., and Martin Kessler, eds. *Rhetorical Criticism: Essays in Honor of James Muilenburg.* Pittsburgh Theological Monograph Series I. Pittsburgh: Pickwick Press, 1974.

Jameson, Fredric R. "The Symbolic Inference." In *Representing Kenneth Burke*, edited by Hayden White and Margaret Brose, 68–91. Baltimore: Johns Hopkins University Press, 1982.

Jarratt, Susan C. "The First Sophists and Feminism: Discourse of the 'Other.'" *Hypatia* 5 (1990): 27–41.

————. *Rereading the Sophists: Classical Rhetoric Refigured.* Carbondale: Southern Illinois University Press, 1991.

Jaspert, Bernd. "Sachkritik und Widerstand. Das Beispiel Rudolf Bultmanns." *Theologische Literaturzeitung* 115 (1990): 161–82.

Jobling, David, and Tina Pippin, eds. *Ideological Criticism of Biblical Texts.* Semeia 59. Atlanta: Scholars Press, 1992.

Johnson, Barbara. *The Critical Difference: Essays in the Contemporary Rhetoric of Reading.* Baltimore: Johns Hopkins University Press, 1980.

Johnson-Odim, Cheryl, and Margaret Strobel, eds. *Expanding the Boundaries of Women's History: Essays on Women in the Third World.* Bloomington: Indiana University Press, 1992.

Jones, A. H. M. *Athenian Democracy.* Baltimore: Johns Hopkins University Press, 1957.

Jones, Kathleen. *Compassionate Authority: Democracy and the Representation of Women.* New York: Routledge, 1993.

Kahl, Brigitte. "Der Brief an die Gemeinden in Galatien: Vom Unbehagen der Geschlechter und anderen Problemen des Andersseins." In *Kompendium feministischer Bibelauslegung*, edited by Luise Schottroff and Marie-Therese Wacker, 603–11. Gütersloh: Chr. Kaiser Gütersloher Verlagshaus, 1998.

————. "No Longer Male: Masculinity Struggles Behind Gal. 3:28?" Paper presented at the Society of Biblical Literature Panel on Gal. 3:28, Orlando, Florida, November 1998.

Kandal, Terry R. *The Woman Question in Classical Sociological Theory.* Miami: Florida University Press, 1988.

Keegan, T. J. *Interpreting the Bible: A Popular Introduction to Biblical Hermeneutics.* New York: Paulist Press, 1985.

Kelly, Joan. *Women, History, and Theory.* Chicago: University of Chicago Press, 1984.

Kemp, Peter. "From Ethics to Bioethics." In *Questioning Ethics: Contemporary Debates in Philosophy*, edited by Richard Kierney and Mark Dooley, 283–93. New York: Routledge, 1999.

Kennedy, George A. *Classical Rhetoric and Its Christian and Secular Tradition from Ancient to Modern Times*. Chapel Hill: University of North Carolina Press, 1980.

———. *New Testament Interpretation Through Rhetorical Criticism*. Chapel Hill: North Carolina University Press, 1984.

Kim, Yong-Bok. *Messiah and Minjung: Christ's Solidarity with the People for New Life*. Hong Kong: Christian Conference of Asia, 1992.

King, Ursula, ed. *Religion and Gender*. Oxford: Oxford University Press, 1995.

Kinukawa, Hisako. *Women and Jesus in Mark: A Japanese Feminist Perspective*. Edited by Letty M. Russell. Maryknoll, N.Y.: Orbis Books, 1994.

Kitzberger, Ingrid Rosa, ed., *The Personal Voice in Biblical Interpretation*. New York: Routledge, 1998.

Klauck, Hans-Josef *1. Korintherbrief*. Würzburg: Echter Verlag, 1984.

———. "Gemeindestrukturen im ersten Korintherbrief." *Bibel und Kirche* 40 (1985): 9–15.

Koester, Helmut. *Introduction to the New Testament*. 2 vols. Philadelphia: Fortress Press, 1982.

Kraditor, Aileen S. *Up from the Pedestal: Selected Writings in the History of American Feminism*. Chicago: Quadrangle Books, 1968.

Kraftschick, Steven. "Why Do the Rhetoricians Rage?" In *Text and Logos: The Humanistic Interpretation of the New Testament*, edited by Theodore W. Jennings, 55–79. Atlanta: Scholars Press, 1990.

Lamberts Bendroth, Margaret. *Fundamentalism and Gender, 1875 to the Present*. New Haven: Yale University Press, 1993.

Lang, F. "Die Gruppen in Korinth nach 1. Korinther 1–4." *Theologische Beiträge* 14 (1983): 68–79.

Laqueur, Thomas. *Making Sex: Body and Gender from the Greeks to Freud*. Cambridge, Mass.: Harvard University Press, 1990.

Lategan, Bernard C., and Vorster, Willem S. *Text and Reality: Aspects of Reference in Biblical Texts*. Semeia Studies. Philadelphia: Fortress Press, 1985.

Lausberg, Heinrich. *Handbuch der literarischen Rhetorik: Eine Grundlegung der Literaturwissenschaft*. 2d rev. ed. Munich: Max Huber, 1973.

Lentricchia, Frank. *Criticism and Social Change*. Chicago: University of Chicago Press, 1983.

Lieu, Judith. "Circumcision, Women, and Salvation." *New Testament Studies* 40 (1994): 358–70.

Lionnet, Francoise. *Postcolonial Representations: Women, Literature, Identity*. Ithaca, N.Y.: Cornell University Press, 1995.

List, Elisabeth. *Die Präsenz des Anderen: Theorie und Geschlechterpolitik*. Gender Studies. Frankfurt: Edition Suhrkamp, 1992.

Lloyd, Genevieve. *The Man of Reason: "Male" and "Female" in Western Philosophy*. Minneapolis: University of Minnesota Press, 1984.

Lovejoy, Alexander. O. *The Great Chain of Being: A Study of the History of an Idea.* 1936. Reprint, Cambridge: Harvard University Press, 1976.

Lucaites, John Louis, Celeste Michelle Condit, and Sally Caudill, eds. *Contemporary Rhetorical Theory: A Reader.* New York: Guilford Press, 1999.

Lüdemann, Gerd. *Paulus.* Vol. 2, *Antipaulinismus im frühen Christentum.* Forschungen zur Religion und Literatur des Alten und Neuen Testaments 130. Göttingen: Vandenhoeck & Ruprecht, 1983.

Lyal, Francis. *Slaves, Citizens, Sons: Legal Metaphors in the Epistles.* Grand Rapids, Mich.: Zondervan, 1984.

Lyndon Shanley, Mary, and Carol Pateman, eds. *Feminist Interpretations and Political Theory.* University Park: Pennsylvania State University Press, 1991.

Lyon, David. *Postmodernity.* Minneapolis: University of Minnesota Press, 1994.

Lyons, George. *Pauline Autobiography: Toward a New Understanding.* Atlanta: Scholars Press, 1985.

Mack, Burton. *Rhetoric and the New Testament.* Minneapolis: Fortress Press, 1990.

Malina, Bruce. "Rhetorical Criticism and Social-Scientific Criticism: Why Won't Romanticism Leave Us Alone?" In *Rhetoric, Scripture, and Theology: Essays from the 1994 Pretoria Conference,* edited by Stanley E. Porter and Thomas H. Olbricht, 72–101. Sheffield: Sheffield University Press, 1996.

Mandelbaum, Maurice. *The Anatomy of Historical Knowledge.* Baltimore: Johns Hopkins University Press, 1977.

Marsden, George. *Fundamentalism and American Culture: The Shaping of Twentieth-Century Evangelicalism, 1870–1925.* New York: Oxford University Press, 1980.

Marshall, Gloria A. "Racial Classifications: Popular and Scientific." In *The "Racial" Economy of Science: Toward a Democratic Future,* edited by Sandra Harding, 116–27. Bloomington: Indiana University Press, 1993.

Marty, Martin E., and R. Scott Appleby, eds. *Fundamentalisms Observed.* Chicago: University of Chicago Press, 1991.

Matthews, Shelly. *Ladies First: The Function of Gentile Noble Women in Early Jewish and Christian Religious Propaganda.* Stanford: Stanford University Press, forthcoming.

McCutcheon, Russell T. *Manufacturing Religion: The Discourse on Sui Generis Religion and the Politics of Nostalgia.* New York: Oxford University Press, 1997.

McDonald, Dennis. *There Is No Male and Female: The Fate of a Dominical Saying in Paul and Gnosticism.* Philadelphia: Fortress Press, 1987.

———. "Corinthian Veils and Gnostic Androgynes." In *Images of the Feminine in Gnosticism,* edited by Karen L. King, 276–92. Philadelphia: Fortress Press, 1988.

McGrew Bennett, Anne, "The Woman's Bible: Review and Perspectives." In *Women and Religion, 1973: Pre-printed Papers for the Working Group on Women and Religion,* compiled by Joan Arnold Romero, 39–43. Tallahassee, Fla.: AAR, 1973.

McKnight, Edgar V. *The Bible and the Reader: An Introduction to Literary Criticism.* Philadelphia: Fortress Press, 1985.

Meeks, Wayne A. *The First Urban Christians: The Social World of the Apostle Paul.* New Haven: Yale University Press, 1983.

————. *The Moral World of the First Christians*. Philadelphia: Westminster Press, 1986.

————. "Understanding Early Christian Ethics." *Journal of Biblical Literature* 105 (1986): 3–11.

————. "The 'Haustafeln' and American Slavery: A Hermeneutical Challenge." In *Theology and Ethics in Paul and His Interpreters: Essays in Honor of Victor Paul Furnish*, edited by Eugene H. Lovering, Jr. and Jerry L. Sumney, 232–53. Nashville: Abingdon Press, 1996.

Meese, Elizabeth A. *Crossing the Double Cross: The Practice of Feminist Criticism*. Chapel Hill: University of North Carolina Press, 1986.

Merton, Robert K. *The Sociology of Science: Theoretical and Empirical Investigations*. Edited by Norman W. Storer. Chicago: University of Chicago Press, 1973.

Mickelsen, Alvera, ed. *Women, Authority, and the Bible*. Downers Grove, Ill.: Inter-Varsity Press, 1986.

Miller, C. R. "Genre as Social Action." *Quarterly Journal of Speech* 63 (1984): 28–42.

Miller, J. Hillis. "Presidential Address 1986: The Triumph of Theory, the Resistance to Reading, and the Question of the Material Base." *PMLA* 102 (1987): 281–91.

Mitchell, Margaret M. *Paul and the Rhetoric of Reconciliation: An Exegetical Investigation of the Language and Composition of 1 Corinthians*. Tübingen: J. C. B. Mohr, 1991.

Mohanti, S. P. "Us and Them: On the Philosophical Bases of Political Criticism." *Yale Journal of Criticism* 2, 2 (1998): 1–31.

Moller Okin, Susan. *Women in Western Political Thought*. Princeton: Princeton University Press, 1979.

Montgomery, James A. "Present Tasks of American Biblical Scholarship." *Journal of Biblical Literature* 38 (1919): 1–14.

Moon, Warren G. "Nudity and Narrative: Observations on the Frescoes from the Dura Synagogue." *Journal of the American Academy of Religion* 40 (1992): 587–658.

Morgenstern, Julian. "The Society of Biblical Literature and Exegesis." *Journal of Biblical Literature* 61 (1942): 1–10.

Morrison, Toni. *Beloved*. New York: Plume, New American Library, 1988.

Morrow, Raymond A. with David D. Baron. *Critical Theory and Methodology*. Thousand Oaks, Calif.: Sage Publications, 1994.

Mosala, Itumeleng J. *Biblical Hermeneutics and Black Theology in South Africa*. Grand Rapids, Mich.: Eerdmans, 1989.

Mulkay, Michael. *Science and Sociology of Knowledge*. London: Allen, 1979.

Munro, Winsome. *Authority in Paul and Peter: The Identification of a Pastoral Stratum in the Pauline Corpus and I Peter*. Society for New Testament Studies Monograph Series 45. Cambridge: Cambridge University Press, 1983.

Murphy, Cullen. "Women and the Bible." *The Atlantic Monthly* 272, 2 (August 1993), 64.

Myers, Ched. *Binding the Strong Man: A Political Reading of Mark's Story*. Maryknoll, N.Y.: Orbis Books, 1988.

Nations, Archie L. "Historical Criticism and the Current Methodological Crisis." *Scottish Journal of Theology* 36 (1983): 59–71.

Natoli, Joseph, ed. *Tracing Literary Theory.* Urbana: University of Illinois Press, 1987.

Natter, Wolfgang, Theodore R. Schatzki, and John Paul Jones III, eds. *Objectivity and Its Other.* New York: Guilford Press, 1995.

Nelson, John S. "Political Theory as Political Rhetoric." In *What Should Political Theory Be Now? Essays from the Shambaugh Conference on Political Theory,* edited by John S. Nelson, 169–240. Albany: State University of New York Press, 1983.

Nelson, John S., Allan Megill, and Donald McCloskey, eds. *The Rhetoric of the Human Sciences: Language and Argument in Scholarship and Public Affairs.* Madison: University of Wisconsin Press, 1987.

Newton, Judith, and Deborah Rosenfelt, eds. *Feminist Criticism and Social Change: Sex, Class, and Race in Literature and Culture.* New York: Methuen, 1985.

Nikoloff, James B., ed. *Gustavo Gutiérrez: Essential Writings.* Minneapolis: Fortress Press, 1996.

Odell-Scott, D. W. "Let the Women Speak in Church: An Egalitarian Interpretation of I Cor. 14:33b-36." *Biblical Theology Bulletin* 13 (1983): 90–93.

Oden, Robert A., Jr. "Hermeneutics and Historiography: Germany and America." In *SBL 1980 Seminar Papers,* edited by Paul J. Achtemeier, 135–57. Chico, Calif.: Scholars Press, 1980.

Orr, William F., and James Arthur Walther. *I Corinthians: A New Translation.* Anchor Bible 32. New York: Doubleday, 1976.

Osiek, Carolyn. *What Are They Saying about the Social Setting of the New Testament?* New York: Paulist Press, 1984.

Parker, Patricia. *Literary Fat Ladies: Rhetoric, Gender, Property.* London: Methuen, 1987.

Patte, Daniel. *Ethics of Biblical Intrepretation: A Reevaluation.* Louisville: Westminster/John Knox Press, 1995.

Patterson, Orlando. *Freedom in the Making of Western Culture.* New York: HarperCollins Publishers, 1991.

Patton, J. "Causation and Creativity in Rhetorical Situations: Distinctions and Implications." *Quarterly Journal of Speech* 65 (1979): 36–55.

Patrick, Dale, and Allen Scult. *Rhetoric and Biblical Interpretation.* Sheffield: Almond Press, 1990.

Perelman, Chaim, and Luci Olbrechts-Tyteca. *The New Rhetoric: A Treatise on Argumentation.* Translated by John Wilkinson and Purcell Weaver. Notre Dame, Ind.: University of Notre Dame Press, 1969.

Perrot, Michelle. *Writing Women's History.* Cambridge: Blackwell, 1992.

Petersen, Norman R. *Literary Criticism for New Testament Critics.* Philadelphia: Fortress Press, 1978.

———. *Rediscovering Paul: Philemon and the Sociology of Paul's Narrative World.* Philadelphia: Fortress Press, 1985.

Phillips, Gary. "Exegesis as a Critical Praxis: Reclaiming History and Text from a Postmodern Perspective." *Semeia* 51 (1990): 7–50.

Pieper, Annemarie. *Ethik und Moral: Eine Einführung in die praktische Philosophie.* Munich: Kösel, 1985.

Plaskow, Judith. "We Are Also Your Sisters: The Development of Women's Studies in Religion." *Women's Studies Quarterly* 21, 1 (1993): 9–21.

Pogoloff, Stephen M. *Logos and Sophia: The Rhetorical Situation of 1 Corinthians.* Society of Biblical Literature Dissertation Series 134. Atlanta: Scholars Press, 1992.

Poland, Lynn M. *Literary Criticism and Biblical Hermeneutics: A Critique of Formalist Approaches.* Chico, Calif.: Scholars Press, 1985.

Poovey, Mary. "Feminism and Deconstruction." *Feminist Studies* 14 (1988): 51–66.

Porter, Frank C. "The Bearing of Historical Studies on the Religious Use of the Bible." *Harvard Theological Review* 2 (1909): 253–76.

Porter, Stanley E., and Thomas H. Olbricht, eds. *Rhetoric and the New Testament: Essays from the Heidelberg Conference.* Journal for the Study of the New Testament Supplemental Series 90. Sheffield: JSOT Press, 1993.

Pratt, Mary Louise. "Interpretative Strategies/Strategic Interpretations: On Anglo-American Reader Response Criticism." In *Postmodernism and Politics,* edited by Jonathan Arac, 26–54. Theory and History of Literature 28. Minneapolis: University of Minnesota Press, 1986.

Prelli, Lawrence J. "The Rhetorical Construction of Scientific Ethos." In *Rhetoric in the Human Sciences,* edited by Herbert W. Simons, 48–68. Newbury Park, Calif.: Sage Publications, 1989.

Prozesky, Martin. "South Africa's Contribution to Religious Studies." *Journal of Theology for Southern Africa* 70 (1990): 9–20.

Pryse, Marjorie and Hortense J. Spillers, eds. *Conjuring: Black Women, Fiction, and Literary Tradition.* Bloomington: University of Indiana Press, 1985.

Ratcliffe, Krista. *Anglo-American Feminist Challenges to the Rhetorical Traditions: Virginia Woolf, Mary Daly, Adrienne Rich.* Carbondale: Southern Illinois University Press, 1996.

Redmond, Sheila. "Christian 'Virtues' and Recovery from Child Sexual Abuse." In *Christianity, Patriarchy, and Abuse: A Feminist Critique,* edited by Joanne Carlson Brown and Carole R. Bohn, 70–88. New York: Pilgrim Press, 1989.

Ricoeur, Paul. *Hermeneutics and the Human Sciences.* Edited and translated by John B. Thompson. Cambridge and New York: Cambridge University Press, 1981.

———. "History and Rhetoric." *Diogenes* 168 (1994): 7–24.

Robbins, Vernon K. "Using a Socio-Rhetorical Poetics to Develop a Unified Method: The Woman Who Anointed Jesus as a Test Case." In *SBL 1992 Seminar Papers,* edited by Eugene H. Lovering, 302–19. Atlanta: Scholars Press, 1992.

———. *Exploring the Texture of Texts: A Guide to Socio-Rhetorical Interpretation.* Valley Forge, Pa.: Trinity Press International, 1996.

Rommelpacher, Birgit. *Dominanzkultur: Texte zu Fremdheit und Macht.* Berlin: Orlanda Frauenverlag, 1995.

Rorty, Richard. *Philosophy and the Mirror of Nature.* Princeton: Princeton University Press, 1979.

Rosaldo, Renato. *Culture and Truth: The Remaking of Social Analysis.* Boston: Beacon Press, 1989.

Rose, Douglas D., ed. *The Emergence of David Duke and the Politics of Race.* Chapel Hill: University of North Carolina Press, 1992.

Rossi, Pietro, ed. *Theorie der modernen Geschichtsschreibung.* Frankfurt: Suhrkamp, 1987.

Royalty, Robert M., Jr. "The Rhetoric of Revelation." In *SBL 1997 Seminar Papers,* 596–617. Atlanta: Scholars Press, 1997.

Russell, Letty M., ed. *Feminist Interpretation of the Bible.* Philadelphia: Westminster Press, 1985.

Sanders, B. "Imitating Paul: I Cor 4:16." *Harvard Theological Review* 74 (1981): 353–63.

Sanders, James A. "Hermeneutics." Supplemental volume to *The Interpreter's Dictionary of the Bible: An Illustrated Encyclopedia,* 402–7. Nashville: Abingdon, 1976.

Saunders, Ernest W. *Searching the Scriptures: A History of the Society of Biblical Literature, 1880–1980.* Chico, Calif.: Scholars Press, 1982.

Schmeller, Thomas. *Brechungen: Urchristliche Wundercharismatiker im Prisma soziologisch orientierter Exegese.* Stuttgart: Verlag Kath. Bibelwerk, 1989.

Schmidt, K. L. "Ekklesia." In *Theological Dictionary of the New Testament.* Vol. 3, edited by Gerhard Kittel, 514–16. Grand Rapids, Mich.: Eerdmans, 1964.

Schmithals, Walter. *An Introduction to the Theology of Rudolf Bultmann.* Minneapolis: Augsburg Press, 1968.

Schneiders, Sandra. *The Revelatory Text: Interpreting the New Testament as Sacred Scripture.* New York: HarperSanFrancisco, 1991.

Schoedel, William R., and Robert L. Wilken, eds. *Early Christian Literature and the Classical Intellectual Tradition: In Honorem Robert Grant.* Théologie Historique 53. Paris: Editions Beauchesne, 1979.

Schottroff, Luise. "Nicht viele Mächtige: Annäherungen an eine Soziologie des Urchristentums." *Bibel und Kirche* 40 (1985): 2–8.

Schrag, Calvin O. *Communicative Praxis and the Space of Subjectivity.* Bloomington: Indiana University Press, 1986.

Schüssler Fiorenza, Elisabeth. "Women in the Pre-Pauline and Pauline Churches." *Union Seminary Quarterly Review* 33 (1978): 153–66.

———. "For the Sake of Our Salvation: Biblical Interpretation as Theological Task." In *Sin, Salvation, and the Spirit: Commemorating the Fiftieth Year of the Liturgical Press,* edited by Daniel Durken, 21–39. Collegeville, Minn.: Liturgical Press, 1979.

———. "Women in Early Christianity: Methodological Considerations." In *Critical History and Biblical Faith in New Testament Perspectives,* edited by T. J. Ryan, 30–58. Villanova, Pa.: CTS Annual Publication, 1979.

———. *The Book of Revelation: Judgment and Justice.* 1985. 2d ed. with a new epilogue, Minneapolis: Fortress Press, 1998.

———. "Missionaries, Apostles, Coworkers: Rom 16 and the Reconstruction of Women's Early Christian History." *Word and World* VI (1986): 420–33.

————. "The Politics of Otherness: Biblical Interpretation as a Critical Praxis for Liberation." In *The Future of Liberation Theology: Essays in Honor of Gustavo Gutiérrez*, edited by Mark H. Ellis and Otto Maduro, 311–25. Maryknoll, N.Y.: Orbis Books, 1989.

————. "Text and Reality—Reality as Text: The Problem of a Feminist Historical and Social Reconstruction Based on Texts." *Studia Theologica* 40 (1989): 19–34.

————. *Revelation: Vision of a Just World.* Minneapolis: Fortress Press, 1991.

————. *But She Said: Feminist Practices of Biblical Interpretation.* Boston: Beacon Press, 1992.

————. *Discipleship of Equals: A Feminist Ekklesialogy of Liberation.* New York: Crossroad, 1993.

————. *In Memory of Her: A Feminist Theological Reconstruction of Christian Origins.* 10th anniversary ed. New York: Crossroad, 1993.

————. *Jesus: Miriam's Child, Sophia's Prophet. Critical Issues in Feminist Christology.* New York: Continuum, 1994.

————. *Bread Not Stone: The Challenge of Feminist Biblical Interpretation.* 1984. 10th anniversary edition. With a new afterword by the author. Boston: Beacon, 1995.

————. *Sharing Her Word: Feminist Biblical Interpretation in Context.* Boston: Beacon Press, 1998.

————, ed. *Aspects of Religious Propaganda in Judaism and Early Christianity.* Notre Dame, Ind.: University of Notre Dame Press, 1976.

————, ed. *Searching the Scriptures* or *A Feminist Introduction* and *A Feminist Commentary.* 2 vols. New York: Crossroad, 1993–1994.

————, ed. *The Power of Naming: A Concilium Reader in Feminist Christian Theology.* Maryknoll, N.Y.: Orbis Books, 1996.

Schüssler Fiorenza, Elisabeth, and Kwok Pui-Lan, eds. *Women's Sacred Scriptures.* Concilium 1998/3. Maryknoll, N.Y.: Orbis Books, 1998.

Schüssler Fiorenza, Elisabeth, and Shawn Copeland, eds. *Feminist Theology in Different Contexts.* Concilium 1996/1. Maryknoll, N.Y.: Orbis Books, 1996.

Schütz, John Howard. *Paul and the Anatomy of Apostolic Authority.* London: Cambridge University Press, 1975.

Scroggs, Robin. *The Text and the Times: New Testament Essays for Today.* Minneapolis: Fortress Press, 1993.

Segovia, Fernando F. "Introduction: Pedagogical Discourses and Practices in Biblical Criticism: Toward a Contextual Biblical Pedagogy." In *Teaching the Bible: The Discourses and Politics of Biblical Pedagogy,* edited by Fernando F. Segovia and Mary Ann Tolbert, 1–28. Maryknoll, N.Y.: Orbis Books, 1998.

Segovia, Fernando F., and Mary Ann Tolbert, eds. *Reading from this Place: Social Location and Biblical Interpretation in the United States.* Vol. 1. Minneapolis: Fortress Press, 1995.

Sennett, Richard. *Authority.* New York: Vintage Books, 1980.

Shapiro, Susan. "Rhetoric as Ideology Critique: The Gadamer-Habermas Debate Reinvented." *Journal of the American Academy of Religion* 62, 1 (1994): 123–50.

Shaw, Rosalind. "Feminist Anthropology and the Gendering of Religious Studies." In *Religion and Gender,* edited by Ursula King, 65–76. Oxford: Oxford University Press, 1995.

Showalter, Elaine, ed. *The New Feminist Criticism: Essays on Women, Literature, and Theory.* New York: Pantheon Books, 1985.

Singer, Peter, ed. *Ethics: An Oxford Reader.* New York: Oxford University Press, 1994.

Smit, D. J. "The Ethics of Interpretation: New Voices from the USA." *Scriptura* 33 (1990) 16–28.

———. "The Ethics of Interpretation and South Africa." *Scriptura* 33 (1990) 29–43.

———. "The Bible and Ethos in a New South Africa," *Scriptura* 37 (1991) 51–67.

Smith, C. R., and S. Lybarger, "Bitzer's Model Reconstructed." *Communication Quarterly* 44 (1996): 197–313.

Smith, Dorothy E. *The Conceptual Practices of Power: A Feminist Sociology of Knowledge.* Boston: Northeastern University Press, 1990.

Smith, Wilfred Cantwell. "The Comparative Study of Religion: Whither and Why? In *The History of Religions: Essays in Methodology,* edited by Mircea Eliade and Joseph Kitagawa. Chicago: University of Chicago Press, 1959.

Soelle, Dorothe. "Rudolf Bultmann und die politische Theologie." *In Rudolf Bultmann: 100 Jahre,* edited by Hartwig Thyen et al., 62–79. Oldenburger Vorträge. Oldenburg: H. Holzberg, 1985.

Sorkin Rabinowitz, Nancy, and Amy Richlin, eds. *Feminist Theory and the Classics.* New York: Routledge, 1993.

Spelman, Elizabeth V. *Inessential Woman: Problems of Exclusion in Feminist Thought.* Boston: Beacon Press, 1988.

Spencer Richard A., ed. *Orientation by Disorientation: Studies in Literary Criticism and Biblical Literary Criticism.* Pittsburgh Theological Monograph Series 35. Pittsburgh: Pickwick Press, 1980.

Spender, Dale. *Women of Ideas and What Men Have Done to Them.* London and Boston: Ark Paperbacks, 1983.

Spivak, Gayatri Chakravorty. *In Other Worlds: Essays in Cultural Politics.* New York: Methuen, 1987.

Stambaugh, John E., and David L. Balch. *The New Testament in Its Social Environment.* Philadelphia: Westminster Press, 1986.

Stamp, Dennis. "Rhetorical Criticism of the New Testament: Ancient and Modern Evaluation of Argumentation." In *Approaches to New Testament Study,* edited by Stanley E. Porter and David Tombs, 129–69. Sheffield: Sheffield Academic Press, 1995.

Starr, Lee Anna. *The Bible Status of Women.* New York: Fleming Revell, 1926.

Stendahl, Krister. "Biblical Theology, Contemporary." In *The Interpreter's Dictionary of the Bible,* vol. 1, edited by Keith Crim, 418–32. Nashville: Abingdon, 1962.

———. "Method in the Study of Biblical Theology." In *The Bible in Modern Scholarship: Papers Read at the 100th Meeting of the Society of Biblical Literature, December 28–30, 1964,* edited by J. Philip Hyatt, 196–209. Nashville: Abingdon, 1965.

————. "The Bible as a Classic and the Bible as Holy Scripture." *Journal of Biblical Literature* 103 (1984): 3–10.

————. *Meanings: The Bible as Document and as Guide.* Philadelphia: Fortress Press, 1984.

Stenger, W. "Beobachtungen zur Argumentationsstruktur von I Cor 15." *Linguistica Biblica* 45 (1979): 71–128.

Stiver, Dan R. *The Philosophy of Religious Language: Sign, Symbol, and Story.* Cambridge: Blackwell, 1996.

Strobel, Regula. "Brot Nicht Steine: Elisabeth Schüssler Fiorenzas Hermeneutik in der Pfarrarbeit." *Fama* 14 (1998): 6–7.

Struthers Malbon, Elizabeth. "Fallible Followers: Women and Men in the Gospel of Mark." *Semeia* 28 (1983): 29–48.

Stuhlmacher, Peter. *Historical Criticism and Theological Interpretation of Scripture: Toward a Hermeneutics of Consent.* Philadelphia: Fortress Press, 1977.

Sugirtharajah, R. S. "Introduction: The Margin as a Site of Creative Revisioning." In *Voices from the Margin: Interpreting the Bible in the Third World*, edited by R. S. Sugirtharajah, 1–8. Rev. ed. Maryknoll, N.Y.: Orbis Books, 1995.

Suskin Ostriker, Alicia. *Feminist Revision and the Bible.* Cambridge: Blackwell, 1993.

Sutton, Jane. "The Death of Rhetoric and Its Rebirth in Philosophy." *Rhetorica* 4 (1986): 203–26.

Talbert, Charles H. "Paul's Understanding of the Holy Spirit." In *Perspectives on the New Testament: Festschrift Stagg*, edited by Charles H. Talbert, 95–108. Macon: Mercer University Press, 1985.

Taubes, Jacob. *Die politische Theologie des Paulus: Vorträge, gehalten an der Forschungsstätte der evangelischen Studiengemeinschaft in Heidelberg, 23.–27. Februar 1987.* Edited by Aleida Assmann and Jan Assmann. Munich: Wilhelm Fink Verlag, 1993.

Taylor, Carole Ann. "Positioning Subjects and Objects: Agency, Narration, Rationality." *Hypatia* 8 (1993): 55–80.

Taylor, Mark C., ed. *Critical Terms for Religious Studies.* Chicago: University of Chicago Press, 1998.

Terry, Ralph Bruce. *A Discourse Analysis of First Corinthians.* Arlington: University of Texas and Summer Institute of Linguistics, 1995.

Theissen, Gerd. *The Social Setting of Pauline Christianity: Essays on Corinth.* Philadelphia: Fortress Press, 1982.

Thiele, Johannes. "Bibelauslegung im gesellschaftlich-politischen Kontext." In *Handbuch der Bibelarbeit*, edited by Wolfgang Langer, 106–14. Munich: Kösel Verlag, 1987.

Thiemann, Ronald F. "Toward an American Public Theology: Religion in a Pluralistic Theology." *Harvard Divinity Bulletin* 18, 1 (1987): 4–6, 10.

————. *Religion in Public Life: A Dilemma for Democracy.* Washington, D.C.: Georgetown University Press, 1996.

Thiselton, Anthony C. *The Two Horizons: New Testament Hermeneutics and Philosophical Description.* Grand Rapids, Mich.: Eerdmans, 1980.

————. *New Horizons in Hermeneutics: The Theory and Practice of Transforming Biblical Reading.* London: HarperCollins, 1992.

Thomas Culver, Elsie. *Women in the World of Religion.* Garden City, N.Y.: Doubleday, 1967.

Thompson, John B. *Studies in the Theory of Ideology.* Cambridge: Polity Press, 1984.

Thomson, James C., Jr., Peter W. Stanley, and John Curtis Perry. *Sentimental Imperialists: The American Experience in East Asia.* New York: Harper Torchbooks, 1981.

Tolbert Roberts, Jennifer. *Athens on Trial: The Antidemocratic Tradition in Western Thought.* Princeton: Princeton University Press, 1994.

Tompkins, Jane P., ed. *Reader-Response Criticism: From Formalism to Poststructuralism.* Baltimore: Johns Hopkins University, 1980.

Tracy, David. *Plurality and Ambiguity: Hermeneutics, Religion, and Hope.* New York: Harper & Row, 1987.

Trible, Phyllis. *God and the Rhetoric of Sexuality.* Philadelphia: Fortress Press, 1978.

————. *Texts of Terror: Literary-Feminist Readings of Biblical Narratives.* Philadelphia: Fortress Press, 1984.

————. *Rhetorical Criticism: Context, Method, and the Book of Jonah.* Minneapolis: Fortress Press, 1994.

Troeltsch, Ernst. *The Social Teaching of the Christian Churches.* Vol. 1. New York: Macmillan, 1931.

Vetterling-Braggin, Mary, ed. *Sexist Language: A Modern Philosophical Analysis.* Totowa, N.J.: Littlefield, Adams and Co., 1981.

Vickers, Brian. *In Defence of Rhetoric.* Oxford: Clarendon Press, 1988.

Vielhauer, Philipp. "Paulus und die Kephaspartei in Korinth." *New Testament Studies* 21 (1975): 341–52.

Wachterhauser, Brice R. *Hermeneutics and Modern Philosophy.* Albany: State University of New York Press, 1986.

Wallace, Ruth A., ed. *Feminism and Social Theory.* Newbury Park, Calif.: Sage Publications, 1989.

Walzer, Michael. *Interpretation and Social Criticism.* Cambridge, Mass.: Harvard University Press, 1987.

Waterman, Leroy. "Biblical Studies in a New Setting." *Journal of Biblical Literature* 66 (1947): 1–14.

Watson, Duane F. "Rhetorical Criticism of the Pauline Epistles since 1975." In *Currents in Research: Biblical Studies* 3 (1995): 219–48.

Watson, Duane F., and Alan J. Hauser. *Rhetorical Criticism of the Bible: A Comprehensive Bibliography with Notes on History and Method.* Biblical Interpretation Series 4. Leiden: Brill, 1994.

Weedon, Chris. *Feminist Practice and Poststructuralist Theory.* London: Blackwell, 1987.

Wendland, Heinz-Dietrich. *Die Briefe an die Korinther.* Das Neue Testament Deutsch 7. Göttingen: Vandenhoeck & Ruprecht, 1965.

Wengst, Klaus. *Pax Romana: Anspruch und Wirklichkeit.* Munich: Chr. Kaiser Verlag, 1986.

West, Gerald. *Biblical Hermeneutics of Liberation: Modes of Reading the Bible in the South African Context.* Pietermaritzburg: Cluster Publications, 1991.

White, Hayden. *Metahistory: The Historical Imagination in Nineteenth-Century Europe.* Baltimore: Johns Hopkins University Press, 1973.

———. "Historicism, History, and the Figurative Imagination." *History and Theory* 14 (1975): 43–67.

———. *Tropics of Discourse: Essays in Cultural Criticism.* Baltimore: Johns Hopkins University Press, 1978.

———. "The Value of Narrativity in the Representation of Reality." *Critical Inquiry* 7 (1980): 5–28.

———. "The Politics of Historical Interpretation: Discipline and De-sublimation." In *The Politics of Interpretation,* edited by W. J. T. Mitchell, 119–43. Chicago: University of Chicago Press, 1983.

White, L. J. "Historical and Literary Criticism: A Theological Response," *Biblical Theology Bulletin* 13 (1983): 28–31.

Wiebe, Donald. "The Politics of Religious Studies." *Bulletin of the Council of Societies for the Study of Religion* 27, 4 (1998): 95–98.

———. *The Politics of Religious Studies: The Continuing Conflict with Theology in the Academy.* London: Macmillan, 1999.

Wilder, Amos N. "Scholars, Theologians, and Ancient Rhetoric." *Journal of Biblical Literature* 75 (1956): 1–11.

———. *Early Christian Rhetoric: The Language of the Gospel.* Cambridge, Mass.: Harvard University Press, 1971.

Willis, Wendell Lee. *Idol Meat in Corinth: The Pauline Argument in I Corinthians 8 and 10.* Society of Biblical Literature Dissertation Series 68. Chico, Calif.: Scholars Press, 1981.

———. "An Apostolic Apologia? The Form and Function of I Corinthians 9." *Journal for the Study of the New Testament* 24 (1985): 33–48.

Winter, Bruce W. *Philo and Paul among the Sophists.* Cambridge: Cambridge University Press, 1997.

Wobbermin, Georg. "Zwei theologische Gutachten in Sachen des Arier-Paragraphen- kritisch beleuchtet." *Theologische Blätter* 12 (December 1933): 356–59.

Woolf, Virginia. *Three Guineas.* New York: Harcourt, Brace, Jovanovich, 1966.

Wrong, Dennis H. *Power: Its Forms, Bases, and Abuses.* New York: Harper & Row, 1979.

Wuellner, Wilhelm. "Where Is Rhetorical Criticism Taking Us?" *Catholic Biblical Quarterly* 49 (1987): 448–63.

———. "Hermeneutics and Rhetorics: From Truth and Method to Truth and Power." *Scriptura* 3 (1989): 1–54.

Young, Katherine K. "Having Your Cake and Eating It Too: Feminism and Religion." *Journal of the American Academy of Religion* 67, 1 (1999): 167–84.

Zinsser, Judith P. *History and Feminism: A Glass Half Full.* New York: Twayne Publishers, 1993.